LITERATURE, JOURNALISM AND THE AVANT-GARDE

Journalism played a role of unparalleled importance in the evolution of modern literary forms and techniques in Arabic literature. *Literature, Journalism and the Avant-Garde* explores the role of journalism in Egypt in shaping the development of modern Arabic literature from its inception in the mid-nineteenth century to the present day.

This book seeks to re-map the Egyptian literary scene over recent decades by focusing on the independent, frequently dissident journals that became the real hotbed of innovative literary activity inflected by politics as censorship and licensing laws drove experimentation underground. It is in this context that the journal became, paradoxically, the 'traditional' forum for innovative literature. Using a broad range of original Arabic sources read against avant-garde theory and Bourdieu's theory of fields, the author shows how the journal became the lifeblood of a whole literary sub-field able to operate (semi-) autonomously of establishment institutions. It is the vibrant dynamic powered by literary journalism and the dialectic between literary margin and mainstream that this book seeks to reconstruct.

While broad in historical scope, *Literature, Journalism and the Avant-Garde* emphasizes the enduring influence of the 'sixties generation' – the subject of increasing scholarly interest – and the pivotal role of the avant-garde journal *Gallery 68* in fostering a sense of literary modernism in Egyptian and, to a larger extent, Arabic fiction.

Elisabeth Kendall studied and researched at Oxford and Harvard Universities. Her core research interests lie in twentieth-century Arabic and Turkish literature, especially experimental movements. She is a lecturer in Arabic and Turkish at Edinburgh University.

ROUTLEDGE STUDIES IN MIDDLE EASTERN LITERATURES

Routledge Studies in Middle Eastern Literatures is a monograph series devoted to aspects of the literatures of the Near and Middle East and North Africa both modern and pre-modern. It is hoped that the provision of such a forum will lead to a greater emphasis on the comparative study of the literatures of this area, although studies devoted to one literary or linguistic region are warmly encouraged. It is the editors' objective to foster the comparative and multi-disciplinary investigation of the written and oral literary products of this area.

1. SHEHERAZADE THROUGH THE LOOKING GLASS
Eva Sallis

2. THE PALESTINIAN NOVEL
Ibrahim Taha

3. OF DISHES AND DISCOURSE
Geert Jan van Gelder

4. MEDIEVAL ARABIC PRAISE POETRY
Beatrice Gruendler

5. MAKING THE GREAT BOOK OF SONGS
Hilary Kilpatrick

6. THE NOVEL AND THE RURAL IMAGINARY IN EGYPT, 1880–1985
Samah Selim

7. IBN ABI TAHIR TAYFUR AND ARABIC WRITERLY CULTURE
A ninth-century bookman in Baghdad
Shawkat M. Toorawa

8. RELIGIOUS PERSPECTIVES IN MODERN MUSLIM AND JEWISH LITERATURES
Edited by Glenda Abramson and Hilary Kilpatrick

9. ARABIC POETRY
Trajectories of modernity and tradition
Muhsin J. al-Musawi

10. MEDIEVAL ANDALUSIAN COURTLY CULTURE IN THE MEDITERRANEAN
Three ladies and a lover
Cynthia Robinson

11. WRITING AND REPRESENTATION IN MEDIEVAL ISLAM
Muslim horizons
Julia Bray

12. NATIONALISM, ISLAM AND WORLD LITERATURE
Sites of confluence in the writings of Mahmūd al-Masadī
Mohamed-Salah Omri

13. LITERATURE, JOURNALISM AND THE AVANT-GARDE
Intersection in Egypt
Elisabeth Kendall

LITERATURE, JOURNALISM AND THE AVANT-GARDE

Intersection in Egypt

Elisabeth Kendall

Routledge
Taylor & Francis Group
LONDON AND NEW YORK

First published 2006
by Routledge
2 Park Square, Milton Park, Abingdon, Oxon, OX14 4RN

Simultaneously published in the USA and Canada
by Routledge
605 Third Avenue, New York, NY 10017

Routledge is an imprint of the Taylor & Francis Group, an informa business

Typeset in Times New Roman by
Newgen Imaging Systems (P) Ltd, Chennai, India

British Library Cataloguing in Publication Data
A catalogue record for this book is available from the British Library

Library of Congress Cataloging in Publication Data
A catalog record for this book has been requested

ISBN13: 978–0–415–38561–9 (hbk)

CONTENTS

Acknowledgements viii

Introduction 1

1 Literary journalism in Egypt: its emergence and development 8

2 Literary journalism in Egypt: increasing politicization 53

3 The theoretical basis of the avant-garde in 1960s Egypt 86

4 The sixties generation and its politics of literature 110

5 The sixties generation in search of a specific literary identity 140

6 The establishment of a new literary paradigm: the 1970s and beyond 188

Appendix A: the blossoming of literary journalism in the early twentieth century 229
Appendix B: Gallery 68 *particulars* 233
Appendix C: list of Egyptian journals mentioned in the text 242
Bibliography 248
Name index 263
Subject index 271

ACKNOWLEDGEMENTS

I would like to offer my profound thanks to the following people and organizations, who played critical roles at various stages in the evolution of this book: Dr M. M. Badawi and Dr Robin Ostle who first roused my enthusiasm for deeper research into Arabic literature; Idwār al-Kharrāṭ who generously gave me access to his private collection of avant-garde journals and put me in touch with many of the writers involved; Jamīl 'Aṭiyya Ibrāhīm for his invaluable guidance and entertaining company; Prof. Alan Jones and Prof. Carole Hillenbrand for their unfailing support and encouragement; Prof. Derek Hopwood whose vision ensured that the library of St Antony's College, Oxford, was furnished with so many rare runs of Arabic journals; Dr Yaseen Noorani and Dr Laleh Khalili for their incisive comments on various parts of the manuscript; Dr Paul Starkey and Dr Philip Sadgrove for offering helpful suggestions and encouragement at an early stage; the British Academy, James Mew Fund, Kennedy Memorial Trust and Queen's College, Oxford for their generous funding and finally, but most importantly, to Simon Palethorpe and my parents whose cheerful tolerance saw me through the highs and lows of this project. Any shortcomings remain entirely my own.

INTRODUCTION

Journalism played a role of unparalleled importance in the evolution of modern literary forms and techniques in Arabic, yet, as Ed de Moor has pointed out, 'this area of research is still no man's land in Arabic studies', a fact confirmed by the total lack of entries for these fora in the *Encyclopedia of Arabic Literature*.[1] This neglect is mainly due to an instinctive tendency to associate literary developments with particular books which exemplify them, although these books may appear up to a decade or more later than the initial journalistic exposure of the same. Added to this is the practical difficulty of tracking down certain runs of journals, especially of the more peripheral but often hugely influential avant-garde variety, which were often hand-written, copied by stencil and handed out in cafés. Yet the immediacy, currency and low cost of the journalistic medium as a whole meant that it could have an enormous impact and nurturing effect on intellectual and literary circles. Independent journals in particular, often published non-periodically to circumvent licensing laws, became a real hotbed of innovative literary activity as the state's encroaching grip on the cultural field pushed literary experimentation underground. It is the vibrant dynamic powered by literary journalism that this book seeks to reconstruct.

The cultural field, in Egypt as elsewhere in the Arab world, has always been broadly reliant on and inseparable from the greater field of power. This has been amply evidenced since the very beginnings of Arabic journalism in Egypt, which originally emerged as a vehicle for military and bureaucratic communication in the early nineteenth century. This political–literary overlap was entrenched at an early stage and spanned a whole range of journalistic activity: from the early official press translations and adaptations of European literature, which were motivated by long-term political strategies of national improvement and guidance, to the independent satirical journals of Ya'qūb Ṣanū' and 'Abd Allāh al-Nadīm, which registered political protest through vivid dramatic sketches. Early journalists identified the press as a powerful instrument of mass education

1 Ed de Moor, 'The Rise and Fall of the Review *Shi'r*', *Quaderni Di Studi Arabi*, no. 18, Venice, 2000, p. 96.

and hence of political opportunity. Intimately bound up with this desire to influence the masses was the need to get one's message across in an entertaining and memorable way, for example, by using stories, poems and dramatic sketches. As the journalistic field blossomed, writers and poets naturally turned to journalism as the most obvious profession from which to earn a living whilst practising their art. Moreover, through publication in a journal, literary texts naturally gained the opportunity of (additional) political definition, for the journal naturally set them against the context of a plurality of voices in which texts, literary or otherwise, resonated against one another in a single space and time.

The cultural and political fields remain closely intertwined today, with journalism acting as both the organ of political dissemination by cultural means, and, vice versa, as the organ of cultural dissemination by political means. This cultural–political overlap has recently received high-profile exposure in the wranglings expressed in the mainstream press over the selection of an Egyptian writers' delegation for the 2004 Frankfurt Book Festival; and, yet more spectacularly, in Sun' Allāh Ibrāhīm's very public rejection of the national Arab Novel Prize in 2003 in condemnation of the Egyptian regime's collaboration with the United States and Israel (see Chapter 6).

On a general level, this book explores the role of journalism in Egypt in effecting and promoting the development of modern Arabic literature from its inception in the mid-nineteenth century until the late twentieth century. On a more specific level, this book examines the role of the independent journal (or 'little magazine') in fostering literary developments, concentrating on the 1960s and the pivotal role of the avant-garde journal *Gallery 68* (see Appendix B). The 1960s saw a storm of modernist forms and techniques unleashed into the literary field which represented a turning point in modern Arabic literature. By the 1970s, the journal had become, paradoxically, the 'traditional' forum for avant-garde literature. In fact, we discover a whole literary sub-field that continued throughout the 1980s and 1990s, acting as the life blood of innovation since it was able to operate (semi-) autonomously of establishment institutions. Drawing on Bourdieu's theory of fields, this book seeks to re-map the Egyptian literary scene over recent decades by focusing on the independent, frequently dissident, journals that were the real hotbed of literary experimentation and made a lasting impact by propelling Arabic literature into the '(post)modern' era. In particular, this book demonstrates the enduring influence of 'the sixties generation' and its journal *Gallery 68*.

Before providing a brief synopsis of each chapter, it is useful to set out the way in which this book employs certain terminology. The use of the expression 'sixties generation' (*jīl al-sittīnāt*) reflects a general tendency in Egyptian criticism to periodize by generation, with the terms 'seventies generation' and 'nineties generation' also in common usage. Although this kind of periodization has been refuted by some critics, as well as several of the writers thus categorized, it has nevertheless become embedded in Arab critique and it is in recognition of this currency that it is used here. However, it is important to note that not all writers who are hailed as members of the sixties generation actually started writing in the 1960s and that many of them continued to write and develop their literary ideas beyond the 1960s. A single writer might belong to several literary generations, with his work exemplifying various period styles, not necessarily in chronological order. Nor can one speak of a specifically sixties aesthetics; elements of the modernist currents showcased by the sixties generation and its journal *Gallery 68* already emerged among experimental writers in the 1940s. The importance of recognizing the nuances within such umbrella terminology was spelled out by Zakī Najīb Maḥmūd as early as the 1950s:

> In Egypt there is an apostasy of which I know no like in European literatures. It is that men of letters are divided between old and young according to their age. . . . The matter would be righted if we were to understand old and young age in literature in a different sense. The old in literature are those who follow a specific system in their understanding of literature and artistic innovation, once the rules of that system have been settled for a while. There is no difference between those who follow this system, whether old or young. All of them are old in literary terms for they look back in time, emulating the aims and devices of their forebears. The young of literature are those who create a new school with which to defy the prevailing old system. In such a case, there is no difference between young and old; all of them are young in literary terms for they are a new plant opening its leaves to the sun and fresh air.[2]

Yet, while it may be inaccurate to use generations for rigid chronological periodization, one can still view the generation as the 'spearhead' of a period, 'a band of likeminded innovators who succeed in displacing the art of their predecessors'.[3] In this context, the sixties generation may be viewed as the spearhead of the cocktail of generations and decades through which modernist forms and techniques were introduced into prose literature in Egypt, but it cannot be viewed as solely responsible for this. Moreover, the primary criterion by which to link this generation must be experience rather than age, for age disregards all political and social differences as well as origin and talent. Sociological age-groups are more important than biological age-groups, for 'the fate of a person is decided by the years of his youth rather than the date of his birth. Youth here means that point of experience around which a generation crystallizes in the life of its people, declares its presence and makes itself felt'.[4] For the sixties generation in Egypt, that shared experience culminated in the 1967 defeat by Israel.

2 Zakī Najīb Maḥmūd, 'Old and Young Men of Letters', editorial to *al-Thaqāfa*, no. 15, Oct. 1951.
3 Ulrich Weisstein, *Comparative Literature and Literary Theory: Survery and Introduction*, (1973), p. 89.
4 Eduard Wechssler, *Die Generation als Jugendreihe und ihr Kampf um die Denkform* (1930), p. 25.

Other familiar-sounding critical terminology used in this study should be treated with care, since it may require a more flexible understanding than that accorded it in a distinctly 'Western' framework. 'Modernist', for example, is used here to refer to broad areas of experimental innovation in the Arabic short story,[5] encompassing a wide variety of techniques which in 'Western' critique might be deemed specifically 'modern' or 'post-modern', as well as referring to some techniques which find no comparison in the Euro-American literary tradition. 'Modernity', by contrast, is used simply to indicate a frame of mind epitomized by an openness to change and to question brought on by fundamental shifts in Egyptian and Arab society.

This study has favoured the term 'avant-garde' over 'post-modern' for several reasons. The term 'post-modern' is particularly problematic in the context of Egyptian experimentalism, owing to the co-emergence and co-existence of literary elements which in 'Western' critique might be considered either specifically 'modern' or specificially 'post-modern'. The fact that 'post-modern' is usually translated into Arabic as *mā ba'da al-ḥadātha* (that which comes after Modernism) renders the term particularly meaningless, since there can be no such hard and fast chronological boundaries alluding, by implication, to a particular literary baggage. The term 'avant-garde', as used here, avoids the pitfall of monolithic categorization. It is not intended to invoke the so-called historical Avant-Garde of early twentieth-century Europe. Rather, it is employed in a supra-historical sense that goes back to its original meaning. Originally a military term meaning advance guard or crack troops, it was appropriated for culture by Saint-Simon in the 1820s; here, it is employed to indicate that a work or writer is advancing away from dominant norms of taste and style towards a new literary future. This stresses the fact that innovation is necessarily part of a literary continuum in the literal avant-garde sense of 'going ahead (of what has gone before)'. This notion is also captured in the Arabic rendition of 'avant-garde', *ṭalī'ī*, which likewise implies 'rising out / forging ahead (of what has gone before)'. This identifies the avant-garde as a liminal space of contestation and change. It is a space that can be occupied by different aesthetics at different times.

The term 'journal' has been used in this study in preference to 'magazine' or 'periodical' on account of its semantic link to 'journalism'. 'Literary journalism' is adopted here in its broadest sense to refer simply to any press content pertaining to creative literature, be it serialized novels, poems, short stories, plays, critical articles and studies, the texts of panel discussions and

5 For example, a move away from clear-cut moral positions and omniscient external narration; the blurring of distinctions between genres; fragmented forms, random collages of disparate materials; an emphasis on impressionism and subjectivity – how we see, not what we see; a move towards literary minimalism; a rejection of the distinction between high and popular art.

debates, and so on. John Weightman provides a sound definition of a specialist literary journal as

> a periodical corresponding to the actual literary production of the day, serving as a forum or a show-case for writers, enabling collective literary moods or fashions to acquire consistency, and protecting literary values against the encroachments of commercialism or politics.[6]

There are two points to take into consideration, however, when applying this definition of a literary journal to the Egyptian context. First, the notion of 'periodical' is not always applicable, since censorship, licensing laws and suspension orders often precluded a journal's ability to publish periodically. Second, rather than protecting literary values against the encroachment of politics, Egyptian literary journals were frequently government sponsored, especially after the 1960s, and intentionally harnessed the talents of intellectuals and writers to propagate a socialist agenda. Even where Egyptian writers formed their own independent literary journals specifically to protect the literary field 'against the encroachments of commercialism or politics', this must not be equated with avoiding politics – quite the reverse: such a stance was itself a political statement and often necessitated political confrontation.

The first two chapters of this book provide the contextual historical framework for the intersection between literature, journalism and the avant-garde that became so successful in the 1960s and beyond. Organized chronologically, they trace the link between fictional literature and the press in Egypt. The decision over which journals to class as literary is inevitably somewhat subjective and the chapter does not claim to provide an exhaustive review. Chapter 1 covers the period from the inception of an Egyptian press in the mid-nineteenth century up to the golden age of literary journalism in the 1930s and 1940s. Chapter 2 continues by reviewing the increasing politicization of both literature and the press itself in the 1950s and 1960s in the wake of the 1948 Palestinian tragedy and the 1952 revolution in Egypt. This sets the scene for the emergence of a culture of negation among the sixties generation of avant-gardists using the journal as their weapon.

Chapter 3 analyses the theoretical context of the sixties generation's literary output, drawing various parallels with critical analysis of avant-garde activity in Europe and the United States. It identifies the basic social preconditions for the emergence of this avant-garde and discusses the role of the journal as an effective medium for experimentation. The short story genre – as the hub of 1960s experimentation – is the focus of the subsequent analysis in which a selection of broad trends exemplifying the new literary sensibility is sketched out, including brief

6 John Weightman, 'The Role of the Literary Journal', *The Times Literary Supplement*, 6 June 1980, p. 638.

translated examples from the literature itself. Finally, this chapter investigates the role of the avant-garde in relation to the future.

Chapter 4 looks at the dialectical relationship between the literary margin and mainstream by exploring the relationship between *Gallery 68* (the focal point of the sixties 'rebels') and the politico-cultural establishment in Egypt using Bourdieu's theory of fields. It examines the key questions surrounding the sixties generation – What was their position in the literary field and how rebellious were they towards the literary heritage? What role did politics play in their literature? What were their fundamental mutual aspirations? Exactly how introverted and coherent were sixties writers? And where did all this lead?

Chapter 5 is based on the belief that it is impossible to understand fully the literary works of a period without reconstructing the mood of the age by placing works within the context of the most potent debates of their time. This chapter therefore examines the literary controversies fuelled by the sixties generation, controversies which were taken up by subsequent journals and remain relevant today, for the structure of the literary field has endured and reproduced itself. Debate centred around three main areas: the extent to which the new literature relied on a perceived foreign cultural hegemony; the extent to which the new literature broke ties to its Arab heritage; and the extent to which the new literature demonstrated commitment and reflected reality. Although not nearly as contested as the debates stirred up around the short story at this time, poetry consituted a fourth area of controversy and is dealt with at the end of Chapter 5.

Chapter 6 looks at the struggle for legitimacy between avant-gardists and those holding dominant positions in the literary field. Serving as the conclusion to the work, it traces the gradual canonization of sixties writers and their literature as their marginal position in the Egyptian literary field shifted towards the mainstream, leaving space and reason for others to take on the literary struggle from the margins. With the cultural establishment under Sadat flexing its muscles, the incentive and need for new platforms from which to launch literary campaigns against current norms grew more intense. This chapter explores how, from the late 1970s, experimental Egyptian writers confronted this cultural challenge by launching a whole stream of non-periodic avant-garde journals, along the lines practiced so successfully by *Gallery 68*. This forum for expression became an established part of the Egyptian literary scene and a crucial part of Egypt's literary dynamic. These journals are examined as an autonomous sub-field (within the greater literary field and the even greater field of power politics), identifying certain common features and focal points that cut across various different aesthetics. The struggle for legtimacy (public recognition or critical acclaim), as it was understood, experienced and realized by this autonomous sub-field, is mapped out. Finally, examples are furnished to evidence the canonization of sixties' writers in Egypt's current cultural scene, as life at the literary margins continues to pass to others.

Conventions

Transliteration is undertaken according to the guidelines of the *International Journal of Middle East Studies*. The names of people are also transliterated according to this system, except where a standard English version of the name already exists (e.g. Naguib Mahfouz, not Najīb Maḥfūẓ).

Although Arabic journal titles are often untranslatable, nevertheless translations – however inadequate – have been provided in the interests of those who do not read Arabic. The title of an Arabic journal is followed by its translation and dates of publication only on its first mention in each chapter. For journals prior to 1920, the date of appearance only is provided in most cases.

1

LITERARY JOURNALISM IN EGYPT

Its emergence and development

This chapter on the emergence and development of literary journalism in Egypt is designed to trace the historical tradition out of which the strong avant-garde assertion by the so-called sixties generation emerged. While much of this contextualization chapter derives from secondary sources, many Arabic sources are brought before an English readership for the first time. Moreover, the pressing need for an overview of the evolution and impact of the very potent genre of literary journalism, in Egypt as elsewhere in the Arab world, has for too long remained a scholarly oversight. Hence this chapter aims to outline the link between fictional literature and the Arabic language press in Egypt, from its inception in the mid-nineteenth century until the Second World War. It will not be possible to mention all those journals that played a part in the marriage between literature and journalism, but the focus will be on those journals that played a key role in furthering the development of literary tastes and norms.

Embryonic literary journalism

A necessary prerequisite for the emergence of literary journalism in Egypt was Muḥammad ʻAlī's educational programme which produced the conditions in which an intellectual group could begin to emerge during Ismāʻīl's reign. It was Muḥammad ʻAlī who founded the Bulaq state-run printing press in 1819–20,[1] the School of Languages in 1835 and who sent Egyptians on educational missions to Europe – Rifāʻa Rāfiʻal-Ṭahṭāwī and ʻAlī Mubārak, who were heavily involved in the embryonic press and dominated the process of transmitting European knowledge to Egypt during 1830–70, both studied with one of the educational missions in France. One of the initial aims of these missions was to train Egyptians in

1 Abū al-Futūḥ Muḥammad Riḍwān, *Taʾrīkh Maṭbaʻat Būlāq* (1953), p. 348. Cited in Philip Sadgrove, *The Development of the Arabic Periodical Press and its Role in the Literary Life of Egypt, 1798–1882*, unpublished PhD thesis, University of Edinburgh (1984). See ch. 1 of Sadgrove's thesis for a history of the introduction of printing and journals in the Middle East, including a review of the early foreign language press in Egypt.

printing skills. Although the primary aim of Muḥammad 'Alī's programme was the formation of a group of technicians to serve the state, especially in the armed forces, it generated an interest in the collection of European books in general among those students who had been sent to Europe and in Muḥammad 'Alī himself, which in turn led to the creation of the first small state libraries in Egypt[2] and a growing translation movement to make European works in the arts as well as sciences available to readers of Arabic. Muḥammad 'Alī's reforms enabled a new generation of Egyptian intellectuals to emerge as the educational and cultural leaders of modern Egypt.

Education was neglected and development of the press delayed during the fifteen years between the death of Muḥammad 'Alī in 1848 and the accession of Ismā'īl to the viceregal throne in 1863. 'Abbās I (1848–54) in particular is said to have considered the reading of newspapers 'an increasing disgrace'.[3] Ismā'īl, who had himself been a member of an early educational mission to Europe, realized the importance of reviving and strengthening the administrative and educational apparatus, a process that was aided by rapid economic growth in the 1860s. With a buoyant cotton market following the American Civil War (1860–5), and Egypt's economic and financial development heralded by the Suez Canal project, Europeans flooded into the country.

Under Ismā'īl, the education budget increased tenfold. The *Dīwān al-Madāris* (the Schools' Bureau) was reconstituted, primary and secondary education were expanded and support was provided for learned societies, libraries, academies, teacher training and the reform of the Azhar curriculum; the *Dār al-'Ulūm* teachers' college, founded in 1872, went on to play a leading role in the revival of Arabic literature in Egypt; meanwhile, the *Jam'iyyat al-Ma'ārif* (Society of Knowledge), formed in 1868, aimed to spread education and culture through translation and publication and its early success enabled it to build its own press. Especially important were the re-opening of the School of Languages and the resumption of educational missions to Europe.[4] Many members of the new group of officials and professionals had been politically and culturally influenced by the European mission schools in which they had trained. Thus the environment was right for development of the arts – Ismā'īl supported the opening of a comedy theatre in Ezbekiyya in 1868, followed by the opening of the Cairo Opera in 1869. Alexandria too boasted two theatres in the 1870s. Development of the theatre and journalism was accelerated by the influx of Syrians who flocked to Egypt encouraged by Ismā'īl's patronage of the arts. The Syrians, in general, had a high level of cultural sophistication and many had acquired knowledge of European languages during their training in

2 P. J. Vatikiotis, *The History of Egypt from Muhammad Ali to Sadat* (1980), p. 95.
3 Aḥmad Maghāzī, *al-Ṣiḥāfa al-Fanniyya fī Miṣr, Nash'atu-hā wa-Taṭawwuru-hā, 1798–1924* (1978), p. 47.
4 From £6,000 under Sa'īd Pasha to over £75,000 in 1875. P. J. Vatikiotis, op. cit. (1980), p. 120.

Syrian missionary schools.[5] Urban life was also influenced by the many foreigners who arrived to work in Ismāʿīl's newly established institutions.

This government-directed intellectual and cultural renaissance under European influence was essential for the provision of both writers and readers needed for the rise of journalism. Many of those trained in the School of Languages headed by Rifāʿa Rāfī al-Ṭaḥṭāwī became leaders in the emerging field of journalism. For example, at the end of the 1860s ʿAbd Allāh Abū al-Suʿūd became editor of *Wādī al-Nīl* (The Nile Valley, 1866),[6] while Muḥammad ʿUthmān Jalāl published the short-lived[7] *Nuzhat al-Afkār* (The Recreation of Ideas, 1870) together with Ibrāhīm al-Muwayliḥī and was also responsible for translating much European fiction; and Ṣalāḥ Majdī, an able poet, contributed regularly to early scholarly journals like *Rawḍat al-Madāris* (The Schools' Training Ground, 1870).

The Arabic language too was in need of modification to meet the requirements of the modern age. The scientific and technical nature of the books to be translated under Muḥammad ʿAlī necessitated a clear and simple style of Arabic. The emergence of Egyptian journalism helped to precipitate simplification of the language. As well as regular issues necessitating rapid typesetting, a simpler language would broaden the potential readership, especially at this early stage of development of the educational system. In any case, the temporary nature of journals (as opposed to books) in addition to their initial function of communicating news and instructions precluded the use of overly ornate prose. This paved the way for the emergence of the editorial which attempted to develop arguments and express opinions more clearly and logically, in contrast to the at times tortuous ramblings of earlier traditional writing. Orality, however, remained a feature of the language for longer than one might have expected since newspapers were read aloud in cafés and other gatherings, and this affected the style and treatment of ideas. Yet this orality, together with the inclusion of satirical cartoons at an early stage, meant that the impact of journals was greater than one might otherwise have expected at a time when the literacy rate was very low.

Just over a decade after the French departure from Egypt, *Jurnāl al-Khidīw* (The Khedive's Journal, 1813)[8] was launched, published in Turkish and Arabic.

5 For a study of Beirut as the initial hub of Arabic language press activity in the nineteenth century, see Dagmar Glaß, *Der Muqtaṭaf und seine Öffentlichkeit* (2004), Vol. 1, pp. 74–90.

6 Scholars vary between 1867 (e.g., Philippe de Ṭarrāzī) and 1866 (e.g., ʿAbd al-Laṭīf Ḥamza and Ibrāhīm ʿAbduh). I have opted for the earlier date since it is possible that more numbers of the journal came to light.

7 It was suppressed by the Khedive after only the second issue owing to its critical remarks. See ʿQiṣṣat al-Ṣiḥāfa', unattributed article, *al-Kātib*, no. 8, Nov. 1961, p. 123.

8 1813 according to ʿAbd al-Laṭīf Ḥamza, *Qiṣṣat al-Ṣiḥāfa al-ʿArabiyya fī Miṣr* (1967), p. 44; ca. 1822 according to I. ʿAbduh, *Taṭawwur al-Ṣiḥāfa al-Miṣriyya, 1798–1981* (1982), p. 335; 1827 according to P. J. Vatikiotis, op. cit. (1980), p. 99. I have opted for the earlier date on the assumption that more issues were discovered by Ḥamza. Although it predates the establishment of the Bulaq press, it was originally handwritten, appearing only monthly; it later became weekly and finally daily in 1821.

Primarily intended to report news of the Khedive's decisions and decrees to high government officials and provincial governors, it occasionally included stories from *A Thousand and One Nights*.[9] This journal was eventually replaced by *al-Waqā'i' al-Miṣriyya* (Egyptian Events, 1828) whose readership reached beyond officials to the educated class, being distributed for free among students of public institutions, though it rarely appeared more than three times a week. Among those involved in editing this journal were leading figures in education and literature such as Aḥmad Fāris al-Shidyāq and Rifā'a Rāfi' al-Ṭaḥṭāwī. The latter was appointed editor in 1842 and under him it took on a more organized format and the Arabic content was placed in the prominent position formerly reserved for the Turkish. The editorials became more analytical and instructive as opposed to simple eulogies of the Pasha of Egypt, and some literary and educational material was introduced. But it soon fell into neglect under 'Abbās I before being suppressed under Sa'īd's rule (1854–63). Ismā'īl revived it and, years later, under the editorship of Muḥammad 'Abduh briefly in the early 1880s, it became a daring organ of Egyptian opinion.[10]

Muḥammad 'Alī had also launched a military newspaper and an agricultural journal, but Egypt still witnessed no independent journalistic ventures in Arabic. It was under Ismā'īl that an embryonic Arabic literary journalism began to take root. News and commentary on literature and the arts began to appear in the daily newspapers, although this amounted to little more than superficial generalization at this stage. The late 1860s saw the launch of the first semi-independent newspaper *Wādī al-Nīl*, edited by 'Abd Allāh Abū al-Su'ūd but sponsored by Ismā'īl with the initial aim of defending his Europhile policies. Yet it found space to publish extracts from recognized literary and historical works as well as announcing forthcoming publications. It also provided regular reports on European operatic and theatrical activity in Egypt, thereby proving instrumental in implanting the idea of an Arab theatre; and it was Abū al-Su'ūd's son, Muḥammad 'Unsī, a regular contributor to *Wādī al-Nīl*, who was apparently the first to conceive a project for the establishment of an Arab National Theatre.[11] *Wādī al-Nīl* was probably inspired by Aḥmad Fāris al-Shidyāq's *al-Jawā'ib* (Responses, 1861), which eventually relocated from Istanbul to Egypt in 1883. *Al-Jawā'ib* owed much to al-Shidyāq's breadth of cultural experience and his fluent style, and many of the Arabic words he coined to replace transliterated European terms gained currency.[12] Although rudimentary, the literary journalism in *Wādī al-Nīl* and *al-Jawā'ib* was invaluable in both responding to and provoking cultural interest; one scholar concludes that 'what these two journals had to say on science and

9 'Abd al-Laṭīf Ḥamza, *Qiṣṣat al-Ṣiḥāfa al-'Arabiyya* fī Miṣr (1967), p. 44.
10 'Izz al-Dīn al-Amīn, *Nash'at al-Naqd al-Adabī al-Ḥadīth fī Miṣr* (1970), pp. 88–90.
11 P. Sadgrove, *The Egyptian Theatre in the Nineteenth Century, 1799–1882* (1996), pp. 105–6.
12 'Umar al-Dasūqī, *Nash'at al-Naqd al-Ḥadīth wa-Taṭawwuru-hu* (1976), pp. 56–7.

literature was the best that there was in Near Eastern journalism at that time'.[13] After criticizing the government, *Wādī al-Nīl* was forced to continue under the title *Rawḍat al-Akhbār* (The News Pasture, 1874) with al-Su'ūd's son, Muḥammad 'Unsī, as editor-in-chief.[14] It ceased in 1878 with the death of al-Su'ūd, indicating how firmly journalism relied on personalities at this early stage.

The rise of journalism as a general cultural rather than purely political and administrative phenomenon was much aided by Rifā'a Rāfi' al-Ṭaḥṭāwī and 'Alī Mubārak who founded and financed scholarly journals in which research could be published and ideas exchanged as part of Ismā'īl's educational development programme. The most important of these was the fortnightly educational–pedagogic journal, *Rawḍat al-Madāris*, founded by 'Alī Mubārak and initially edited by Rifā'a Rāfi' al-Ṭaḥṭāwī, whom Ḥamza calls 'the first pioneer of Egyptian journalism.'[15] On his death, the journal was edited by his son, 'Alī Fahmī Rifā'a, until its closure in 1877. Al-Taḥṭāwī himself, having been heavily influenced by his French as well as traditional Azharī education, took some of the first steps to revolutionize Arabic literature. Through his translations of French poetry and his introduction of patriotic songs into the Egyptian army and schools, he helped to revive strophic poetic forms to cater for contemporary themes, harnessing the *muwashshaḥ* and simple *zajal* forms.[16] His journal provided a focal point for many of the intellectual leaders of Ismā'īl's reign,[17] and its role in broadening the horizons of the rising generation of intellectuals was aided by it being distributed free of charge among students.[18] Rather than just a forum for opinions and ideas, *Rawḍat al-Madāris* marks the dawn of Egyptian journalism as a literary outlet. Both scientific and literary books were serialized in it and it was the first Egyptian journal to publish part of a play, an adaptation of a Molière play by 'Uthmān Jalāl serialized in three parts – no other play appeared in the press for another decade.[19] The most remarkable feature of Jalāl's Molière translations was the simple vernacular quality of their Arabic.[20] However, these beginnings were modest: unlike its Beirut counterparts, the style of *Rawḍat al-Madāris* was still dominated by rhymed prose (*saj'*), and although its circulation increased nearly threefold it still

13 'Izz al-Dīn al-Amīn, op. cit. (1970), p. 94.

14 Ami Ayalon, *The Press in the Arab Middle East: A History* (1995), p. 41.

15 'Abd al-Laṭīf Ḥamza, *Qiṣṣat al-Ṣiḥāfa al-'Arabiyya fī Miṣr* (1967), p. 51.

16 Shmuel Moreh, *Modern Arabic Poetry, 1800–1970: The Development of its Forms and Themes Under the Influence of Western Literature* (1976), pp. 15–20.

17 For example, 'Abd Allāh Fikrī, Muḥammad Qadrī, Ismā'īl al-Falakī, Ṣāliḥ Majdī, Ḥamza Fatḥ Allāh and the poet Ismā'īl Ṣabrī.

18 Lūwīs 'Awaḍ, *The Literature of Ideas in Egypt*, Part 1 (1986), p. 30.

19 P. Sadgrove, *The Egyptian Theatre in the Nineteenth Century, 1799–1882* (1996), p. 101.

20 H. A. R. Gibb, 'Studies in Contemporary Arabic Literature: I. The Nineteenth Century', *Bulletin of the School of Oriental Studies*, Vol. 4, no. 4, 1928, p. 745.

rarely exceeded 700.[21] In fact, in the decade prior to the British occupation, only 3 of the 33 newspapers and journals published were billed as primarily scientific, literary or satirical; the rest were purely political.[22] Even where literature was specifically included and encouraged, this tended to fall within the rubric of a general educational programme aimed at moral and intellectual improvement.[23]

Jamāl al-Dīn al-Afghānī's presence in Egypt in the 1870s helped to inspire early protest movements demanding greater independence from Turkey and Europe and a stronger Egyptian identity. Protest increased after the establishment of European fiscal control in 1876 which suggested the imminent threat of European domination. It was natural that writers should have felt a greater sense of urgency to reach the public at this time of increasing nationalist fervour. Thus an independent press began to develop as a vehicle for nationalist protest. The rise of an independent press at this time was possible since the necessary infrastructure, including postal and telegraph systems as well as the Reuter's news wire service, was now in place. Running a journal presented a business opportunity for smaller entrepreneurs – it required little investment and could be run by a couple of people.[24] The Syrian emigrés were instrumental in this early development of Egyptian journalism and in fact owned approximately 20 per cent of Egypt's newspapers and journals before the First World War.[25] Yet even this high statistic does not do justice to the role of Syrians in the development of Egyptian literary journalism, for they dominated the cultural press, particularly in Alexandria, until at least the end of the nineteenth century. The Syrians Salīm and 'Abduh al-Ḥamwī founded the first independent Arabic journal in Alexandria, *al-Kawkab al-Sharqī* (The Eastern Star, 1873), a political and literary weekly that was soon closed down by Ismā'īl. Several subsequent Syrian initiatives met similar fates.[26] Despite an active interest in the theatre, Syrian journalists such as Salīm al-Naqqāsh

21 'Abd al-Laṭīf Ḥamza, *Qiṣṣat al-Ṣiḥāfa al-'Arabiyya fī Miṣr* (1967), p. 48.

22 Sāmī 'Azīz, *Jadwal Iṣdār al-Ṣuḥuf.* Appendix to *al-Ṣiḥāfa al-Miṣriyya wa-Mawqifu-hā min al-Iḥtilāl al-Injilīzī* (1968).

23 Aḥmad Ibrāhīm al-Hawwārī, *Naqd al-Riwāya al-'Arabiyya fī Miṣr* (1978), pp. 28–9. Cited in Samah Selim, *The Novel and the Rural Imaginary in Egypt, 1880–1985* (2004), p. 11.

24 Beth Baron, *The Women's Awakening in Egypt: Culture, Society and the Press* (1994), p. 58.

25 Thomas Philipp, *The Syrians in Egypt 1725–1975* (1985), p. 98. Cited in B. Baron *The Women's Awakening in Egypt: Culture, Society and the Press* (1994), p. 16. Maghāzī writes more negatively of the role of the Syrian emigrés, claiming that they only devoted themselves to journalism and the theatre inasmuch as this did not endanger their means of subsistence in Egypt, especially prior to the British occupation, since they had come to Egypt in the first place in search of freedom and a living. Aḥmad Maghāzī, op. cit. (1978), p. 103.

26 Salīm al-Naqqāsh and Adīb Isḥaq founded the weekly *Miṣr* (Egypt, 1877), published first from Cairo, then from Alexandria. While both men were active supporters of the theatre in Egypt, as followers of al-Afghānī, their newspaper concentrated on opposing European control and was suppressed more than once for its bold criticism of the government. Another pupil of al-Afghānī, Mikha'īl 'Abd al-Sayyid, founded *al-Waṭan* (The Nation, 1877) in Cairo, which ran until the British banned it in 1884. Meanwhile, al-Naqqāsh and Isḥaq also launched *al-Tijāra* (Trade, 1878) in Alexandria, which carried fierce articles by al-Afghānī, Muḥammad 'Abduh and 'Abd

and Adīb Isḥāq focused their journals overwhelmingly on politics, opposing European control and expounding the views of al-Afghānī and Muḥammad 'Abduh. Unlike European journals in Egypt at the time, Arabic journals still approached the theatre as fundamentally something of news interest rather than specifically literary interest.[27]

The real birth of Egyptian journalism with both a political and literary impact was achieved through the efforts of Ya'qūb Ṣanū' and 'Abd Allāh al-Nadīm who identified with ordinary Egyptians in a way in which the Syrians could not. Both men expressed their political opposition through satirical journalism. It was just before the 'Urābī revolt that conditions were right for their papers to flourish – Egyptian national consciousness had reached fever pitch with the imminent threat of European domination and at the same time Egypt had reached a high enough level of cultural sophistication for such journals to succeed with many new ideas having taken root influenced by almost a century of close contact with Europe. Although the literacy rate in the 1880s was still under 8 per cent, Hafez points out that '. . being a member of an educated minority drove those who were literate to think deeply about both their cultural and political role'.[28]

Ṣanū' and al-Nadīm: two pioneers of satirical literary journalism

The roots of Ṣanū''s journalism lay in his activities in the theatre at the turn of the 1870s. Muḥammad Muṣṭafā Badawī writes, 'in Egypt the birth of modern drama coincided with the rise of national consciousness, and this provided an incentive not simply to Arabize, but to Egyptianize foreign works as well'.[29] Hence we find

Allāh al-Nadīm attacking European control in Egypt. It was suppressed by the authorities in 1879, prompting them to establish yet other outlets in the form of *Miṣr al-Fatāh* (Young Egypt, 1879), *al-'Asr al-Jadīd* (The New Era, 1880) and *al-Maḥrūsa* (The Protected One, 1880); this latter was taken over by Ilyās Ziyāda in 1909, under whom it took on a more literary rather than political character. Another Alexandrine paper, *al-Waqt* (Time, 1879), was launched by Lebanese theatre activist Salīm Taqlā, who also founded the generally pro-Ottoman *al-Ahrām* (The Pyramids, 1876), initially Alexandria based. The Syrian Salīm al-'Anḥūrī founded the bi-weekly *Mir'āt al-Sharq* (Mirror of the East, 1879). It was taken over by Ibrāhīm al-Laqqānī, a disciple of al-Afghānī, and kept reemerging despite being banned frequently. *Mir'āt al-Sharq* under al-Laqqānī played an important role in gathering young talent such as Shaykh 'Alī Yūsuf, who went on to edit Salīm Fāris al-Shidyāq's *al-Qāhira* (Cairo, 1885) and eventually founded his own journal, *al-Ādāb* (Refined Culture, 1887), a short-lived literary weekly, before shifting his emphasis to politics as editor of *al-Mu'ayyad* (The Endorsed, 1889).

27 P. Sadgrove, *The Egyptian Theatre in the Nineteenth Century*, (1996), pp. 73 and 100.

28 Sabry Hafez, *The Rise and Development of the Egyptian Short Story, 1881–1970*, unpublished PhD thesis, London University (1979), p. 16. Hafez estimates that 8.3 per cent of the population was literate by the 1880s, but this figure is probably over-optimistic given that the UNESCO figure for 1907, nearly two decades later, is only 7.3 per cent. UNESCO study: *Progress of Literacy in Various Countries* (1953).

29 M. M. Badawi, *Early Arabic Drama* (1988), p. 68.

that prominent men in the early theatre such as Ya'qūb Ṣanū', Salīm al-Naqqāsh, Adīb Isḥaq and 'Abd Allāh al-Nadīm turned to political journalism and became involved in the Egyptian nationalist movement. Ṣanū''s publication of *Abū Naḍḍāra* (The Man with Spectacles, 1877)[30] was a continuation of his theatrical activity in that it contained theatrical sketches and dialogues incorporating narrative and satirical elements. Their popular appeal was fuelled by the fact that Ṣanū' derived much of his inspiration from letters sent to him by the Egyptian public. Ṣanū' succeeded in capturing the tone of Egyptian national consciousness and hostility towards the Khedive and the British in a language with which people could easily identify. He was more concerned with recording his train of thought than with classical correctness, discovering a simple journalistic style which exploited the versatility of the vernacular. His language would tend towards the classical or the vernacular according to the requirements of his dialogues and theatrical pieces. Although this was not the only Egyptian journal to be making use of the vernacular,[31] it was the first to use several colours and one of the first to use photographs alongside its many caricatures. Such devices would have helped to increase its circulation and make it accessible even to those with a low level of literacy – distribution of some issues reached 1,050 copies. The first run of *Abū Naḍḍāra*, however, lasted only two months and Ṣanū' was eventually exiled in June 1878 for having incurred the wrath of the Khedive through his satire.[32] The power of *Abū Naḍḍāra* stemmed from its potent fusion of popular political, linguistic, visual and humorous characteristics. Ṣanū' continued to advocate Egyptian nationalism from Paris, still through satirical sketches,[33] in a series of similarly named satirical journals, such as *Abū Ṣaffāra* and *Abū Zummāra*, as well as variations featuring the original *Abū Naḍḍāra*.

'Abd Allāh al-Nadīm too employed his skills as a poet and orator for political purposes. A leading agitator of the 'Urābī revolt, his weekly journal *al-Tankīt wa-l-Tabkīt* (Banter and Blame, 1881) proved a potent outlet for the views and ideas he represented. Ḥamza describes al-Nadīm as 'the journalist *extraordinaire* of the nineteenth century'.[34] His deep social and political conscience won him popular appeal; he exposed the suffering of the Egyptian masses, in particular the

30 Sanū' changed the name of this journal at least four times, but it essentially remained *Abū Naḍḍāra* until 1910. Ṣanū' also launched other journals but these were of less significance for the rise of literary journalism. For example, *al-Waṭan al-Miṣrī* (The Egyptian Nation, 1882), *al-Munṣif* (The Righteous Man, 1888), *al-Tawaddud* (Friendship, 1904), *al-'Ālam al-Islāmī* (The Islamic World, 1903).

31 *Al-Maymūn* (The Monkey, 1879) was a humorous daily written in the Egyptian vernacular which ran for four years.

32 L. 'Awaḍ, *The Literature of Ideas in Egypt*, Part 1 (1986), p. 71.

33 For example, *Abū Naḍḍāra* (8–15 Aug. 1885) parades before readers the characters of the Queen of England and the Russian Emperor in an attempt to expose the ambitions of British colonialism; *Abū Naḍḍāra* (3–20 March 1886) presents a theatrical piece comprising five sketches in a harsh tone telling of the nationalist tragedy of Egypt, complaining of racial discrimination and attacking the English slave trade in Sudan. Cited in Aḥmad Maghāzī, op. cit. (1978), p. 125.

34 'Abd al-Laṭīf Ḥamza, *Qiṣṣat al-Ṣiḥāfa al-'Arabiyya fī Miṣr* (1967), p. 77.

fallāḥīn, and dealt with the problems, anxieties and aspirations of the common man. Yet his journal was popular among many different groups. This stemmed from the convergence of three factors in al-Nadīm: knowledge of traditional Arab culture, knowledge of European literature and thought[35] and wide experience of Egyptian life. With regard to the traditional, most of al-Nadīm's fictional work in his journals was highly didactic, as was the norm at this time since didacticism was a major justification for literature. At the same time, he introduced modern European concepts into his fiction, such as irony, allegory and several levels of meaning, and he found a new means of satire in the transliteration of foreign words. Moreover, like Ṣanū', he used the vernacular for much of his writing, especially for his fictional sketches and episodes. The popularity of this was demonstrated when al-Nadīm declared his intention to discontinue using the vernacular – the reading public responded by inundating his journal with letters requesting him to continue. The success of his journal lay in the new style resulting from the fusion of these factors, 'a style which the learned will not despise and the ignorant will not need to have interpreted'.[36]

The first issue of *al-Tankīt wa-l-Tabkīt* contained four of al-Nadīm's new didactic fictional episodes and these continued in most issues until the national question reached boiling point in August 1881 and henceforth occupied most of the space. These episodes were constructed around middle class characters and scenes and were often crudely didactic.[37] While many critics consider these episodes to be the first examples of the modern Egyptian short story, this is probably an exaggeration of their literary merit. Yet their early marriage of fiction and politics at the altar of Egyptian nationalism proved a true harbinger of the direction Egyptian literary development was to take over the following decades.

In late 1881, al-Nadīm renamed his journal *al-Ṭā'if* (The Wanderer) and moved it from Alexandria to Cairo to become the official organ of the 'Urabī revolt. The urgency of the times meant that pure political content now dominated, with classical Arabic now the exclusive vehicle, since the vernacular had been used primarily to parody earthy peasant characters in the sketches. After the fall of the 'Urābī revolt in September 1882, al-Nadīm was forced to lie low, but he returned to journalism in Egypt a decade later with the launch of another satirical opposition journal, *al-Ustādh* (The Master, 1892). This time al-Nadīm directed his satirical wit against the British, rather than the Khedive and Europe in general as had previously been the case. The effectiveness of al-Nadīm's fictional episodes – based on

35 Al-Nadīm was educated in Alexandria; he was also influenced by Europeans whom he knew in Alexandria and by European literature in translation.

36 *al-Tankīt wa-l-Tabkīt*, 6 June 1881. Quoted in Pierre Cachia, *An Overview of Modern Arabic Literature* (1990), p. 48.

37 For example, 'Majlis Ṭibbī li-Muṣāb bi-l-Afranjī', *al-Tankīt wa-l-Tabkīt*, 6 June 1881, allegorically warns of the evils of Europeanization. A swindler tempts a respectable young Arab into sinful actions until he contracts syphilis. This and other episodes are more fully discussed by S. Hafez in his PhD thesis (1979), pp. 43–54, to which I am greatly indebted.

his winning formula of concern for everyday issues, didacticism, politics and fiction – is shown by their continued popularity in *al-Ustādh*. While many of the character types and themes remained the same as before,[38] we see the growing use of allegory in an attempt to veil the meaning from the British. Yet, recognizing the potency of this literature, it was pressure from the British that forced al-Nadīm into hiding in June 1893. The important role al-Nadīm played in inspiring the rise of literary journalism resulted from the fact that he was 'mainly a writer who came to journalism from literature, and who combined both with clear political insight and a strong desire to play a major role in his country's life'.[39] His didactic fictional episodes established a firm link between journalism and short fictional forms which others, such as Muḥammad al-Muwayliḥī, were to continue and build upon in the future.

A further major achievement of Ṣanū' and al-Nadīm's journalism was to imbue a flexibility into the Arabic language, manipulating it as a paradic tool to suit their literary and communicative aims. Moreover, Samah Selim credits Ṣanū' and al-Nadīm with single-handedly installing the Egyptian *fallāḥ* as a modern literary character, despite the appearance of this figure in popular drama in Egypt prior to the nineteenth century. Although many critics have pointed to the literary flaws in Ṣanū' and al-Nadīm's experiments, Selim rightly points out that such criticisms tend to spring from an essentially teleological perspective on genre development which views Egyptian writers as building on a European ideal.[40] Badawī describes Ṣanū''s theatrical sketches as too 'brief to possess any dramatic structure, too caricature-like to allow for any characterization or deep psychological insight, too directly political to be works of art'.[41] However, if one views genre formation as rooted in complex and contested social ideologies and social experiences, as Selim suggests, then the various notions of language, character and narrative stance to emerge at the hands of Ṣanū' and al-Nadīm acquire their own logic and may be viewed as 'a deliberate articulation of representational authority and autonomous creativity' rather than flawed attempts at a literary ideal.[42] On a more general level, the rebellious journals of Ṣanū' and al-Nadīm proved inspirational for others attempting to revitalize Egyptian culture and society. A century later, Aḥmad Rayyān in his avant-garde journal *al-Naddāha* (The Caller) praised al-Nadīm's journalism as a motivating and revolutionary force, a model of positive and influential interaction with the Egyptian public which had helped to inspire his own experiment;[43] and one avant-garde writer

38 For example, the campaign against narcotics, alcohol and gambling; satire of Europeanized Egyptians; exposing the suffering of the poor.

39 S. Hafez, PhD thesis (1979), p. 38.

40 See S. Selim, *The Novel and the Rural Imaginary in Egypt* (2004), pp. 25–56, for an excellent study on the construction of the *fallāḥ* in the drama and dialogue of Ṣanū' and al-Nadīm.

41 M. M. Badawi, *Early Arabic Drama* (1988), p. 34.

42 S. Selim, op. cit. (2004), p. 23.

43 Aḥmad Rayyān, ''Abd Allāh al-Nadīm wa-*l-Tankīt wa-l-Tabkīt*', *al-Naddāha*, no. 2, n.d. (1979?), pp. 9–11.

from the so-called 'sixties generation', Muḥammad Ibrāhīm Mabrūk, actually named his anti-establishment journal *al-Nadīm*.

Ṣanū' and al-Nadīm set the tone and model for the subsequent development of satirical literary journalism in Egypt. Muḥammad al-Najjār's *al-Arghūl* (The Musical Pipes, 1894) provided a vehicle for the didactic *zajal*[44] of poets like Muḥammad Imām al-'Abd, 'Izzat Ṣaqr, Khalīl Naẓīr and al-Najjār himself. Other potent examples are Ibrāhīm al-Muwayliḥī's *Abū Zayd* (Abu Zayd, 1901) and *Ḥimārat Munyatī* (The Donkey of My Desire, 1897), founded by the *zajal* poet Muḥammad Tawfīq. Satirical poems with a vernacular flavour appeared in nearly every issue of *Ḥimārat Munyatī*, attacking public figures and contemporary policies, at the same time challenging formal distinctions between classical and vernacular poetry by adhering to classical syntax but with colloquial inflection.[45] Al-Najjār's *Al-Arghūl* meanwhile claimed to keep its distance from politics, although it was clearly pro-Khedive. In contrast to Tawfīq's use of the vernacular in *Ḥimārat Munyatī*, al-Najjār stressed the need for *zajal* to rely on the classical language, although *al-Arghūl* did include some vernacular poems sent in by readers.[46] Many satirical journals, however, sank into a cheap and vulgar humour devoid of the inspirational and reformative purpose behind Ṣanū' and al-Nadīm's work.[47]

As nationalist sentiments intensified with the 1904 Entente, the 1906 Danshaway incident and Cromer's replacement by Kitchener, the climate was right for the emergence of another hard-hitting satirical newspaper, *Khayāl al-Ẓill* (The Shadow Play, 1907), which Maghāzī identifies as 'a clear extension of Ṣanū''s illustrated satirical journals'.[48] Like Ṣanū''s journals, *Khayāl al-Ẓill* also published *zajal* verse and theatrical pieces linked to contemporary political events, most notably a four-part serialization set around the Danshaway incident, but the journal was closed the following year.[49] Satirical journalism, which

44 *Zajal* refers a rhymed strophic poem in non-classical Arabic, the rhythm of which derives from classical metrical patterns.

45 Marilyn Booth, 'Poetry in the Vernacular', in M. M. Badawi (ed.) *Modern Arabic Literature* (1992), pp. 468–9.

46 M. Booth, 'Colloquial Arabic Poetry, Politics and the Press in Modern Egypt', *International Journal of Middle Eastern Studies*, Vol. 24, 1992, pp. 425–9.

47 A. Jundī, op. cit. (1967), p. 312.

48 A. Maghāzī, op. cit. (1978), p. 167. Muḥammad Mas'ūd and Ḥāfiẓ 'Awaḍ preceded *Khayāl al-Ẓill* with *Hā... Hā... Hā* (Ha Ha Ha, 1907), a one-off publication which acted like a learning experience for the reader, providing an article explaining caricature as well as explaining the satirical message behind the cartoons published.

49 'Riwāya Siyāsiyya Shi'riyya li-Aḥad Masjūnī Danshaway', *Khayāl al-Ẓill*, nos. 1–4, 15 March–15 April 1907; and no. 10, 18 May 1907. Ibid., p. 173. It may be to this theatrical piece that Aḥmad Ḥamrūsh referred when he mentioned sifting through the archives of the National Theatre in the 1960s to look for historical political plays about Egypt and deciding to stage one he had found about the Danshaway incident. 'Aḥmad Ḥamrūsh: Rūḥ al-Taḥaddī warā' Izdihār Masraḥ al-Sittīniyyāt', interview, *al-Bayān*, 22 July 2002. Online. Available HTTP: http://www.albayan.co.ae/albayan/2002/07/22/sya/34.htm

abounded in times of political unrest, flared up dramatically after the First World War with hopes of liberation from the British Protectorate. A particularly influential fusion of literary and political concerns was effected at this time by Bayram al-Tūnisī in the Alexandrine press. Al-Tūnisī's own journal *al-Misalla* (The Obelisk, 1919) provided an outlet for his provocative poetry alongside that of other *zajal* poets who attacked the government and king in a potent vernacular. Although al-Tūnisī was banished in October 1919, *zajal* became a regular feature in the popular press of the 1920s and 1930s, with several journals having their own resident *zajal* poet, performing a function similar to today's editorial columnist.[50]

In fact, al-Tūnisī continued to contribute to the Egyptian press, even in absentia. Not only did he target the political establishment, he also directed his satire against traditional forms of discourse, even while using them. For example, a *maqāma*, as well as caricaturing a group, became a parody of its own formal and thematic 'rules'.[51] Al-Tūnisī also stood apart for incorporating motifs and forms from oral folk literature into his poetry as part of his attempt to incorporate workers and peasants into the liberal nationalist programme, and Booth believes that his *zajal* represents 'the modern apex of that genre'. The poet Aḥmad Shawqī, who had himself fallen victim to al-Tūnisī's satire, reportedly considered al-Tūnisī and his folk literature to be the greatest threat to Arabic poetry.[52] The three volumes of poetry and two of prose dialogue that were published during al-Tūnisī's lifetime were all republications of material first published in the press, often years earlier.

Following the 1923 Constitution and an increase in press freedom, satirical journalism was in a position to blossom further. The most influential subsequent journal was doubtless *Rūz al-Yūsuf* (Rose al-Yūsuf, 1925–). Founded by the actress Fāṭima al-Yūsuf for weekly news about the theatre and arts, it soon became more famous for its political satire and became Egypt's best-selling journal. High profile men of letters such as Ibrāhīm al-Māzinī, 'Abbās Maḥmūd al-'Aqqād, Muḥammad Luṭfī Jum'a and Zakī Ṭulaymāt would contribute work without remuneration over the years to come. Novelist, short story writer and journalist Iḥsān 'Abd al-Quddūs testifies to the enormous influence of *Rūz al-Yūsuf* on his rapid early development as a writer, owing to the fact that his mother, Fāṭima al-Yūsuf, 'in publishing her journal would always rely on new generations of writers and journalists'.[53]

50 M. Booth, 'Colloquial Arabic Poetry, Politics and the Press in Modern Egypt', *International Journal of Middle Eastern Studies*, Vol. 24, 1992, pp. 429–31.

51 For an excellent treatment of Bayram al-Tūnisī and his contribution to Egypt's literary development, see Booth's lengthy and detailed study, *Bayram al-Tunisi's Egypt: Social Criticism and Narrative Strategies* (1990).

52 Ibid., pp. 3–10.

53 Interview with Iḥsān 'Abd al-Quddūs, 22 Nov. 1983. In Rushdī al-Dhawwādī, *Aḥādīth fī al-Adab* (1986), pp. 53–8. Al-Quddūs became *Rūz al-Yūsuf's* editor-in-chief in 1945 before moving to *Akhbār al-Yawm* in 1966.

Literary journalism under the British occupation

The introduction of the first Press Law in late 1881 gave the government the right to suspend a publication to protect public order, morals or religion. While in practice this did not differ greatly from the previous perils posed by royal will, of more significance for the development of literary journalism was the weighty insurance now payable by journal owners. Although both Dufferin and Cromer stated in reports that reasons for maintaining freedom of the press outweighed those for press restrictions,[54] contrary to common belief the Press Law remained in active operation until 1894.[55] As such, literary journalism continued in an extemporized rather than written form, thanks to groups of cultured men who met in cafés or private houses to discuss literature and the arts. Plays too were sometimes performed in cafés. At the same time, the theatre continued to rise under men like Yūsuf al-Khayyāṭ, Sulaymān al-Qardāḥī and Aḥmad Abū Khalīl al-Qabbānī. Matti Moosa writes, 'During the period of despondency after the failure of the 'Urābī revolt and the British occupation of Egypt, the majority of the literate or semiliterate public turned to fiction to escape political reality. And at just this time the Syrian belle-lettrists and journalists were busily engaged in the translation of Western fiction'.[56] In reality, Syrians and other foreigners who enjoyed the protection of nations granted immunities under the Capitulations System were relatively unimpeded by the Press Law.

However, no journal specializing wholly in literature or the theatre was founded until about a quarter of a century later, despite a growing interest in cultural journalism. In the decade before the British occupation, only 9 per cent of newspapers, journals and periodicals were scientific, literary or satirical; the rest were political. In the first decade of occupation, this rose to 75 per cent.[57] Sāmī 'Azīz believes this is because the complexity of issues facing Egypt under European occupation made general journalism more important than specialist journalism, which would monopolize the talents of writers and distract readers from other important issues.[58] Maghāzī, on the other hand, attributes the lack of any specialist literary journal at this time to a lack of imagination on the part of journalists and littérateurs – they simply did not recognize the latent power of fiction and thus failed to exploit freedom of the press for the development of literary journalism. He writes that plenty of nationalists shared the opinion of many Europeans that granting freedom of the press was dangerous.[59] Rather than

54 A. Maghāzī, op. cit. (1978), p. 122.

55 For a discussion of press freedoms at this time, see Sāmī 'Azīz, Khalīl Ṣābāt and Yunān Labīb Rizq, *Ḥurriyyat al-Ṣiḥāfa fī Miṣr, 1798–1924* (1972).

56 Matti Moosa, *The Origins of Modern Arabic Fiction* (1983), p. 24.

57 Calculated from *Jadwal Iṣdār al-Ṣuḥuf*. Appendix to Sāmī 'Azīz, *al-Ṣiḥāfa al-Miṣriyya wa-Mawqifu-hā min al-Iḥtilāl al-Injilīzī* (1968).

58 Quoted in A. Maghāzī, op. cit. (1978), p. 120.

59 Ḥasan Ḥusnī, the owner of *al-Nīl*, argued against freedom of the press in his newspaper, 29 Sept. 1892.

persist, the grumbling journalists were content to let matters take their own course and be led by them.[60]

While it is true that the journalistic climate was somewhat freer under the British than it had been beforehand and that stability under the British occupation was conducive to the flourishing of the arts, Maghāzī probably overstates his case. The British were not averse to clamping down on those who opposed Britain's rights or challenged her position in Egypt – under Dufferin, one paper after another was closed[61] while others were warned for having criticized Britain's harsh policy.[62] Viewed from an alternative perspective, however, censorship might be deemed to have had some slight positive influence on the rise of fiction in journalism since it was a means of veiling opposition – hence al-Nadīm's heavily allegorical fictional episodes in *al-Ustādh* – yet, even then, British pressure forced the journal's closure. As for the lack of a journal specializing wholly in literature and the arts, Sabry Hafez writes that 'the press was more interested in enhancing its position in society by adopting and defending its public morality than in the promotion of narrative works'.[63] However, a major reason for this must be that it was not yet a practical venture. The reading public was extremely limited and press publications very expensive, both to produce and to purchase – a monthly review cost between 1 and 2 per cent of the annual per capita income.[64] It was therefore natural that readers should wish to find various diverse subjects covered in the same journal, rather than face the expense of buying more than one. This was doubtless a major reason for the short-lived nature of many subsequent journals specializing in literature and the arts.

The two principal general cultural journals in Egypt at the end of the nineteenth century were *al-Muqtaṭaf* (The Selection, 1876 Beirut, moved to Cairo 1885) and *al-Hilāl* (The Crescent Moon, 1892), both of which manifested an increasing interest in literature. Salāma Mūsā, in his autobiography, testifies to the enormously influential role played by these journals in providing him and his peers with intellectual stimulation and innovative inspiration during their formative years.[65] The primary aim of *al-Muqtaṭaf* was to familiarize Arab readers with Western thought as a means to progress, mainly through science, and Mūsā attributes his adoption of a more telegraphic and less ornamental style of writing to *al-Muqtaṭaf*'s scientific focus.[66] *Al-Muqtaṭaf* began to include poetry after the move to Cairo, following a call by a female reader (Oct. 1885) for more contemporary compositions since she felt that classical poetry did not cater adequately for modern life. Henceforth, *al-Muqtaṭaf* became a forum for readers'

60 A. Maghāzī, op. cit. (1978), pp. 120–3.
61 For example, *al-Ṭā'if*, *al-Mufīd*, *al-Safīr*, *al-Najā* and *al-Zamān*.
62 For example, *al-Waṭan*, *Rawḍat al-Iskandariyya*, *Mir'āt al-Sharq* and *al-Burhān*.
63 S. Hafez, *The Genesis of Arabic Narrative Discourse* (1993), p. 85.
64 Ibid., p. 84.
65 Salāma Mūsa, *The Education of Salāma Mūsā* (1961), p. 123.
66 Ibid., p. 38.

technophile poetry,[67] in keeping with the scientific orientation of its editors, Ya'qūb Ṣarrūf and Fāris Nimr, who understood poetry as an alternative source of knowledge. In a long essay entitled 'Poetry and Poets' (Dec. 1891), they defined poetry as a 'mirror of the soul' with the power to enchant the spirit. It was Ṣarrūf and Nimr who advocated that Arabic poetry be revolutionized through borrowing from European poetry.[68] Both Aḥmad Shawqī and Ḥāfiẓ Ibrāhīm had published poems in *al-Muqtaṭaf* before 1900 and Shawqī's historical play, *'Alī Bey*, and his *Shawqīyyāt* had received rudimentary reviews in it by the same date. After 1900, the number of poems published in *al-Muqtaṭaf* increased and included work by future household names such as Muṣṭafā Luṭfī al-Manfalūṭī, Ma'rūf al-Ruṣāfī and Muṣṭafā Ṣādiq al-Rāfi'ī.

Yet narrative fiction in *al-Muqtaṭaf* before the turn of the twentieth century was still scarce, partly owing to the paucity of good writers at this time, but mainly because the editors were science oriented – Ya'qūb Ṣarrūf, the editor-in-chief, felt that the effort of translating a novel would be better spent translating something more useful. In 1882, still in its Beirut period, *al-Muqtaṭaf* had attacked the reading of fiction, claiming that it spread immorality, wasted time and corrupted the taste of young people.[69] By 1890, however, it had moderated its stance and accepted fiction that was didactic, moralistic and informative. The growing popularity of literary journalism during this period is clearly apparent in Shāhīn Makāriyūs' *al-Laṭā'if* (Jokes, 1886), an offshoot of *al-Muqtaṭaf* that ran monthly for ten years,[70] when it announced its intention to increase its literary studies and stories.[71] *Al-Muqtaṭaf* itself became more receptive to literature towards the end of the 1890s, once worthy works were being produced by writers such as Ibrāhīm and Muḥammad al-Muwayliḥī, Ḥāfiz Ibrāhīm, Aḥmad Taymūr and Muṣṭafā Luṭfi al-Manfalūṭī. On a more practical level, Ṣarrūf realized that concentrating solely on scientific subjects could jeopardize sales, and the popularity of fiction in *al-Hilāl* was doubtless noted. In 1900, al-Manfalūṭī sent a letter to *al-Muqtaṭaf* on behalf of many readers demanding literary works and Ṣarrūf enlarged his journal accordingly.

This demand was symptomatic of the rise of a new artistic and literary sensibility. Ṣarrūf himself began to contribute Arabic translations of English literature to al-Muqtaṭaf,[72] as well as writing four novels of his own during this opening

67 For example, the following issue of *al-Muqtaṭaf* (Nov. 1885) published a reader's poem describing modern technical innovations like the air balloon, raliway and telegraph.

68 D. Glaß, op. cit. (2004), pp. 241–2. NB This work by Glaß provides the first truly comprehensive study of *al-Muqtaṭaf*, locating it within its surrounding social and political milieu.

69 'Ḍarar al-Riwāyāt wa-l-Ash'ār al-Ḥubbiyya', *al-Muqtaṭaf*, Aug. 1882. Cited in S. Hafez, *The Genesis of Arabic Narrative Discourse* (1993), p. 85.

70 *Al-Laṭā'if* resurfaced as *al-Laṭā'if al-Muṣawwara* (Illustrated Jokes, 1915–49).

71 *al-Laṭā'if*, April 1889.

72 For example, Sir Walter Scott's *Talisman* in 1886 and *Tancred of Beaconsfield* in 1900. Cited in D. Glaß, op. cit. (2004), p. 243.

decade of the twentieth century. Eventually, serialized novels were introduced to *al-Muqtaṭaf* via a separate supplement, which could also be ordered as a paperback whole. Nevertheless, conservative attitudes towards literature had not yet vanished and 1905–7 saw an ongoing debate over the moral dangers of reading novels.[73] It is thus unsurprising that literary criticism barely featured in *al-Muqtaṭaf* in these early decades. Ṣarrūf and Nimr made various attempts to awaken a more critical approach to books, and they bewailed the lack of contemporary Arab criticism in contrast to European mastery of the same.[74] Yet criticism was defined as pointing out the merits and defects in an author's work, and it was this notion of 'criticism of literature' rather than more contemporary concepts of 'literary criticism' that persisted in the literary press for several decades to come. Yet in terms of injecting impetus into literary life, the German scholar Dagmar Glaß does not exaggerate the role of *al-Muqtaṭaf* when she asserts that 'the Arabic novel has not least this editorial policy and marketing to thank for its acceptance and current place in literary life'.[75]

Heavily influenced and impressed by the *al-Muqtaṭaf* model during his formative years, the Lebanese intellectual Jūrjī Zaydān established *al-Hilāl*, which still persists as something of an institution in Egyptian, indeed Arab, literary life. In contrast to *al-Muqtaṭaf*, Zaydān placed the emphasis of his journal onto the cultural-historical rather than the scientific,[76] and dedicated one of its five sections to fictional prose, accompanied by pictures, adding a further 'story' section in 1896. In real terms, this amounted to a significant amount of literature since the journal was published fortnightly until 1904, when it adopted its present form of 10 monthly issues plus 2 books. Zaydān was himself a novelist and serialized all of his novels in *al-Hilāl*. Like *al-Muqtaṭaf*, *al-Hilāl* did not forget to stress the moral and reformative role of these fictional works and Zaydān intended that they should 'cultivate the mind, refine the emotions, inform [one's] morality and broaden the sphere of choice'.[77] That didactic concerns still took precedence over literary concerns is evidenced by *al-Hilāl*'s insistence that the author of a historical novel should not manipulate historical fact to serve his artistic aims, thus severely limiting artistic license and inspiration. However, the fact that these historical narratives appeared with the description 'Humour' indicates that they were not published purely for their edifying role. The growing popularity of literary journalism in this period is proved by the fact that the number of subscriptions to *al-Hilāl* doubled after the serialization of Zaydān's *Armanūsa*

73 Interestingly, this debate occurred in the journal's 'Household Administration' section, indicating the level at which fiction was pitched. A. H. al-Ḥawwārī, *Naqd al-Riwāya al-'Arabiyya fī Miṣr* (1978), pp. 28–9. Cited in S. Selim, op. cit. (2004), p. 11.

74 'al-Naqd' (essay), *al-Hilāl*, Dec. 1887. Cited in D. Glaß, op. cit. (2004), pp. 308–9.

75 Ibid., p. 243.

76 Ibid., p. 165.

77 *al-Hilāl*, 15 Feb. 1897.

al-Miṣriyya (Armanusa the Egyptian Woman) in 1895.[78] This technique of working fiction out of history was subsequently adopted by many future writers, including Faraḥ Anṭūn, Muḥammad Farīd Abū Ḥadīd and 'Abbās Khiḍr. Zaydān's novels also incorporated romantic elements (*al-tashwīq*), which both encouraged and facilitated the process of reading at this early stage. Such romantic elements were to prove popular in the future, especially in Maḥmūd Kāmil's journals of the 1930s and 1940s. Moreover, it was in *al-Hilāl* that the study of Arab literary history was first undertaken on a large scale.[79]

Other literary genres were also covered in *al-Hilāl*. Like many of his compatriots from the Levant, Zaydān was keen to encourage and report the activities of literary theatre troupes and he called on young men to establish troupes in Cairo along the lines of those in Alexandria,[80] requesting government funding for such initiatives.[81] *Al-Hilāl* also aimed to inspire theatrical activity through the translation of plays, in particular by Corneille and Molière. Nor was poetry neglected, with articles and poems by a whole host of now-famous poets featuring in the journal's early years, among them Khalīl Muṭrān, Jibrān Khalīl Jibrān, Aḥmad Shawqī, Amīn al-Rīḥānī and Muṣṭafā Ṣādiq al-Rāfi'ī. One critic has described Jibrān's articles in al-Hilāl as prose poetry representing 'a new kind of modern artistic publication'.[82] In short, as Moosa claims, *al-Hilāl* provided 'an important source of inspiration for young writers, poets, historians and littérateurs of every stripe and age'.[83]

Thus, at the beginning of the twentieth century, new fictional forms were taking shape, blending traditional Arabic forms with a new innovatory style and content to produce something authentically Egyptian in character. Epitomizing this fusion – accomplished through journalism – is Muḥammad al-Muwayliḥī's *Ḥadīth 'Īsā Ibn Hishām aw Fatra min al-Zamān* (The Story of 'Īsā Ibn Hishām or A Period of Time). This work developed out of a series of articles beginning in *al-Muqaṭṭam* newspaper in the mid-1890s and continuing in *Miṣbāḥ al-Sharq* (Light of the East, 1898), a weekly journal founded by Muḥammad al-Muwayliḥī's

78 A. Ḥ. al-Ṭamāwī, *al-Hilāl: mi'at 'ām min al-taḥdīth wa-l-tanwīr, 1892–1992* (1992), p. 39.

79 Following the publication of a review of a European book, *History of the Arabs and their Literature*, in which the reviewer commented that the Arabs themselves lacked any such literary science (*al-Hilāl*, 1 Aug. 1893), Jūrjī Zaydān began publishing a long series of articles in 1894 under the heading *Tārīkh Ādāb al-Lugha al-'Arabiyya* which were later collected into four volumes (1911–14). P. Cachia, op. cit. (1990), p. 89.

80 *al-Hilāl*, June 1897. Cited by A. Maghāzī, op. cit. (1978), p. 143.

81 *al-Hilāl*, 1 Jan. 1898.

82 A. Ḥ. al-Ṭamāwī, *al-Hilāl: mi'at 'ām min al-taḥdīth wa-l-tanwīr, 1892–1992* (1992), pp. 77–82. In May 1905, many pages were devoted to Muṭrān's *al-Janīn al-Shahīd* (The Martyred Embryo), which comprised hundreds of verses. The subject matter was still traditionally moralistic, warning against the evils of alcohol through the story of a girl's intoxication, seduction, pregnancy and subsequent abortion. Nevertheless, the poem has been described as innovatory, leading Arabic poetry towards romanticism.

83 M. Moosa, op. cit. (1983), p. 158.

father, Ibrāhīm. The work was not published in book form until 1907, by which time it had been severely edited and included none of the *al-Muqaṭṭam* material.[84] This provides firm evidence of the important role played by journalism in creating a relatively free environment in which literary forms and works could develop. Ḥamza believes that journalism, as the prose platform of social reformers, set the precedent for the first Egyptian narrative of modern times being of a social nature. He writes that 'this journalism was itself an intellectual awakening paving the way for the emergence of Egyptian fiction' and he cites *Ḥadīth 'Īsā Ibn Hishām* as the first evidence of this.[85]

Unlike other forms of literary journalism in *Miṣbāḥ al-Sharq*, such as the publication of Arabic literature from the classical canon, *Ḥadīth 'Īsā Ibn Hishām* was truly innovative, employing the traditional *maqāma* form but endowing it with a modern content. Ṣanū''s and al-Nadīm's fictional episodes satirizing political and social institutions provided a precedent for various scenes in *Ḥadīth 'Īsā Ibn Hishām*, but al-Muwayliḥī's work proved superior in both its narrative quality and episodic structure. The fictional episodes were not published for literary interest alone; Roger Allen writes, 'the principal purpose behind *Fatra min al-Zamān* was to enable him [Muḥammad al-Muwayliḥī] to discuss issues of current interest through the characters in his story and to reflect the editorial policy of his newspaper on various subjects'.[86] In fact it reflected all four of the policies consistently advocated by *Miṣbāḥ al-Sharq*: Pan-Islamism based on the Ottoman caliphate; support for Muḥammad 'Abduh's views on religious reforms; ridicule of the blind imitation of Western customs and opposition to the British occupation. The fact that episodes closely reflected events reported in the journal helped to establish a firmer link between literature and everyday issues and played an important role in developing and popularizing fictional writing. While the work's social and political relevance ensured its immediate popularity, it also inspired other similar literary attempts, such as the *maqāmāt* of Ibrāhīm al-Muwayliḥī and Ḥafiẓ Ibrāhīm. Ultimately, it was to become a landmark of Egyptian literature, penetrating the national curriculum; Allen now believes that its weak narrative thread might even be seen as a precursor to the fragmented narratives of recent decades.[87]

The more conservative side of literary journalism at the turn of the twentieth century may be perceived in *al-Bayān* (Information, 1897), founded by Ibrāhīm al-Yāzijī and Bashāra Zalzāl. This began as a monthly, but by September 1897 the popularity of cultural journalism induced it to publish fortnightly and to

84 See Roger Allen, 'Muḥammad al-Muwayliḥī's Coterie: The Context of *Ḥadīth 'Īsā Ibn Hishām*', *Quaderni di Studi Arabi*, no. 18, 2000, pp. 51–60, which discusses some of the differences between the four subsequent book editions of the original series of articles. NB The complete works of Muḥammad al-Muwayliḥī were published in Cairo by the Supreme Council for Culture in 2002.

85 'Abd al-Laṭīf Ḥamza, *Adab al-Maqāla al-Ṣuḥufiyya*, Vol. III (1957–63), pp. 98–9.

86 R. Allen, *A Period of Time* (1992), p. 47.

87 R. Allen, 'Muḥammad al-Muwayliḥī's Coterie: The Context of *Ḥadīth 'Īsā Ibn Hishām*', *Quaderni di Studi Arabi*, no. 18, 2000, p. 59.

increase the number of pages by a third in order to include more scientific and literary studies, generally penned by Ibrāhīm al-Yāzijī, Qastakī al-Ḥamasī and Najīb al-Ḥaddād. The literary content comprised mainly poetry, and the regular question and answer section often included discussions of popular early poetry as well as matters of grammar and language. It occasionally revealed a more progressive attitude, as demonstrated in Najīb al-Ḥaddād's harsh criticism of Arabic poetry and praise for European poetry in his seminal article, 'Between Arabic Poetry and Foreign Poetry'.[88] *Al-Bayān* also recognized the need for linguistic development as a prerequisite for literary development and ran a series of robust articles on 'Language and the Age'.[89]

Al-Ḍiyā' (Light, 1898) was the name under which *al-Bayān* continued until it finally ceased in 1906. In the opening article of the first issue, al-Yāzijī wrote that although there were more than fifty journals in circulation in Cairo at this time, most were concerned primarily with international politics and contained little to which Egyptians could really relate.[90] *Al-Ḍiyā'* increased the emphasis on literature, introducing a new section for fictional narrative (*riwāyāt*), which accounted for about one-third of the journal. As in *al-Hilāl*, the *riwāyāt* were introduced as 'Humour', indicating a move away from the disapproving attitude towards literature intended for entertainment. These were usually detective or police stories translated from English by Nasīb al-Mash'alānī. Occasionally, however, original stories would appear by writers such as Labība Hāshim, Salīm al-'Aqqād, Khalīl al-Jāwīsh, Ibrāhīm Barakāt and Ilyās al-Ghaḍbān. Nevertheless, an underlying conservative attitude towards fiction was still apparent inasmuch as readers were often told that the events of a story were true, even for some of the translated stories.[91] In response to readers' demands, the amount of poetry published increased dramatically.[92] The journal also published numerous articles on linguistic issues such as etymology, transliteration and translation, as well as a number of progressive articles on an eclectic range of subjects – 'Journalism in the West' dealt with the weapon of caricature and with the journalistic article as a separate genre, and an article on the relationship between the writer and his work provided an early warning against overt subjectivity in literary criticism.[93] A regular section reviewing contemporary publications, including Arabic cultural journals published abroad as well as foreign-language journals published in Egypt, is a treasure trove for modern researchers.

88 *al-Bayān*, 1 Sept. 1897.

89 *al-Bayān*, 1 June 1897–1 Jan. 1898.

90 *al-Ḍiyā'*, 15 Sept. 1898.

91 'Abbās Khiḍr, 'Min Awā'il Kuttāb al-Uqṣūṣa fī Miṣr', *al-Qiṣṣa*, March 1965, p. 32.

92 At first, *al-Ḍiyā'* published only about five poems (*qaṣā'id* and *muwashshaḥāt*) annually. After a year, however, al-Yāzijī wrote of readers' demands for more contemporary poetry. Between September 1899 and March 1900, five of the leading articles were about poetry, and by 1904 the number of poems published annually, both original and translated, had at least doubled.

93 *al-Ḍiyā'*, 15 May 1906.

Representative of the occidentalist perspective of literary journalism at the turn of the twentieth century – and extremely influential within a certain intellectual elite – was Faraḥ Anṭūn's fortnightly *al-Jāmi'a al-'Uthmāniyya* (The Ottoman Community, 1899)[94] in Alexandria. Salāma Mūsā testifies to *al-Jāmi'a*'s role in providing him with 'a new perspective, and even a new inspiration'. He credits Anṭūn's presentation of French literature with influencing him to 'a boundless veneration for European literature', a tendency which subsequently proved important and influential in Mūsā's own journals, which in turn wielded enormous influence on the future direction of Egyptian culture and literature. While, at this time, *al-Hilāl*'s outlook was largely Eastern oriented, *al-Muqtaṭaf* lacked literary content and *Miṣbāḥ al-Sharq* focused on traditional Arab culture, *al-Jāmi'a* was 'like an explosion. It generated light and energy and power. It enlightened our minds, and it motivated our first gropings towards a new society, efforts modelled on those of the French writers of the late eighteenth century'.[95]

The early twentieth century

Despite the fact that the British occupiers closed many secondary schools, the reading public had risen from no more than 30,000 at the start of the occupation to over 100,000 during the reign of 'Abbās II (1892–1914).[96] While it is estimated that there were fewer than 5,000 subscribers to Egyptian newspapers in 1882, this number was said to be over 20,000 by 1897, and the actual public among whom these newspapers circulated could have been as large as 200,000.[97] The attention of most readers, however, was focused on politics and, by the end of the nineteenth century, bodies of political opinion had begun to cluster around newspapers which became the mouthpieces of political parties. Significantly, it was the parties that formed around the papers rather than vice versa. Given the huge impact that rising nationalist awareness was to have on literary development in Egypt,[98] the most important of these mainly political papers are mentioned in the following section.

Al-Muqaṭṭam (The Muqattam Hills, 1889) was a pro-British daily, launched by the Lebanese Fāris Nimr and Ya'qūb Ṣarrūf and financed by Cromer to counter

94 This title was shortened to simply *al-Jāmi'a* after the journal's first year and it was relaunched in America after Anṭūn moved there in 1907. Upon his return in 1911, *al-Jāmi'a* was revived in Cairo until Anṭūn's death in 1922. Rizq Ṣafūrī, 'Min A'lām al-Fikr al-'Arabī: Faraḥ Anṭūn wa-l-Fikr al-'Arabī fī al-'Aṣr al-Ḥadīth', *al-Bayādir*, no. 845, n.d. Online. Available HTTP: http://albayader.com/index.asp?cat=27&issue=845

95 S. Mūsā, *The Education of Salāma Mūsa* (1961), pp. 39–40.

96 A. Maghāzī, op. cit. (1978), p. 121.

97 'Kuttāb al-Jarā'id wa-l-Majallāt', *al-Hilāl*, Oct. 1897. Cited by S. Hafez, *The Genesis of Arabic Narrative Discourse* (1993), p. 84. NB Such figures are now impossible to confirm and must be treated with caution.

98 See Yasir Suleiman and Ibrāhīm Muhawi (eds.) *Literature and Nation in the Middle East* (2006). See also S. Selim's chapter on 'Novels and Nations', op. cit. (2004), pp. 66–90.

al-Ahrām's support for the French. As the nationalist movement developed, its writers and thinkers gathered around *al-Mu'ayyad* (The Endorsed, 1889), edited by Shaykh 'Alī Yūsuf and sponsored by the Khedive. Kelidar describes Yūsuf as 'a true and native son of Egypt', adding that he 'knew better than most of his rivals how to appeal to the minds of his countrymen'.[99] Its contributors boasted many men of talent including Sa'd Zaghlūl, Muḥammad 'Abduh, Muṣṭafā Kāmil, who was to spearhead the call for a university,[100] Ibrāhīm al-Laqqānī and Ḥāfiẓ 'Awaḍ, who went on to found *Hā Hā Hā* and *Khayāl al-Ẓill* (see the earlier section on satirical journalism). The importance of the Arabic language, together with the need for improvements in education, became favourite topics of *al-Mu'ayyad*. Many progressives featured among its contributors, including Qāsim Amīn, whose provocative treatise on women's emancipation was serialized in it, Rashīd Riḍā, editor of the Islamic reformist journal *al-Manār* (The Minaret, 1898),[101] Muḥammad Kurd 'Alī, who went on to edit *al-Muqtabas* (Acquired Knowledge, 1906), the Islamic reformist Muḥammad 'Abduh and the Iraqi poet Jamīl Ṣidqī al-Zaḥāwī.[102] *Al-Mu'ayyad* published many of Muṣṭafā Luṭfī al-Manfalūṭī's early fictional pieces which were not collected into book form until the second decade of this century.[103] Like al-Nadīm's fictional episodes, al-Manfalūṭī's also contained didactic and reformative elements, but unlike al-Nadīm, Hafez writes that his awareness of the national identity was not strong enough to truly inspire readers.[104] Nevertheless, the elegant refinement and fluency of his poetic and emotionally charged language would inspire the young littérateurs who were to become *Jamā'at al-Madrasa al-Ḥadītha* (The Modern School) in the 1920s.[105] *Al-Mu'ayyad*'s circulation figures testify to its popularity,[106] although its readership was sharply dented when another nationalist paper opposing the British, *al-Liwā'* (The Standard, 1900), was founded by Muṣṭafā Kāmil. *Al-Liwā'* too was sponsored at first by the Khedive, but, whereas *al-Mu'ayyad* adjusted its political stance after the Khedive signed the *entente cordiale* with the British in 1904, *al-Liwā'* maintained its strong nationalist stance. It became one of the most influential political papers of the early twentieth century, together with Luṭfī

99 Abbas Kelidar, 'Shaykh 'Alī Yūsuf: Egyptian Journalist and Islamic Nationalist', in M. R. Buheiry (ed.) *Intellectual Life in the Arab East, 1890–1939* (1981), p. 14.

100 'Izz al-Dīn al-Amīn, op. cit. (1970), p. 96.

101 *Al-Manār*, in which Riḍā spread Muḥammad 'Abduh's reformist Islamic views, emphasized the need to interpret Islam to suit modern society as a means to achieve pan-Arab nationalism until Riḍā's death in 1935.

102 A. Kelidar, op. cit. (1981), p. 16.

103 Most of al-Manfalūṭī's pieces collected in *al-Naẓarāt* (vol. I, 1910; vol. II, 1912; Vol. III 1920) and *al-'Abarāt* (1915) had been published in newspapers and periodicals many years earlier, especially in *al-Mu'ayyad*.

104 S. Hafez, PhD thesis (1979), p. 68.

105 Ḥusayn Fawzī. In Muḥammad Shalabī, *Ma' Ruwwād al-Fikr wa-l-Fann* (1982), p. 81.

106 It is estimated that *al-Mu'ayyad*'s circulation had risen to 6,000 by 1896. A. Ayalon, op. cit. (1995), p. 109.

al-Sayyid's daily *al-Jarīda* (The Newspaper, 1907), whose journalists Cachia deems the first firm and consistent intellectual supporters of nationalism in Egypt.[107]

Al-Jarīda frequently complemented its political current affairs content with original Arabic fiction, in addition to much translation from European literature. The main themes of this were nature (especially in the work of Luṭfī al-Sayyid himself), the Egyptian countryside and intellectual meditations, for example on the value of human life, happiness and European civilization. *Al-Jarīda* provided an outlet for contemporary young poets such as 'Abd al-Raḥmān Shukrī, Aḥmad al-Kāshif, Ibrāhīm al-Miṣrī, Abū Shādī, Aḥmad Shawqī and many more; Ḥamza lists twenty-eight poets and his list does not claim to be exhaustive.[108] After the appearance of Muṣṭafā Ṣādiq al-Rāfi'ī's book *Tārīkh Adab al-'Arab* (The History of the Arabs' Literature) in 1912, *al-Jarīda* became the battleground for the ensuing debate between the old, spearheaded by al-Rāfi'ī, and the new, represented by Ṭāhā Ḥusayn and Muḥammad Ḥusayn Haykal among others. Many thought-provoking articles were published during the course of which Ṭaha Ḥusayn, whose articles took pride of place in the paper, became well known as a literary critic.[109] Ḥamza writes that *al-Jarīda*'s encouragement of literary criticism aimed to root Egyptian literature firmly in modern times. This nascent literary criticism tried to distinguish between objective and subjective criticism and helped to free Egyptian literature from its old themes and excesses.[110]

The increasing preoccupation with and articulation of nationalistic sentiments in these newspapers began to be reflected in literary as well as political life, as Luṭfī al-Sayyid's nationalist ideology was carried forward by Salāma Mūsā and Muḥammad Ḥusayn Haykal. Egyptian nationalism favoured the creation of an Egyptian literature set in Egyptian surroundings with Egyptian characters. Some Egyptian nationalists also favoured use of the Egyptian colloquial in the educational system and literary expression. Haykal's *Zaynab* (Zaynab, 1913), frequently hailed as the first Arabic novel,[111] was serialized in *al-Jarīda* and fulfilled both these requirements: it was set in rural Egypt and the dialogue was written in the Egyptian colloquial. It received favourable reviews in the press and its model was followed by several other Egyptian novels, also answering *al-Jarīda*'s call for a national Egyptian literature.

Despite journalism's predominant interest in political affairs, there was still an enormous increase in the number of cultural journals published around the

107 P. Cachia, op. cit. (1990), p. 12.

108 'Abd al-Laṭīf Ḥamza, *Adab al-Maqāla al-Ṣuḥufiyya*, Vol. VI (1957–63), pp. 65–6.

109 Ṭaha Ḥusayn's articles in *al-Jarīda* included 'About the Language' (26 April 1913) and 'The Life of Literature' (19, 21, 26, 29 Jan., 7, 8, Feb., 8 March 1914).

110 'Abd al-Laṭīf Ḥamza, *Adab al-Maqāla al-Ṣuḥufiyya*, Vol. VI (1957–63), pp. 180–1.

111 *Zaynab* tends to be judged the first Arabic novel when the nineteenth century European novel is upheld as the ideal model. In fact, numerous novels of sorts – didactic, historical and recreational, as well as adaptations from European literature – were produced before *Zaynab*. See S. Selim, op. cit. (2004), pp. 62–70. Also see R. Allen, 'The Beginnings of the Arabic Novel', in M. M. Badawi (ed.) *Modern Arabic Literature* (1992), pp. 190–2.

turn of the twentieth century. One scholar is even led to describe the publication of *al-Muqtabas* in Cairo in 1906 rather than Damascus as 'essentially superfluous', given the richness of cultural journalism already in existence in Cairo.[112] Appendix A provides a flavour of the remarkable proliferation of literary journalism at this time, yet one must beware of assuming cultural content merely from a journal's title. This period witnessed an instability, if not confusion, about the definition of the terms *adab* (now generally considered 'literature') and *fann* (now generally considered 'art'). In the loosest interpretation, these categories were held to cover any topic bar politics and religion.[113] In fact, much narrative fiction was actually published under the more light-hearted rubric of fukāhāt (humour) or *musāmarāt* (nightly tales),[114] with the latter cropping up frequently in the titles of the journals themselves.

This rise of Egyptian literary journalism was influenced, at least in part, by the model provided by foreign literary journalism in Egypt, which flourished as never before during the British occupation. French literary journalism proved particularly prolific, perhaps because the Egyptian cultural elite had by this time become expert at the French language, or perhaps because the French were more concerned to maintain their cultural ties with Egypt now that the British were in occupation. Maghāzī cites twenty influential French journals in Egypt that were concerned with literary and artistic issues during this period.[115] Several Egyptian journals included regular reviews and round-ups of what the contemporary French press had to say on cultural and literary matters.

Meanwhile, the search for new forms and themes in Arabic poetry was gathering pace, with literary journalism playing a key role in the propagation of new poetic ideas. One of the prime movers in the poetic revolution was the Lebanese poet Khalīl Muṭrān. Having gained valuable journalistic skills whilst working at *al-Ahrām* in the 1890s and publishing in *al-Hilāl, al-Mu'ayyad* and other journals,[116] Muṭrān was best able to expound his project for poetic renewal by founding his own journals. Through the fortnightly *al-Majalla al-Miṣriyya*

112 Samir Seikaly, 'Damascene Intellectual Life in the Opening Years of the Twentieth Century: Muḥammad Kurd 'Alī and *al-Muqtabas*', in M. R. Buheiry (ed.) *Intellectual Life in the Arab East, 1890–1939* (1981), p. 127.

113 See *al-Hilāl*, 15 Aug. 1894, p.752 for evidence on confusion over the word *adab*. In fact, there are broader examples of journal titles which one might now consider misleading: *al-Mathaf* (The Museum,1893) had nothing whatsoever to do with artefacts and an advertisement on the front page that 'the fine arts' (*al-funūn al-jamīla*) featured among the contents simply indicated the inclusion of a picture or two to supplement an article; *al-Fūtūghrāf* (The Photograph, 1903) dealt with politics and current affairs rather than the cinema or photography, and *al-Tamthīl* (Acting/Representation,1899) with politics rather than the theatre. See A. Jundī, op. cit. (1967), p. 224 and A. Maghāzī, op. cit. (1978), p. 130.

114 See S. Selim's analysis of 'Abd al-Muḥsin Ṭaha Badr's typology of the novel at this time, op. cit. (2004), pp. 62–70.

115 A. Maghāzī, op. cit. (1978), pp. 179–88.

116 Jamāl al-Dīn al-Ramādī, *Khalīl Muṭrān: Shā'ir al-Aqṭār al-'Arabiyya* (n.d.), p. 25.

(The Egyptian Journal, 1900) and after it the daily *al-Jawā'ib al-Miṣriyya* (Egyptian Responses, 1903),[117] Muṭrān called for the organic unity of the Arabic poem. Influenced by his knowledge of Western, in particular French, poetry, he injected new themes into the fixed rhyme and metre of the conventional Arabic *qaṣīda*, as well composing strophic verse. His main achievement was to revolutionize the internal form of the poem, such that language, meaning and images were able to interact as part of a whole, rather than being manipulated merely to fulfil external formal criteria.[118] The journalistic medium proved especially effective in inculcating such renewal because, rather than isolating the poems in the ivory tower of a *diwān*, it interspersed them with subject matter that was directly relevant to contemporary life – Muṭrān himself wrote articles on economics, science, agriculture and history and his journal tackled the pressing issues of the day, even publishing Qāsim Amīn's provocative treatise, *al-Mar'a al-Jadīda* (The New Woman). Muṭrān was to have a decisive influence on the future course of poetry, influencing both the *Dīwān* poets, such as 'Abd al-Raḥmān Shukrī, 'Abbās Maḥmūd al-'Aqqād and Ibrāhīm 'Abd al-Qādir al-Māzinī, and in particular the *Apollo* group of the 1930s under Aḥmad Zakī Abū Shādī.

Interest in the theatre was also gathering pace in the press, particularly among Syrian and Lebanese journalists in Egypt, such as Salīm Sarkīs whose fortnightly journal, *Sarkīs* (Sarkis, 1905) was one of the first to publish the complete text of an original Arabic play.[119] *Sarkīs*' main focus was the theatre and Sarkīs himself presented a progressive stance on theatre criticism, as exemplified in his perceptive and objective comments on Iskandar Faraḥ's new play *Mary Tudor*,[120] at a time when exaggerated eulogy tended to prevail. The journal even sponsored theatre evenings, in which poets and orators were also invited to participate and declaim, and it championed the rights of dramatists against the greed of theatre proprietors. Sarkīs enlisted the support of a number of prominent writers including Jūrjī Zaydān, Khalīl Muṭrān, Sulaymān al-Bustānī and Muḥammad al-Muwayliḥī, but writers from the younger generation also contributed, among them Aḥmad Nasīm, Aḥmad al-Kāshif and Mayy Ziyāda.[121] The journal was one of the first to introduce special issues dedicated to events or prominent literary figures, such as Khalīl Muṭrān and Ḥāfiẓ Ibrāhīm. As well as stories, serialized novels, rudimentary critical studies and articles on the arts, there was a dedicated poetry section. The vital nurturing role of literary journalism is evidenced by the

117 It ran until 1907 according to M. M. Badawi (1975), 1904 according to Mounah A. Khouri (1971) and 1905 according to S. Moreh (1976). Since the journal suffered financial difficulties, it may be that it was suspended at times, but resurrected again.

118 S. Moreh, *Modern Arabic Poetry 1800–1970* (1976), pp. 58–9.

119 *Ḥawla Sarīr al-Marīḍ*, written by Sarkīs himself, was a philosophical, symbolic one act play, reminiscent of Ṣanū''s symbolic dramas. *Sarkīs*, July 1912. Cited in A. Maghāzī, op. cit. (1978), p. 156.

120 *Sarkīs*, 15 Nov. 1905, p. 438. Cited in A. Maghāzī, op. cit. (1978), p. 149.

121 A. H. al-Ṭamāwī, *Fuṣūl min al-Ṣiḥāfa al-Adabiyya* (1989), pp. 194–8.

fact that some contributed poems by Muṭrān and Ibrāhīm were never published in their complete works. *Sarkīs* was also effective in stirring and disseminating new literary ideas by recording debates and discussions between writers and intellectuals in literary salons, clubs and cafés. The journal proved popular and resilient, continuing until Sarkīs' death in 1926, despite being forced to suspend publication several times.

Another influential general cultural journal of this period was the Syrian Muḥammad Kurd 'Alī's *al-Muqtabas* (Acquired Knowledge, 1906), a monthly which was particularly keen to introduce Egyptian readers to Western writers through both expository articles and translation. The opening editorial pre-empted the opening manifestos of the great cultural journals of the 1930s, promising to provide readers with truths from East and West, with old and new, and to avoid politics and religion in order to remain free from prejudice and bias.[122] *Al-Muqtabas* tirelessly reiterated the need for reform and renewal in the face of Arab decline. Yet with regard to language, Kurd 'Alī himself began by using traditional *saj'* (rhymed prose), thereby falling into the very kind of mechanical perpetration of tradition which he opposed. However, he responded to criticism, evolving a more clear and direct style suited to the propagation of new concepts.[123] In fact, *al-Muqtabas* even criticized the use of *saj'* in new literary works such as Ḥāfiẓ Ibrāhīm's *Layālī Saṭīḥ*, (Nights of Saṭīḥ, 1906), which employed the *maqāma* form as a vehicle for social criticism, at a time when other journals such as *al-Hilāl* and *al-Manār* issued gushing welcomes.[124] Both Egyptian and Syrian authors contributed to *al-Muqtabas*, among them Aḥmad Taymūr, Aḥmad Zakī and Ṭāhir al-Jazā'irī, before it relocated to Damascus in 1909.

One of the first major journals of the twentieth century to present itself as dedicated solely to literature and the arts was *al-Zuhūr* (Blossomings, 1910), a monthly founded and edited by Anṭūn al-Jumayyil with Amīn Taqī al-Dīn joining as co-editor the following year. Encouraged by the opening of the Egyptian University in 1908, *al-Zuhūr* aimed to provide training and encouragement for budding young writers and to forge links between Arab writers of different regions. To this end, it introduced numerous writing competitions and won a broad reputation, a strategy which became popular among journals in the 1930s and 1940s. Al-Ṭamāwī likens the poetry section to a literary market-place in which poets from various Arab regions were able to publish their poetic responses to other poems. Original poems telling of human emotions and experience

122 Opening editorial to *al-Muqtabas*, Jan. 1906 (Muḥarram 1324).

123 Samir Seikaly, 'Damascene Intellectual Life in the Opening Years of the Twentieth Century: Muḥammad Kurd 'Alī and *al-Muqtabas*', in M. R. Buheiry (ed.) *Intellectual Life in the Arab East, 1890–1939* (1981), pp. 127–8.

124 *al-Muqtabas*, Oct. 1908, p. 598; *al-Hilāl*, July 1908, p. 583; *al-Manār*, Aug. 1908, p. 530. Cited in H. A. R. Gibb, 'Studies in Contemporary Arabic Literature: IV. The Egyptian Novel', *Bulletin of the School of Oriental and African Studies*, Vol. 7, no.1, 1933, p. 6.

dominated over the old-style poetry composed for social and political occasions, and these were published alongside translations and Arabization of European poetry.[125] Like the great periodicals of the 1930s, *al-Zuhūr* aimed to present a balanced selection of literature featuring both the European literary canon and contemporary original Arabic literature. The journal also examined modes of literary criticism, reviewed books and provided news and comment on contemporary literary life.

The rapid development of interest in the theatre at this time was particularly well catered for in *al-Zuhūr* and, as the practice of publishing plays before performing them spread, *al-Zuhūr* began to write criticisms of these, focusing on literary practice rather than the provision of theatre news which was now commonplace. *Al-Zuhūr* reflected nationalist sentiments in its call for an indigenous literature and its demand for the establishment of a theatre school in Egypt. It stressed the need for state intervention to protect the 'serious' theatre from the loose translation of plays and the use of the vernacular. One prominent study, aimed at encouraging budding young actors, examined Jūrj Abyaḍ as a role model under the sweeping title 'The First Eastern Actor'.[126] European role models were also paraded before readers and the same issue provided extracts from Racine's *Andromaque* together with a comparative study of the way in which Homer, Virgil and Racine treated this character. *Al-Zuhūr* was also the first journal to serialize a Shakespeare play, *Julius Caesar*.[127] By the time the journal ceased in 1913, it had made a significant contribution to Egyptian literary life and to the development of the theatre in particular. Its mission was picked up by *Jam'iyyat Anṣār al-Tamthīl* (The Society for the Friends of Drama), founded in 1914.

As part of its effort to promote a serious Egyptian theatre, *Jam'iyyat Anṣār al-Tamthīl* published a monthly journal dedicated to the Egyptian theatre, the first of its kind: *al-Adab wa-l-Tamthīl* (Literature and Drama, 1916). The cover depicted Muḥammad 'Uthmān Jalāl and Aḥmad Abū Khalīl al-Qabbānī and advertised its aim as the establishment of an independent Egyptian theatre. The fact that it ran to only two issues indicates that the market was not yet strong enough to support such specialist journals. Like many of the short-lived specialist literary journals in the decades to come, *al-Adab wa-l-Tamthīl* communicated firm notions of its literary role and duty in its opening editorial, which issued a damning indictment of the vulgar new vaudeville theatre. As part of its attempt to rescue the 'serious' theatre, an article on the acting profession provided a general classification of dramatic roles, analyzing their requirements to ensure that only those qualified tried to enter the acting profession. This journal evidences the beginning of interest in and study of the roots of Egyptian dramatists and the

125 A. Ḥ. al-Ṭamāwī, *Fuṣūl min al-Ṣiḥāfa al-Adabiyya* (1989), pp. 279–307.

126 *al-Zuhūr*, April 1910, pp. 65–7. Cited by A. Maghāzī, op. cit. (1978), p. 159.

127 *al-Zuhūr*, Nov. 1912–Jan. 1913. By popular demand, *al-Zuhūr* published the whole play at once in August 1913.

foundations of the Arab theatre of music and dance, which had maintained interest in dramatic performance at a time when many translated and adapted texts were of poor quality. In *al-Adab wa-l-Tamthīl*, we see the first technical, as opposed to literary, criticism of plays. It went beyond *al-Ẓuhūr*'s theatre studies in that it developed a more precise and specialist language.[128]

Shortly after the appearance of *al-Zuhūr* and responding to the same desire for literary renewal, 'Abd al-Raḥmān al-Barqūqī launched the monthly *al-Bayān* (Information, 1911). As a more general cultural journal, it published articles on a wide variety of subjects ranging from mysticism to Bolshevism, but its prominence on the literary scene can be ascertained from the eminent names featuring among its contributors: 'Abbās Maḥmūd al-'Aqqād, Ibrāhīm al-Māzinī, Muḥammad Ḥusayn Haykal and Muḥammad al-Sibā'ī. *Al-Bayān*'s literary content included poetry, travelogues and short stories, and it played a significant role in the translation movement. In 1919, al-Barqūqī declared his intention of publishing a complete short story in every issue in response to readers' demands for this.[129] These were generally translated from European languages and would occasionally be followed by a commentary. For example, an untitled story by Turgenev was accompanied by a lengthy commentary in which the story was shown to be a psychological study, elucidating the differences between Russia and Western European nations.[130] This identification with the hopes and aspirations of Russians foreshadowed the interest shown in Russian writers by *Jamā'at al-Madrasat al-Ḥadītha* (The Modern School) which crystallized around the journal *al-Fajr* in the mid-1920s. In fact, the short story writer Ḥusayn Fawzī testifies to the great influence exerted by *al-Bayān*'s translations from Western literature on the education of the young writers who were to form 'The Modern School' a decade later.[131] Yet Salāma Mūsā criticized the reactionary linguistic attitude of *al-Bayān*, describing al-Barqūqī's language as 'old-fashioned' and 'dead'.[132]

Probably the most important progressive new journal of the war period to devote significant space to literature was 'Abd al-Ḥamīd Ḥamdi's *al-Sufūr* (The Unveiling, 1915). This weekly emerged as a more specialist literary journal, catering for something approaching an avant-garde. Its aim was 'the creation of a literary awakening aimed at freeing the mind, delivering Egyptian nationalism from weak elements, and freeing women from the chains of ignorance and unsound traditions'.[133] It published early work by eminent writers such as Muḥammad Ḥusayn Haykal, Manṣūr Fahmī, Ṭāhā Ḥusayn, Ḥusayn Fawzī and

128 A. Maghāzī, op. cit. (1978), pp. 220–34.
129 *al-Bayān*, Jan. 1919.
130 *al-Bayān*, June 1919.
131 Ḥusayn Fawzī, in M. Shalabī, *Ma' Ruwwād al-Fikr wa-l-Fann* (1982), p. 81.
132 S. Mūsā, *The Education of Salāma Mūsā* (1961), p. 159.
133 B. Baron, *The Women's Awakening in Egypt* (1994), p. 34.

Aḥmad Ḍayf. Many contributors were pupils of Luṭfī al-Sayyid who wished to continue to develop the emerging literary forms and propagate the modern outlook of *al-Jarīda* after its closure in 1914. One of the journal's founder members was Muṣṭafā 'Abd al-Rāziq, who ran an influential and progressive literary salon and whom Hafez calls 'a neglected pioneer'. The innovative narrative texts he published in *al-Sufūr* were remarkable for their simple language and high level of verisimilitude, yet none was collected into his subsequent works, possibly because writing narrative fiction was not yet deemed serious enough to be compatible with 'Abd al-Rāziq's subsequent government position.[134] This proves the vital role of literary journalism in providing an outlet for work which might never otherwise have come to light and in enabling other talent to crystallize around such work.

Al-Sufūr called for Egyptians to free themselves from tradition and adopt a style suited to contemporary requirements in their search for an authentic Egyptian literature. It advised its readers to study Egyptian poets and writers, whilst embracing European literature.[135] The first issue published an article criticizing Muṣṭafā Luṭfi al-Manfalūṭī's works for their crude didacticism and incoherent structure. This indicates the emergence of a new literary sensibility in which the organic unity of a work began to take precedence over the verbal acrobatics it showcased. *Al-Sufūr* was of particular significance in encouraging short story writers,[136] with Muḥammad Taymūr providing a role model through his regular stories which appeared throughout 1917 under the general title *Mā Tarā al-'Uyūn* (What Eyes See), which did not emerge in book form until 1922. The title demonstrates that the stories aimed to reflect social reality and, although some of the themes had been tackled previously by al-Nadīm, Taymūr's treatment was more artistic, although his simple *fuṣḥā* dialogue lacked the impact of al-Nadīm's vivid colloquial dialogue.[137] Hafez explains this change in literary sensibility through a change in priorities: 'Unlike the preceding writers whose fictional achievements were somehow incidental to their reformative and polemic goals, Taymūr's prime aim was to create a new literary genre'.[138] In *al-Sufūr*, Taymūr repeatedly affirmed the independence of each story in *Mā Tarā al-'Uyūn* in order to distinguish them from the episodic *maqāma*. Many stories published by Muḥammad Taymūr in *al-Sufūr* and other journals were not republished in collections because he considered them too immature. This confirms the importance of literary journalism as a training ground or nursery both for writers and for the development of modern literary

134 S. Hafez, *The Genesis of Arabic Narrative Discourse* (1993), pp. 149–52.

135 Yaḥyā Ḥaqqī, *Fajr al-Qiṣṣa al-Miṣriyya* (1975), p. 76.

136 Sayyid Ḥāmid al-Nassāj, 'Ḥawla Qaḍiyyat al-Riyāda fī al-Qiṣṣa al-Miṣriyya', *Nādī al-Qiṣṣa*, June 1970.

137 S. Hafez, PhD thesis (1979), pp. 80–5.

138 Ibid., p. 78.

genres in Egypt. It was *al-Sufūr* that provided sustenance for *Jamā'at al-Madrasa al-Ḥadītha* in its early years.[139]

In general, literary journalism in the early twentieth century consisted of the encyclopaedic presentation of information rather than close criticism and debate. An exaggerated, subjective and superficial style of literary appreciation still dominated, although meaning was no longer sacrificed at the altar of an elaborate language. The communicative imperative of new reports and the evolution of the journalistic article had done much to encourage a more succinct and lucid prose style. Nevertheless, Maghāzī accuses journals such as *al-Hilāl, Sarkīs* and *al-Zuhūr* of failing in their literary duties, especially with regard to the theatre. He blames collaboration between the largely Syrian proprietors of journals and theatres for focusing their attention on outward performance rather than inner depth, as material concerns distracted them from their pursuit of a pure literary journalism aimed at nurturing Egypt's cultural renaissance. The editors of these three journals were all Syrian, just as those who had revitalized the theatre after Ṣanū' had been. Maghāzī argues that these Syrians had a vested interest in either maintaining the status quo or developing it to suit their own artistic potential rather than specifically to serve Egypt's nationalist and social concerns. Maghāzī thus believes that literary journalism in Egypt lost its way for a long while.[140] Maghāzī doubtless exaggerates the Syrian nature of these journals. Many of the actual contributors were Egyptian and the common denominator linking both articles and the various emerging literary genres developing in journals in the early twentieth century was concern for and critique of Egyptian society as it faced external challenges. If the amount of space allocated to original Egyptian literature was relatively small, this was probably due partly to the lack of quality literature being produced at this early stage and partly to legitimate financial concerns which necessitated coverage of a wide variety of topics to ensure adequate marketability. One might instead conclude that the Syrians had a positive impact on Egyptian literary development by providing successful models of literary journalism, thus helping to stimulate early Egyptian interest in literature and the theatre and pave the way for more home-grown literary journals.

One might have expected literary journalism to flourish during the First World War – with men either wishing to express their hopes and fears through art and literature or simply immersing themselves in it to escape reality. However, public taste came to prefer the escapism of slapstick comedies and cabaret which had spread with the arrival of British troops in Cairo. Moreover, strict censorship and paper shortages hampered the development of journalism in general and specialist literary journals in particular since the latter were more of a luxury. Salāma Mūsa and Shiblī Shumayyil's cultural weekly *al-Mustaqbal* (The Future, 1914)

139 Y. Ḥaqqī, op. cit. (1975), p. 76, and Ḥ. Fawzī, in M. Shalabī, op. cit. (1982), pp. 81–2.
140 A. Maghāzī, op. cit. (1978), pp. 138–54.

was one such journal to be forced to cease after only sixteen issues; although its financial position was becoming pressing with the ever increasing price of newsprint, in fact it was government pressure that caused it to close owing to its 'extreme modernism'.[141] The fact that a couple of literary periodicals continued to publish during the war despite the difficulties indicates how popular fiction was becoming in Egypt, among the literate elite at least, for it is estimated that over 91 per cent of the population was still illiterate at this time.[142]

The golden age of literary journalism: the mid-1920s to the Second World War

As the quest for national and political identity matured, encouraged by advances such as the 1919 revolution and the 1923 constitution, a new more subjective fictional writing emerged in the 1920s, designed to reflect intellectuals' perceptions of national identity and, in doing so, to play a role in shaping that identity. Gershoni identifies two main strains in the literature of Egypt's modernizing cultural process: Westernized Egyptianist and Islamic-Arab, both of which were played out overwhelmingly in the press. Until the end of the First World War, the tension between these two systems was slack as they were still in the early stages of intellectual formation, waging a common battle against the traditional cultural systems which they aimed to supersede. In the 1920s, the Westernized Egyptianist focus for national culture came to dominate the press, only to be marginalized by the Islamic-Arab focus during the 1930s and 1940s. Gershoni attributes this cultural shift to setbacks in the parliamentary Egyptianist order which resulted in the loss of political hegemony by the secular pro-Western elite. At the same time, wide scale urbanization had produced a surge in the ranks of intellectuals and readers hailing from a social stratum that identified more with an Islamic-Arab culture than with the secular Egyptianist national culture with its Western orientation.[143]

There are two problems with Gershoni's model. First, the internal dynamics of the two main modernizing strains are underemphasized, as is the blurring between them; the Westernized Egyptianist strain, for example, is presented as monolithic, united against both the traditional cultural system and the neo-traditional Islamic-Arab modernizing strain. Yet the cultural press of the time bears witness to varying emphases, divergences and debates within the common goal of propagating a modern Egyptian national culture. Second, cultural development is stressed as

141 It was pro-evolution and robustly secular, revealing all the fire of Salāma Mūsā's youth, which had become somewhat tamed by the time he launched his great periodical *al-Majalla al-Jadīda* (The New Journal, 1929). S. Mūsā, *The Education of Salāma Mūsā* (1961), pp. 125, 129–30.

142 Majdī Wahba, *Cultural Policy in Egypt* (UNESCO study, 1972), p. 11.

143 See Israel Gershoni, 'The Evolution of National Culture in Modern Egypt: Intellectual Formation and Social Diffusion, 1892–1945', *Poetics Today*, Vol. 13, no. 2, Summer 1992, pp. 325–50.

a two-way process between consumers and producers. However, while the newly educated urbanized classes may have favoured an Islamic-Arab oriented culture, the decisive role of this 'public' in 'reevaluating and reconstructing' Egyptian cultural products along Islamic-Arab lines, as Gershoni would have it, is highly questionable given that fewer than 15 per cent of Egyptians were literate at this time.[144]

Rather than categorizing the 1920s as the Westernized Egyptianist era of literary journalism followed by the heyday of Islamic-Arab literary journalism in the 1930s and 1940s, it would appear more sensible to interpret the widespread cultural shift identified by Gershoni under the broader rubric of an emerging nascent popular market for cultural consumption. What we actually see is the splintering of literary journalism into general and specialist fields. Public opinion may indeed have opted for a culture that was more anti-secular and anti-Western in the 1930s and 1940s, but this does not indicate that the pursuit of a Western-influenced national Egyptian(ist) literature was dead or dying. As the market for journalism expanded, certain cultural periodicals began to cater to and reflect popular Islamic-Arab leanings,[145] but the more literary-oriented journals generally remained keen to introduce Western cultural material, if not always as part of a nationalist programme, certainly as part of a desire to satisfy readers' voracity for information and general curiosity. Meanwhile, in the literary field, more specialist journals emerged in which successive avant-gardes continued to develop a pro-secular national Egyptian culture, heavily influenced by Western culture. Whilst the latter specialist literary journals may not necessarily have reflected nor interacted with popular opinion on culture, they could nevertheless potentially wield great influence on the future direction of Egyptian literature.

144 In 1927, the illiteracy rate was still 85.9 per cent, dropping only to 85.2 per cent in 1937. Donald C. Mead, *Growth and Structural Change in the Egyptian Economy* (1967), Statistical Appendix 301, Table 11–A–6.

145 For example, as well as the obviously Islamic journals like *al-Ikhwān al-Muslimīn* (The Muslim Brotherhood), launched in 1933, we find *al-Rābiṭa al-Sharqiyya* (The Eastern League), launched in 1928 and edited by Aḥmad Shafīq with the help of 'Alī 'Abd al-Rāziq. It aimed to link the cultural renaissances in 'Eastern countries' and featured contributions by Ṭaha Ḥusayn and Manṣūr Fahmī as well as poems by the famous Iraqi poet-philosopher Jamīl Ṣidqī al-Zahāwī in his twilight years. Meanwhile, one of the most ardent advocates of an Islamic-Arab direction for Egyptian culture was Muḥibb al-Dīn al-Khaṭīb. Of his journals, *al-Zahrā'* (The Most Brilliant, 1924–30) had a particularly strong literary orientation. It declared its intention to study the Arabs, Islam and the East on the inside cover and the opening editorial stressed 'concern for our historical traditions, our national customs, our national characteristics and our native tongue'. In literary terms, it concerned itself primarily with poetry, publishing many poems by Aḥmad Shawqī, Khalīl Muṭrān and Abū Shādī. Among its contributors were Aḥmad Taymūr, Tawfīq al-Yāzijī, 'Alī Adham, Muṣṭafā Ṣādiq al-Rāfi'ī and Khalīl Jibrān. While defining its objective as 'to watch over the current renaissance in Egypt, the Arab nation and the Islamic world', al-Khaṭīb still stressed the importance of adopting the sources of strength from foreign civilizations, though it published very little European literature. Opening editorial to *al-Zahrā'*, 15 Muḥarram 1343 (1924).

Here, it is worth pondering the respective roles of general cultural and specialist literary journals. Just as in Victorian England, the rise of general cultural periodicals coincided with the coming of age of a growing middle class, curious to find out about new or rapidly developing subjects like geology, anthropology and sociology, in Egypt, the newly emerging educated class, whose national consciousness had been awakened and horizons expanded through contact with the West, was eager for knowledge on a variety of cultural matters. And while in Victorian England, formal university studies were generally limited to classics and maths, in Egypt in the first half of this century, the newly founded universities taught only mainstream subjects while the Azhar remained a bastion of traditional learning despite curriculum reforms. Hence the range of material found in the general cultural journals was both popular and valuable, with literary material increasingly included as part of the journal's desire to secure readers through both its pedagogical and entertainment value.[146] By 1928, *al-Muqtaṭaf* had even added 'literature' to its English subtitle alongside science.[147] Meanwhile, on the pages of *al-Hilāl*, heavyweight writers and intellectuals abounded, among them Ṭaha Ḥusayn, Aḥmad Amīn, Maḥmūd 'Abbās al-'Aqqād, 'Abd al-Qādir al-Māzinī and Muḥammad Ḥusayn Haykal, especially with Salāma Mūsā at the editorial helm 1923–9. Yet 'Alī Shalash warns against mistaking general cultural journals, such as *al-Muqtaṭaf* and *al-Hilāl*, for literary journals. To illustrate this point, he presents a table showing that only about one-third and never more than one-half of their content comprised literary material.[148] However, if the percentage of literary subject matter is similarly calculated for other major journals, which Shalash does deem literary, it is found to be little more.[149] Hence the nature of the literary content must play a role in our categorization. General cultural journals tended to lack a specific sense of duty within the literary field; their literary content was of a more tried and tested nature, rather than experimental, intended to respond to popular demand, rather than to provoke debate.

The blossoming of general cultural journals was boosted in the mid-1920s with the decision of the two leading political dailies, *al-Siyāsa* (the organ of the Liberal-Constitutionalists) and *al-Balāgh* (the organ of Wafdists), to

146 Shalash actually refers to *al-Thaqāfa* and *al-Risāla*, as 'free universities'. *al-Majallāt al-Adabiyya fī Miṣr: Taṭawwuru-hā wa-Dawru-hā, 1939–52* (1988), p. 150.

147 D. Glaß, op. cit., p. 244.

148 This is calculated according to the literary content of the January issues of *al-Muqtaṭaf* and *al-Hilāl*, 1940–9. A. Shalash, *al-Majallāt al-Adabiyya fī Miṣr: Taṭawwuru-hā wa-Dawru-hā, 1939–52* (1988), pp. 7–8; Table, p. 35.

149 25 per cent in *al-Majalla al-Jadīda*, 42 per cent in *Majallatī*, 45 per cent in *al-Thaqāfa* and 55 per cent in *al-Risāla*. I have calculated these statistics based on issues taken at six-monthly intervals for the first five years of the journals' lives (two and a half years for *Majallatī*), since it is arguably in these first years that the journals were at their best and their editors at their most devoted.

publish weekly sister journals devoted to literary and cultural matters.[150] *Al-Siyāsa al-Usbū'iyya* (Weekly Politics, 1926–31, 1937–49)[151], edited by leading novelist and intellectual Muḥammad Ḥusayn Haykal, quickly became one of the pillars of Egypt's intellectual renaissance.[152] Haykal intended the journal to be 'a link between the thoughts of the Arab East and between all Arabic speakers' and a forum for the exchange of opinions in complete freedom.[153] It echoed *al-Jarīda's* call for a national Egyptian literature, with Haykal himself publishing a series of articles entitled 'Egyptian Art'[154] and later drafting a special manifesto exhorting the creation of a specifically Egyptian literature.[155] Its literary content included travelogues, articles about European poets and authors, poems[156] and a couple of regular literary sections, one on the theatre, and the long-running 'Story of the Week', usually translated from a European language. The journal ceased for six years in the 1930s,[157] but Haykal continued to produce irregular supplements to the daily *al-Siyāsa* in which he published his work on the life of the Prophet Muḥammad. This might be seen as a professional decision to cater to market tastes rather than merely as a growing urge among intellectuals to spread an Islamic-Arab as opposed to Western-oriented culture, as Gershoni argues.

It is significant that the market was buoyant enough to support another major political daily's launch of a sister weekly with a strong literary orientation. *Al-Balāgh al-Usbū'ī* (The Weekly Report, 1926–30) began under the editorship of 'Abd al-Qādir Ḥamza eight months after its rival. In his opening editorial, Ḥamza described his journal as 'an instrument of calm reflection' and 'a refuge for thoughts and pens'.[158] He denied the need for a manifesto since the new weekly was merely an extension of the already well-established literary page of its sister daily.[159] Like *al-Siyāsa al-Usbū'iyya*, it published a couple of poems and

150 Literary journalism had already become a solid feature of more politically oriented cultural journals such as Muḥammad al-Marṣafī's *al-Jadīd* (The New, 1928–9), Ismā'īl Maẓhar's *al-'Uṣūr* (The Ages, 1927–30) and Ḥāfiẓ 'Awad's *Kawkab al-Sharq* (Star of the East, 1924–39), which the tireless literary experimenter Lūwīs 'Awaḍ later singled out as a great encouragement to him in the formative years of his youth. L. 'Awaḍ, *The Literature of Ideas in Egypt*, Part 1 (1986), p. 211.

151 The second run of *al-Siyāsa al-Usbū'iyya* probably included significant breaks, for Ḥamza gives its closure date as 1931, *Qiṣṣat al-Ṣiḥāfa al-'Arabiyya fī Miṣr* (1967), p. 169; and Shalash as 1938, *al-Majallāt al-Adabiyya fī Miṣr: Taṭawwuru-hā wa-Dawru-hā 1939–1952* (1988), p. 37.

152 See Charles D. Smith, *Islam and the Search for Social Order in Modern Egypt* (1983) for Haykal's role in Egypt's intellectual life.

153 See A. Ḥ. al-Ṭamāwī, *Fuṣūl min al-Ṣiḥāfa al-Adabiyya* (1989), pp. 331–4.

154 *al-Siyāsa al-Usbū'iyya*, 12 Dec. 1927–7 Jan. 1928.

155 'Da'wa ilā Khalq Adab Qawmī', *al-Siyāsa al-Usbū'iyya*, 28 June 1930.

156 The most popular poets were Jamīl Ṣidqī al-Zahāwī, Aḥmad Shawqī, 'Alī Maḥmūd Ṭaha, Ibrāhīm Zakī and Ibrāhīm Nājī.

157 Feb. 1931–Jan. 1937.

158 *al-Balāgh al-Usbū'ī*, 26 Nov. 1926.

159 Salāma Mūsā praised the literary content of the daily *al-Balāgh*, which he helped to edit and which serialized three of his own books, including *al-Tajdīd fī al-Adab al-Injilīzī al-Ḥadīth* (Innovation in Modern English Literature, n.d.). S. Mūsa, *The Education of Salāma Mūsā* (1961), p. 125.

short stories in every issue, both original and translated, including several summaries of Shakespeare plays. Another regular section saw literary giants such as ʻAbbās Maḥmūd al-ʻAqqād and Muṣṭafā Ṣādiq al-Rāfiʻī provide readers with book reviews – these were later gathered into a book, providing a snapshot of contemporary literary taste.[160] Both *al-Siyāsa al-Usbūʻiyya* and *al-Balāgh al-Usbūʻī* were culturally oriented supplements rather than specialist literary journals. Their significance lay largely in their general educational impact born of widespread circulation,[161] long life span and heavyweight regular writers,[162] for they were too diverse and general to inspire directly any progressive new literary departure or cultural turning point. Nevertheless, they helped prepare the ground and rouse enthusiasm for the growing boom in literary journalism which peaked in the 1930s. According to Ḥamza, they were a valuable repository for all the opinions and thoughts which accompanied Egypt's cultural renaissance.[163]

It is possible to identify certain common denominators and shared ambitions among the most important general cultural journals to spring up in the late 1920s and 1930s.[164] These journals revealed a general sense of purpose, usually loosely defined, and believed themselves to be responding to a genuine public need. This sense of duty is revealed in mutual claims of indulgence towards journalistic competition and intellectual opponents, indicating that literary journalism had matured to include more discussion alongside direct didacticism. Salāma Mūsā, who left *al-Hilāl* in 1929 to become editor of *al-Majalla al-Jadīda* (The New Journal, 1929–44)[165] declared his intention to publish opposing views, provided

160 *Sāʻāt bayna al-Kutub* (Hours among Books), 1929.

161 The circulation of *al-Siyāsa al-Usbūʻiyya* at one point in the late 1920s exceeded that of the original daily *al-Siyāsa*. Al-Ṭamāwī judges it the most important cultural journal of the inter-war period before Ḥāfiẓ Maḥmūd took over as editor in December 1937. A. Ḥ. al-Ṭamāwī, *Fuṣūl min al-Ṣiḥāfa al-Adabiyya* (1989), p. 332.

162 Regular writers for *al-Siyāsa al-Usbūʻiyya* included Ḥasan Maḥmūd, Muḥammad Farīd Abū Ḥadīd, Zakī Muḥammad Ḥasan, Ḥāfiẓ ʻAfīfī, ʻAlī ʻAbd al-Rāziq, Ṭāhā Ḥusayn, Fikrī Abāẓa, Aḥmad al-Sāwī Muḥammad and Maḥmūd Tawfīq Diyāb. Those for *al-Balāgh al-Usbūʻī* included Ḥāfiẓ Ibrāhīm, Maḥmūd Taymūr, Muṣṭafā Ṣādiq al-Rāfiʻī, ʻAbbās Maḥmūd al-ʻAqqād, Zakī Mubārak, Muḥammad al-Sibāʻī and Nabawiyya Mūsa.

163 ʻAbd al-Laṭīf Ḥamza, *Qiṣṣat al-Ṣiḥāfa al-ʻArabiyya fī Miṣr* (1967), p. 171.

164 The core group of general cultural journals referred to here are deemed to have had significant impact on the literary field: *al-Majalla al-Jadīda* (The New Journal, 1929–44), *al-Risāla*, (The Dispatch, 1933–53), *Majallatī*, (My Journal, 1934–45), *al-Thaqāfa* (Culture, 1939–53). NB Other journals carried deceptive names, for example, Mary ʻAbduh's *al-Rāwī al-Jadīd* (The New Storyteller, 1934–45) in which literary material generally comprised less than 20 per cent.

165 Scholars appear at odds over the date this journal ended. This doubtless results from confusion between the weekly (launched 1934) and the monthly, which carried the same name. The monthly ceased in 1941, but the weekly was taken over by the Society of Art and Freedom in Dec. 1941 and handed over to them officially in Aug. 1942. It ceased in late 1942 but was restarted by the same society in 1943 with Yūnān himself now named editor-in-chief. It subsequently emerged fortnightly, not weekly, and became monthly from Feb. 1943 until its final closure by military decree in April 1944. See Sāmīr Gharīb, *al-Siryāliyya fī Miṣr* (1986),

that they were well argued and defended.[166] The prevailing attitude was summed up well by Aḥmad Amīn, in the opening editorial to *al-Thaqāfa* (Culture, 1939–53):[167] 'With regard to our fellow journal owners, we feel only that we are different battalions in a single army'.[168]

These journals' manifesto-like opening editorials also revealed certain shared objectives: to renew culture (*tajdīd*), to enrich it and to enlighten readers (*tathqīf*). In introducing the new (*al-jadīd*),[169] they also showed concern to nurture the nation's roots, whether emphasized as Egyptian or as Islamic-Arab. An integral part of this strategy of renewal was the desire to link East with West to varying degrees, an ideal that was repeated *ad nauseam*. Cultural progress and the pursuit of Egyptian nationalism tended to be associated with learning from European models, with Salāma Mūsa's *al-Majalla al-Jadīda* one of the most ardent advocators: 'The good of the nation and its progress are dependent on turning towards Europe rather than Asia. Moreover, we believe that if we do not adopt and imitate this European civilization, it will inundate us and destroy us'.[169] Yet the very next issue published the text of a lecture by Ibrāhīm al-Miṣrī warning against the polarization of the literary field into those seeking purely Arab roots and those chasing purely foreign influences in their quest for an Egyptian literature at the expense of nurturing an actual Egyptian identity.[171] Aḥmad al-Sāwī Muḥammad, editor of *Majallatī* (My Journal, 1934–45)[172] echoed this view, defining his journal's mission as 'to catch up with Western literature which soars in an aeroplane while our literature creeps along like a tortoise'.[173] Likewise, Aḥmad Amīn at *al-Thaqāfa* unequivocally stated that 'the best thing for the East

pp. 26–7. NB *Al-Majalla al-Jadīda* (monthly) was forced to cease publication Sept. 1931–Nov. 1933, owing to the turmoil caused by the 1931 Press Law, after which Mūsā spent some time in prison. See Salāma Mūsā's opening editorial to *al-Majalla al-Jadīda*, Sept. 1931 (actually published Oct. 1933).

166 Opening editorial to *al-Majalla al-Jadīda*, 1 Nov. 1929.

167 Most scholars give the end date of *al-Thaqāfa* as 1952, which is where most library-stocked volumes end, but a final issue dedicated to the short story appeared on 5 Jan. 1953.

168 Opening editorial to *al-Thaqāfa*, 3 Jan. 1939.

169 That readers were eager to embark on this voyage of self-discovery and renewal is clear from a reader survey undertaken in *al-Majalla al-Jadīda* (Nov. 1929) to choose the top ten Arabic books published in the preceding three decades. Seven of those chosen broke with old traditions and conventions, with Qāsim Amīn's *Taḥrīr al-Mar'a* (The Liberation of Women) topping the list and Ṭāhā Ḥusayn's highly controversial *Fī al-Shi'r al-Jāhilī* (On Pre-Islamic Poetry) third.

170 Opening editorial to *al-Majalla al-Jadīda*, 1 Nov. 1929. Yet it must be stressed that Salāma Mūsā's admiration for the West was not blind to the evils of imperialism; in his autobiography, he accused the British of perpetrating 'crimes that are beyond the bounds of imagination' against Egypt. S. Mūsā, *The Education of Salāma Mūsā* (1961), p. 167.

171 Ibrāhīm al-Miṣrī, 'Ayna huwa al-Adab al-Miṣrī?', *al-Majalla al-Jadīda*, Dec. 1929, pp. 228–9.

172 Most library collections mark *Majallatī*'s dates as 1934–7 and these are the only numbers to which I have gained access. However, both al-Nassāj and Shalash date the journal 1934–45 so one must assume that further runs appeared.

173 Opening editorial to *Majallatī*, 1 Dec. 1934.

is to become acquainted with all that is in the West'.[174] The editor of *al-Risāla* (The Dispatch, 1933–53), on the other hand, Aḥmad Ḥasan al-Zayyāt, showed greater concern to maintain links with the Arab past. While still eager for readers to assimilate Europe's high literature,[175] he ran regular articles on past Islamic literature and history and sought to defend the purity of the Arabic language, in particular from Turkish influences, in accordance with his view of an Arab-centric Islam.[176] Nevertheless, at least one writer later testified that *al-Risāla* 'expanded the Arab worldview to include the best of European literature'.[177]

The editors of all four of the journals mentioned in the previous paragraph had spent time in Europe. Consequently, translated work featured heavily and would often be published as part of their journals' pedagogical role, offering a model for both the reader and the aspiring writer. Muḥammad Ḥusayn Haykal commented that the inter-war period was 'on the verge of becoming the age of translation',[178] with almost every issue of every journal containing something adapted or translated from a foreign language. *Al-Hilāl* and *al-Majalla al-Jadīda* published many Russian short stories throughout the 1930s and often advertised the fact on the front cover, indicating market demand. *Al-Thaqāfa*'s translated work was particularly far-reaching and included writers from India, Persia, Turkey and China. Such extensive use of translation[179] increased both the number and knowledge of the reading public and was invaluable in familiarizing readers with modern Western literary conventions. However, Hafez points out that this flood of translations also had disadvantages – the huge press demand for translation meant that unqualified translators could be published, there was confusion between translation and summary, and even some fake translations appeared.[180]

Original Egyptian literature was also published and encouraged, aided by short story and novel competitions, some of which clearly aimed to encourage the

174 Opening editorial to *al-Thaqāfa*, 3 Jan. 1939.

175 Opening editorial to *al-Risāla*, 15 Jan. 1933.

176 See Dennis Walker, 'Turks and Iraq's Impact on Early Egyptian Pan-Arabs: Aḥmad Ḥasan al-Zayyāt', *Journal of Arabic, Islamic and Middle Eastern Studies*, Vol. 2, no. 1, 1995, pp. 64–5. In fact, *al-Risāla* devoted much space throughout 1944 to a fierce contestation of 'Abd al-'Azīz Fahmī's suggestion (*al-Muṣawwar*, March 1944) to Romanize the Arabic alphabet. NB This idea had been touted previously, in 1930, by Maḥmūd 'Azmī who insisted (in vain) that any article he wrote for *al-Majalla al-Jadīda* be published in Romanized letters. S. Musa, *The Education of Salāma Mūsā* (1961), p. 165.

177 Interview with Rustum al-Kīlānī, 13 June 1983, in R. al-Dhawwādī, *Aḥādith fi al-Adab* (1986), p. 111.

178 Cited in A. Shalash, *al-Majallāt al-Adabiyya fī Miṣr: Taṭawwuru-hā wa-Dawru-hā, 1939–52* (1988), p. 78.

179 For example, 114 of the 136 short stories published in *al-Riwāya* in its first year were translations. Cited in S. Hafez, PhD thesis (1979), p. 191.

180 For example, M. Luṭfī Jum'a's works in *al-Riwāya* throughout 1938. Cited in S. Hafez, PhD thesis (1979), p. 191.

production of a national Egyptian literature.[181] Short stories and serialized novels became staples of these influential cultural journals, with the former particularly prolific in *al-Risāla* and the latter in *al-Thaqāfa*, which serialized three historical novels by Muḥammad Farīd Abū Ḥadīd in its first two years. It is significant to note how many seminal works of Egyptian literature first came to light in the press. Ṭāhā Ḥusayn's *al-Ayyām* (The Days, 1926) and *Maḥmūd Ṭāhir Lāshīn's Ḥawwā' bi-lā Ādam* (Eve without Adam, 1934) were both serialized in *al-Hilāl*, while *al-Majalla al-Jadīda* devoted a whole issue to the publication of Mahfouz's novel, *'Abath al-Aqdār* (The Games of Fate, 1939).[182] Shalash even suggests that it was the Egyptianist Pharaonic focus of *al-Majalla al-Jadīda* that turned Mahfouz's attention to writing three novels about Ancient Egypt at the beginning of his literary career.[183] Further evidence of journalism's influence on a prominent novelist is provided by the serialization of al-Ḥakīm's applauded *Yawmiyyāt Nā'ib fī-l-Aryāf* (The Diary of a Country Prosecutor, 1937) in *al-Riwāya. Yawmiyyāt Nā'ib* is an episodic novel comprising a series of pictures from Egyptian country life strung together by a weak murder plot. This structure is explained by the fact that it was originally serialized in thirteen parts under the general heading 'Egyptian Pictures'. It seems probable that al-Ḥakīm wrote the novel an episode at a time specifically for periodical publication since the journal held a competition for readers to guess the murderer, although the murder case ended up unresolved. Had al-Ḥakīm planned the story in advance, it seems unlikely that such a competition, which received hundreds of entries, would have been held. In fact, this important novel may not have been written at all, had it not been for the encouragement of the press. Al-Hakīm later admitted to *al-Riwāya*'s editor, Aḥmad Ḥasan al-Zayyāt: 'But for you, I might never have turned my mind to this matter and the curiosities of those days would have been lost for ever'.[184] The role of the Egyptian periodical in Egyptian literature would seem as significant as that of the Victorian periodical in English literature: Had it not been for periodicals, Saintesbury thought that 'more than half the most valuable books of the age in some departments, and a considerable minority of the most valuable in others, would never have appeared as books at all'.[185]

181 *Majallatī* (15 Jan. 1936) offered a prize for the best Egyptian story on condition that the events related were autobiographical or biographical, hinting that exaggeration should be avoided. *Al-Thaqāfa* (12 March 1940) too held a competition for the best novel, provided that the action took place in an Egyptian or Eastern setting; one of the winners was the young Naguib Mahfouz.

182 *al-Majalla al-Jadīd*a, Sept. 1939.

183 A. Shalash, *al-Majallāt al-Adabiyya fī Miṣr: Taṭawwuru-hā wa-Dawru-hā, 1939–52* (1988), p. 143.

184 *al-Risāla*, 22 June 1942, p. 649.

185 Cited in Walter E. Houghton, 'Periodical Literature and the Articulate Classes', in J. Shattock and M. Wolff (eds) *The Victorian Periodical Press: Sightings and Soundings*, p. 23.

The booming popularity of literary journalism precipitated the emergence of several specialist literary journals in the 1920s[186] and the number proliferated in the 1930s.[187] These can be divided into two groups: populist and progressive. The former aimed primarily to entertain the public rather than to nurture the evolution of new and more experimental literary techniques. This literary populism was typified by Muṣṭafā al-Qashāshī's *al-Riwāyāt al-Jadīda* (New Novels, 1936–45), which thrived on amusing stories, poor quality translations and summaries,[188] together with the journals of Maḥmūd Kāmil which led the Romantic trend in the 1930s and early 1940s.[189] The success of Maḥmūd Kāmil's romances in his journal *al-Jāmi'a* (The University, 1930–48)[190] encouraged him to launch another journal totally devoted to stories, *Majallat al-'Ashar Qiṣaṣ* (The Ten Story Journal, 1936–7), which he subsequently expanded into *Majallat al-'Ishrīn Qiṣṣa* (The Twenty Story Journal, 1937–45). The stories published were full of ardent passions and coincidences and were designed more to indulge popular public taste rather than to refine it. As with the general cultural journals of the 1930s, Western cultural hegemony is again clearly marked in the opening editorial of this newly expanded journal, with Maḥmūd Kāmil rationalizing the need for an Egyptian journal devoted to the short story on the grounds that this was now the dominant genre in Europe and America.[191] As part of the desire to learn from Western models, but also to entertain readers, these journals published many translated works of fiction – the back cover of *al-Riwāya al-Jadīda* even advertised that each issue carried a foreign story – although the quality might vary from Maxim Gorky to Agatha Christie. Nevertheless Maḥmūd Kāmil has been praised as 'a pioneer of Egyptian fiction and an exemplary model for the complete man of culture'.[192] This is probably a fair description in the context of the 1930s, and Hafez concurs that Maḥmūd Kāmil's journals 'played an important role in popularizing the Egyptian short story and bringing it to the

186 For example, *al-Qiṣaṣ* (Stories, 1922–3), *al-Fajr* (The Dawn, 1925–7), *al-Masraḥ* (The Theatre, 1925–7), *al-Nāqid* (The Critic, 1927–8).

187 For example, *al-Shi'r* (Poetry, 1930), *al-Qiṣaṣ* (Stories, 1930–1) in Alexandria, *Apollo* (Apollo, 1932–4), *Majallat al-'Ashar Qiṣaṣ* (The Ten Story Journal, 1936–7) which became *Majallat al-'Ishrīn Qiṣaṣ* (The 20 Story Journal, 1937–45), *al-Riwāya* (The Novel, 1937–9, 1952–3), *Adabī* (My Literature, 1936–7) in Alexandria, *al-Kātib* (The Writer, 1937–8). NB One should be aware that several other journals bore literary titles or had famous literary men as their editors, but cannot be classed as predominantly literary journals.

188 A. Shalash, *al-Majallāt al-Adabiyya fī Miṣr: Taṭawwuru-hā wa-Dawru-hā, 1939–52* (1988), p. 123.

189 Ibid., p. 154.

190 1930–48 according to Shalash, *al-Majallāt al-Adabiyya fī Miṣr: Taṭawwuru-hā wa-Dawru-hā, 1939–52* (1988), p. 8; 1932–9 according to Hafez, PhD thesis (1979), p. 576; 1934–48 according to Sayyid Ḥāmid al-Nassāj, *Ittijāhāt al-Qiṣṣa al-Miṣriyya al-Qaṣīra* (1978), p. 363. I have selected the widest possible dates on the assumption that additional runs were found.

191 A. Shalash, *Dalīl al-Majallāt al-Adabiyya fī Miṣr: Biblīyūghrāfiyya 'Āmma, 1939–52* (1985), p. 60.

192 M. Shalabī, op. cit. (1982), p. 211.

literary limelight'.[193] In fact, the simple and melodramatic appeal of Maḥmūd Kāmil's romance continued after the Second World War in a number of other journals such as *Qiṣaṣ al-Shahr* and *Riwāyāt al-Usbū'*, and many of his stories from this period only materialized in books in the early 1960s.[194]

Naturally, the broader commercial potential of these more populist journals meant that they tended to have longer life spans. The more progressive specialist literary journals, on the other hand, were usually short lived owing to the commercial inviability of catering to a narrow specialist market. Yet they provided a nurturing environment for budding young writers and poets in which they could develop their ideas and publish their experiments without an overly expedient concern for popular approval. *Al-Riwāya* (The Novel, 1937–9, 1952–3) was the most prominent journal of the 1930s to be devoted to the technical advance of Arabic fiction.[195] Published by the editor of *al-Risāla*, Aḥmad Ḥasan al-Zayyāt, it extended the latter's aim of bridging East and West, proclaiming its pages a meeting place between the genius of the East and the genius of the West.[196] As well as furnishing readers with works by well-known foreign authors, with al-Zayyāt's own translations of Maupassant's short stories becoming a regular feature, it also presented material from lesser-known countries such as Brazil, Armenia and Germany. The work of talented young Egyptian writers such as Tawfīq al-Ḥakīm, Naguib Mahfouz and Shukrī 'Ayyād was published alongside that of prominent men of letters such as Ṭaha Ḥusayn and members of the Council for Composition, Translation and Publication. Yet *al-Riwāya* cannot be considered truly avant-garde in the sense of attempting to crystallize or consolidate a particular new literary worldview. The two key journals of this period to take on an avant-garde role in this sense and exact long-term influence on the literary scene despite their short lives were *al-Fajr* (The Dawn, 1925–7) for the short story and *Apollo* (Apollo, 1932–4) for poetry.

Published weekly by *al-Madrasa al-Ḥadītha* (The Modern School), *al-Fajr* effected the first truly potent fusion of literature, journalism and the avant-garde. Although Aḥmad Khayrī Sa'īd had applied for permission to launch *al-Fajr* in 1918, bureaucratic complications, political unrest and fund-raising issues meant that the journal did not actually appear until January 1925. Sabry Ḥāfez writes that *al-Madrasa al-Ḥadītha* 'did not start as a proper literary school but as a gathering of enthusiastic young writers' with a common dream of publishing their own journal.[197] This journal was urgently needed to link young writers sharing similar views and to draw attention to the group's work. Only in the articles and

193 S. Hafez, PhD thesis (1979), p. 426.

194 Sayyid Ḥāmid al-Nassāj, op. cit. (1978), p. 18.

195 In fact, the first journal of the 1930s to be devoted entirely to Egyptian narrative literature was *al-Qiṣaṣ* (Stories, 1930–1) in Alexandria, yet it was only half the size of *al-Riwāya* and soon fizzled out.

196 Opening editorial to *al-Riwāya*, 1 Feb. 1937.

197 S. Hafez, PhD thesis (1979), p. 132.

stories published in *al-Fajr* did their ideas on literature crystallize enough for the group to become a proper literary school. Aḥmad Khayrī Sa'īd called it 'the first journal of its kind destined to play a small but significant role in the artistic and literary renaissance'[198] and through it he was able 'to destroy all the chains shackling those who love the short story'.[199]

Despite deliberately eschewing any claim to a political role, *al-Fajr* nevertheless provides a prime example of the political impetus behind the rise of literary journalism. The journal was financed by the National Party and the group's call for a national literature (*adab qawmī*) and intellectual independence echoed the nationalists' call for political independence. Although the group had initially intended to publish translations rather than their own stories, they were encouraged by the fact that some members, in particular Maḥmūd Taymūr, had begun to write relatively mature stories.[200] The emphasis therefore shifted from simply importing European material to actually reproducing European ideas in a local Egyptian context to create a specific Egyptian modernity able to stand side by side with the hallowed European modernity. The journal's aims were eventually defined as follows:[201]

> We want Egypt to have an Egyptian literature, an Egyptian art and an Egyptian thought. We condemn every thought conceived out of the minds of others. For us, there is no difference between he who thinks with an occidental mind, he who thinks with a pre-Islamic mind and he who does not think at all. Such men are mere imitators.

Yet in publishing their own Egyptian literature, European, in particular Russian, literature was not neglected: for example, 'Abd al-Ḥamīd Salīm wrote a number of articles introducing Russian writers and discussing Russian schools of literature. In fact, their own work drew heavily on translated Western literature; Ḥusayn Fawzī, himself a member of the group, described them as 'some young men, [who] from their readings in foreign languages, sensed things of which there was no trace in the Arabic literature they had memorized and studied at school. The idea was to attempt to write in these foreign styles using the Arabic language' and 'to develop and renew our national literature to keep apace of the times, deriving contemporary beliefs and forms from Western literature'.[202] Publishing their own work in *al-Fajr* was important because, despite the talent of those involved, Lāshīn was the only one to re-publish his works in book form. This

198 Quoted in Y Ḥaqqī, op. cit. (1975), p. 79.

199 S. Ḥ. al-Nassāj, op. cit. (1978), *Nādī al-Qiṣṣa*, no. 2, June 1970.

200 Aḥmad Khayrī Sa'īd, quoted in Y. Ḥaqqī, op. cit. (1975), p. 79.

201 Aḥmad Khayrī Sa'īd, *al-Fajr*, no. 24. Cited in Boutros Hallaq, 'Articulation du Particulier et de l'Universel chez Yaḥyā Ḥaqqī et *al-Madrasa al-Ḥadītha*', *Quaderni di Studi Arabi*, no. 18, 2000, p. 62.

202 Ḥusayn Fawzī. In M. Shalabī, op. cit. (1982), pp. 81–2.

highlights the role of literary journalism in building up writers' confidence in these early years and making room for those lacking in artistic confidence whose works might not otherwise have come to light.

Boutros Hallaq, however, criticizes *al-Madrasa al-Ḥadītha*'s writers for 'living more in books than in reality', describing the lives of ordinary Egyptians in a purely photographic way, focusing on external aspects at the expense of the internal. Their attempts to compensate for this deficiency by treating the universal aspects of human characters, a feature they admired greatly in Russian literature, produced only abstract results. By contrast, Yaḥyā Ḥaqqī later succeeded in overcoming *al-Madrasa al-Ḥadītha*'s impasse by successfully capturing the dialectical nature of the relationship between the universal and the particular. Hence Hallaq places the writers of *al-Fajr* outside 'the sphere of literary modernity' and concludes that 'they succeeded only in being scouts, not founders'.[203] While Hallaq's appraisal may be largely correct, technically at least, it rather misses the point of an avant-garde: the group represented a step on the way to the maturation of modern Arabic fictional narrative, rather than an end in itself, something to which Ḥaqqī's work indeed testifies from its position further along the continuum of literary evolution. *Al-Fajr* certainly marked a departure for Egyptian literature; Ḥusayn Fawzī described its writers as 'very different from the aristocracy of the first group [*al-Sufūr*]...a kind of literary bohemianism (*ṣa'laka*)...his group represented a true revolt against the official literature existing at this time'.[204] At the very least, *al-Fajr* helped to gain wider acceptance of a more serious approach to creative literature in general and the short story in particular, helping to familiarize readers with certain artistic conventions of narrative. *Al-Fajr*'s significance lay in its introduction of European ideas about creative literature and its role in society, shifting the focus from a work's political relevance to its artistic form, whilst retaining its social and didactic role. *Al-Fajr* paved the way for well-established, respectable journals, such as *al-Muqtaṭaf* and *al-Hilāl*, to publish more short stories and to encourage authors to write them.[205] Thus it lived up to its slogan, 'a journal of destruction and construction'. By the time *al-Fajr* came to an end in January 1927, the group had expanded greatly to comprise more than twenty short story writers in addition to several critics and translators. Such groups of writers and intellectuals clustered around journals must have provided an important stimulus in these early stages of the rise of Arabic narrative genres.[206]

The time for poetry came in the 1930s when Abū Shādī formed the Apollo society, publishing a monthly review by the same name. This was probably the

203 B. Hallaq, op. cit. (2000), pp. 63–5.

204 Ḥ. Fawzī. In M. Shalabī, op. cit. (1982), pp. 81–2.

205 S. Hafez, PhD thesis (1979), pp. 134–8.

206 Lāshīn found it difficult to write after the closure of *al-Fajr* and the break up of *al-Madrasa al-Ḥadītha*. S. Hafez, PhD thesis (1979), p. 138.

first weighty journal in the Arab world to be devoted entirely to the revivification of Arabic poetry.[207] The group's aims were to combat the literary authorities; to replace fighting between writers with co-operation and brotherhood; to elevate Arabic poetry and guide poetic efforts in an honourable direction; to raise the literary, social and material level of poets and to defend their interests and honour; and to support the artistic renaissance in poetry.[208] Abū Shādī wrote of the error of those who continued 'ineffectual theoretical research into the kingdom of poetry and the traditional delusions that permeate it which the Apollo group was set up to destroy'.[209] In the opening editorial to *Apollo*'s third year, Abū Shādī wrote that, initially, the journal had relied on several famous poets, but it now recognized that 'dozens of gifted poets are unknown, for people look at who is speaking and not at what is being said'. *Apollo* vowed to work towards destroying 'these useless traditions' through 'its liberal principles and tightly-knit group'.[210] *Apollo* was open to various literary tastes and types, even allowing Maḥmūd 'Abbās al-'Aqqād space in the first issue to attack its 'Western' title,[211] and it took especial pride in its encouragement of innovative young poets. Abū Shādī personally scouted tirelessly for new talent, discovering the young student poets Ṣāliḥ Jawdat, Mukhtār al-Wakīl and Muḥammad al-Ḥamrashī,[212] and the last issue contains a poem by Lūwīs 'Awaḍ at age 19. *Apollo* was even willing to tackle the thorny issue of prose poetry, for example in the publication of Ramzī Miftāḥ's article entitled 'Prose Poetry and the Philosophy of Rhythm'.[213] As such, *Apollo* inevitably provoked fierce debate between old and new to the extent that several conservative poets planned to establish a rival group with its own journal to challenge *Apollo*.[214]

207 Shalash suggests that the reason for so few journals specializing in poetry was that the new trend of renewal and modernization expressed so often in journals' manifestos naturally favoured the new forms of narrative prose as opposed to the well-entrenched genre of poetry, *al-Majallāt al-Adabiyya fī Miṣr: Taṭawwuru-hā wa-Dawru-hā, 1939–52* (1988), p. 77. This reason seems trivial, however, given that new trends in poetry (presently romantic and later blank verse) were as different from the old style of poetry as the short story was from the *maqāma*. It may be that the translation movement, which provided essential impetus and material for literary journals, favoured narrative prose at this stage for the simple reason that this is often more straightforward to understand, translate and consume than poetry. In any case, renewal in Arabic poetry had already been taken on in the New York journal *al-Funūn* (The Arts, 1913–18) and continued during the 1920s through *al-Rābiṭa al-Qalamiyya* (The Pen Club, 1920–31), a group formed by the poets Jibrān Khalīl Jibrān and Mīkhā'īl Nu'ayma.

208 Kamāl Nash'at, 'Dawr Madrasat *Apollo* wa-Mabādi'u-hā', *al-Majalla*, June 1967, p. 34.

209 *Apollo*, March 1933, p. 705. Ibid.

210 *Apollo*, Sept. 1934, p. 4. Ibid., p. 35.

211 *Apollo*, Sept. 1932, pp. 44–6. Robin Ostle, 'The Apollo Phenomenon', *Quaderni di Studi Arabi*, no. 18, 2000, p. 74.

212 Ṣāliḥ Jawdat. In M. Shalabī, op. cit. (1982), p. 98.

213 *Apollo*, Nov. 1933.

214 These poets were Muḥammad al-Harāwī, Aḥmad al-Zīn, Ḥasan al-Ḥātim, 'Abd al-Jawād Ramaḍān. *Apollo*, June 1933.

In general though, *Apollo* became the journal of Romantic poets both inside and outside Egypt – a prolific contributor was the Tunisian poet al-Shābbī. It was usually divided into about twelve sections, each devoted to a different type of poetry, such as lament, love poetry, nature poetry and even philosophical poetry and children's poetry, as well as a section for criticism. Abū Shādī avoided polemical factionalism in literary criticism and active involvement in politics; *Apollo* was 'a clear attempt to bridge the factionalism and quarrels which bedevilled the political and cultural life of newly independent Egypt'.[215] However, it was discontinued in December 1934 after financial difficulties and political opposition.

Both Aḥmad Shawqī and Ḥāfiẓ Ibrāhīm, who had dominated the neoclassical style of poetry, died in 1932 and the launch of *Apollo* that same year had heralded a new era in Arabic poetry. Despite the brevity of its existence, *Apollo* had extended encouragement and patronage to promising young poets and greatly stimulated the Romantic movement, and as such it had a significant impact on the course of modern Arabic literature. The poet Ṣāliḥ Jawdat testified to *Apollo*'s great influence on his early development and described the journal as 'an upheaval in the history of poetry with huge repercussions... it raised poetry up from the level of partisan and worldly objectives, stripped it of its link to occasions, and made it faithful to the face of life, love and humanity'.[216] Even more telling perhaps is that poets more receptive to formal innovations than Jawdat (who fought free verse until his death in 1976) also acknowledged their debt to *Apollo*: both Aḥmad Ḥijāzī and Ṣalāḥ 'Abd al-Ṣabūr, heavyweights of the poetic scene in the 1960s and 1970s, wrote their first poems under the influence of *Apollo*'s Romantics before moving on to free verse and realist themes. Even after having come such a long way in their own poetic development, these two poets still published anthologies of *Apollo* poets Ibrāhīm Nājī and 'Alī Maḥmūd Ṭaha respectively in 1970.[217] The far-reaching impact of *Apollo* is, moreover, clearly demonstrated by the fact that a group of largely unpublished young poets in Alexandria in the 1960s decided to model themselves as 'The New Apollo'.[218]

It was the more avant-garde specialist literary journals like *al-Fajr* and *Apollo* that really propelled literary evolution. Hence one cannot evaluate the significance of a journal in proportion to its life span, as several critics, including Shalash, have done. Shalash attributes a journal's longevity and success overwhelmingly

215 R. Ostle, 'The Romantic Poets', in M. M. Badawi (ed.) *Modern Arabic Literature* (1992), p. 110.

216 Ṣ. Jawdat. In M. Shalabī, op. cit. (1982), p. 99.

217 See Richard Jacquemond, 'La Poesie en Égypte aujourd'hui: etat des lieux d'un champ "en crise"', *Alif*, no. 21, 2001, p. 195.

218 For example, Fu'ād Ṭamān, Sa'īd Nāfi', Fahmī Ibrāhīm, Aḥmad 'Abd al-'Aẓīm al-Shaykh, Muḥammad Rafīq Khalīl, 'Azīza Kātū. Aḥmad Faḍl Shablūl, 'al-Mashhad al-Shi'rī al-Skandarī', *Middle East Online*, 19 Sept. 2002. Online. Available HTTP: http://www.middle-east-online.com/?id=8267

to its editorial quality,[219] yet the editors of the short-lived *al-Fajr, Apollo* and *al-Riwāya* were unquestionably devoted and able. In explaining the demise of specialist literary journals, the emphasis must be shifted onto other factors. On the one hand, the more successful brand of literary journalism was a victim of its own popularity. Writers and translators simply could not keep apace of demand; after 1937, *Majallat al-'Ishrīn Qiṣṣa* and *al-Riwāya* alone demanded over 50 stories a month. As a result, literary quality deteriorated and such journals became less desirable. On the other hand, the more progressive specialist literary journals concerned with developing literary techniques catered for an intellectual elite which was too narrow to provide the necessary financial support. As a result, they tended either to cease publication altogether or to lose their distinct literary focus. However, it was just such journals that often exerted influence out of all proportion to their brief existences. They fertilized Egyptian literature at grass-roots level, giving would-be writers the opportunity not only to publish, but to develop their writing and crystallize their ideas in a productive atmosphere of group interaction.

Nevertheless, the range of material found in more general journals was both popular and valuable and their bulk meant that the relatively small percentage of them devoted to literature in reality added up to a substantial amount of material.[220] Half a century later, the leftist avant-garde writer Rushdī Ṣāliḥ reflected nostalgically on the weighty cultural journals of the 1920s and 1930s, in which the writer of literary articles and essays of opinion was given the space to develop his arguments.[221] Nor were talented young writers entirely neglected: Naguib Mahfouz published in all of *al-Majalla al-Jadīda, al-Risāla* and *al-Thaqāfa* as well as in the more specialist *al-Riwāya* during the war period.[222] It was possible for journals to straddle the gap between the broadly conceived categories of general and specialist journals employed here. *Al-Majallat al-Jadīda*, for example, was a general cultural periodical with a long life span which nevertheless played an active role in the formation of a literary avant-garde. It had always demonstrated a progressive literary orientation under Salāma Mūsā but became the mouthpiece of the *Jamā'at al-Fann wa-l-Ḥurriyya* (The Society of Art and

219 A. Shalash, *al-Majallāt al-Adabiyya fī Miṣr: Taṭawwuru-hā wa-Dawru-hā, 1939–52* (1988), pp. 106–34.

220 Per month, *al-Thaqāfa* published ca. 65 A4-sized pages on literature, *al-Majalla al-Jadīda* ca. 30 A5-sized pages, *Majallatī* ca. 90 A5-sized pages and *al-Risāla* ca. 84 A4-sized pages (once it had become weekly).

221 Rushdī Ṣāliḥ. In M. Shalabī, op. cit. (1982), p. 21.

222 Yet some young writers felt that they were being blocked by established writers who dominated the major cultural journals. Al-'Aqqād's arrogant response to just such a letter of complaint from a young poet, Kamāl Nash'at, all but justified the issues raised. Al-'Aqqād advised the young poet to take responsibility for himself and not to expect great writers to read his work, for while the young might profit from reading the works of mature writers, the reverse was not true. Maḥmūd 'Abbās al-'Aqqād, 'Iḥtikār al-Adab' (editorial), *al-Risāla*, 18 May 1942.

Freedom) in late 1941, with the license transferred officially to Ramsīs Yūnan in 1942.[223] Yūnān had published a seminal article in *al-Risāla* (4 Sept. 1939), preparing Arab readers for the subsequent encounter with surrealism in literature and art, and under his leadership *al-Majalla al-Jadīda* became home to a new kind of surrealist writing expressing inner fantasy as a means of exposing external reality.[224] Literature formed an integral part of the group's bold Marxist programme which led to its closure by military decree in 1944.[225] Thus, by the 1940s, literary journalism had gained a momentum of its own and was no longer reliant on nationalist zeal to act as its essential impetus, though the cultural and political fields remained ever more closely bound up. Al-Zayyāt's overview of *al-Risāla*'s achievement might be more appropriately applied to the impact of these general cultural journals en masse: they helped to 'awaken and unite the Arabs, educate a class of men of letters, and cultivate a nation of readers'.[226]

223 *Al-Majallat al-Jadīda* had previously become the mouthpiece of a group of literary-minded Coptic youth for a brief spell in 1939.

224 Yūsuf al-Shārūnī, 'al-Lā-Ma'qūl fī Adabi-nā al-Yawma' (part 2), *al-Majalla*, Dec. 1964, pp. 36–7.

225 Sāmīr Gharīb, op. cit. (1986), pp. 26–7.

226 Editorial to the thousandth number of *al-Risāla*, 1 Sept. 1952.

2

LITERARY JOURNALISM IN EGYPT

Increasing politicization

This chapter provides a brief overview of those journals to have played a significant role in the development of literary tastes, norms and techniques during the 1950s and 1960s as the Egyptian cultural field became increasingly politicized. As Chapter 1 has shown, the strong intertwinement of the literary and political fields had already been firmly established and evidenced over the preceding decades, with journalism acting as the potent melting pot for this fusion. However, politicization, both of the literature itself and of the cultural apparatus surrounding it, grew ever stronger in the wake of the 1948 Palestinian tragedy and the 1952 revolution in Egypt. This trend set the scene for the emergence of a culture of negation among writers of the 1960s and beyond who employed the journal as the weapon through which to spread their experimental and controversial work.

From the Second World War to the 1952 revolution

In general, literary journalism suffered during the Second World War as it had during the First. Paper shortages forced many journals to shrink or cease publication completely.[1] Moreover, war news and politics began to encroach on the literary sections.[2] The war years did, however, increase interest in reading,[3] resulting from the contradictory desires to both keep abreast of and to escape war realities. People no longer went out so frequently owing to blackouts and a lack of new material at cinemas and theatres. Some literary-minded young men during this period founded new journals or revived old ones in an attempt to attract new young writers, but such journals quickly became distracted from specifically

1 For example, *al-Riwāya* was incorporated into *al-Risāla* in 1940, and Majallat *al-'Ishrīn Qiṣṣa* into *al-Jāmi'a* in 1939.

2 For example, *al-Risāla* published only five short stories over the two-year period 1943–4.

3 M. 'Abd al-Ghanī Ḥasan, writing in *al-Muqtaṭaf* (March 1943, p. 334) remarked: 'Those involved in writing or publishing these days will observe among readers of Arabic a great interest in what the presses publish on various matters of learning and culture'. Cited by 'Alī Shalash, *al-Majallāt al-Adabiyya fī Miṣr: Taṭawwuru-hā wa-Dawru-hā, 1939–52* (1988), pp. 58–9.

literary matters.[4] After the war, the proportion of literary material generally increased again, but it did not match up to its heyday in the 1930s, with the exception of *al-Muqtaṭaf* which witnessed a literary revival under the editorship of Ismā'īl Maẓhar (1946–9) before its closure in 1952. Most of *al-Hilāl*'s famous writers in fact wrote on non-literary subjects and literary journalism rarely occupied more than a quarter of the journal; *al-Majalla al-Jadīda* finally ceased for good by military order in 1944 as the war ended. *Al-Risāla*'s literary focus waned and several of its writers were headhunted to the weekly newspaper *Akhbār al-Yawm* (The News of the Day, 1944–) while others left to join *al-Kātib al-Miṣrī* (The Egyptian Writer, 1945–8). After the war, al-Zayyāt shifted *al-Risāla*'s emphasis onto conveying his 'progressively more rigorous supra-Egyptian Arab identifications to educated Egyptian youth, the new generation that was to conduct messianic pan-Arabism under Nasser'.[5] Yet al-Zayyāt still recognized the need to encourage Arab literary talent, particularly through foreign role models, and translation remained a priority on the literary agenda: 'If we want... our literature to flourish in the present as it did in the past,... we must support it with the literature of the European nations and link it to modern trends in thought.... Our literature will never be a world literature if it is not impregnated by world literatures. Imitation is the strongest influence on literature'.[6] *Al-Thaqāfa* was one of the stalwarts in carrying forward this translation movement during the 1940s, and it raided the literatures of India, Turkey, Persia, China and Japan as well as the usual European traditions.

Generally, however, *al-Risāla* and *al-Thaqāfa* began to lose touch with the younger generation in their twilight years. In fact, a group of young men including 'Izz al-Dīn Ismā'īl, Fārūq Khūrshīd, 'Abd al-Raḥmān Fahmī and the poet Ṣalāḥ 'Abd al-Ṣabūr attempted to reinvigorate *al-Thaqāfa* in late 1952. Their efforts to forge stronger bonds between culture, politics and the public paid off as circulation tripled. However, conservative elements of the Committee for Composition, Translation and Publication baulked at leaving the journal to the inflammatory articles of these young men who encouraged poetic renewal and use of the vernacular in dialogue and it was eventually closed down in the first week of 1953, just as its long-promised special issue on the short story was published and its popularity was on the increase.[7]

4 For example, As'ad Ḥusni revived *al-Usbū'* (The Week, originally 1933) in 1939, intending it as a forum for the work of budding young writers, but it soon became caught up in politics.

5 Dennis Walker, 'Turks and Iraq's Impact on Early Egyptian Pan-Arabs: Aḥmad Ḥasan al-Zayyāt', *Journal of Arabic, Islamic and Middle Eastern Studies*, Vol. 2, no. 1, 1995, p. 60.

6 Editorial to *al-Risāla*, 23 April 1945. Cited in A. Shalash, *al-Majallāt al-Adabiyya fī Miṣr: Taṭawwuru-hā wa-Dawru-hā, 1939–52* (1988), p. 271. For a full study of the literary role of *al-Risāla*, see Ṣalāḥ al-Dīn Ḥamza, *Majallat al-Risāla wa-Dawru-hā fī al-Nahḍa al-Adabiyya al-Ḥadītha 1933–53* (1982).

7 Personal testimony of 'Izz al-Dīn Ismā'īl, a member of *al-Thaqāfa*'s final editorial board. 'Izz al-Dīn Ismā'īl, 'al-Mushkilāt allatī Tuwājihu al-Majallāt al-Adabiyya fī Miṣr', *al-Ādāb*, Dec. 1974, p. 34.

A new generation of literary journals sprang up to replace those that had waned during the war. Several were designed primarily for entertainment and were modelled on Maḥmūd Kāmil's literary journals of the 1930s.[8] Such journals lacked the usual manifesto-like opening editorials clearly elaborating a sense of mission. While they claimed to encourage Egyptian writers who could find nowhere to publish their stories,[9] in practice this meant continuing to support and propagate romanticism in its dominance over realism in literature. Hafez writes that, unlike Maḥmūd Kāmil's journals a few years earlier, which had familiarized readers with the conventions of the short story when serious works were in short supply, these later journals of the 1940s and early 1950s tried to continue sentimentality after its positive role had been played out.[10] *Al-Thaqāfa* had recognized this by 1951 and printed a series of articles by Salāma Mūsā entitled 'Misguided Literature' attacking such sentimental romanticism.[11] Mūsā's attitude reflected the growing politicization of literature towards the end of the 1940s: 'the man of letters in our present age would in fact betray his responsibilities if he were not to make politics on of his main concerns, too.... And therefore his literary work is necessarily transformed into miltant, political literature'.[12]

One of the most influential literary journals of this period was doubtless Ṭaha Ḥusayn's *al-Kātib al-Miṣrī* (The Egyptian Writer, 1945–8). Its opening manifesto resembled that of the great general cultural journals of the 1930s inasmuch as Ḥusayn emphasized Egypt's position as a Mediterranean country and expressed his hope that the journal would become a forum for mutual cultural exchange between East and West, as well as providing a cultural link between the Arab nations themselves. Like *al-Majalla al-Jadīda* and *al-Thaqāfa* before it, *al-Kātib al-Miṣrī* promised to remain open 'to literary and cultural trends of any persuasion, from any nation and in any language'.[13] In terms of Western material, a clear bias was shown towards French literature and thought; articles on this subject were contributed by university professors like Tawfīq Shaḥḥāṭa and Raymond Francis as well as by Ṭāhā Ḥusayn himself. English literature was dealt with by intellectuals like Lūwīs 'Awaḍ and Rashād Rushdī. 'Awaḍ's Marxist interpretations of English authors in *al-Kātib al-Miṣrī* were later collected and published as a book.[14] His article introducing T. S. Eliot (Jan. 1946) was of huge significance in encouraging early attempts at free verse, inspiring young poets such as

8 For example, Ḥusayn 'Afīfī's *al-Qiṣṣa* (The Story, 1945–6), Muḥammad Muḥyī al-Dīn Farḥāt's *Qiṣaṣ al-Shahr* (Stories of the Month, 1945–6), Faraj Jibrān's *al-Nadīm al-Qiṣaṣī* (al-Nadīm the Storyteller, 1946–7), Ḥusayn al-Qabbānī's *al-Mahrajān* (The Festival, 1947–8) and Tawfīq al-Shimālī's *Riwāyāt al-Usbū'* (Stories of the Week, 1949–54).

9 For example, *al-Nadīm al-Qiṣaṣī*, 1 Oct. 1946, p. 15.

10 Sabry Hafez, PhD thesis (1979), p. 438.

11 *al-Thaqāfa*, 17 Dec. 1951. Cited in M. M. Badawi, *Modern Arabic Literature and the West* (1985), p. 11.

12 Salāma Mūsā, *The Education of Salāma Mūsā* (1961), p. 161.

13 *al-Kātib al-Miṣrī*, Oct. 1945.

14 Lūwīs 'Awaḍ, *Fī al-Adab al-Injilīzī* (1950).

Ṣalāḥ ʻAbd al-Ṣabūr, although it was actually Ibrāhīm Nājī who first presented Eliot to Arab readers in *al-Majalla al-Jadīda* seven years earlier (Aug. 1939). Jabrā Ibrāhīm Jabrā writes that Eliot

> fascinated many of the new Arab authors mainly because he seemed to be an articulate and concise advocate of their incipient thoughts.... For Arab poets who, however rebellious, were never forgetful of tradition, Eliot's concept of tradition was truly dynamic. Tradition for him was kept alive by the interaction between the new and the old through individual talent, which acted as a catalyst.[15]

Other modernist European writers such as Joyce, Kafka, Sartre and Camus, whose ideas on existentialism and engagement were pivotal in the development of modern Arabic literature, were also introduced critically for the first time in *al-Kātib al-Miṣrī*,[16] as well as some writers from further afield such as black American writer Richard Wright. The journal vowed to encourage, train and criticize young experimental writers, a task which Ḥusayn undertook both by publishing their work and by writing about them. Hafez attributes *al-Kātib al-Miṣrī* with 'revolutionizing the study of literature' and 'popularizing the academic,'[17] and he singles out some of the original creative works it published for their innovative qualities.[18] It is uncertain whether the termination of *al-Kātib al-Miṣrī* in May 1948 was voluntary or government enforced, but the political situation was certainly unfavourable; the journal's publishing house was run by Egyptian Jews and faced frequent accusations of Zionism in the climate of fervent Arab nationalism exacerbated by the Palestinian war. Despite the fact that it lasted less than three years, Lūwīs ʻAwaḍ describes *al-Kātib al-Miṣrī* as 'probably the finest cultural organ Egypt has ever known'[19] while sixties avant-gardist and now established novelist Bahā' Ṭāhir reveals, 'Certainly it was *al-Kātib al-Miṣrī* that influenced me and my generation.... it was inherited from one generation to another' and he remembers copies being swapped among students while at university in the 1960s.[20] Half a century later, the valuable contribution

15 Jabrā Ibrāhīm Jabrā, 'Modern Arabic Literature and the West', in I. J. Boullata (ed.) *Critical Perspectives on Modern Arabic Literature* (1980), p. 13.

16 Among the most important introductions to existentialism as a literary philosophy were translated articles by Jean-Paul Sartre and other young French writers in *al-Kātib al-Miṣrī*, Oct. 1947, Feb. 1947, May 1947 and May 1948. Of particular importance was Ṭaha Ḥusayn's review of Sartre's 'Qu'est-ce Que La Littérature' (June 1947, pp. 9–21), which introduced the idea of literary commitment, a term that would be adopted by socialists to suit their political agenda.

17 S. Hafez, PhD thesis (1979), p. 475.

18 Ibid. Yaḥyā Ḥaqqī's *Ṣūra* (Jan. 1946) and *Warā' al-Sitār* (July 1947); Ḥasan Maḥmūd's *Mughāmir* (March 1946); Darwīsh al-Jamīl's *Yajib an Na'īsh* (Nov. 1946).

19 L. ʻAwaḍ, *The Literature of Ideas in Egypt*, Part 1 (1986), p. 134.

20 Bahā' Ṭāhir, taped interview, Cairo, 1 May 1996.

of this journal to Egypt's literary development was recently recognized and it was enshrined by its republication in collected volumes.[21]

Soon after the closure of *al-Kātib al-Miṣrī*, another serious specialist literary journal emerged, edited by the famous Romantic poet Ibrāhīm Nājī, who had published prolifically in several journals throughout the 1930s and 1940s.[22] *Al-Qiṣṣa* (The Story, 1949–55) was 'a reaction to the domination of lightweight story magazines which restricted themselves to the entertainment element of fiction'.[23] Although it devoted some space to poetry and drama, its primary aim was to rescue the short story from frivolous romance. To this end, it published many articles by Nājī and Taymūr among others, dealing with the theory of narrative fiction. Nājī appealed for 'narrative fiction in its true sense... born of a refined sensitivity to experience'.[24] The ideal story should leave the reader with a lasting impression, imparted through the psychological depth of its characterization and the meaningful inclusion of even apparently insignificant detail.[25] Like the great cultural periodicals of the 1930s, *al-Qiṣṣa* also published foreign stories to act as models for Egyptian narrative. Great Russian writers such as Dostoyevsky were particular favourites and Nājī summarized many stories and plays himself. As well as publishing about 15 of his own short stories in *al-Qiṣṣa*, Nājī also serialized his only novel *Zāzā* in it. However, he was unable to implement his theories on narrative fiction practically and his stories lacked the artistic elements which he required of others[26] and the journal in no way matched the progressive and powerful intellectualism of *al-Kātib al-Miṣrī*. Although the journal declined after Nājī left in July 1951, it had proved a focal point of encouragement for young writers. In the same way that young lawyers had clustered around the journals of Maḥmūd Kāmil, himself a lawyer, so a group of literary-minded young medical students and doctors like Nājī clustered around *al-Qiṣṣa*, including the young Yūsuf Idrīs who went on to lead the Arabic short story in the 1950s and 1960s.[27]

Meanwhile, more conservative literary currents were represented in *al-Kitāb* (The Book, 1945–53). 'Ādil al-Ghaḍbān declared his journal's pride in the Arab past and its intention 'to build our modern literature on our classical literature', although he added that this process should be open to the influences of the modern age and the West. Like other cultural journals of the period, *al-Kitāb* aimed to publish what was best in both Eastern and Western cultures, relying on 'liberal thought' and 'an honourable pen'.[28] It drew on the talents of a number of

21 *al-Kātib al-Miṣrī*, Cairo: General Egyptian Book Organization, 1998.

22 For example, *al-Jāmi'a, Ḥakīm al-Bayt, al-Rāwī, al-Majalla al-Jadīda, Majallatī* and *al-Risāla*.

23 A. Shalash, *al-Majallāt al-Adabiyya fī Miṣr: Taṭawwuru-hā wa-Dawru-hā, 1939–52* (1988), p. 152.

24 *al-Qiṣṣa*, 5 Oct. 1949, p. 28.

25 Ibid.

26 A. Shalash, *al-Majallāt al-Adabiyya fī Miṣr: Taṭawwuru-hā wa-Dawru-hā, 1939–52* (1988), p. 122.

27 Other young contributors were Ṣalāḥ Ḥāfiẓ, Zakariyyā al-Ḥijāwī and Muḥammad Yusrī Aḥmad.

28 *al-Kitāb*, Nov. 1945.

famous writers,[29] publishing stories, poems, reviews of plays and cultural news from both the Arab world and Europe, as well as numerous penetrating studies on literature and criticism. The critical articles in *al-Kitāb* and *al-Kātib al-Miṣrī* were generally more theoretical than those of *al-Riṣāla* and *al-Thaqāfa*, which focused largely on recounting the life and works of particular writers. The importance of *al-Kitāb* as a publishing outlet and a forum for literary ideas and debate increased after the termination of *al-Kātib al-Miṣrī* in May 1948. It began to publish the work of younger poets like Adūnīs, ʻAbd al-Wahhāb al-Bayātī and Nāzik al-Malā'ika, although it published none of their free verse. This was an exciting time for poetic developments in Arabic, with the first attempts at free verse, but much of this activity was occurring in the Levant. A journal dedicated to poetry did emerge in Egypt, Muḥammad Muṣṭafā al-Manfalūṭī's *al-Shā'ir* (The Poet, 1950–1), but it lacked a precise manifesto proclaiming cohesive aims and a progressive will. It undertook no fundamental study on the nature of the revival in Arabic poetry and initiated no debates on the relation between poetic form and content. It remained primarily concerned with the Romantic Movement which had already been the focus of *Apollo* nearly twenty years earlier.

Responding to a growing urgency among intellectuals to link literature to life, Mufīd al-Shūbāshī launched *al-Adīb al-Miṣrī* (The Egyptian Man of Letters, 1950). The opening editorial reproached Egyptian writers and poets for imitating both Western and bygone Arabic literature instead of being inspired by their own contemporary society.[30] In common with many of the afore-mentioned journals, it aimed to introduce Egyptians to the most important trends in European literary thought and to reach conclusions in a clear and analytical way.[31] Lūwīs ʻAwaḍ, for example, published a series of articles about D. H. Lawrence in which he introduced psychoanalysis as a critical method, concluding that Lawrence's work was 'diseased'.[32] In its attempts to propagate the notions of social and political commitment elaborated by thinkers such as Sartre, it proved 'extremely influential within a certain elite'[33] despite running to only six issues owing to financial difficulties. *Al-Adīb al-Miṣrī*'s writers spanned generations, and included those who had participated in mainstream journals like *al-Risāla* and *al-Thaqāfa* alongside those who participated in the more marginal journals of the far left.[34]

29 For example, ʻAbbās Maḥmūd al-ʻAqqād, Maḥmūd Taymūr, Ṭāhā Ḥusayn, Ibrāhīm al-Māzinī, Tawfīq al-Ḥakīm, Salāma Mūsā, Mikhā'īl Nuʻayma, Khalīl Muṭrān and the new young writer Shukrī ʻAyyād.

30 *al-Adīb al-Miṣrī*, Jan. 1950. Cited in A. Shalash, *Dalīl al-Majallāt al-Adabiyya fī Miṣr: Biblīyūghrāfiyyā ʻĀmma, 1939–52* (1985), p. 7.

31 *al-Adīb al-Miṣrī*, Feb. 1950. Cited in A. Shalash, *Dalīl al-Majallāt al-Adabiyya fī Miṣr: Biblīyūghrāfiyyā ʻĀmma, 1939–52* (1985), p. 8.

32 *al-Adīb al-Miṣrī*, Jan., Feb., and March 1950. Cited in A. Shalash, *Dalīl al-Majallāt al-Adabiyya fī Miṣr: Biblīyūghrāfiyyā ʻĀmma, 1939–52* (1985).

33 Maḥmūd Amīn al-ʻĀlim, taped interview, Cairo, 3 May 1996.

34 Among its contributors were ʻAbd al-Ḥamīd Yūnus, Lūwīs ʻAwaḍ, Abū Shādī, Ibrāhīm Nājī, Nuʻmān ʻĀshūr, ʻAlī al-Rāʻī, Yūsuf al-Shārūnī, Muḥammad Saʻīd al-ʻAryān, Anwar Fatḥ Allāh and Aḥmad ʻAbbās Ṣāliḥ.

In fact, the 1940s witnessed a flurry of activity and organization among the far left with the birth of several radical cultural groups, many of which published their own journals. Marxist ideology, together with the groups and journals which formed around it, greatly influenced the development of modern Egyptian literature.[35] One of the forerunners of this movement was a group of Marxist young men, *Jamā'at al-Fann wa-l-Ḥurriyya* (The Society of Art and Freedom), founded in September 1939 by Jūrj Ḥunayn. Among the group's more prominent members were Ramsīs Yūnān, Kāmil al-Tilmisānī and Fu'ād Kāmil, all of whom were both writers and artists.[36] The group launched a monthly intellectual journal, *al-Taṭawwur* (Development, 1940), edited by Anwar Kāmil, describing contemporary Egyptian society as 'diseased' and 'unbalanced' and aiming 'to struggle against the inherited values that were put in place to exploit the energies of the individual in his material and spiritual life'.[37] *Al-Taṭawwur* published some of the earliest examples of surrealist tendencies in Arabic literature in the short stories of Albert Quṣayrī and the poems of Jūrj Ḥunayn, both of whom were French educated and wrote much of their work in French, as well as translating foreign thinkers and poets such as Sigmund Freud, Bernard Hollander, Paul Eluard and Arthur Rambeau, so that Egyptian intellectuals could keep apace of their foreign counterparts in the quest for social justice.[38] Despite its claim, 'We do not call on people to embrace specific principles that become a firm incontestable creed after a generation or less',[39] in reality its clear Marxist principles led to its demise. *Al-Taṭawwur* declined rapidly after the fourth issue, having been advised by the censor, 'Write what you like, but put it under a cold shower before publishing it'. Thus its demise was not so much a matter of finance (it had a circulation of 1,000), but of having half of its material suppressed by the censor, and the journal ceased after only seven issues.[40]

The group re-emerged, minus Anwar Kāmil who had split to form another group, *Jamā'at al-Khubz wa-l-Ḥurriyya* (The Society of Bread and Freedom), on the pages of the weekly *al-Majalla al-Jadīda* in late 1941. After Ramsīs Yūnan took over the latter's license from Salāma Mūsā in 1942, the journal hosted an increasingly bold political agenda, announcing itself as 'a journal for social struggle and renewal' and attacking prominent writers such as Tawfīq al-Ḥakīm and Maḥmūd 'Abbās al-'Aqqād for their failure to link art to life. It printed articles on Marxist thought by writers such as Lūwīs 'Awaḍ and Yūsuf al-Shārūnī and was finally closed by military decree after a picture of Lenin appeared on the cover of

35 Rif'at al-Sa'īd has devoted a two-volume study to the phenomenon of leftist journalism in Egypt, 1925–52, *al-Ṣiḥāfa al-Yasāriyya fī Miṣr*, Vol. 1, 1925–48 (1974); Vol. 2, 1948–52 (n.d.).

36 Yūsuf al-Shārūnī, 'al-Lā-Ma'qūl fī Adabi-nā al-Yawma' (part 2), *al-Majalla*, Dec. 1964, pp. 36–7.

37 *al-Taṭawwur*, no. 1, Jan. 1940, p. 1.

38 'Alī Kāmil, 'al-Fikr fī Khidmat al-Mujtama' ', *al-Taṭawwur*, no. 1, Jan. 1940, p. 22.

39 Advertisement for *al-Taṭawwur* placed at the front of *al-Majalla al-Jadīda*, Feb. 1940.

40 Hishām Qishṭa, introduction to republication of *al-Taṭawwur*, Cairo: al-Kitāba al-Ukhrā, n.d.

its final issue.[41] Yet the influential role model such activity provided for future experimental groups was demonstrated half a century later. *Al-Kitāba al-Sawdā'* (Black Writing, 1988), the publication of the *Aṣwāt* group of avant-garde poets, included work by both Ramsīs Yūnān and Jūrj Ḥunayn; and Hishām Qishṭa's avant-garde journal *al-Kitāba al-Ukhrā* (Alternative Writing, 1991–2001) forcefully declared its appreciation of the influential role played by the Society of Art and Freedom and proclaimed the continuing relevance of its intellectual and creative values in Egypt's cultural evolution.[42] The republication of *al-Taṭawwur* as a single volume in the 1990s signifies the subsequent canonization of this avant-garde.

A general and more immediate effect of the Marxist journals to spring up in the 1940s and 1950s was to encourage realism in literature and attention to social themes. One of the most important of these journals in literary terms was *al-Fajr al-Jadīd* (The New Dawn, 1945–6).[43] Its stated aim was 'to spread liberal culture and progressive views, and not only to propagate these generally, but to interact with them in order to create a new culture rooted in social reality', and hence create a balanced and liberated Egyptian society.[44] This journal, launched by Raymond Douek and Ṣādiq Sa'd, was in fact the secret cultural arm of Paul Jacot des Combe's Marxist study group which was itself an offshoot of the Partisans of Peace, a group of foreign activists that had formed in Egypt in the mid-1930s. The journal was edited by Rushdī Ṣāliḥ, who had been recruited when Douek and Ṣādiq infiltrated *Jamā'at Nashr al-Thaqāfa al-Ḥadītha* (The Society for the Spread of Modern Culture) in the early 1940s.[45] From the very beginning, *al-Fajr al-Jadīd* linked the struggle for a liberal and modern culture with the national struggle for freedom and peace and, in time, its focus became overwhelmingly political rather than literary, as reflected in its subtitle which changed from 'the journal of liberal culture' to 'the journal of national and intellectual liberation'. In July 1946 most of its writers were jailed after clashes between trade union leaders and the government and it ceased publication. Despite *al-Fajr al-Jadīd*'s short life, it had provided young writers with a focal point around which to crystallize their ideas and sparked the launch of another Marxist journal, *al-Jamāhīr* (The Public, 1947–8), in opposition to it. Some of *al-Fajr al-Jadīd*'s writers, including Abụ Sayf Yūsuf and Rushdī Ṣāliḥ, its editor, continued to write in *Rābiṭat al-Shabāb* (The Youth League,

41 Samīr Gharīb, *al-Siryāliyya fī Miṣr* (1986), pp. 26–7.

42 *al-Kitāba al-Ukhrā*, no. 3, Dec. 1992.

43 For a fuller treatment of *al-Fajr al-Jadīd*, see Rif'at al-Sa'īd, *al-Ṣiḥāfa al-Yasāriyya fī Miṣr, 1925–1948* (1974), pp. 112–49.

44 *al-Fajr al-Jadīd*, 1 June 1945. Cited in A. Shalash, *al-Majallāt al-Adabiyya fī Miṣr: Taṭawwuru-hā wa-Dawru-hā, 1939–52* (1988), p. 69.

45 Douek and Sa'd also got to know Nu'mān 'Āshūr, 'Abd al-Raḥmān al-Sharqāwī, Sa'd Makkāwī and others through this society. Rif'at al-Sa'īd, *al-Ṣiḥāfa al-Yasāriyya fī Miṣr, 1925–1948* (1974), pp. 111–13.

1947–50),[46] the organ of the Wafdist Vanguard, as well as having a regular voice in *al-Kātib* (The Writer, 1950–1), the organ of the peace movement. One of the more culture-oriented of the Wafdist Vanguard's subsequent journals was *al-Nās* (The People, 1951), edited by 'Uthmān al-'Antablī, the arts editor of the daily *al-Miṣrī* (The Egyptian, 1936–54). It featured Rushdị Ṣāliḥ, Aḥmad Shawqī al-Khaṭīb and Aḥmad Abū al-Fatḥ but ran to only three issues.[47] What this muddled rash of leftist journals clearly demonstrates is the inextricable intertwinement of the cultural and political fields in Egypt.[48]

Yūsuf al-Shārūnī states that a post-war movement, similar to the Society of Art and Freedom based around *al-Taṭawwur* but more Egyptian and more literary, crystallized in 1948 and expressed itself in a number of journals, among them *al-Fuṣūl* (The Seasons, 1944–54?).[49] Edited by Zakī 'Abd al-Qādir, who ran regular literary salons, it exercised a strong influence on the younger generation. Among those to make their journalistic debut on its pages were Aḥmad Bahā' al-Dīn, a young law student who went on to become a prominent political writer and editor of *Ṣabāḥ al-Khayr* (Good Morning, 1951–), *al-Sha'b* (The People, 1956–9) and *Akhbār al-Yawm* (The News of the Day, 1944–)[50] and Aḥmad Ḥamrūsh, a Free Officer who played a central role in the cultural establishment, editing numerous journals and directing the National Theatre during the 1960s.[51]

However, the most influential avant-garde journal of the 1940s in purely literary terms was probably the weekly *al-Bashīr* (The Herald, 1948–50) after a group of young writers and poets rented its publication license for a brief period.[52] Among those to cluster around *al-Bashīr* were Yūsuf al-Shārūnī, Badr al-Dīb, 'Abbās Aḥmad, Aḥmad 'Abbās Ṣāliḥ, Fatḥī Ghānim and Maḥmūd Amīn al-'Ālim. In common with future avant-gardes, their rhetoric emphasized the

46 The first issue, dated 20 March 1947, is actually numbered 154. This journal was taken over by the Wafdist Vanguard under the editorship of Muṣṭafā Mūsā for these years before it was closed and those involved were arrested. Lam'ī al-Muṭī'ī, 'al-Ṭalī'a al-Wafdiyya Wajh Taqaddumī li-l-Wafd', Wafd Party website. Online. Available HTTP: http://hezb.alwafd.org/index.php?option=com_content&task=view&id=124&Itemid=67

47 Ibid.

48 Other journals may have had famous literary men as their editors but were essentially poltical, for example, satirical poet Ḥusayn Shafīq al-Miṣrī's *al-Ayyam* (The Days, 1941–8) and critic Muḥammad Mandūr's *al-Ba'th* (The Revival, 1944–6). Cited in A. Shalash, *al-Majallāt al-Adabiyya fī Miṣr: Taṭawwuru-hā wa-Dawru-hā, 1939–52* (1988), pp. 7–9.

49 Y. al-Shārūnī, 'al-Lā-Ma'qūl fī Adabi-nā al-Yawma' (part 2), *al-Majalla*, Dec. 1964.

50 Amīn al-Ghaffārī, 'Taḥiyya ilā Dhikrā Mīlād al-Ustādh Aḥmad Bahā' al-Dīn', *al-'Arabī*, Year 11, no. 895, 8 Feb. 2004. Online. Available HTTP: http://www.al-araby.com/articles/895/040208-11-895-opn01.htm

51 'Aḥmad Ḥamrūsh: Rūḥ al-Taḥaddī warā' Izdihār Masraḥ al-Sittīniyyāt', unattributed interview, *al-Bayān*, 22 July 2002. Online. Available HTTP: http://www.albayan.co.ae/albayan/2002/07/22/sya/34.htm

52 Ibrāhīm Manṣūr, taped interview, Cairo, 1 May 1996. This explains why the first issue, dated 2 Oct. 1948, is actually numbered 351.

severance of ties to their predecessors, with the opening manifesto, which was barely a page long, featuring the leitmotif 'we are lost sons' five times, and the verb 'we reject' six times. The group's revolutionary plan of action was simple: 'The point is now, the way is action and experiment, and the goal is absolute and free expression'.[53] Hafez writes that, 'the experimentation of the *Bashīr* group was one of the most profound in modern Egyptian literature, for it did not confine itself to one form or genre and was receptive to many ideas and techniques'.[54]

Influenced by Western writers such as Kafka, Eliot and Strindberg, *al-Bashīr*'s writers pre-empted the literary avant-garde of the 1960s. Hafez points out that Fatḥī Ghānim did not include the experimental works of his *Bashīr* period in any of his collections until 1964, on account of the prevailing literary mood of realism based on socialist commitment. Their significance therefore lies in 'their pioneering role in expressing the early and pressing need for new modes of discourse at the time of their first publication in periodicals'.[55] Likewise, three short stories by Yūsuf al-Shārūnī first published in *al-Bashīr* were recognized two decades later as marking 'a new page, a turning point in the history of the short story,'[56] although the literary climate discouraged him from writing in such a vein for another fifteen years. Comments made by the short story writer Yaḥyā al-Ṭāhir 'Abd Allāh in the 1980s testify to the truly avant-garde nature of some of the work of the *Bashīr* group: 'I marvelled when I read stories, unsigned and unpublished, and found them to be very contemporary works. I later learned that their author was Badr al-Dīb and that he had written them at the end of the forties'.[57]

Fatḥī Ramlī took over *al-Bashīr*'s franchise in April 1950. Its new more conservative (if equally ambitious) aim was 'to spread culture and knowledge and to cement bonds of friendship between all nations in order that hope and peace might prevail on earth'.[58] Within two months, the journal was dominated by the socialist organization HDTW, *al-Ḥaraka al-Dīmūqrāṭiyya li-l-Taḥrīr al-Waṭanī* (The Democratic Movement for National Liberation) whose writers and artists included Ibrāhīm and Kamāl 'Abd al-Ḥalīm and Muḥammad Yusrī Aḥmad.[59] Two decades later Maḥmūd Amīn al-'Ālim, who reportedly wrote *al-Bashīr*'s original manifesto, looked back on the power of the journalistic outlet, describing it as 'the bridge which mankind constructs to unite judgement and authority, wisdom and government; the point of fusion for theoretical and practical criticism;

53 Opening editorial to *al-Bashīr*, no. 351, 2 Oct. 1948.

54 S. Hafez, PhD thesis (1979), pp. 476–7.

55 Ibid., p. 493.

56 Ghālī Shukrī, *Ṣirā' al-Ajyāl* (1971), p. 137.

57 Yaḥyā al-Ṭāhir 'Abd Allāh. Interview conducted by S. Gharīb, *al-Mustaqbal al-'Arabī*, no. 2. Reprinted in *Khaṭwa*, no. 3 (special issue commemorating Yaḥyā al-Ṭāhir 'Abd Allāh), n.d. (1981?), p. 61.

58 Gh. Shukrī, *Ṣirā' al-Ajyāl* (1971), p. 137.

59 R. al-Sa'īd, *al-Ṣiḥāfa al-Yasāriyya fī Miṣr, 1950–1952* (n.d.), pp. 31–3. NB Rif'at al-Sa'īd was himself a member of HDTW.

the tool which the group uses to express and propagate its opinion'.[60] Some young members of the *Bashīr* group were to have an enormous impact on the Egyptian literary field. Maḥmūd Amīn al-'Ālim, for example, co-wrote the seminal and highly influential Marxist work *Fī al-Thaqāfa al-Miṣriyya* (On Egyptian Culture, 1955) and eventually became head of the Egyptian publishing house, Akhbār al-Yawm, while Idwār al-Kharrāt led the literary avant-garde in the 1960s and beyond and went on to sit on the Supreme Council for Culture.

Thus, during the 1940s, literary journalism continued to flourish despite (and also in response to) the climate of inflation, unemployment, strikes and general economic disruption. This can be attributed to the following factors: writers and readers had become reasonably familiar with literary genres of European origin; famous writers were willing to write for literary journals despite the rewards of current affairs journalism; literary quarrels among writers during the war period had given literary journalism a new stimulus; and the concept of the literary journal had become a firmly rooted part of the Egyptian cultural scene. On a more practical level, literacy had now spread to approximately one quarter of the population,[61] and the founding of Alexandria University at the beginning of the 1940s and 'Ayn al-Shams University in Cairo at the beginning of the 1950s supplied literary journals with new writers, as well as extending the potential market for them.

However, in Egypt, as elsewhere in the Arab world, the literary field was and remains subject to the greater field of political power. Tensions ran high, with cultural activities indelibly bound up with the nationalist struggle, both Egyptian and pan-Arab, as governments sought to tighten their grip on power. Politics rose to the fore, not just in editorials and articles, but also in the work of poets and fiction writers. The 1948 Palestinian war exacerbated tensions and Ibrāhīm 'Abd al-Hādī's government pursued a massive campaign of arrest and torture. When martial law was lifted in 1949, journals again became involved in the nationalist struggle, especially satirical journals such as *Ākhir Sā'a* (The Final Hour, 1934–83) and *Rūz al-Yūsuf* (Rose al-Yusuf, 1925–). Their influence on public opinion was enormous – according to 'Abd al-Laṭīf Ḥamza, *Rūz al-Yūsuf* undertook the most significant campaign in journalistic history, helping to topple the monarchy and instigate the 1952 revolution.[62] Censorship, arrest and imprisonment extended even to literary journals, with Nu'mān 'Āshūr and Salāma Mūsā among those arrested. Rather than folding prematurely for purely financial reasons, specialist literary journals were now disappearing for political reasons. This reinvigorated politicization of the literary field reflected the climate of fervent nationalist hopes in the run up to the 1952 revolution. For the next two decades and beyond, the literary and political fields were to become ever more

60 M. Amīn al-'Ālim, *Rūz al-Yūsuf*, 28 Oct. 1968, pp. 14–15.

61 22.8 per cent in 1947, rising to 29.7 per cent by 1960. Figures from Majdī Wahba, *Cultural Policy in Egypt* (UNESCO Study, 1972), p. 11.

62 'Abd al-Laṭīf Ḥamza, *Qiṣṣat al-Ṣiḥāfa al-'Arabiyya fī Miṣr* (1967), p. 161.

closely bonded, both in terms of the socially and politically committed literature produced and in terms of the cultural climate in which this production was controlled.

In the wake of the 1952 revolution

While the Wafd government of 1951–2 had been laudably attentive to educational and cultural matters with Ṭāhā Ḥusayn as Minister of Education, the early years of the revolutionary regime halted this development. Many of the Marxist writers, poets and artists of The Democratic Movement for National Liberation (HDTW), which had cooperated with the Free Officers' movement in the July 1952 revolution, began to fall out with the new regime. Factionalism among the far left intensified with the Soviet Union's condemnation of the Officers' movement as an American plot. In January 1953, all political parties were banned, their assets and printing equipment confiscated and eight journals banned, including the organ of HDTW.[63]

A breakaway group comprising some of those who had clustered around the avant-garde journal *al-Bashīr* in the late 1940s now launched *al-Ghad* (Tomorrow, 1953, 1959, 1985–6), which integrated a strong literary and artistic element into its Marxist programme, deeming this a 'weapon against the oppressive reality that was strangling us, a weapon against political oppression and social injustice'.[64] It was edited by the painter and writer, Ḥasan Fu'ād, and the franchise was owned by Ibrāhīm and Kamāl 'Abd al-Ḥalīm, who ran Dār al-Fikr publishing house. Kamāl, himself a poet, also headed HDTW's office for writers and artists, many of whom clustered around the new journal.[65] *Al-Ghad* aimed to defend nationalist culture against suppression, backwardness, division, isolation from the concerns of the Arab nation, consumerism and indifference for the ultimate purpose of improving quality of life so that 'no Arab is unable to eat, be educated or live'.[66] It ran to only three issues before the authorities closed it and many of HDTW's leaders were arrested on charges of attempting to topple the regime, but it represented the beginning of a new trend, not just in literature and poetry, but in Egyptian thought.[67] Leading novelist Bahā' Ṭāhir backs this up, revealing, 'For me and for others it was something revolutionary . . . it had great influence'.[68] As well as introducing colloquial poetry by Ṣalāḥ Jāhīn and Fu'ād Ḥaddād, many great future writers published some of their earliest works here,

63 Marina Stagh, *The Limits of Freedom of Speech: Prose Literature and Prose Writers in Egypt under Nasser and Sadat* (1993), p. 16.

64 Muḥammad Ṣidqī, 'Sa-ya'tī Dā'im-an', *al-Ghad* (III), no. 2, Nov. 1985, p. 114.

65 Aḥmad al-Qaṣīr, 'Kamāl 'Abd al-Ḥalīm: Basāṭat al-'Umq', *Akhbār al-Adab*, no. 560, 4 March 2004. Online. Available HTTP: http://www.akhbarelyom.org.eg/adab/issues/560/1000.html

66 Ḥasan Fu'ād, 'al-Fann fī Sabīl al-Ḥayāh' (editorial looking back at the 1950s *al-Ghad), al-Ghad* (III), no.1, 1985 (no month).

67 Kamāl 'Abd al-Ḥalīm, taped interview, Cairo, 3 May 1996.

68 B. Ṭāhir, taped interview, Cairo, 1 May 1996.

among them ‘Abd al-Raḥmān al-Sharqāwī, Aḥmad Bahā’ al-Dīn, Yūsuf Idrīs, Fatḥī Ghānim, Iḥsān ‘Abd al-Qaddūs and Ṣalāh ‘Abd al-Ṣabūr. *Al-Ghad* was the first to call for state prizes for literature, grants to enable writers to devote all their time to writing, and cultural institutions for provincial writers.[69] *Al-Ghad* re-emerged for three issues in 1959 before Ḥasan Fu’ād and his colleagues were arrested, their publishing house closed and all its goods sequestrated. With the termination of *al-Ghad* in 1953, Ḥasan Fu’ād played a major role in the design and choice of politically engaged young writers for *Ṣabāḥ al-Khayr* (Good Morning, 1956–), while more hard-line communist literature and thought continued in *al-Hadaf* (The Objective, 1956–8). Edited by Aḥmad Ḥamrūsh, a Free Officer with links to the Communist Party, it was a progressive cultural journal in which Ḥasan Fu’ād again played an active role and published his paintings. Al-‘Ālim refers to it as ‘one of the tribunes of democratic thought – in its poetry, literary criticism and intellectual articles’.[70]

Over the course of the 1950s, the number of newspapers and journals published in Egypt almost halved.[71] Following pro-democracy demonstrations in March 1954 protesting the authoritarian tactics of the new regime, many leading literary figures were imprisoned as part of a crackdown on communists. This was followed by the dissolution of the executive of the Union of Journalists in April 1954 and, a month later, a decree was issued confirming the ban on forty-two independent journals.[72] As a result, much experimental writing was published in Lebanese and Syrian journals, which played an important role in the development of Arabic literature at this time.[73] This meant that remaining outlets for literary journalism in Egypt were even more important. Yet the only great cultural journal of the pre-revolutionary era to benefit from some continuity was *al-Hilāl*, with Ṭāhir al-Ṭināḥī as editor 1950–61. Al-Ṭamāwī writes that the most important literary material in *al-Hilāl* at this time was autobiographical work by writers such as Maḥmūd Taymūr, Amīna al-Sa‘īd, Yūsuf al-Sibā‘ī and Aḥmad Amīn.[74] Meanwhile, *al-Hilāl* also promoted some new writers, such as Aḥmad Khamīs and Muḥammad al-Asmar, and its importance in familiarizing Egyptian readers with Western literature continued and was recognized by Ṭāhā Ḥusayn in his speech at the Damascus conference of Arab writers in 1957, in which he detailed

69 M. Ṣidqī, op. cit. (1985), p. 115.

70 M. Amīn al-‘Ālim, taped interview, Cairo, 3 May 1996.

71 From 422 in 1951 to 246 in 1960. S. Hafez, PhD thesis (1979), p. 186.

72 M. Stagh, op. cit. (1993), pp. 16–18.

73 Of particular importance were *al-Adīb, al-Ādāb, Adab, Ḥiwār, Shi‘r* and *Mawāqif* in Lebanon; *al-Ḥadīth, al-Nāqid* and *al-Ma‘rifa* in Syria. *Al-Ādāb* (The Literary Arts, 1953–) became a haven for writers and poets throughout the Arab world. Founded by Suhayl Idrīs, it attempted to restore Sartre’s original meaning of *engagement* to the Arab interpretation of *iltizām* which had become synonymous with literary principles of socialist realism. See Verena Klemm, ‘Literary Commitment Approached through Reception Theory’, in V. Klemm and B. Gruendler (eds) *Understanding Near Eastern Literatures* (2000), p. 149.

74 A. Ḥ. al-Ṭamāwī, *al-Hilāl: mi’at ‘ām min al-taḥdīth wa-l-tanwīr*, 1892–1992 (1992), p. 52.

all the international literature published in *al-Hilāl*. Debates over the provenance of Egyptian drama in *al-Hilāl* in the 1950s reflected renewed enthusiasm for Egyptian independence in this post-revolutionary era. Aḥmad Amīn claimed the shadow plays of Ibn Danyāl as a precedent for the Egyptian theatre and called upon Egyptian playwrights to derive inspiration from these instead of imitating Western drama.[75] While scholars such as 'Alī al-Rā'ī and 'Abd al-Ḥamīd Yūnus began to research Ibn Danyāl, others, including Zakī Ṭulaymāt who summarized several classics of Western drama in *al-Hilāl*, refused to accept any form of theatre in Egypt prior to that imported from the West.[76]

The 1950s saw a powerful surge in committed literature (*al-adab al-multazim*) embodying the social and political ideologies that had given rise to the 1952 revolution with the maturing effects of the large-scale translation by Gorky, Maupassant, Chekhov and others during the 1940s now apparent in the ever-popular short story. The social and political content of the new literature meant that publication of it in the daily or weekly press was apt and natural. Among the most important such outlets were *Rūz al-Yūsuf*, which continued to publish a story each week, while its section 'Art and Life' exemplified the prevalent mood of literary commitment, printing pieces by Ḥasan Fu'ad after the strangulation of the *al-Ghad* experiment;[77] *al-Miṣrī* (The Egyptian, 1936–54) under Aḥmad Abū al-Fatḥ, which serialized 'Abd al-Raḥmān al-Sharqāwī's seminal novel *al-'Arḍ* (The Land, 1952), now a canonical work exemplifying the socialist political agenda of the revolutionary era; Muṣṭafā and 'Alī Amīn's weekly *Akhbār al-Yawm* (The News of the Day, 1944–), which continued to feature prominent writers such as Tawfīq al-Ḥakīm, 'Abbās Maḥmūd al-'Aqqād, Ibrāhīm al-Māzinī, Maḥmūd 'Azmī, Muḥammad al-Ṭābi'ī and Zakī 'Abd al-Qādir and the newly emerged newspaper *al-Jumhūriyya* (The Republic, 1953–), which also included a prominent literary section. Ghālī Shukrī, a well-known Egyptian literary critic and journalist who came to prominence in the 1960s, testifies to the important role such weeklies could play in the literary formation of younger generations. Shukrī admits to being 'fascinated' by Rushdī Ṣāliḥ's articles in *al-Jumhūriyya*, such as his series of critical articles comparing Tawfīq al-Ḥakīm's plays to foreign plays.[78] *Al-Jumhūriyya* became the battleground of an important controversy, beginning in 1954, over the relation of form and content in literature. The dispute was really about 'commitment' with Ṭāhā Ḥusayn and al-'Aqqād representing the old generation who argued that form and content were inseparable, while Maḥmūd Amīn al-'Ālim and 'Abd al-'Azīz Anīs were among those representing the new, arguing that content dictated form and was thus the most important

75 *al-Hilāl*, July 1952.
76 *al-Hilāl*, Jan. 1955.
77 See M. Ṣidqī, op. cit. (1985).
78 Gh. Shukrī, *Min al-Arshīf al-Sirrī li-l-Thaqāfa al-Miṣriyya* (1975), p. 28.

element of a literary work; the style and language of a work should simulate the everyday.[79] While al-ʻĀlim's seminal work of Marxist literary theory, *Fī al-Thaqāfat al-Miṣriyya* (1955), co-authored with Anīs, was first published in Beirut not Cairo, his views made waves on the Egyptian literary scene and al-ʻĀlim continued to provoke literary debate in Egypt by publishing regularly in *Rūz al-Yūsuf* and Yūsuf al-Sibāʻī's *al-Risāla al-Jadīda* (The New Dispatch, 1954–8)[80] before his arrest in 1959.

However, the newspaper of most significance in promoting the new literature in the post-revolutionary era was *al-Masā'* (Tonight, 1956–) under the editorship of the left-wing officer Khālid Muḥyī al-Dīn. In its first 15 months, it published 37 colloquial poems inspired largely by the Suez crisis,[81] indicating the continuing role of the press as a bridge between politics and literature. Ghālī Shukrī testifies to the valuable openness to more innovative writers exercised by *al-Masā'* and *Ṣabāḥ al-Khayr* (Good Morning, 1951–) under the editorship of Aḥmad Bahā' al-Dīn at the end of the 1950s.[82] Those who wrote for these journals were able to escape 'the prison of bitter reality in Egyptian journalism,' while others writing for journals like *al-Jīl* (The Generation, 1951–60) suffered the effacement of three out of every four articles. Ghālī Shukrī complains that Mūsā Ṣabrī, editor of *al-Jīl*, would ask him to write about Iḥsān ʻAbd al-Qaddūs, Yūsuf al-Sibāʻī or Yūsuf Ghurāb instead of Yūsuf Idrīs, ʻAbd al-Raḥmān al-Sharqāwī, Alfred Faraj or Ṣalāḥ ʻAbd al-Ṣabūr, since he considered what the latter wrote to be incomprehensible.[83] Despite the removal of Khālid Muḥyī al-Dīn and other Leftists from *al-Masā'* in 1959, its progressive literary content, prominently placed on the back page, continued to provide a valuable forum for progressive writers and intellectuals in the 1960s after ʻAbd al-Fattāḥ al-Jamal became cultural editor. Literary journalism in the 1950s still retained its importance as a training ground for writers. The selected work of many writers did not begin to appear in book form until a decade or more after they began to publish in newspapers and journals. Many of ʻAbd al-Raḥmān Fahmī's short stories in journals of the early 1950s did not appear in book form until 1969;[84] ʻAbd al-Ghaffār Makkāwī started publishing in journals like *al-Shahr* and *al-Ādāb* in the early 1950s, but his collections were not published until 1967; Shukrī ʻAyyād had

79 For a more detailed discussion, see Mahmud Ghanayim, 'Maḥmūd Amīn al-ʻĀlim: Between Politics and Literary Criticism' *Poetics Today*, Vol. 15, no. 2, Summer 1994, pp. 322–4.

80 *Al-Risāla al-Jadīda* was edited by Yūsuf al-Sibāʻī, an ex-army officer and novelist who became head of the Supreme Council for Arts and Letters after its establishment in 1956. It was in this journal that Naguib Mahfouz's famous trilogy first saw the light of day when its serialization began in 1955.

81 Marilyn Booth, 'Colloquial Arabic Poetry, Politics and the Press in Modern Egypt', *International Journal of Middle Eastern Studies*, Vol. 24, 1992, p. 419.

82 For example, Aḥmad al-Khamīsī published his first story in *Ṣabāḥ al-Khayr* in 1962 when he was only fourteen.

83 Gh. Shukrī, *Min al-Arshīf al-Sirrī li-l-Thaqāfa al-Miṣriyya* (1975), p. 43.

84 S. Ḥ. al-Nassāj, op. cit. (1978), p. 19.

begun publishing in 1937 in *al-Jāmi'a* and *al-Riwāya* and he published regularly in *al-Miṣrī* during the 1950s before his first collection appeared in 1957; Nu'mān 'Āshūr started publishing in the late 1940s in *Rūz al-Yūsuf*, *al-Miṣrī* and *al-Taḥrīr*, but his first collection did not appear until 1959. The work of Muḥammad Yusrī Aḥmad provides a microcosmic example of the invaluable role of journal publication in shaping future literary trends. Although he published more than twenty stories in various journals, in particular *al-Qiṣṣa* in the 1950s, his work was never published in book form. Nevertheless he drew out the talent in others, especially in the young Yūsuf Idrīs who went on to lead developments in the short story in the 1960s.[85]

The latter half of the 1950s witnessed a surge in cultural activity. A more widespread interest in cultural matters was made possible partly by the dramatic increase in the number of students in higher education – from just over 3,000 in 1926 to over 15,000 in 1946 to just over 80,000 by 1960[86] – but also by increasing state intervention. Following the establishment of the Ministry of National Guidance in 1953, the foundation of the Supreme Council for the Arts, Letters and Sciences in 1956 led to the organization of several cultural and literary committees which launched competitions, discovered new talent and granted fellowships to young writers. Statistical analysis shows that publishers gave more scope to new writers during the 1950s, especially from 1955–60, than they did during the 1960s, and that new writers in the 1950s were more successful in continuing publication than those of the 1960s. Stagh attributes this to rising government concern for cultural activities and relatively low government oppression after 1955.[87] Another factor that fuelled interest in cultural matters was the launch of a new cultural radio station, 'Programme Two', in May 1957. It had been called for by 'an elite group of leading intellectuals' and was headed by Fatḥī Raḍwān.[88] The popularity of 'Programme Two' led to it being broadcast on short-wave as well as medium-wave, despite the fact that it dealt with 'weighty subjects' and demanded of listeners 'a great capacity for concentration and comprehension'.[89] The climate was right for the successful launch of the journals *al-Adab* (Literature, 1956–66), *al-Majalla* (The Journal, 1957–71) and *al-Shahr* (The Month, 1957–61).

Al-Shahr, edited by Sa'd al-Dīn Wahba, was a democratic, progressive and tolerant cultural journal, and it provided an outlet for the new wave of poetry,[90] including poetry by the young Sayyid Ḥijāb who was one of the founding editors of the avant-garde journal *Gālīrī 68* (hereafter referred to as *Gallery 68*, 1968–71) and who eventually became a celebrity colloquial poet and lyricist. Among those

85 The publishing details of some of the authors mentioned are supplied by S. Hafez, PhD thesis (1979), pp. 343–5.

86 P. J. Vatikiotis, op. cit. (1980), p. 443.

87 M. Stagh, op. cit. (1993), pp. 49–53.

88 'Anbā' wa Ārā' ', *al-Majalla*, June 1957.

89 Editorial to *al-Majalla*, March 1959.

90 M. Amīn al-'Ālim, taped interview, Cairo, 3 May 1996.

who published regularly in it were Muḥammad Mandūr, Shukrī 'Ayyād and Maḥmūd Amīn al-'Ālim. Although it was forced to close owing to difficulties caused by the nationalization of press and publishing houses and problems of finance,[91] nevertheless, young writers of the 1960s admit to its influence on their early development.[92] Sa'd al-Dīn Wahba, initially a short story writer who went on to become a prominent dramatist and screen play writer, continued to extend his encouragement to experimental young writers over the years to come, for example by organizing a broad distribution base for *Gallery 68*.[93]

The most influential literary journals of the late 1950s were, however, *al-Adab* and *al-Majalla*. Both lamented the lack of quality in literary journalism: *al-Adab* wrote that 'all are agreed that it [journalism] has grown estranged from literature',[94] while *al-Majalla* wrote that 'superficial gutter journalism has succeeded in killing elevated journalistic production'.[95] *Al-Adab* was the journal of Amīn al-Khūlī's society, *al-Umanā'* (The Guardians) and its slogan was 'art for life'. It was here that the concept of 'art for art's sake' was first attacked and 'committed literature' became the watchword of numerous articles,[96] with each issue beginning with a piece by 'The Guardians' under the general title 'Of Art and Life'. One editorial directly stated that socialism was the declared 'badge and slogan' of *al-Adab* and that 'journalism is the most attentive to it [socialism], the most able to establish it and in all of this, artistic journalism has the strongest sentiments, the most mature consciousness and the most correct sense of duty'.[97] Yet 'Alī Shalash was able to publish articles on 'The Crisis in the New Poetry' in 1959, warning of the dangers of poetry becoming too politically engaged at the expense of artistic values.

In its opening manifesto, *al-Adab* described itself as 'a literary sacrifice for the glory of Egypt and the East', aiming to appeal to all generations through having been inspired by 'the eternal spirit of Egypt'.[98] Its oft-touted lofty aims, however, did tally with its literary content. For example, its promise 'to bring the fruits of lofty human production near to those who love art and literature' was exemplified in a series of articles on poetry by M. M. Badawi in 1957, while its ambition 'to supply artistic talent with that which will kindle it and cause it to mature' was fulfilled through its introduction of new literary ideas through translation, with the presentation of prominent Western writers such as Kafka, Woolf and Joyce as well as some literature from further afield (e.g. China, India, Romania and

91 Shukrī 'Ayyād, taped interview, Cairo, 29 April 1996.
92 For example, B. Ṭāhir, taped interview, Cairo, 1 May 1996.
93 Jamīl 'Aṭiyya Ibrāhīm, taped interview, Cairo, 30 April 1996; and I. Manṣūr, taped interview, Cairo, 1 May 1996.
94 'al-Adab fī Ṣiḥāfati-nā', *al-Adab*, April 1956.
95 'al-Fujūr al-Ṣiḥāfī', *al-Majalla*, July 1957.
96 For example, the leading article of Dec. 1961, written by *al-Umanā'*, was entitled 'Politics and Literature'.
97 Editorial to *al-Adab*, April 1961.
98 Opening editorial, *al-Adab*, March 1956.

Guatemala). It was not intended as a profit-making venture and promised never to resort to mindless entertainment as a means to increase circulation.[99] These aims were reiterated in the editorial to the first issue of the journal's fourth year, a special issue dedicated to the study of literary and artistic development in Egypt, which further promised to purify journalism's 'rotten filth'.[100]

Typically, the annual editorials of 'The Guardians' were flowery and repetitive, despite frequent affirmations in these same editorials that literature had matured beyond verbosity and ornamentation. But the quality of its regular writers, including 'Abd al-Ḥamīd Yūnus, Suhayr al-Qalamāwī, 'Abd al-Raḥmān Fahmī, Bint al-Shāṭi', Muḥammad 'Afīfī Maṭar and Shukrī 'Ayyād generally provided high literary quality. *Al-Adab* maintained a balance between East and West, with explanatory articles about Western giants such as Thomas Mann, Ibsen and D. H. Lawrence in addition to home-grown giants like 'Abd Allāh al-Nadīm. The publication of original Arabic literature tended to favour the short story and poetry, but occasional one-act plays and verse dramas appeared, and drama became a popular subject of study in 1959. After the establishment of the government committee for folk literature under Ḥusayn Mu'nis in 1956, *al-Adab* provided an important forum for debate on the value of the folk arts during 1957. This debate extended to the relative merits of the classical and colloquial languages and involved prominent literary figures such as 'Abd al-Ḥamīd Yūnus, 'Afīf al-Nimr, Muḥammad Kamāl al-Dīn Yūsuf, Jūrj Ṭarābīshī, Rajab Mursī and Naguib Mahfouz. The fact that *al-Adab* lasted a decade owed more to the devoted editorship of Amīn al-Khūlī than to the paltry subsidy provided by the Ministry of Culture,[101] and it is no surprise that it should have come to an end in 1966, shortly after al-Khūlī's death, despite a brief attempt to resurrect it at the end of the 1960s.

Al-Adab was soon complemented by *al-Majalla*, a monthly launched by the Ministry of Culture under the editorship of Muḥammad 'Awaḍ Muḥammad for the first eight months until Ḥusayn Fawzī took over. It served more as a vehicle for learned studies on literature and culture more generally, featuring many prominent writers,[102] rather than as an actual publishing outlet for young authors and poets, and months could pass without the publication of any creative literature.[103] As in *al-Adab*, folk literature proved a popular topic and cropped up in

99 Opening editorial, *al-Adab*, March 1956.

100 Editorial to *al-Adab*, April 1959. The opening editorial to *al-Adab's* sixth year again reiterated its desire to promote 'a belief in the majesty, honour, influence and position of art, for art is no longer that wanton pastime nor dissolute entertainment', editorial to *al-Adab*, April 1961.

101 'Izz al-Dīn Ismā'īl, 'al-Mushkilāt allatī tuwājihu al-Majallāt al-Adabiyya fī Miṣr', *al-Ādāb* (Beirut), Dec. 1974, p. 24.

102 For example, Fatḥī Raḍwān, Yaḥyā Ḥaqqī, 'Abd al-Ḥamīd Yūnus, Ibrāhīm Zakī Khūrshīd, Muḥammad Mandūr, Suhayr al-Qalamāwī, Maḥmūd Taymūr, Mufīd al-Shūbāshī, 'Abd al-Raḥmān al-Sharqāwī and Rushdī Ṣāliḥ.

103 For example, *al-Majalla* published no Egyptian fiction in March, April and May, 1957.

almost every issue of the journal during 1957. Also like *al-Adab, al-Majalla* broadened the horizons of literary interest, dealing at various times with literature from countries as diverse as Sweden, India, Hungary and Algeria. English and French literature was dealt with by scholars like Lūwīs 'Awaḍ and Rashād Rushdī,[104] and the journal also featured many articles on the literature of the Arab past. Unlike *al-Adab*, literary content typically comprised only one-third of the journal,[105] with the rest consisting of a whole host of cultural subject matter from dance and cinema to politics and history. *Al-Majalla* aptly described itself as 'a lighthouse of thought and knowledge'.[106]

Echoing the didactic principles to abound in the great periodicals earlier in the century, *al-Majalla*'s sense of its mission to provide cultural guidance rather than secure commercial success is apparent from its response to a reader. While readers had indicated their desire for more rigid regular sections and for more articles on Arabic literature and tradition rather than music and dance, *al-Majalla* reacted by vowing to expand the amount of material on art and music, albeit from a more general perspective, on the grounds that its mission was to spread culture rather than to pander to readers. It also agreed to extend the space devoted to Arabic literature, but only with genuinely new studies and analysis.[107] Although it was not until Yaḥyā Ḥaqqī took over *al-Majalla* in the 1960s that it really took off as a progressive and experimental literary outlet, its literary content increased after 'Alī al-Rā'ī took over as editor in March 1959, especially with regard to drama. He aimed to publish a complete literary work in each issue, beginning with plays, and to introduce new sections for drama and the cinema.[108] This was doubtless both a cause and a result of a considerable revival of interest in the theatre in the 1950s and 1960s, with several prose writers now turning their hands to drama, including Yūsuf Idrīs, Alfred Faraj, 'Abd al-Raḥmān al-Sharqāwī and Nu'mān 'Āshur, whose colloquial play *al-Nās illī Taḥt* (The Folks Downstairs) in 1956 made the theatre directly relevant to contemporary Egypt. Not only were financial rewards much greater in the theatre, but many writers felt that drama offered closer ties to the public.[109]

Strengthening literature's ties to the public had become something of a literary imperative by the 1960s for those espousing the prevailing socialist realist interpretation of literary engagement. The Nasserist state had started to harness

104 For example, 'Egypt in English Romantic Poetry' by Rashād Rushdī, *al-Majalla*, Feb. 1957; 'Existentialism in French Literature' by L. 'Awaḍ, *al-Majalla*, March 1957.

105 In its first year, the proportion of *al-Majalla* devoted to literature exceeded 50 per cent only once (July 1957) and fell below 10 per cent only once (Dec. 1957). Typically, literary content amounted to about one-third of the journal, which was a significant amount given that it comprised 136 A4-sized pages.

106 Editorial to *al-Majalla*, Sept. 1957.

107 Editorial to *al-Majalla*, Feb. 1958.

108 Editorial to *al-Majalla*, March 1959.

109 S. H. al-Nassāj, op. cit. (1978), p. 28.

intellectuals to promote its social and political agenda, recognizing that a cultural revolution, aimed at awakening the masses, was a prerequisite for the successful realization of the socio-economic revolution.[110] Yves Gonzalez-Quijano points out that while researchers such as Stagh tend to assume the polarization of state and intellectuals over the issue of freedom of expression, with a blanket judgement deeming all restrictions and censorship negative, in fact large elements of the political and intellectual elites believed in the right to control or at least to guide the cultural consumption of the masses.[111] And journalism was the obvious melting pot through which intellectuals and writers could impart their social and political concerns to readers, under the increasingly paternalistic eye of the state.

Institutionalization: the 1960s

With the start of the 1960s, Egyptian critic Sayyid Ḥāmid al-Nassaj identifies the end of a literary era: 'Our Egyptian society, after the period of social revolution and the beginning of practical socialist application...changed tangibly in every way, necessitating a new mode of thought, a new art and a new literature'.[112]

With the political and cultural fields inextricably entwined, the political disillusionment and unrest that dominated the 1960s was inevitably reflected in the cultural domain. Progressive literary activity suffered a setback in the first half of the decade following the arrest of Egyptian communist and left-wing intellectuals in 1959 after Nasser's dispute with the Iraqi leader, Qāsim, who had strong leftist leanings. Nationalization, taxation and land reforms began on a massive scale and, with literary development still strongly bound up with journalism, the nationalization of the press in May 1960 was bound to have a resounding impact on the literary field. Al-Nassāj cites the changed nature of the journalistic field after 1960 as a principal reason for ending his study of the Egyptian short story in 1961.[113] Yet this tightening of the state's grip on journalistic activity coincided with the inundation of the literary field with short story writers, doubtless stirred to put pen to paper by the political furore surrounding them.

Nationalization turned out to be a double-edged sword as far as the literary field was concerned, with some positive benefits making themselves felt around the mid-1960s, and the negative effects gradually emerging towards the end of the 1960s, culminating in the increasing stagnation of cultural activity in the 1970s. Nationalization was accompanied by massive investment in the field of culture, with hefty grants allocated to strategic publishing projects. While both dailies and

110 See Richard Van Leeuwen, 'Literary Journalism and the Field of Literature: the Case of *Akhbār al-Adab*', *Quaderni di Studi Arabi*, no. 18, 2000, p. 153.

111 Yves Gonzalez-Quijano, 'Pour une Sociologie du Fait Littéraire dans le Monde Arabe: à propos de *The Limits of Freedom of Speech* par Marina Stagh', *Arabic and Middle Eastern Literatures*, Vol. 3, no. 1, 2000, p. 89.

112 S. H. al-Nassāj, op. cit. (1978), pp. 29–30.

113 Ibid., p. 27.

weeklies increased their cultural sections, several new cultural journals, both general and specialist, were established under the auspices of the Ministry of Culture in the mid-1960s. The appointment in 1963 of Muḥammad Aḥmad Khalaf Allāh, himself recently released from prison for his bold thinking, as the director of the Ministry of Culture's journals gave literary journalism a fresh impetus. This was aided by the release from prison the following year of many leftist journalists and intellectuals whose impact was immediately felt on the pages of *al-Majalla* and the Ministry's various new journals. One of the most interesting elements of the literary field under Nasser, as Yves Gonzalez-Quijano points out, is that many writers who suffered repression and censorship at the hands of the regime nevertheless chose to collaborate actively with it, acting as both victims and perpetrators of the state apparatus.[114] By late 1965, the right within the Ministry of Culture again stepped up its campaign against leftists, many of whom were dismissed from their journalistic employ. The Ministry of Culture's grants scheme (*tafarrugh*), which peaked in 1965,[115] helped some such dismissed writers avoid unemployment since grant allocation was influenced by sympathetic intellectuals like Yaḥyā Ḥaqqī and Anwār al-Ma'dāwī. Yet leftist intellectuals again sustained mass arrests in 1966, including several talented young writers, poets and journalists such as Jamāl al-Ghīṭānī, 'Abd al-Raḥmān al-Abnūdī, Sayyid Ḥijāb, Ghālī Shukrī and Sabry Hafez,[116] all of whom would later contribute to the avant-garde journal *Gallery 68*.

In the early 1960s, meanwhile, literary momentum was mainly maintained by *al-Masā'* and *al-Majalla*, with the appointment of 'Abd al-Fattāḥ al-Jamal as editor of the cultural page of the former in 1960 and Yaḥya Ḥaqqī as editor of the latter in 1962. Al-Jamal opened *al-Masā'* to the creative and critical works of the younger generation instead of commissioning professional journalists. He also asked Ḥaqqī to contribute a weekly column as well as recommending many young writers to Ḥaqqī. When Ḥaqqī could not find room for writers in *al-Majalla*, he would send them to al-Jamal who was more open to experimentation than the more cautious and selective Ḥaqqī. Since al-Jamal's page appeared five or six times a week, he could publish as much interesting modern work in a month as *al-Majalla* published in a year. One critic writing in the mid-1960s described *al-Masā'* as 'the Cairo paper most concerned with fiction', despite the disappearance of its literary supplement.[117] Many young writers of the 1960s testify to the crucial role played by *al-Masā'* in their literary development: Jamīl 'Aṭiyya Ibrāhīm speaks of *al-Masā'*'s 'great influence on our generation' as the only regular outlet for their work, given that *al-Majalla* only published a 'truly modern

114 Y. Gonzalez-Quijano, 'Pour une Sociologie du Fait Littéraire dans le Monde Arabe: à propos de *The Limits of Freedom of Speech* par Marina Stagh', *Arabic and Middle Eastern Literatures*, Vol. 3, no. 1, 2000, p. 88.

115 Twenty-one in 1965–6. M. Wahba, *Cultural Policy in Egypt* (UNESCO Study, 1972), p. 77.

116 Gh. Shukrī, *Min al-Arshīf al-Sirrī li-l-Thaqāfat al-Miṣriyya* (1975), pp. 91–6.

117 Fakhrī Fāyid, 'al-Qiṣṣat al-'Arabiyya fī al-Shahr', *al-Qiṣṣa*, July 1965, p. 148.

story' every three months or so.[118] Jamāl al-Ghīṭānī categorically states that ''Abd al-Fattāḥ al-Jamal was the first one to give us a push'.[119] The service of *al-Masā'* to Egyptian literature is summed up by Hafez when he writes, 'it is possible to posit that without al-Jamal in charge of the cultural page of *al-Masā'*, some of the young writers who were reluctant to banish their work to Beirut would have found it extremely difficult to publish or to develop and continue as writers'.[120]

Under Ḥaqqī, the literary content of *al-Majalla* almost doubled, comprising about half the journal during his first six months as editor and rising to almost two-thirds in the following six months.[121] This literary content was still overwhelmingly in the form of studies and articles, although each issue published at least some original literature, typically two poems and a short story plus the occasional play. Literary studies were wide ranging, taking in the ancient and modern in both East and West. Alongside the usual staples of English and French literature, more marginal writers were also introduced, from Czechoslovakia, Cyprus and Greece for example. It also presented a selection of the material current in foreign literary journals 'to surround the reader with a variety of intellectual currents' as well as in other Arab literary journals 'to increase cultural links between Arab nations'.[122] This was in line with the role Ḥaqqī had outlined for *al-Majalla* in his first editorial when he described the journal as 'an international club which opens its doors to all races and to which every humble member may bring the best treasures of his nation and language'.[123] The studies and articles were usually carefully focused, avoiding the superficial generalization and sweeping statements of earlier literary journalism. Ḥaqqī justifiably wrote that '*al-Majalla*... confines itself to the heart of the matter and keeps its distance from empty ornamentation, haste and triviality'.[124]

Despite *al-Majalla*'s heavy bias towards literary content, its attention to other areas of culture such as the arts, architecture, music and archaeology increased after the launch of its sister journal, *al-Masraḥ* (The Theatre, 1964–70), which focused on both the theatre and cinema.[125] This diversity was probably partly responsible for the journal's lengthy existence. Ḥaqqī wrote that during the decade since *al-Majalla*'s inception in 1957, Egypt had witnessed a renaissance in the theatre, the performing arts, folklore, writing and translation as well as the penetration of Arabic literature onto the international literary scene,[126] and it

118 J. I. Ibrāhīm, taped interview, Cairo, 30 April 1996.

119 Jamal al-Ghīṭānī, taped interview, Cairo, 30 April 1996.

120 S. Hafez, PhD thesis (1979), pp. 542–3.

121 During Ḥaqqī's first six months as editor, literary content averaged 51 per cent, rising to an average of 64 per cent in the following six months.

122 *Majallat al-Majallāt* section in *al-Majalla*, Jan. 1963.

123 Editorial to *al-Majalla*, May 1962.

124 Editorial to *al-Majalla*, Jan. 1968.

125 *Al-Masraḥ* was published as *al-Masraḥ wa-l-Sīnimā* (Dec. 1968 – July 1969) until *al-Sīnimā* was published independently in Aug. 1969.

126 Editorial to *al-Majalla*, July 1967.

is fair to judge that *al-Majalla*, with its long life and consistently high quality, had a hand in inspiring these achievements.

In *al-Majalla*'s later years, the amount of original Arabic literature it published increased, with poetry proving especially popular. This coincided with the appointment of Shukrī 'Ayyād as deputy editor in September 1967.[127] 'Izz al-Dīn Ismā'īl, however, complains that the rising young generation of writers remained virtually ignored. Although an entire issue was devoted to them in August 1966, it was as though this issue was 'written off' in order to relieve the persistent pressure of these young voices. He writes that Ḥaqqī's editorial policy had become dated by the end of the 1960s to the extent that *al-Majalla* became irrelevant and was forced to close in 1971, despite an attempt to revamp it over its last ten months under the new editorial policy of 'Abd al-Qādir al-Qiṭṭ.[128] Several rising experimental writers of the 1960s, however, testify to the valuable encouragement and inspiration extended to them by Ḥaqqī even after his retirement.[129]

Another journal to span the whole of the 1960s was *al-Kātib* (The Writer, 1961–80), a semi-official weekly acting as the organ of the peace movement and 'published by a vague sort of agreement with the government'.[130] It was edited by Aḥmad Ḥamrūsh assisted by Rif'at al-Khayyāṭ, although after July 1962 it was Muḥammad Mandūr who wrote the editorials. The opening manifesto told of a crisis in Egyptian culture, a claim that would become a leitmotiv of journal manifestoes for decades to come. *Al-Kātib* saw itself 'a humble new cultural platform which may lead intellectuals to reconsider culture' and the manifesto was generally conservative, pointing out and presenting ways of avoiding a number of cultural pitfalls: it warned against using Egyptian backwardness as an excuse to adopt Western trends, which it deemed alien and confused, but at the same time it was wary of a totally isolationist Egyptian culture; it criticized art for art's sake and aimed 'to consolidate the link between culture and life'; it warned against cultural fragmentation in the name of specialization, and against simplistic value judgements favouring either high or popular culture instead of allowing their peaceful coexistence; it advocated a sensible balance between maintaining the cultural heritage and allowing for cultural development, 'taking the present as the starting point in the search for both yesterday and tomorrow'.[131]

127 Before Shukrī 'Ayyād's appointment as deputy editor in September 1967, Ḥaqqī's editorial committee comprised at various times Anwar al-Ma'dāwī, Fu'ād Dawwāra, Yūsuf al-Shārūnī, Kamāl Mamdūḥ Ḥamdī, Muḥammad Sāmī Farīd and 'Abd al-Fattāḥ al-Dīdī. On 'Ayyād's appointment, a number of new names joined: Badr al-Dīn Abū Ghāzī, Fu'ād Zakariyyā, 'Abd al-Ghaffār Makkāwī and 'Ādil Thābit.

128 I. al-Dīn Ismā'īl, 'al-Mushkilāt allatī tuwājihu al-Majallāt al-Adabiyya fī Miṣr', *al-Ādāb*, Dec. 1974.

129 Taped interviews with B. Ṭāhir (Cairo, 1 May 1996), J. al-Ghīṭānī (Cairo, 30 April 1996), I. Manṣūr (Cairo, 1 May 1996), J. A. Ibrāhīm (Cairo, 30 April 1996).

130 Sh. 'Ayyād, taped interview, Cairo, 29 April 1996. In fact, it appeared under the auspices of *al-Taḥrīr* (Freedom) publishing house until 1964 when it was officially absorbed by the Ministry of Culture.

131 'Li-mādhā Majallat *al-Kātib*', opening editorial to *al-Kātib*, April 1961.

Al-Kātib was more literary in its pre-1964 phase, publishing numerous critical studies of both Arabic and Western literature. Lūwīs ʿAwaḍ and Ramsīs ʿAwaḍ were frequent contributors on English literature, Ṣaqr Khaffāja wrote regularly on Greek literature, Amīd al-Imām contributed numerous translations and abridgements of English, American and Irish literature, and one of the earliest Egyptian introductions to the new novel in France was undertaken in three articles by ʿAbd al-Munʿim al-Ḥifnī.[132] However, that the general attitude towards modernist currents remained overwhelmingly conservative is apparent in a number of articles.[133] While the journal included numerous studies, with Arabic drama and various foreign literatures proving the most popular subject matter, the publication of original Arabic literature in the 1960s was in fact more scarce – most issues published only one Arabic short story, if that, and poetry rarely occupied more than ten of *al-Kātib*'s 192 pages. After being absorbed by the Ministry of Culture in 1964, a completely new editorial board was introduced. Aḥmad ʿAbbās Ṣāliḥ became editor-in-chief and his committee included the likes of Yūsuf Idrīs and Nuʿmān ʿĀshūr. In this new post-1964 phase, *al-Kātib* clearly stated its support for socialism and pan-Arabism[134] while its literary content decreased. Poetry and drama remained more popular subjects of study than the novel or short story, and virtually no Arabic short stories were published until further changes were made to the editorial board in April 1965. At this point, although the monthly Arabic short story was reinstated, the number of literary studies dwindled greatly, so that *al-Kātib* became largely a journal of politics and economics,[135] and after the June 1967 defeat, even the monthly Arabic short story disappeared.[136]

With the surge in cultural activity in the mid-1960s, the debate between old and new resumed, taking the form of right versus left. Debate was stirred up with the Ministry of Culture's launch of the monthly *al-Shiʿr* (Poetry, 1964–5), with Muḥammad ʿAbd al-Qādir al-Qiṭṭ, who was relatively sympathetic towards the new poetry, at the helm and Ghālī Shukrī, leftist intellectual and ardent supporter of the new poetry, as administrative editor. In welcoming the arrival of *al-Shiʿr*, Yaḥyā Ḥaqqī assessed the contemporary poetic scene in rather negative conservative terms, writing that both old and new trends in poetry

> generally express the same thing, although neither addresses the emotions of the nation, uniting past and present. A fruitless struggle

132 Articles on Alain Robbe-Grillet and Michel Butor, *al-Kātib*, July, Aug. and Sept. 1963.

133 For example, Muḥammad Mandūr's 'The Absurd is a Futile Revolt against Art and Life' and Aḥmad Kamāl Zakī's 'The Non-Literature', *al-Kātib*, March 1963.

134 This emphatic commitment was made clear in a lengthy editorial (Jan. 1964) addressed to Arab intellectuals, and was borne out by the huge number of articles devoted to these topics over the next few years.

135 From mid-1965, the proportion of *al-Kātib* devoted to literature was rarely more than 25 per cent and frequently under 10 per cent. However, its literary focus increased greatly from the mid-1970s.

136 The monthly Arabic short story reappeared briefly Sept. to Dec. 1968, and this may in part be influenced by the emergence of *Gallery 68*.

> ensues between the two groups and both of them lose some of their power and impact. Colloquial poetry then creeps into the field, chasing away the dusts of war and imagining that it is the one that will inherit the earth. One of the greatest hopes pinned on *al-Shi'r* is that it will work towards illumination through the appreciation of poetry, its honour and its mission in society.[137]

Al-Shi'r's mission, as perceived by Ḥaqqī, was: to redefine concepts of poetry which would preserve the language whilst endowing it with a new role in modern Arab society; to familiarize readers with the great poets of both East and West through competent translation; to treat a variety of schools of poetical theory and criticism; and to encourage emerging talent.[138] Ḥaqqī's hopes were largely met and in *al-Shi'r*'s opening editorial, 'Abd al-Qādir al-Qiṭṭ emphasized the journal's desire to overcome the perceived crisis in poetry by taking a neutral stance in the struggle between old and new. Unlike Ḥaqqī, however, *al-Shi'r* regarded this struggle as a positive phenomenon, necessary both for the future development of poetry and for the protection of poetry from the unbridled acceptance of everything new.[139] But under Ghālī Shukrī's influence, this neutral stance was soon lost. Shukrī had been disappointed by the poor quality of the poems published in the first issue, despite the high standard of the critical studies. In order to improve the journal's quality, he felt compelled to increase the publication and criticism of more innovative poetry at the expense of the conventional.[140] *Al-Shi'r*'s leftist inclination was fuelled by contributions from some of the many leftists released from prison in April 1964. Eventually, growing pressure from the right led 'Abd al-Qādir al-Qiṭṭ to suggest that Shukrī moderate the amount of poetry by leftists and unknowns,[141] despite the fact that al-Qiṭṭ was himself sympathetic to such poetry.[142] In fact, the liberalism of al-Qiṭṭ was to prove a valuable asset to Egyptian poetry in the culturally lean years of the early 1980s through his editorship of the journal *Ibdā'* (Creativity, 1983–2002).

Al-Shi'r's openness to new talent and opinions is demonstrated by the fact that eleven of those who were to contribute to the avant-garde journal *Gallery 68* had previously published poems or studies in *al-Shi'r*, despite the latter lasting for less than two years. By the time *al-Shi'r* had ceased at the end of 1965, leftists had infiltrated cultural institutions and members of the Poetry Committee included leading proponents of '*al-shi'r al-jadīd*' (the new poetry). 'Izz al-Dīn Ismā'īl is puzzled by the sudden closure of *al-Shi'r* given that it fulfilled a definite need

137 Editorial to *al-Majalla*, Jan. 1964.

138 Ibid.

139 Editorial to *al-Shi'r*, Jan. 1964.

140 Gh. Shukrī, *Min al-Arshīf al-Sirrī li-l-Thaqāfa al-Miṣriyya*, pp. 86–7.

141 Ibid., p. 88.

142 Al-Qiṭṭ had published poems sent by post by unknowns. 'Abd al-Qādir al-Qiṭṭ, introduction to Muḥammad Mihrān al-Sayyid's first collection, *Badal-an min al-Kidhb* (1967), p. 5.

among intellectuals and its circulation reached 8,000 issues. He presumes that it must have fallen victim to the usual problems of finance and distribution.[143] However, given that three other Ministry of Culture-sponsored journals were also closed down within the space of a month,[144] its closure most likely resulted from a conscious policy decision. Moreover, with regard to *al-Shi'r* in particular, the Poetry Committee, dominated by the conservative right, set out to dampen the journal's leftist and innovative appeal. The Committee called an extraordinary meeting, resulting in a memorandum which proclaimed new poets to be against Islam and the Arabic language, supporters of class war and indifferent to traditional morals. The Committee asserted its right 'to oversee all publication and broadcasting media through which these poisons reach the people'.[145] Shortly afterwards, Shukrī was dismissed from the journal and his place taken by Maḥmūd Ḥasan Ismāʻīl and 'Abduh Badawī. '*Al-Shi'r* journal somersaulted like a clown and became the mouthpiece of a clique within the Poetry Committee'.[146] Nothing could more clearly demonstrate the subjugation of the literary field to the greater field of power politics.

Al-Risāla and *al-Thaqāfa*, resurrected briefly (1963–5) by the Ministry of Culture, were returned to their pre-revolution editors, Aḥmad Ḥasan al-Zayyāt and Muḥammad Farīd Abū Ḥadīd respectively. They were dominated by the conservative right, whom Shukrī acrimoniously described as lacking in talent to the extent that the two journals 'had to recourse to administrative officials in the Ministry's secretariat to scribble pages any which way'.[147] Although Shukrī himself wrote a weekly section on world culture for *al-Thaqāfa*, he was careful to separate such work, which he considered 'a refuge from unemployment', from true journalism,[148] demonstrating the careful path intellectuals had to tread to maintain a semblance of autonomy. One of *al-Thaqāfa*'s more valuable contributions was an article by Ibrāhīm Fatḥī which rose above the polarization in contemporary debate about socialist realism. Fatḥī tried to promote the understanding of newly emerging trends in the short story by explaining that realism should derive from life, rather than from politics or philosophy.[149] The mature and considered approach of this article is indicated by the decision of the non-periodic journal *Mawqif* to reprint it nearly two decades later in 1981. Meanwhile, *al-Risāla* contributed to the right's battle against the left, for example through Maḥmūd Shākir's staunch weekly attacks on Lūwīs 'Awaḍ's series of articles in *al-Ahrām* which examined the depiction of the Hereafter in various literatures.

143 I. al-Dīn Ismāʻīl, 'al-Mushkilāt allatī tuwājihu al-Majallāt al-Adabiyya fī Miṣr', *al-Ādāb*, Dec. 1974.
144 *al-Funūn al-Sha'biyya, al-Thaqāfa* and *al-Risāla*.
145 A summary of this memorandum is provided in Gh. Shukrī, *Min al-Arshīf al-Sirrī li-l-Thaqāfa al-Miṣriyya* (1975), p. 89.
146 Ibid., p. 91.
147 Ibid., p. 88.
148 Ibid., p. 84.
149 Ibrāhīm Fatḥī, 'al-Wāqi'iyya al-Ishtirākiyya', *al-Thaqafa*, July 1964.

Al-Qiṣṣa (The Story, 1964–5) was another of the Ministry of Culture's new journals of the mid-1960s, edited by Maḥmūd Taymūr with the assistance of Tharwat Abāẓa. In common with other journals, it claimed an unbiased approach and an intention to publish promising young writers, yet much of the content was a continuation of the romantic vein established almost three decades earlier in the journals of Maḥmūd Kāmil. The opening editorial displayed the kind of narrow outmoded view of the short story that *Gallery 68* was keen to dispel: Taymūr described European fiction as 'the adopted mother' of modern Arabic fiction, balancing this claim with the point that European fiction had in the past drawn inspiration from early Arabic fiction.[150] This simplistic view of Egyptian literature was compounded by Muḥammad 'Abd al-Ḥalīm 'Abd Allāh in the same issue when he asserted that 'the blossoming of Arabic fiction in Egypt... is nothing but the natural result of the completion of the marriage between Arabic culture and other cultures'.[151] This idea that Egyptian literature was reaching maturity through its ever closer approximation to foreign, more specifically Western, literatures was widespread yet erroneous, as will be demonstrated in Chapter 4.

Al-Qiṣṣa acted mainly as a publishing outlet, with over 100 different Egyptian writers appearing in its twenty issues.[152] Several translated foreign stories were also included in each issue from lands as diverse as South America, India, the Far East and Scandinavia as well as the more familiar Russian, French and English material. Studies, both translated and original, introduced readers to Kafka, Steinbeck, Faulkner and Conrad among others, and Ṭaha Maḥmūd Ṭaha wrote a regular section on English literature. At this time, the short story was the overwhelmingly popular medium and only one novel, by Tharwat Abāẓa, was serialized in the journal. Abāẓa himself, while expressing confidence in the future of the short story, voiced his fear for the fate of the Egyptian novel. He announced that *al-Qiṣṣa* aimed to serialize more novels by young writers, and encouraged critics to take more of an interest in the novel.[153] However, this aspiration came to nothing since the journal ceased abruptly after the following issue.

Mohammad Shaheen dismisses *al-Qiṣṣa* on the grounds that it published 'the kind of fiction which would have no positive effect on the development of the art', at least no longer by the mid-1960s. Stories generally unfolded chronologically through an author–narrator, and Shaheen laments the fact that '*al-Qiṣṣa* set a bad example for short story writers,' both in Egypt and in the Arab world at large, since Egyptian writers were generally looked upon as pioneers.[154] Literary criticism was neglected and in fact, Maḥmūd 'Abd al-Ḥalīm 'Abd Allāh had

150 Opening editorial to *al-Qiṣṣa*, Jan. 1964.

151 Maḥmūd 'Abd al-Ḥalīm 'Abd Allāh, 'Mushkilāt fī Ḥayāti-nā al-Adabiyya', *al-Qiṣṣa*, Jan. 1964, p. 63.

152 Particularly prolific in *al-Qiṣṣa* were Maḥmūd al-Badawī and Ṣūfī 'Abd Allāh, although Taymūr did find space to publish a good many stories of his own.

153 Tharwat Abāẓa, 'Bayna al-Qiṣṣa wa-l-Qurrā' ', *al-Qiṣṣa*, July 1965, p. 153.

154 Mohammad Shaheen, *The Modern Arabic Short Story: Shahrazad Returns* (1989), pp. 16–17.

affirmed in the first issue that the critic was not an essential factor in the literary equation.[155] Despite mention of the intention to start a special section for literary criticism, this never materialized and criticism rarely progressed beyond published comments by readers, with a few notable exceptions.[156]

Shaheen's judgement of *al-Qiṣṣa*'s narrative as 'dated three decades back', tales and anecdotes rather than short stories,[157] may be overly harsh, for the journal did at times promoted more interesting new work. Among those published in *al-Qiṣṣa* were Jamāl al-Ghīṭānī, Muḥammad Ḥāfiẓ Rajab, Ibrāhīm Aṣlān, Aḥmad Hāshim al-Sharīf and Muḥammad al-Bisāṭī, all of whom were later to contribute to the avant-garde journal *Gallery 68*. Muḥammad 'Abd al-Ḥalīm 'Abd Allāh wrote a short piece in defence of the rising young generation of writers, condemning the public indifference that forced them to shout to 'provoke the public and break the silence... Young writers prefer whistles of mockery to complete silence'.[158] Yet he did underestimate and oversimplify the complex dynamic of literary change at work in the 1960s: as proof that the claim to be a 'generation without forefathers' was false, he divided contemporary writers neatly into five generations based on age and patronizingly concluded that the youngest generation of writers would find their forefathers as soon as their anxiety calmed and they found themselves.[159] Taymūr too acknowledged the literary scene's need for 'the flame of youth with its novelty, curiosity and rebellion'[160] and the growing number of new young writers led to the publication of a special issue devoted to avant-garde writers (*al-ṭalā'i'*) in June 1965. Although the stories selected were by no means the most radically experimental of the time and the collection suffered from rudimentary superficial criticism which would have benefited neither the readers nor the writers themselves, nevertheless, as *al-Qiṣṣa* itself pointed out, the publication of a special issue devoted to avant-garde writers was itself something of an experiment at the time. *Al-Majalla* was to refer to the example set by *al-Qiṣṣa* in its own special issue on 'Avant-Garde Short Story Writers' the following year (Aug. 1966).

Meanwhile, the high profile that the folk arts had achieved by the mid-1960s was recognized by the Ministry of Culture's launch of *al-Funūn al-Sha'biyya* (The Folk Arts, 1965, 1967–71). As the journal itself observed, 'Not a day goes by without the reader finding a news item, article, suggestion or comment specific in some respect to folk arts'.[161] *Al-Funūn al-Sha'biyya* was intended to

155 M. 'Abd al-Ḥalīm 'Abd 'Allāh, 'Mushkilāt fī Ḥayāti-nā al-Adabiyya', *al-Qiṣṣa*, Jan. 1964, p. 65.

156 For example, Gh. Shukrī's studies on the work of Yūsuf al-Sibā'ī (Jan. and Feb. 1965) and the meaning of tragedy (March 1965); 'Abbās Khiḍr's study of Maḥmūd Ṭāhir Lāshīn (July 1965).

157 M. Shaheen, op. cit. (1989), p. 2.

158 M. 'Abd al-Ḥalīm 'Abd Allāh, 'Qaṣṣāṣ min Jīl bi-lā Asātidha', *al-Qiṣṣa*, July 1964, p. 101.

159 M. 'Abd al-Ḥalīm 'Allāh, 'Mushkilāt fī Ḥayāti-nā al-Adabiyya', *al-Qiṣṣa*, Jan. 1964, p. 66.

160 Editorial to *al-Qiṣṣa*, June 1965.

161 Aḥmad Ādam, 'Jawlat al-Funūn al-Sha'biyya bayna al-Majallāt', *al-Funūn al-Sha'biyya*, Jan. 1965, p. 133. *Al-Funūn al-Sha'biyya* found ready contributors, including Suhayr al-Qalamāwī, Rushdī Ṣāliḥ, Nabīla Ibrāhīm, Aḥmad al-Ḥafnī, Fawzī al-'Antīl, Maḥmūd Fahmī Ḥijāzī and Aḥmad Ādam.

reflect culturally the recent empowerment of ordinary people and it emphasized culture as common property rather than elitist: 'This journal is of the people and for the people'. It displayed optimistic confidence in Arab society's adoption of socialism and described itself as a new departure following a successful transition period. It identified for itself three tasks: to study folklore using scientific methodology; to study the development of the folk arts in the new post-revolution socialist society; and to identify folk elements in high literature.[162] The journal's celebration of a common deep-rooted Arab heritage was a cultural extension of the regime's pan-Arab ambitions. The Ministry's hand was apparent in the editorials of 'Abd al-Ḥamīd Yūnus, which stressed commitment to socialist principles and incorporated much praise for the glories of the 1952 revolution and the achievements and policies of the Ministry of Culture amid the discussions of folk art. Nevertheless, like *al-Qiṣṣa* and *al-Shi'r*, *al-Funūn al-Sha'biyya* ceased abruptly without explanation after July 1965, and did not relaunch until after the June defeat in 1967 when a slight relaxation in press control may be observed.

One of the most successful and widely read leftist journals[163] was the monthly *al-Ṭalī'a* (The Avant-Garde, 1965–77), which supported a broad base of cultural interest that included literature. Although Shukrī 'Ayyād dismisses it as no more than an attempt by the regime to contain the left through Muḥammad Ḥasanayn Haykal at *al-Ahrām*,[164] in fact, under the literary supervision of Ghālī Shukrī, it did publish a few important literary studies at the end of the 1960s in which it recognized a significant literary phenomenon gathering pace among the rising young generation of writers. A special issue (Sept. 1969) was devoted to investigating the social roots, motives and influential factors behind the creativity of young Egyptian writers through the analysis of a basic questionnaire. Several of the writers questioned were at that time involved in the avant-garde journal *Gallery 68*. A similar study was undertaken three months later after a similar questionnaire was circulated to young writers in the Arab world at large. Nevertheless, the difficulties hampering the active encouragement of new experimental literature in the late 1960s are made clear when Ghālī Shukrī reveals that he was forced to use the names of respectable members of the older generation, such as Laṭīfa al-Zayyāt, to front his literary pages in *al-Ṭalī'a*.[165] When Ghālī Shukrī left Egypt in 1972, Fārūq 'Abd al-Qādir took over the literary side *of* *al-Ṭalī'a*, which launched a literary supplement the same year. Interestingly, *al-Ṭalī'a* was revived in the 1980s as an independent journal siding with the

162 Muḥammad 'Abd al-Qādir Ḥātim, 'Hādhihi al-Majalla', *al-Funūn al-Sha'biyya*, Jan. 1965, pp. 3–5.

163 See Elie Chalala, 'Egyptian Ideological Press Continues Decline', *al-Jadīd*, Vol. 2, no. 3, Jan. 1996.

164 Sh. 'Ayyād, taped interview, Cairo, 29 April 1996.

165 Gh. Shukrī, taped interview, Cairo, 3 May 1996.

margin against the literary establishment in a bid to counter the cultural crisis for which it held Sadat responsible.[166]

The Ministry of Culture's *al-Fikr al-Mu'āṣir* (Contemporary Thought, 1965–71), edited by Zakī Najīb Maḥmūd, took a predictably optimistic view of the future of Egyptian culture. The opening editorial stressed that Egypt's current difficulties were merely teething troubles in the transition to socialism and confidently stated that 'the world is on the threshold of a new birth that will change many aspects of life, bringing them in line with scientific progress, conquering space on the one hand and plumbing the depths of the human soul on the other'. It also reiterated many of the by now familiar clichés of cultural journalism, celebrating Egypt as a crucible of Western and Eastern thought throughout the ages, advocating the free exchange of ideas and discouraging extremes of either acceptance or rejection.[167] Although its interests were broad ranging, the third of the journal's four sections was devoted to literature and criticism and, as promised, incorporated a good mix of subject matter from East and West. It took a relatively sympathetic, if not particularly analytical, approach to the new poetry, a stance which is typified in the opening editorial which blithely informed readers that a certain amount of obscurity was to be expected in poems dealing with the secrets of the soul.[168]

Ḥaqqī's annual opening editorials in *al-Majalla* during the 1960s were also upbeat and encouraging, full of fighting spirit and hopeful of the rising new generation of writers and it is on these pages that we feel the true pulse of contemporary intellectual feeling. He wrote of Egypt's battle to progress, modernize and raise her profile and of *al-Majalla's* principal aim being 'to work towards achieving victory in this battle by opening its pages to the best scholars and literary men of this nation'. According to Ḥaqqī, 'her [*al-Majalla's*] ultimate joy lies in every rising talent blossoming on her pages'.[169] He enjoined Egyptian writers to 'emanate first and foremost a strong love for their nation and a burning desire to serve it... exceeding the good in pursuit of the best'.[170] *Al-Majalla* reflected

166 *Al-Ṭalī'a* was resurrected as a non-periodic journal in May 1984 and was published without official subsidies. Although the opening editorial of this first issue declared the aim of publishing six times annually, in fact it only ran to four issues, the last two of which contained literary supplements, before it again ceased publication in February 1986. This new *al-Ṭalī'a* pointed to the embitterment of intellectuals under Sadat. The opening editorial cited the 1967 defeat as the beginning of crisis and decline, and blamed cultural dearth in the Arab world generally on Egypt's exclusion owing to the return of imperialism under the Americans after the treaty with Israel. The opening editorial to the final issue (Feb. 1986) complained of the 1970s having been dominated by sycophantic literature and literature aimed at consumerism rather than at the intellect.

167 Opening editorial to *al-Fikr al-Mu'āṣir*, March 1965.

168 Ibid. Among *al-Fikr al-Mu'āṣir*'s writers were Jalāl al-'Asharī, Fu'ād Zakariyyā, 'Abd al-Fattāḥ al-Dīdī, 'Alī Adham, Muṣṭafā Māhir, Na'īm 'Aṭiyya and 'Alī Jamāl al-Dīn 'Izzat.

169 Editorial to *al-Majalla*, Jan. 1965.

170 Editorial to *al-Majalla*, Jan. 1966.

the increasing preoccupation of intellectuals with the rising tensions between Egypt and Israel. Ḥaqqī wrote a rousing editorial to the June 1967 issue entitled *Yā Waṭanī* (O My Nation) which was brimming with enthusiasm for the imminent clash with Israel. It listed Egypt's exceptional qualities and exaggerated the degree of pan-Arabism achieved. Ḥaqqī called upon Arabs of all nations to rise up as brothers to fight the mutual enemy and added, 'We shall certainly be victorious, since right and justice are on our side'. The enormous scale of the subsequent Arab defeat at the hands of Israel and 'its helpers,' in which Egypt lost both its army and the Sinai, came as a crushing shock.[171]

After the June 1967 defeat, 'the individual found himself in a situation similar to someone who has turned down a path without knowing where it leads'.[172] *Al-Majalla* and *al-Kātib* provide firm evidence of the defeat's profound effect on Egyptian intellectuals. The entire contents of their July 1967 issues are devoted to subjects related to the June war. In his editorial addressed to 'O My Dear Brother', Ḥaqqī wrote that Egypt had been 'on the verge of completing its long climb up the mountain where it would be met with a smiling horizon' but that the June defeat had flung it back to square one. He added that to write about anything other than Egypt's battle for survival would now seem trivial.[173] In *al-Kātib*, Ḥasan Sulaymān wrote 'there remains for art only one duty',[174] and from then on his journal devoted itself to angry anti-imperialist articles, with only a sprinkling of the usual socialist-oriented literature.

Society was in turmoil for some months after the defeat: Nasser offered to resign, rumours abounded, many new decrees were passed and full details of the defeat were not published until three months later.[175] When the scale of the defeat became clear, intellectuals were deeply shaken. Naguib Mahfouz stated that 'the defeat was the most atrocious event ever to have shaken my being'[176] and that 'everything had lost its rationality... My only concern was to express my anxiety'.[177] Shukrī 'Ayyād wrote that the defeat 'profoundly unhinged the people and left them in a state of disarray which deprived them of all perception of past, present and future,'[178] and 'Abd al-Karīm Darwīsh called the defeat 'a sudden and violent shock which undermined my confidence'.[179] This time the blame was more widely disseminated: by examining the poetry following the 1948 and 1967 defeats, Khalid A. Sulayman observes that poetry following the former defeat

171 Editorial to *al-Majalla*, June 1967.
172 Samir Hegazy, *Littérature et Société en Egypte de la Guerre de 1967 à celle de 1973* (1986), p. 14.
173 Editorial to *al-Majalla*, July 1967.
174 *al-Kātib*, July 1967.
175 S. Hegazy, op. cit. (1986), p. 49.
176 Interview with Naguib Mahfouz (Alexandria, 2 Sept. 1975). In S. Hegazy, op. cit. (1986), p. 50.
177 Ibid., p. 158.
178 Sh. 'Ayyād, *Dirāsa fī 'Ālam Mutaghayyir*. Quoted in S. Hegazy, op. cit. (1986), p. 48.
179 Quoted in S. Hegazy, op. cit. (1986), p. 50.

concentrated on 'putting the whole responsibility for losing the war on the Arab leadership, to such an extent that other aspects of Arab society – such as social and cultural backwardness, freedom of thought and speech...remain[ed] untouched'; in poetry following 1967, 'not only was the Arab leadership criticized, but also Arab society itself'.[180]

Thus, despite a brief surge in cultural activity in the middle of the decade (1964–5), when many leftists had been released and new journals had been launched by the Ministry of Culture, in general the cultural scene was beginning to stagnate. At the end of 1965, four of the Ministry's journals were suddenly closed without explanation. Writing in late 1965 in *al-Qiṣṣa*'s monthly round up of the short story as presented in other Egyptian journals, Fakhrī Fāyid ominously observed that the short story had suffered a setback, disappearing from the pages of weekly and monthly journals.[181] Moreover, his observations were published in what turned out to be the final issue of *al-Qiṣṣa* itself. By 1967, the number of writers receiving Ministry of Culture grants had fallen to only six.[182] Egypt's economic and political life had been deteriorating throughout the 1960s owing to intervention in the Yemen, and as a clash with Israel looked more likely, defence expenditure became a priority at the expense of the cultural budget.[183] The government had resorted to large-scale suppression to keep control, and mass arrests in October 1966 further hampered cultural development, since many of those imprisoned without trial on political charges were young writers, poets and journalists.

After nearly a decade of state control of cultural and literary journals, young experimental writers in particular felt excluded and frustrated. The young novelist Ṣun' Allāh Ibrāhīm complained that, by the end of the 1960s, 'the publishing house had resorted to that sort of censor which life in our society had selected at that time – the censor of the private sector'.[184] Ibrāhīm's own novel, *Tilka al-Rā'iḥa* (1966), which even the sympathetic Ḥaqqī criticized as 'a shameful repulsiveness' resulting from 'its flawed sensibility and vulgarity',[185] was forced to publish in Beirut under the auspices of the journal *Shi'r* (Poetry, 1957–64, 1967–70), after being confiscated in Cairo. In fact, the back cover carried a manifesto which evidences the frustration of young writers at the time. The signatories, Kamāl Qalash, Ra'ūf Mus'ad and 'Abd al-Ḥakīm Qāsim (the latter two would later contribute to *Gallery 68*) wrote bitterly of Egyptian culture being 'controlled by traditional works and superficial, naive phenomena...all our

180 Khalid A. Sulayman, *Palestine and Modern Arabic Poetry*, p. 128. Cited in John M. Asfour, *When the Words Burn: An Anthology of Modern Arabic Poetry, 1945–1987* (1993), p. 69.

181 F. Fāyid, 'al-Qiṣṣa fī al-Shahr', *al-Qiṣṣa*, Aug. 1965.

182 M. Wahba, *Cultural Policy in Egypt* (UNESCO Study), p. 77.

183 Ibid., p. 27.

184 Ṣun' Allāh Ibrāhīm, introduction to the 1986 unexpurgated edition of *Tilka al-Rā'iḥa*, trans. M. Booth, *Index on Censorship*, Vol. 16, no. 9, 1997, p. 22.

185 Y. Ḥaqqī, *al-Masā'*, n.d. (Feb. 1966?). Cited by Ṣun' Allāh Ibrāhīm (1986), Ibid., p. 20.

courage and seriousness has been needed to achieve the kind of self-expression which embodies the creative potential of our particular generation'.[186]

These words demonstrate the profound and sincere desire of young writers to participate in renewing Egyptian culture even before the defeat. It was the shock and scale of Egypt's annihilation by Israel, however, that provoked a significant number of them to assert their voices and dissociate themselves from the establishment which they held responsible for the defeat. This sparked the first of what was to become a whole stream of avant-garde journals – *Gallery 68*. Literary critics and historians have tended to ignore these journals, owing to their short life spans and marginal status. Shalash dismisses them as uninfluential on the grounds that 'the majority of them were closer to youthful rebellions'.[187] However, the very fact that these journals generally represented the younger writer and new experimental trends makes them an important and intriguing literary phenomenon, worthy of deeper study. They did not intend immediate acceptance among the existing reading public; rather, they catered for a small but significant intellectual elite that was able to shape its ideas and visions through them. Some of the young unknowns whom such journals nurtured were to become the intellectual and literary heavyweights of the future.

186 Back cover of Ṣun'Allāh Ibrāhīm, *Tilka al-Rā'iḥa* (1966 edition). Ibid.

187 A. Shalash, *al-Majallāt al-Adabiyya fī Miṣr: Taṭawwuru-hā wa-Dawru-hā, 1939–52* (1988), p. 45.

3

THE THEORETICAL BASIS OF THE AVANT-GARDE IN 1960s EGYPT

This chapter aims to analyse the 1960s avant-garde in Egypt, drawing various parallels with critical analysis of avant-garde activity in Europe and the United States.[1] First, this book's use of the term avant-garde in its generic rather than historically specific sense is explained, together with its social preconditions. The chapter then discusses the role of the journal as an effective medium for avant-garde experimentation and explores why sixties Egypt saw such a strong avant-garde assertion, especially in the journal *Gallery 68* (1968–71). The short story genre – as the hub of sixties experimentation – is the focus of the subsequent analysis in which a selection of broad trends exemplifying the new literary sensibility is mapped out.[2] Finally, this chapter examines the role of the avant-garde in relation to the future.

What is meant by avant-garde?

Originally a military term, then a political term, avant-garde was coined as a cultural term by Saint-Simon in the 1820s and positioned the artist within a consortium of socially conscious individuals urging culture ahead to a better future.[3] The emergence of the artistic avant-garde has been linked time and again to the cultural conditions of bourgeois society. The rise of the bourgeoisie transformed art into a commodity, provoking a reaction in the form of art breaking out of the commercial mould to become marginal. Poggioli believes that the dominant feature of avant-garde literature is its rebellion against linguistic conventionality dating from the commercialization of language in bourgeois capitalist society.[4]

1 This chapter is broadly similar to my article 'The Theoretical Roots of the Literary avant-garde in 1960s Egypt', *Edebiyat*, Vol. 14, nos. 1–2, 2003, pp. 23–59.

2 49 per cent of *Gallery 68* was dedicated to publishing short stories; only 12.5 per cent was used for poetry and 8 per cent for drama. There were no serialized novels, although many of the short story writers published in *Gallery 68* were to become renowned novelists in later years.

3 Estera Milman, 'The Text and Myth of the Avant-garde', *Visible Language*, Vol. 21, nos. 3–4, Autumn 1987, p. 335.

4 Renato Poggioli, *The Theory of the Avant-Garde* (1968), p. 107.

Jochen Schulte-Sasse challenges this view on the grounds that bourgeois capitalist society began in the 18th century, not with the historical avant-garde in the 1920s. Yet if scepticism towards language began back in the eighteenth century, then the term avant-garde fails to distinguish between romanticism, symbolism, aestheticism, the avant-garde and post-modernism.[5] This dilemma is, however, easily solved: either what Poggioli meant by bourgeois capitalist society was *mature* bourgeois capitalist society, thus putting the date of the avant-garde much later, having allowed time for a reaction to build up, and hence bypassing romanticism, symbolism and aestheticism. Or, more probably, Poggioli did not intend the term avant-garde to distinguish between the movements mentioned in the previous sentence in this context, but rather to refer more generally to that which breaks with dominant norms of taste and style. It was in recognition of this dilemma that Ortega y Gasset chose to avoid the term avant-garde altogether, preferring instead to write of 'the new or young art'.[6]

Likewise in Egypt, Idwār al-Kharrāṭ has coined the term *al-ḥassāsiyya al-jadīda* (the new sensibility) to refer to the avant-garde of the 1960s and 1970s. He writes that in Egypt too this avant-garde can to some extent be explained by the rise and decline of the bourgeoisie, followed by Nasserism and further deterioration under Sadat.[7] But one must also take into account the nature of the creative process itself which does not arise out of the writer's isolation from society, but from his interaction with the warring currents within society. I shall therefore focus attention on the avant-garde as a sociological rather than aesthetic phenomenon, since it is the former that provides a unified substratum to avant-garde experimentation (never forgetting that different avant-garde*s* may have different intentions), while the poetics and aesthetics form a rather chaotic complex. The Syrian poet Adūnīs, whose work has greatly influenced poetic experimentation in recent decades in Egypt, writes, 'We will only be able to reach a proper understanding of the poetics of Arab modernity by viewing it in its social, cultural and political context'.[8]

Social transition and the avant-garde

In Egypt at the beginning of this century, the intellectual elite was drawn from the privileged classes, usually the urban bourgeoisie, since it was they who were educated, had more contact with Europeans and could afford to spend time pursuing cultural activities. With the spread of education and a surge in the ranks of the bourgeoisie in the inter-war period, we see writers and intellectuals drawn from much more diverse backgrounds. Jamāl al-Ghīṭānī, one of the leading young

5 Jochen Schulte-Sasse, Foreword to Peter Bürger, *Theory of the Avant-Garde* (1984), p. viii.

6 R. Poggioli, op. cit. (1968), pp. 5–6.

7 Idwār al-Kharrāṭ, Introduction to *al-Karmal*, no. 14, 1984 (special issue dedicated to contemporary Egyptian literature), pp. 4–14.

8 Adonis (Adūnīs), *An Introduction to Arab Poetics* (1990), p. 75.

experimental writers in the 1960s, asserts: 'my generation came from the popular classes, . . . therefore we had a new outlook, a new sensibility; we tried to write in another style'.[9] Paradoxically, the financial circumstances of many of the new breed of writers made them more dependent on the market, and a common means of supporting one's work was to write for the popular commercial press. Yet it is precisely this triumph of popular commercial journalism that 'motivates and justifies the existence of the avant-garde review, which represents a reaction, as natural as it is necessary, to the spread of culture out to (or down to) the vulgar'.[10] Kathleen Tillotson has detected a similar phenomenon in Victorian England: the Industrial Revolution resulted in new urban classes, free popular education with the resulting increases in literacy, the growth of a popular press and the resulting split between pulp fiction and the little review.[11]

New young Egyptian writers began to reflect critically on this dependence of bourgeois culture either on the commercial market or on state patronage (and hence state control). Gradually, therefore, certain writers took a more sceptical approach to language and form in the belief that the aesthetic enjoyment of a work undermines its critical content, while the practical end of quantitative communication spoils the quality of expression. Although we glimpse this before the 1960s, especially among some of the poets of *Apollo* (Apollo, 1932–4) in the early 1930s and writers of the journals *al-Taṭawwur* (Development, 1940) and *al-Bashīr* (The Herald, 1948–50)[12] in the 1940s, it emerges more strongly at the end of the 1960s in *Gallery 68*. By the end of the 1970s, a more uncompromising radicality had emerged in the poetics of *Iḍā'a 77* (Illumination 77, 1977–88). What Bürger writes of the European avant-garde is also true of the Egyptian: 'such literature no longer refers positively to society by critically presenting norms and values, but rather attacks the ossification of society and its language in what amounts to intellectual guerrilla warfare'.[13] It is not so much that art should derive directly from life, but that life should derive from art.

The journal: an effective medium for the avant-garde

The specialist literary journal became the most effective platform from which to wage this guerrilla warfare against the cultural establishment. Poggioli describes little magazines as 'one of the external signs most characteristically avant-garde . . . their most symptomatic characteristics are limited printings and sparse, though highly selective, circulation . . . In sum, their chief characteristic is the noncommercial nature of their publishing: that is their natural condition (and

9 Jamāl al-Ghīṭānī, taped interview, Cairo, 30 April 1996.

10 R. Poggioli, op. cit. (1968), p. 23.

11 David Daiches, *Critical Approaches to Literature* (1961), p. 386.

12 The first issue, dated 2 Oct. 1948, is billed as no. 348, since an existing license was rented by a group of experimental writers and poets for a brief period.

13 J. Schulte-Sasse, op. cit. (1984), p. xii.

the no less natural reason for the failure of each of them or, at least, for their short lives)'.[14] Poggioli is correct in his bracketed afterthought to dissociate failure from short life span since the furore that such journals stirred up frequently outlived them. To condemn short-lived journals as insignificant failures has been a common misconception among Egyptian literary critics and historians. Small is not synonymous with insignificant, as Pollak acknowledges when he deems the role of the avant-garde journal in literature as significant as that of the atom in nuclear physics.[15] Nor is popularity, even among the cultural elite, a safe criterion by which to judge literary quality, in the Arab world in particular. One critic notes that 'the absence of *real* publishers and responsible critics, added to the oppressive effects of censorship, make popularity an extremely dubious criterion by which to judge an Arab author'.[16]

Two possible goals of the avant-garde journal may be identified, the first being 'merely to publish proclamations and programs or a series of manifestos, announcing the foundation of a new movement, explicating its doctrine, categorically and polemically'.[17] This was the case with *al-Taṭawwur* which ran to only five issues in 1940 but in which Jūrj Ḥunayn uncompromisingly proclaimed the intentions of *Jamā'at al-Fann wa-l-Ḥurriyya* (Society of Art and Freedom): 'O intellectuals! O writers! O artists! The hour of great revenge is nigh. O comrades, be cruel!'.[18] The other goal is simply 'to present to a friendly or hostile public an anthology of the collective work in a new tendency or by a new group of artists and writers. Precisely for that reason, we are often dealing with only more or less confessedly special numbers or special collections, which, with a good will or bad, abandon the obligation to appear regularly'.[19] This was the case with *Gallery 68* which ran to eight issues (1968–71), only two of which carried collective editorials, and which acted far more as a publishing outlet than as direct propaganda for a specific group.

Moreover, one should not underestimate the valuable encouragement extended to writers merely from seeing their names and works in print; one American writer confirmed, 'The little magazines are of course totally indispensable. They give the beginning writer his first important step – a chance to see how the thing looks in print. And there's nothing as salutary'.[20] This proved especially true for Egyptian experimental writers, given the state's increasingly suffocating grip on

14 R. Poggioli, op. cit. (1968), pp. 21–2.

15 Felix Pollak, 'The World of Little Magazines', *Arts in Society*, Spring/Summer 1962, p. 102.

16 Mohammed Shaheen, *The Modern Arabic Short Story: Shahrazad Returns* (1989), p. 1.

17 R. Poggioli, op. cit. (1968), p. 21.

18 *al-Taṭawwur*, no. 1, Jan. 1940. Quoted in 'Iṣām Maḥfūẓ, *al-Riwāya al-'Arabiyya al-Ṭalī'iyya* (1982), p. 14.

19 R. Poggioli, op. cit. (1968), p. 22.

20 Stephen Vincent Benét in an unpublished letter to Charles Allen, editor of *The Sewanee Review*, Sept. 1939. Cited in Frederic Hoffmann, Charles Allen and Carolyn Ulrich, *The Little Magazine: A History and Bibliography* (1967), p. 15.

the publishing industry in the late 1960s and 1970s. Thus this avant-garde phenomenon of non-periodic journals blossomed into a successive stream of activity in the late 1970s and early 1980s. In Egypt as in the United States,

> the little magazine spirit... is free and gay and irreverent and deadly earnest and intense, pugnacious and ebullient, often irresponsible, always irrepressible – little magazines may die after a short span of publication, but the *esprit* that gave them birth lives on and begets forever new titles that take their places.[21]

It is such journals which have provided the source material for recent developments in modern Egyptian literature.

Given the growing state hold on the Egyptian publishing industry after the start of nationalization in 1960, the little magazine became an exceptionally vital vehicle of avant-garde assertion. Poggioli defines avant-garde ideology as 'an argument of self-assertion or self-defence used by a society in the strict sense against society in the larger sense. In Egypt, the little magazine fulfilled Poggioli's role of 'society in the strict sense' (or *al-jam'iyya*), trying to assert its voice against the cultural establishment, 'society in the larger sense' (or *al-mujtama'*). In the 1940s, the voice of writers publishing modernist work in journals like *al-Taṭawwur* and *al-Bashīr* was not strong enough to win attention from the cultural establishment; but by the end of the 1960s, the new sensibility had gathered pace. One of the founding editors of *Gallery 68* wrote that 'this generation is in fact facing a threat over which it has almost no power. But it is impelled with a conquering force to face it and to wade into its deluge. This generation, the generation of *68*, refuses to set foot on well-trodden paths'.[22]

Why this avant-garde assertion in the late 1960s?

Statistical analysis undertaken by Marina Stagh shows that publishers were less receptive to new writers during the 1960s than they were in the 1950s, and that those who were published were less successful in continuing to publish than those of the 1950s.[23] Therefore, while more young writers of the 1960s were given the opportunity to publish for the first time, comparatively few of them managed to establish themselves as writers. Part of the reason for this situation must lie in the increased government hold on cultural activity through the nationalization of press and publishing houses that began in 1960. While nationalization involved massive government investment in culture and several new literary journals were

21 F. Pollak, 'Landing in Little Magazines – Capturing a Trend', *Arizona Quarterly*, Vol. 19, no. 2, Summer 1962, p. 52.

22 I. al-Kharrāṭ, Editorial to *Gallery 68*, no. 8, Feb. 1971.

23 Marina Stagh, *The Limits of Freedom of Speech* (1993), pp. 50–2.

established under the auspices of the Ministry of Culture,[24] this boom appears to have been accompanied by a lack of literary discernment and hence a failure to concentrate on fostering true talent.

Several writers active during the 1960s stress that Nasser was largely sympathetic to the cultural elite, cracking down only on the organized political opposition,[25] and he gained a reputation for artistic sensitivity. He listened to classical music, read translated fiction and kept the company of broad-minded intellectuals like Muḥammad Ḥasanayn Haykal and Lūwīs 'Awaḍ. Egyptian novelist Jamīl 'Aṭiyya Ibrāhīm now describes the 1960s as 'a glorious period in Egypt for writers and artists in general. They were not only given a free hand in their production, they were actively encouraged and often subsidized'.[26] One poet and critic who published prolifically in the Beirut journal *Shi'r* in the 1960s writes, 'the sixties were the literary golden age in comparison with the gloom we experience today;... for the sixties was the age of fearless freedom, the age of enthusiasm for life, the book and the pen'.[27] The once rebellious independent journal *al-Ghad*, launched for a third and final time by the 'Abd al-Ḥalīm brothers and Ḥasan Fu'ād in the mid-1980s, published an article which enshrined Nasser as the friend of culture who had turned Egypt into a pioneer and model of culture in the Arab world.[28]

There is, however, a danger of reflecting too nostalgically on the relative freedom of culture under Nasser in the light of Sadat's cultural terrorism. There may also be an element of idealizing the prime days of one's youth, now that another generation is taking centre stage. In 1964, Sabry Hafez at least was moved to write an article on 'The Crisis of Freedom in Contemporary Arabic Fiction'; and despite publishing this in the Beirut journal *Ḥiwār*, he still only made veiled references to circumstances under the Nasser regime. He pointed out that the issue of freedom actually became critical after independence rather than being solved by independence; however, he appears to blame this on Egypt's lack of experience of democracy, having suffered long decades of imperial rule, rather than commenting on the Nasser regime directly.[29] Later, the poet Amal Dunqul complained more openly in a Kuwaiti journal of Nasser's repressive measures being directed against writers and intellectuals,[30] and the literary critic and journalist Ghālī Shukrī recriminated bitterly against right-wing Nasserists controlling culture in a

24 For example, *al-Kātib* 1961–80, *al-Masraḥ* 1964–71, *al-Shi'r* 1964–5, *al-Fikr al-Mu'āṣir* 1965–71, *al-Kitāb al-'Arabī* 1964–71, *al-Ṭalī'a* 1965–77.

25 M. Stagh's interviews with Egyptian writers corroborate my own interviews with Egyptian writers on this point.

26 Fayza Ḥasan, 'Gamil Attiya Ibrāhīm: Keeping the Books', *al-Ahram Weekly*, 20–26 June 1996, p. 26.

27 Riyāḍ Najīb al-Rayyis, *al-Fatra al-Ḥarija: Naqd fī Adab al-Sittīnāt* (1992), p. 14.

28 Fatḥī Raḍwān, ''Abd al-Nāṣir wa-l-Thaqāfa', *al-Ghad*, no. 1, 1985, pp. 17–23.

29 Sabry Hafez, 'Azmat al-Ḥurriyya fī al-Riwāya al-'Arabiyya al-Mu'āṣira', *Ḥiwār*, May–June 1964, p. 52.

30 Interview with Amal Dunqul conducted by Amānī al-Sayyid, *al-Yaqẓa* (Kuwait), no. 524, Oct. 1977. It is worth noting, however, that some of Amal Dunqul's poems critical of the regime were actually published in *al-Ahrām* in 1961.

'battle' against progressive nationalist men of culture.[31] Mohammed Shaheen confirms that 'whatever would be expressed in social, cultural, individual, historical or human terms, that might be taken as directly relevant to politics and government,...was omitted'. While Nasser respected intellectuals, he did not trust their Marxist tendencies, and while he let them work within the institutions, he left real power in the hands of others and thus maintained a control of sorts over the newly nationalized publishing industry. One can sympathize with the bitter tone of the independent Egyptian journal *al-Nādīm*,[32] reflecting on widespread nostalgia in the 1980s for 'those [times] which many now eulogize under the name of the sixties, though their forms of tyranny continue to be inflicted on us'.[33] It is important to remember that, at the time, editors and journalists remained wary of incurring Nasser's wrath. Bahā' Ṭāhir, a leading Egyptian novelist active in the 1960s, remembers that

> to publish creative writing was difficult because one had to publish in the government press. One had to deal with editors, sub-editors, and the like, who themselves exercised censorship, not because they had directives, but out of fear. Both literary and non-literary magazines were very suspicious of the young generation.[34]

The radical leftist critic, Ibrāhīm Fatḥī, was a prime example, discovering upon his release from prison in 1967 that publishing houses were under instructions not to print his work. Only the daily *al-Masā'* broke this siege, so *Gallery 68* provided an essential outlet for his Marxist literary critique.[35] This tallies with Gonzalez-Quijano's observation that mechanisms of censorship were dictated by complex factors internal as well as external to the literary and intellectual fields.[36]

Another problem for writers was that, while the theatre and cinema were well catered for in the Ministry of Culture's journals, experimental narrative and poetry tended to be neglected. A number of Egyptian critics attribute the rise of new trends in the short story in the late 1960s directly to the previous literary generation having devoted most of its experimental energies to drama.[37] Yūsuf al-Shārūnī too affirms that new trends in the short story which erupted at the end

31 Ghālī Shukrī, *Min al-Arshīf al-Sirrī li-l-Thaqāfa al-Miṣriyya* (1975), pp. 5–8, 90–2.

32 *Al-Nādīm* was edited by Muḥammad Ibrāhīm Mabrūk who had joined the editorial board of *Gallery 68* at the end of the 1960s.

33 Editorial to *al-Nādīm*, May 1985.

34 Bahā' Ṭāhir, taped interview, Cairo, 1 May 1996.

35 Hala Halim, 'Ibrāhīm Fatḥī: Curbstone Critic', *al-Ahram Weekly*, no. 602, 5–11 Sept. 2002. Online. Available HTTP: http://weekly.ahram.org.eg/2002/602/profile.htm

36 Yves Gonzalez-Quijano, 'Pour une Sociologie du Fait Littéraire dans le monde arabe: à propos de *The Limits of Freedom of Speech* par Marina Stagh', *Arabic and Middle Eastern Literatures*, Vol. 3, no. 1, 2000, p. 90.

37 For example, Jalāl al-'Asharī, 'al-Qiṣṣa al-Qaṣīra min al-Azma ilā al-Qaḍiyya', *al-Fikr al-Mu'āṣir*, June 1969, and Gh. Shukrī, *Ṣirā' al-Ajyāl* (1971), p. 111.

of the 1960s were in part motivated by the fact that drama had monopolized literary attention in the early 1960s, while the short story, novel and poetry were sidelined.[38] The Ministry's *al-Shi'r* (Poetry, 1964–5) and *al-Qiṣṣa* (Narrative, 1964–5) journals lasted little more than a year, *al-Ṭalī'a* (The Avant-Garde, 1965–77) did not publish its literary supplement until 1972 and meanwhile *al-Adab* (Literature, 1956–66) had ceased publication in 1966. While very few editors in the 1960s, such as 'Abd al-Fattāḥ al-Jamal at *al-Masā'* (Tonight, 1956–) and Yaḥyā Ḥaqqī at *al-Majalla* (The Journal, 1957–71), did encourage and publish young experimental writers, in general there was a distinct lack of outlets for the highly charged literary work of the so-called *jīl al-sittīnāt* (the generation of the 1960s).

Wayne Booth cites political failure as one of the five principal inspirations behind innovative movement,[39] and for the Egyptian avant-garde, the breaking point finally came with the crushing defeat in 1967 in which Egypt lost both her army and the Sinai. The defeat had a profound effect on intellectuals and vindicated the younger generation's criticism of the establishment, whether political, social or cultural. Jamāl al-Qaṣṣāṣ, a young Egyptian poet who began writing at the beginning of the 1970s, reveals

> the reality of the 67 defeat pushed us urgently to gather the pieces of our nation in our poems and to search for new focal points for the Egyptian identity... 1967 was a fundamental point marking the transition from individual thought to collective thought.[40]

Sulaymān Fayyāḍ, a young writer who was to contribute a story to *Gallery 68*, was even moved to entitle one of his collections *Aḥzān Ḥazīrān* (June Sorrows, 1969). Yaḥyā Ḥaqqī, who, together with Naguib Mahfouz, was highly respected among rising young experimental writers, called on intellectuals to restore Egypt's self-confidence, writing 'they are the ones holding the weapon and who should point out the right path at the crossroads.... In the field of cultural exchange, they can achieve unity of the Arab nation where politics fails'.[41] Experimental young writers were keen to take up the challenge, but the outlets for their work were too few and too diffuse to confirm them as a new phenomenon. Frustration and the desire to magnify their impact sparked the first in a whole stream of avant-garde non-periodic journals: *Gallery 68*. Ibrāhīm Manṣūr, the prime mover behind the launch of *Gallery 68*, described the 1967 defeat as the 'triggering point' for this journal.[42]

38 Yūsuf al-Shārūnī, *Dirāsat fī al-Qiṣṣa al-Qaṣīra* (1989), p. 99.

39 Wayne Booth, 'Renewing the Medium of Renewal: Some Notes on the Anxieties of Innovation', in Ihab and Sally Hassan (eds) *Innovation/Renovation* (1983), p. 134.

40 Jamāl al-Qaṣṣāṣ, taped interview, Cairo, 4 November 1994.

41 Editorial to *al-Majalla*, Jan. 1970.

42 Ibrāhīm Manṣūr, taped interview, Cairo, 1 May 1996.

Samir Hegazy detects a direct causal link between the rapid change in social structures in Egypt, 1967–73, and the ascent of the avant-garde short story, which featured so heavily in *Gallery 68*. Disillusionment after the 1967 defeat eroded certain values that had linked the individual to social structures, causing the writer to withdraw and isolate himself from society.[43] However, rather than engineer his own isolation, it would be truer to say that the writer found himself isolated, hence the avant-garde assertion, which was not intended as an affirmation of isolation but as a means of reintegrating the writer and his art into life. Shafīq Maqqār, himself a contributor to *Gallery 68*, explains the dilemma of the avant-garde writer at the end of the 1960s: he is desperate to expose the truth, but is 'fettered by a backwardness which he cannot destroy'. Thus he 'is thrown' into a situation where he cannot compromise by 'floating up to the earth's surface to walk in the sun', but nor does he wish to recede into the dark, 'so he cries out his yearning and distress, caused by circumstances beyond his control'.[44] Writers' cries would naturally be loudest when uttered simultaneously, for example, when gathered into a single outlet such as *Gallery 68*. But given this isolation of the writer (for whatever reason), Hegazy is correct in claiming that the short story proved an attractive medium through which to express the writer's malaise since its economy and brevity enabled him to give the impression of unity in a compressed vision of life, while he perhaps lacked the confidence to embark on the longer novel form; it also assuaged the urgency of the young experimenter to finish and see the effect of his work, and was more suited to the journalistic platform. As one Egyptian writer explained, while the novelist must be a sociologist, historian and psychologist, the short story writer is confined to his individuality.[45] Ghālī Shukrī, who himself came to prominence as a literary critic in the 1960s, also affirms the particular partiality of the avant-gardist to the short story, asserting that it was in journals that this form really developed: 'He who... observes the dozens of groups of fiction writers understands to what extent this art form [the short story] enriched and continues to enrich the young generations that gather beneath its banner'.[46]

The cultural scene deteriorated after 1967 as the reverse outcome of the state monopoly on culture made itself felt. Much state finance for cultural activity was re-allocated for defence and reconstruction of the army, yet state control over publication was tightened.[47] Meanwhile the private publishing houses that had survived Nasser's nationalization were small and weak and as such were incapable

43 S. Hegazy, *Littérature et Société en Egypte de la Guerre de 1967 à Celle de 1973* (1976), pp. 158, 199.

44 Shafīq Maqqār, ' 'An al-Jadīd wa-al-Qadīm wa-Mā Bayna Bayna', *Gallery 68*, no. 7, Oct. 1969, p. 96.

45 Shukrī 'Ayyād, *al-Qiṣṣa al-Qaṣīra fī Miṣr* (1968), p. 36.

46 Gh. Shukrī, *Muḥāwarāt al-Yawm* (1980), p. 146.

47 In 1969, all state publishing enterprises were merged into the large conglomerate *The General Egyptian Book Organization*, and in 1971 centralization reached its peak with the incorporation of the National Library into this.

of cultivating quality and talent. Sadat began to dismantle Nasser's cultural edifice and most of the journals sponsored by the Ministry of Culture were closed down, several of them in 1971.[48] Animosity between writers and the regime grew throughout the Sadat era[49] and in 1973, over 100 leading journalists and writers were suspended. Although censorship was officially lifted in 1974, in practice Sadat found other ways to crack down on criticism. A reshuffle in press and publishing houses in 1974 favoured those who favoured the regime and ousted those with a left-wing record. This informal censorship, which drained the cultural press of left-wing and liberal personalities, turned out to be more effective than a formal one. Part of the problem was that Sadat fancied himself a writer and was thus much more interventionist than Nasser. Outside the censorship authority proper lurked a sophisticated transparent censorship in the form of editors, local censors stationed at journals, favourites of Sadat appointed to the boards of press and publishing houses and reading committees. In other words, censorship became institutionalized. Naguib Mahfouz regretfully remembered that Sadat 'was the opposite to 'Abd al-Nāṣir.... He threw away all he had done'.[50] The passionate antagonism felt by many young experimental writers towards the Sadat regime is still apparent. Jamīl 'Aṭiyya Ibrāhīm, Egyptian novelist, short story writer and one of the founding editors of *Gallery 68*, complained bitterly, 'Sadat was illiterate and surrounded by illiterates, despite having literary pretensions. Sadat worked actively against intellectuals; many were dismissed and forced to emigrate abroad'.[51]

Given these conditions, it is not surprising that in Egypt as in Europe 'the avant-garde image originally remained subordinate, even within the sphere of art, to the ideals of a radicalism that was not cultural but political'.[52] Leading Egyptian novelist and contributor to *Gallery 68*, Bahā' Ṭāhir, reflects on the literary scene for young writers at the end of the 1960s: 'We ate and drank politics at that time. Had we not written it, this would have been a great lie'.[53] As for the impact of this avant-garde activity, what Bürger writes of the European avant-garde is also true of the Egyptian: 'Although the political intentions of the avant-garde movements (reorganization of the praxis of life through art) were never realized, their impact in the realm of art can hardly be overestimated'.[54] Likewise, the dynamic experimental movement that centred around *Gallery 68* proved inspirational for young avant-garde poets of the 1970s, albeit partly through stirring up their opposition to

48 For example, *al-Majalla, al-Qiṣṣa, al-Kitāb al-'Arabī, al-Fikr al-Mu'āṣir and al-Funūn al-Sha'biyya.*

49 Many writers took exception to the violent measures used to quell student demonstrations in 1972.

50 Naguib Mahfouz, quoted in Aḥmad Hāshim al-Sharīf, *Naguib Mahfouz: Muḥāwarāt Qabl Nobel* (1989), p. 17.

51 Jamīl 'Aṭiyya Ibrāhīm, taped interview, Cairo, 30 April 1996.

52 R. Poggioli, op. cit. (1968), p. 9.

53 B. Ṭāhir, taped interview, Cairo, 1 May 1996.

54 P. Bürger, op. cit. (1983), p. 59.

certain aesthetics. Just as Scheunemann has dismissed Bürger's theory of a single unified intention behind European avant-garde activity as untenable,[55] so it was in Egypt – the avant-garde 'seventies' poets objected to what they saw as *Gallery 68*'s overt links to social and political phenomena. Nevertheless, one of these poets, Jamāl al-Qaṣṣāṣ, reveals that *Gallery 68* still had a direct and vital influence on poetic experimentation, encouraging himself and others to form a group of poets and publish *Iḍā'a 77* in 1977. This in turn was followed by at least nine other non-periodic avant-garde journals over the next decade and a host of one-offs, since the need for such activity remained pressing.

Who were the avant-gardists?

Those writers contributing to *al-ḥassāsiyya al-jadīda* (the new sensibility) in the short story in Egypt have come to be known as *jīl al-sittīnāt* (the generation of the sixties). However, *al-ḥassāsiyya al-jadīda* and *jīl al-sittīnāt* are not interchangeable terms since this would mix physical criteria with historical and stylistic criteria. *Gallery 68* itself never referred to its contributors as *jīl al-sittīnāt*, nor even *al-jīl al-jadīd* (the new generation), preferring instead the more fluid term *jīl al-yawm* (today's generation). This is more accurate since the work published in *Gallery 68*, through which the new sensibility finally gained a foothold and crystallized, is characterized by the intersection of various decades and generations. The sixties generation may therefore be viewed as the spearhead of those writers giving expression to *al-ḥassāsiyya al-jadīda*, but not as synonymous with it.[56]

The common denominator shared by sixties' avant-gardists was their disillusionment with the regime, and a sense of isolation from the institutions and establishments which represented it, feelings that were greatly exacerbated by Egypt's annihilating defeat at the hands of Israel in June 1967. This negative disenchantment was coupled with a more positive desire to effect change, and to restore confidence and pride. One young contributor to *Gallery 68* described the avant-gardist as 'he whose most powerful inner force is the will to change; he is necessarily at odds with society and with the institutions and organizations that wish to protect their [own] survival'.[57] The independent journal proved an effective means of constructive action by uniting conflicting avant-garde resonances into an assertive forceful voice.

What was 'the new sensibility'?

While this new sensibility embraced various, even opposing, currents, Idwār al-Kharrāṭ detects four main currents,[58] always allowing that the boundaries

55 Dietrich Scheunemann (ed.) *European Avant-garde: New Perspectives* (2000), introduction.

56 See the introduction to this book for a brief discussion of the use of 'generation'.

57 Usāma al-Ghuzūlī's reply to questionnaire, 'Hākadhā Yatakallamu al-Udabā' al-Shabbāb', *al-Ṭalī'a*, Sept. 1969.

58 I. al-Kharrāṭ, op. cit. (1984), pp. 9–11.

between these currents were blurred and that writers might adhere to more than one. These currents may be seen to have arisen as the result of one or more of four distinct moments identified by Poggioli. However, it is important to remember that avant-garde experimentation cannot entirely be flattened into recognized theoretical positions since 'actual positions and practices are very much more diverse than their subsequent ideological presentations'.[59]

Nihilism/alienation (al-tashyī'/al-tab'īd)

The language of this current is lifelessly economical, unembellished, dry and emotionless with an indifferent rhythm, unswerving from its task of stark documentation. It indicates the impossibility of penetrating to the warm pulse of life. As a result it retreats from the complicated tensions of reality, establishing instead fleshless channels from which to observe reality coldly and indifferently. Yet this trend is itself an active rejection, at once passionate and silent, of reality. 'This dictionary which narrows, defines and denudes is itself loaded with suggestion and has its own cruel poetics'.[60] This current springs from Poggioli's nihilistic moment when the dynamism of the avant-garde drives itself beyond any limit, rejoicing in beating down whatever stands in its way.

Ra'ūf Mus'ad's *Wa-Daqīqa* (Another Minute) exemplifies this cold observation of reality through the eyes of an alienated young man heading for suicide. In common with many *Gallery 68* stories, Mus'ad's protagonist lives alone in a solitary room on the roof, observing life rather than participating in it. The story is framed by the clock of the city square which he watches through his window,

> He was silent.
> Two o'clock. And ten minutes.
> An ambulance.
> Half past two.
> The police station.
> Four thirty.
> A telegram to his father.
> Eight thirty.
> The pension. The bed. His white wrist. His father looking at him.
> Nine thirty.
> His father lit his second cigarette in half an hour. He was leafing through a colour magazine.
> Ten thirty.

59 Raymond Williams, 'Language and the Avant-garde', in Nigel Fabb, Derek Atteridge, Alan Durant and Colin MacCabe (eds) *The Linguistics of Writing: Arguments between Language and Literature* (1984), p. 34.

60 I. al-Kharrāṭ, op. cit. (1984), p. 9.

His father decides to take him to the town.
Eight o'clock in the morning.
The window of his old room, the flies eating the eye of the horse and the eye of the cabbie. A licorice root seller, a child urinating and writing his name with his urine. A madman scratching his face. A student on her way to school gnawing her nails. A goat rubbing its back against the wall. A song on the radio. He took the razor out of his pocket.
Five past eight.[61]

Ibrāhīm Aṣlān's *Fī Jiwār Rajul Ḍarīr* (Next Door to a Blind Man) also depicts the monotonous isolated existence of a solitary alienated young man, living alone in a room on the roof. The story consists of indifferent, superficial sentences, divided into nine chapters over only four pages. The first three chapters are as follows,

-1-
Nothing happened.
-2-
A very few things happened. After much thinking, I thought it best to conclude with the belief that she/it might not be suitable enough.
-3-
Once again I thought about the days that had passed in vain. I thought how numerous the times were that I had proposed to put and end to this matter. I put on my clothes and went out into the road. I saw the people, then I returned to the house.[62]

We wonder whether he is considering putting an end to his life, and indeed he slashes his face with a razor blade during the night. The story's pace and style remain wilfully pedestrian and dispassionate, emphasising the protagonist's solitary and monotonous existence. Nevertheless, he fears that he can see and hear another man living with him (probably his alter ego). This gives rise to the sole instance of dialogue; it occurs between the protagonist and his blind landlord and is extremely economical:

-Is the room comfortable?
I said:
-It's comfortable.
-Is the bed comfortable?
-It's comfortable.
-We have noticed that you are alone, that's why we haven't crowded it out for you.

61 *Gallery 68*, no. 8, Feb. 1971, pp. 45–6.
62 *Gallery 68*, no. 6, April 1969, pp. 5–8.

> I said:
> -I chose this house for its quiet location.
> -From this perspective, it's the best place in town.
> -And I specifically chose the roof because you assured me that it's devoid of residents.
> -We have never allowed anyone to rent it, ever since the house was built, and you ought to know that you are the only resident to whom we have allowed that.
> The wife confirmed her husband's words. I thanked them and left.
>
> (Ibid., p. 7)

Ibrāhīm Manṣūr's *al-Yawm 24 Sā'a* (A Day is 24 Hours) is also about the pointless existence of an alienated young man and again sets its hopeless tone with the first sentence, 'In the morning I didn't go to work because there wasn't any work there.'[63] This protagonist too observes reality as the cold passage of time, noting down times from the bar clock in his notebook whenever the barman suggests that he is drunk. Minute pedestrian detail is dispassionately observed and recounted in dull monotony, focusing in on the occasional odd detail:

> The bus was not crowded but I didn't find a window seat, and I sat on the galabiyya of a man with a face made of rubber because he didn't move his galabiyya when he saw that I was interested in sitting next to him or perhaps he hadn't seen me. The bus conductor didn't have change for the pound I had with me so I got off and the man's galabiyya was creased. I returned again to the station and bought a packet of cigarettes, then another bus came; it wasn't crowded and I found a window seat with no one next to me. I saw a man walking in the street and thought that he was my father but I remembered that he had died, he and my aunt and my aunt's husband. I gave the bus conductor a note worth ten piasters and he gave me the change and I said to myself: some of them have change and some of them don't have change. Such is life.
>
> (Ibid., p. 16)

Likewise, there are several seemingly banal footnotes to the text which reinforce the excessively superficial nature of the protagonist's existence and his inability to integrate into society. The following example also illustrates the strained relationship with the female sex that was so common in *Gallery 68* stories:

> I was walking in the street, I and the Syrian lad who had become my friend, staring at the women. There were many women, some of whom were very ignorant. The Syrian lad said to a beautiful girl who passed him wearing a

63 *Gallery 68*, no. 6, April 1969, p. 16.

> blue dress, 'Multi Bella Senorita', so I stopped and started laughing because the girl might have been Italian. He was angry and said that if I hadn't laughed, the girl would have become his lover (footnote sign).
>
> Footnote: This is not true because I was sitting with a Kuwaiti lad in the Hilton one evening and when a girl brought coffee for me and dinner for him he said something to her which I don't remember and I laughed but the girl still became his lover.
>
> (Ibid., p. 17)

Thus, in this story, the alter ego takes the form of a Syrian friend and again the story closes under the threat of death when the Syrian friend asks the protagonist to shoot him, although the latter refuses.

Internal or inter-dimensional current (al-tayyār al-dākhilī/tayyār al-tawarruṭ)

In contrast to nihilism, this current uses explosive, sensitive language to observe reality from the inside on the assumption that first truth lies in the soul. There is little or no formal dialogue, rather we find confidentialities and ravings. The writer confuses and complicates the language, however absurd the result, for familiar language, 'the language of a decadent bourgeois society', is perceived to block true creativity, and the rule instead is 'dictation by thought, in the absence of any control exercised by reason'.[64] The text gushes forth, only to dwell then on a flash of insight. The plot is extremely brittle and at times superfluous. Time is released from its external chronological boundaries, to be free as in dreams. Hesitation and obscurity are the rule. Boundaries are blurred between internal and external, between reality and fantasy. In an editorial to *Gallery 68*, Kharrāṭ admitted that he and fellow writers were fed up with rationality. Thus the purpose of writing is not communication but illumination with an emphasis on the experience itself, rather than the forms embodying it.[65]

This is the case with Muḥammad Juwaylī's *Baʿda Layla min al-Araq* (After a Night of Araq), consisting only of two pages of internal monologue, yet still incorporating the common ingredients of violent tendencies, a hint of sexual perversion and an alter ego, with time and reality slipping in and out of focus. The final paragraph reads,

> Why does my father's voice grow weaker the older he grows? Perhaps it is the fat assailing his broad chest. Perhaps his veins have swelled up with flesh despite the fact that his eyes are still small and their blue has faded and changed to gloomy grey, . . . why did that fly in particular insist on lingering over my wrist, scratching its head like someone thinking

64 R. Williams, op. cit. (1984), p. 40.

65 I. al-Kharrāṭ, Editorial to *Gallery 68*, no. 8, Feb. 1971.

> about something?...he was looking at me again, he was saying something,...why did the odour of his mother's breast remain in his mouth at that age? Perhaps he was asking about time,...the flies were extremely cold, I wanted to spit on him, slap him hard...he was still looking at me...I wonder if he knows others? Ha...an absurdity.[66]

Khalīl Sulaymān Kalfat's *Māta Ḥāmid Yawma 'Awdati-hi min al-Qāhira* (Ḥāmid Died the Day of His Return from Cairo) is also almost entirely devoid of dialogue, wildly swapping between narrative voices whilst breaking the bounds of time and reality (and punctuation) in a gushing text. Ḥāmid's would-be fiancée, Fāṭima, has poisoned both him and herself:

> She now had half an hour for them both to die – he must not know the cause – the story must die with her – I might be cruel and abominable. I might be a criminal. I might be an ordinary wronged girl violating the law – I might be anything but he deserves it and I deserve it because I am stupid. For billions of light-years she has been stupid, not recognising the two-faced traitor – she said to Ḥāmid you have half an hour to die – Ḥāmid was astonished – what are you saying. Impossible.[67]

At times the plot is completely subordinate to confused ravings, such as here, where the narrative voice is passed to Ḥāmid's friend (or rather, alter ego), Muḥammad:

> It seems that I will not live long after him and his mother and brothers will not live long after him – no one will live, but everyone will live for long centuries and perhaps the dead will rise up – really perhaps the dead will rise up – before our death great things happened – Ḥāmid was always saying this to me: you must be idle and extraordinary things will happen – the sun will come and cry at my feet and forgive me my sins – it will rise from the West too and things will fly without falling back down to earth – great things will inevitably happen – this makes no sense but what's the sense in my dying. His words were clear, obscure, strong, summarising man's degradation with easy girls seducing him – what is the sense in death? Or even, what is the sense in life? For obscure reasons people disappear and for obscure reasons people go and no one takes care of order.
>
> (Ibid., pp. 41–2)

This current appears to spring from what Poggioli terms the activist and agonistic moments. In the activist moment, the writer agitates primarily for the

66 *Gallery 68*, no. 3, July 1968, pp. 49–50.

67 Ibid., pp. 37–48.

sake of agitating, to obtain a reaction. To be free is more important than to be sound or right or justified, and this is achieved by revolutionizing the very medium of innovation, the language in which it is carried out.[68] At times, the writer may be 'more interested in motion than creation...creation often appears as a vulgar variant of aestheticism and sometimes is reduced to nothing more than a kind of "operation" '.[69] The agonistic moment represents the wish to delve ever further, ignoring the ruin of others and welcoming its own ruin as a sacrifice for future progress. This sacrifice 'is conceived in terms of a collective group of men born and growing up at the same moment'[70] – hence the surge of writers (the majority of whom were born in the late 1930s or early 1940s) experimenting in this current in *Gallery 68*, although Kharrāṭ himself (b.1926) is one notable exception who had been a practitioner since the 1940s.

The inspiration of the Arab heritage (istiḥā' al-turāth al-'arabī)

This draws on folklore and the collective memory. The challenge is to ensure that the material drawn from the heritage actually fuses with the artistic vision to create an effective living entity, rather than remaining mere overlay. While Kharrāṭ admits to blurring between the four currents, I would view drawing inspiration from the Arab heritage on a wholly separate level, more as a means than as an end result, as a broad-ranging device rather than a separate current. Yet it is a device that is important and widespread enough to warrant special mention.

New realism (al-tayyār al-wāqi'ī al-jadīd)

This current rejects traditional authority and interrogates the prevailing value system. The form may appear traditional on the surface, but is in fact more severe, precise and ruptured. While conventional writers treat their material as an organic whole, something that has sprung from concrete life, these avant-gardists might remove their concrete material from the functional context that gives it meaning, isolate it and turn it into a fragment. The ruptured fragment of art differs radically from the organic unity of the bourgeois institution of art for it is open to supplementary responses and 'challenges its recipient to make it an integrated part of his or her reality and to relate it to sensuous-material experience [i.e., experience not yet worked-through by narration]'.[71] Fragments are joined with the intent of positing a meaning which does not derive from the original context of the fragments, and which thus varies in differing historical contexts. The resulting work is a self-proclaimed artificial construct based on montage. This current springs from Poggioli's antagonistic moment, agitating against and questioning the status quo.

68 W. Booth, op. cit. (1983), p. 137.
69 R. Poggioli, op. cit. (1968), p. 29.
70 Ibid., p. 68.
71 J. Shulte-Sasse, op. cit. (1984), p. 39.

Aḥmad al-Buḥayrī's *Makān bi-lā Malāmiḥ Mumayyiza* (A Place without Distinguishing Characteristics) recounts several similar trivial exchanges at a bus stop, during which nothing really happens.

> I saw one of my friends waiting for the bus like me so I patted him on the shoulder. He looked at me and smiled wanly. He said that he had just come from a strange place. I feigned surprise and asked him about the details without any real wish to know... but purely to kill time. He said that it was a very strange place and that, throughout his time there, he had experienced a very strange feeling and that he couldn't say more than that. When I asked him – purely to kill time – to describe this place, he said that this place had no distinguishing characteristics.[72]

The bus then comes and the friend departs. After remembering that all his friends are dead, he decides to keep on waiting at the bus stop. A girl arrives.

> I went up to her and patted her on the shoulder. She looked at me and smiled a wan smile. I discovered that I had met her once in Port Said. She told me that she was going to a confined and extremely secluded place. I told her that this was a totally appropriate place in weather such as this. I asked her whether this place was her refuge; she didn't respond.
> (Ibid., p. 38)

The girl then cries copiously, ostensibly to clean her eyes of dust, before the opening scenario is reversed with the protagonist now adopting the role of his friend:

> I tried to say anything purely to kill time, so I told her that I had just come from a strange place. She was surprised and asked me about it so I told her that it was very strange and that, throughout my time there, I had experienced a very strange feeling and that I couldn't say more than that. When she asked me to describe this place for her, I told her that it was a place without any distinguishing characteristics.
> (Ibid.)

The bus then comes and the girl departs. The story then seems to begin again with the protagonist again encountering his friend at the bus stop roughly a week later, but this time the scenarios are intertwined – the friend now adopts the girl's role and the two afore-mentioned places are merged:

> I felt a hand patting me on the shoulder and looked and found my friend with the wan smile so I smiled. He told me that he was going to a confined and extremely secluded place. I told him that this was a totally appropriate place in weather such as this. I asked him whether this place

72 *Gallery 68*, no. 1, April–May 1968, p. 37.

> was his refuge; he didn't respond, so I asked him to describe this place to me. He said that it was without distinguishing characteristics.
>
> (Ibid., p. 39)

After the friend agrees that he has perhaps met the girl before, the bus comes and both the girl and friend depart. The story is brought full circle when the girl arrives again at the bus stop, echoing the opening scenario by now adopting the friend's initial role:

> I was still waiting when I felt a hand patting me on the shoulder. I looked and found the thin girl with the wide eyes so I smiled. She said that she had come from a very strange place so I feigned surprise. I asked her about it and she said that it was a very strange place and that throughout her time there, she had experienced a very strange feeling. When I asked her to describe it, she said that it was a place without distinguishing characteristics.
>
> (Ibid.)

The story ends as it begins, with the protagonist still waiting at the bus stop. The resulting montage of these superficial incidents gives us a deeper awareness of the triviality, passivity and monotony of existence. As the layers build up, the actual story loses importance as the nameless friend and girl emerge merely as projections of the protagonist's own character, while the place(s) without distinguishing features appears to be more of a mental state than a concrete reality.

Similar in style is Ibrāhīm 'Abd al-'Āṭī's *Taqārīr Shāmila wa-Nihā'iyya 'an Ba'd al-Ḥālāt al-Khaṭīra allatī tajlisu fī Hudū' fī Maqhan 'alā Jānib min al-Ahammiyya* (Comprehensive and Final Reports about Some Serious States which Sit Calmly in a Café of Some Significance).[73] We come to realize that the three reports of which the story is comprised, each dealing with a nameless man from a café, are simply telling the same man's story from slightly differing angles. Like Buhayrī's story, inexact repetition is an essential unifying structural thread, in particular the man's various sexual encounters and the severe boredom he suffers. Each report builds up the layers of the story, filling in the gaps like a montage to give a complex impression rather than a complete picture.

Khalīl Sulaymān Kalfat's *Māta Hamad Yawma 'Awdati-hi min al-Qāhira* (Hamad[74] Died the Day of His Return from Cairo)[75] has a different method of rupturing the traditional form of the story. It is introduced by a page-long documentary style section, providing very precise realistic details about the exact geographical setting – the village of Ismā'īliyya in Upper Egypt; in contrast, the reader is later

73 *Gallery 68*, no. 6, April 1969, pp. 9–13.

74 Significantly, the name Hamad carries overtones of torpor and death, unlike the root Ḥamad from which Muḥammad, the name of the protagonist's friend/alter ego, is derived.

75 *Gallery 68*, no. 3, July 1968, pp. 37–48.

challenged to imagine that the story could take place anywhere, even on the moon.[76] The material of the story is also undermined by several footnote-like asides placed mid-text. For example, after a paragraph describing Hamad's father, the resultant picture is immediately ruptured in an aside informing the reader that this could be any father. Likewise, after describing Hamad's would-be fiancée, Fāṭima, the story is again broken by an aside universalising her too in a direct address to the reader, 'You know her of course, otherwise ask about her if you find someone to ask' (ibid., p. 46).

Similarly, at a point of high tension when the protagonist Hamad and his friend Muḥammad are running to the village cemetery so that Hamad, who has been poisoned, can die on his father's grave, the short urgent sentences are suddenly interrupted by a seemingly superfluous aside, assuring the reader that the choice of location 'has no political or patriotic significance'.[77] In fact, the story actually ends with an abrupt alienating aside which emphasizes the story's irrational and obscure features by using a contrasting documentary style: Hamad's tomb is visited by his friend (or rather, alter ego) Muḥammad,

> He threw himself down on his [Hamad's] tomb perhaps until the dawn – it seems that the motives were not emotional and perhaps the truth is that there were no motives at all – the day of Hamad's return from Cairo was an anxious incomprehensible day – it was something belonging to the obscurity of the night – this is all I wanted to say at this point.
>
> (Ibid., p. 48)

Poggioli's moments form a more universal model of avant-gardism than Kharrāṭ's currents for they are entirely supra-historical. In fact, Kharrāṭ himself recognizes the weakness in his formulation when he is at pains to separate modernity from modernism. While modernity (*al-ḥadātha*) is based primarily on the principles of rejection, rebellion and interrogation, *al-ḥassāsiyya al-jadīda* refers to a specific period in the development of Egyptian literature. And while many of the works of the new sensibility practice modernity, others have themselves become patterned formulations and formed new traditions,[78] as the fringe moves to the centre. In other words, they have succumbed to modernism, which Poggioli describes as 'an unconscious parody of modernity,... modernolatry: nothing but the blind adoration of the idols and fetishes of our time'.[79] Although such works represent a form of regression, they actually display the spirit of their time more directly, revealing the modernism of an epoch but not its modernity. For modernity cuts vertically through time; its chronological place is merely the surface representation of a deep internal movement.[80] Thus modernism is condemned to die (hence the birth of post-modernism) but modernity lives on.

76 Ibid., p. 40.
77 Ibid.
78 I. al-Kharrāṭ, op. cit. (1984), p. 11.
79 R. Poggioli, op. cit. (1968), p. 218.
80 Adonis, op. cit. (1990), p. 99.

Schulte-Sasse criticizes Poggioli for subsuming both modernism and the avant-garde under the label 'modernism' and praises Bürger for being more precise in his terminology. For Bürger points out that although there are many similarities between modernism and the avant-garde, yet their strategies of negation remain radically different. While modernism may be understood as an attack on traditional writing techniques, the avant-garde can only be understood as an attack meant to alter the institutionalized commerce with art.[81] This point makes an important distinction between the social roles of the avant-garde and (what Bürger terms) modernism, but in the light of the previous sentence, one might in turn criticize Schulte-Sasse for subsuming both modernism and modernity under the label 'modernism'.

Thus *al-ḥassāsiyya al-jadīda* is not a uniform or rigid model, for the avant-garde does not offer a style as such; rather, it is 'a posture, a set of tactics, a mode of social organization of the arts... Indeed, the avant-garde is likely to generate stylistic pluralism, since it functions socially through movements and tendencies, themselves subject to schism, proliferation, pluralization and dissent'.[82] Indeed, *Gallery 68* stressed its commitment to exposing 'different features, trends and schools' and 'the greatest possible variety, diversity and novelty' among Egyptian avant-gardists.[83] The artist Ḥasan Sulaymān, one of *Gallery 68*'s founders, observed that 'that which links a generation as an artistic school or intellectual current is not a specific philosophy or ideology as much as an emotional initiative with regard to the present'.[84] What unites the various diverse works of *al-ḥassāsiyya al-jadīda* under the umbrella term avant-garde is that they form part of a culture of negation. Kostelanetz posits that 'the term avant-garde is best applied to work that is so different in intention and experience that it renders the old classifications irrelevant'.[85] However, this is not necessarily the case for, in Egypt at least, successive avant-gardes shared parallel experiences (isolation, censorship, mistrust of institutions) and similar intentions (self-assertion, reintegration of art into life). Rather, it is the way of achieving the intention and expressing the experience that subverts conventional deportment and renders the old classifications irrelevant.

This necessarily results in difficulties for the reader and one can sympathize with one American critic who writes exasperatedly of 'a pursuing of the tortured word until it yells for mercy and a squeezing out of meaning until it is too thin and isolated to be understood short of an occupational lifetime. One gets the uneasy feeling that some of these little magazine critics like a particular poem for the very difficulty it presents to the layman'.[86] Kostelanetz falls into this trap of

81 J. Schulte-Sasse, op. cit. (1984), pp. xiv–xv.

82 Malcolm Bradbury, 'Modernisms/Postmodernisms', in Ihab and Sally Hassan (eds) op. cit. (1983), p. 314.

83 Editorial to *Gallery 68*, no. 6, April 1969.

84 Ḥasan Sulaymān, *Gallery 68*, no. 1, April/May 1968, p. 30.

85 Richard Kostelanetz, *The Avant-Garde Tradition in Literature* (1982), p. 6.

86 Paul Bixler, 'Little Magazine, What Now?', *Antioch Review*, Vol. 8, no. 1, Spring 1948, p. 73.

reducing the avant-garde to an intellectual puzzle when he describes literature as language mediated by experience (of other literary works), instead of experience mediated by language. Even the linguistically acrobatic poets of the Egyptian avant-garde journal *Iḍā'a 77* admitted to language as the tool of experience rather than vice versa. When looked at from this latter perspective, what Kostelanetz implicitly criticizes as the avant-gardist's capacity 'to fabricate mountains of literature out of molehills in life'[87] becomes the natural result of profound and complex experience. Yet given that the language *is* difficult to penetrate, whether emotionally or intellectually, the question raised by Kostelanetz's analogy is: do the views at the top merit the climb?

Certainly *Gallery 68* brought to light much experimental work of marked quality and continued to inspire literary experimentation, not merely imitation, well into the following decade. It is also true, however, that a number of the subsequent avant-garde journals printed much material of dubious quality. One critic has described the avant-gardist as 'half-hero, half-fool'[88] and no doubt the following explanation holds true for some of those who published in Egypt's experimental journals: 'Not infrequently,... it is insecurity, combined with an envy of the respectable, that leads the pioneer and rebel... to apologize for his feeling of insecurity with considerable bizarre behaviour and intellectual display... designed to emphasize his uniqueness, his superiority'.[89] *Gallery 68* stands apart from other avant-garde journals for its generally more mature perspective and lack of pretension. Nevertheless, one of *Gallery 68*'s founding editors himself described the *68* generation as rash, foolish and inexperienced, yet sincere and pure.[90] In this journal and others, one can afford to overlook a good deal of adolescence for the sake of some bold and genuine accomplishment.

Generally, the whole culture of negation has some latent positive aspects. Hostility isolates but it also reunites, hence the sectarian spirit of avant-gardism, despite the anarchistic characteristics of the various currents. Moreover, the avant-gardists' obscurity actually disguises their attempt to re-endow art with social relevance in that it symbolizes their antagonism towards art as an institution,[91] having recognized the social inconsequentiality of autonomous art. As such, the obscurity can actually be creative and inspiring – the refusal to provide a meaning is intended to shock the reader into questioning the conduct of his life (although as the reader comes to expect to be shocked, the effect fades). These Egyptian avant-gardists are not trying to isolate themselves, but to reintegrate themselves and their art into a changed society. In fact, in expressing social

87 R. Kostelanetz, 'Avant-garde (1984)', *New England Review and Bread Loaf Quarterly*, Vol. 7, no. 1, Autumn 1984, p. 36.

88 F. Hoffman, 'Little Magazines and the Avant-garde', *Arts in Society*, Fall 1960, p. 23.

89 F. Hoffmann, C. Allen and C. Ulrich, op. cit. (1967), p. 16.

90 I. al-Kharrāṭ, Editorial to *Gallery 68*, no. 8, Feb. 1971.

91 Art as an institution refers to the means of production, distribution, function and the ideas that determine the reception of art.

alienation, isolation and frustration, they do so because they aspire to a 'more just, more liberal value system that is more faithful to man's basic dignity'.[92] This does not mean that the content of the avant-garde work of art should be socially significant, but that art itself should have a social function.

The avant-garde and the future

The function of avant-gardism then is transcendental in that the present is valid only for its potentialities for the future, not as a culmination of the past. This attitude is particularly suited to a crisis-ridden era, such as that following the 1967 defeat. The campaign to shape the future is waged through the avant-garde journal which 'functions as an independent and isolated military unit, completely and sharply detached from the public, quick to act, not only to explore, but also to battle, conquer, and adventure on its own'.[93] This campaign is fought against the present as a culmination of the past, or in other words, against convention and tradition. Since all of these are epitomized by the establishment, by the older generation, the conflict is to some extent (though not wholly) expressed in a father–son antithesis that is best validated by the new generation's deliberate use of an idiom all of its own.

But the intensity of the campaign makes death for the cause a certainty: avant-gardists are 'men destined for the slaughter so that after them others may stop to build'.[94] The sword of slaughter is double edged in that it is wielded by both the avant-garde's instigator and its offspring, the mainstream and the margin, the last generation and the next, the past and the future. The former (in each of the opposing pairs) condemns the avant-gardists as insignificant attention seekers, whose cult of novelty, with the obscurity that results, ensures their popular unpopularity. For the latter (in each of the opposing pairs) the avant-gardists simply outlive their usefulness. For, in appointing itself a mediator through which a golden age can be achieved, the avant-garde implies that it will itself become tradition. In a sense then, one can speak of the conventions of the avant-garde in that deviation becomes the norm, but this occurs in support of a living, dynamic, constantly evolving tradition rather than a static one. While avant-gardism in general lives on, each specific avant-garde is destined to live only a morning as it were. The fact that each successive avant-garde breaks from its inheritance does not disrupt the continuum of literary progress. Like the history of science, literature does not conform rigidly to a cumulative and linear model, but is 'a discontinuous series of drastic reorientations'.[95]

92 I. al-Kharrāṭ, op. cit. (1984), p. 13.

93 R. Poggioli, op. cit. (1968), p. 23.

94 Massimo Bontempelli, *L'Aventura Novecentista: Selva Polemica 1926–1938*. Cited in R. Poggioli, op. cit. (1968), p. 67.

95 Thomas S. Kuhn, 'The Structure of Scientific Revolutions' (essay, 1962). Cited in R. Kostelanetz, op. cit. (1984), p. 33.

So it was then that in Egypt, the seventies generation of poets clustered around *Idā'a 77* rejected what they saw as the overt politicism of the sixties generation epitomized in *Gallery 68*, just as the writers and poets of *Kitābāt* (Writings, 1979–84) a non-periodic journal in the early 1980s, later objected to the poetics of *Idā'a 77*. The cycle continues, with the so-called 'nineties generation'[96] publishing their work in experimental journals like *al-Kitāba al-Ukhrā* (Alternative Writing, 1991–2001) and *al-Jarād* (The Locust, 1994–2000?). Just as those publishing in *Gallery 68* faced criticism from established writers, now that many have themselves become relatively established as writers, they criticize aspects of today's avant-garde. Bahā' Ṭāhir, for example, complains of the new generation's complete indifference to politics. He describes *al-Jarād* as 'an experiment which makes me very sad, because I can't smell or see society in what they are writing'.[97]

Prominent Egyptian novelist Jamāl al-Ghīṭānī, one-time contributor to *Gallery 68* and now editor-in-chief of the famous literary weekly *Akhbār al-Adab* (The Literary News, 1993–) reflects that there has been no literary manifestation to equal that of the 1960s.[98] Writer and journalist, Ibrāhīm Manṣūr, and leading literary critic, Ghālī Shukrī, who were both involved in *Gallery 68*, also agree that successive generations have not formed a comprehensive new outlook. Yet that these writers are not jealously defending the furrows they ploughed in the 1960s is proved by the fact that they all look forward to more fundamental change. Manṣūr speaks of post-*Gallery 68* efforts as 'the conquered literary journalism, conquered not defeated' and Shukrī agrees that these efforts promise the eventual emergence of an entirely new outlook.[99] Al-Ghīṭānī too optimistically reveals, 'Perhaps now, I feel something new in the reality, but completely different'.[100] Therefore *Gallery 68* genuinely has occupied a unique place in Egyptian literary development, for the historical moment which finally triggered this avant-garde venture into literary journalism has not since been matched. The crushing shock of the 1967 defeat focused the 1960s experiment, resulting in an unprecedented urgency to launch this sincere collective attempt to expose the truth of their situation, in all its conflicting artistic expressions.

96 Literary categorization by decade still persists in Egypt, although many of the writers thus defined object to the restrictions implied by this. Nevertheless, once certain fundamental disclaimers have been clarified (as indicated earlier), such categorization may usefully show the 'spearhead' of a literary period.

97 B. Ṭāhir, taped interview, Cairo, 1 May 1996. NB Some of the young poets and writers of *al-Jarād* (The Locust, 1994–2000?) refused even to sit in the same café as the more established writers I was meeting. They waited in the café across the road, then took me to one of their own preferred cafés. Significantly, given their confessed indifference to politics and society, this was situated outside the downtown area of Cairo where the cafés of previous literary generations tended to be located.

98 J. al-Ghīṭānī, taped interview, Cairo, 30 April 1996.

99 Gh. Shukrī and I. Manṣūr, taped joint interview, Cairo, 3 May 1996.

100 J. al-Ghīṭānī, taped interview, Cairo, 30 April 1996.

4

THE SIXTIES GENERATION AND ITS POLITICS OF LITERATURE

Pierre Bourdieu's concept of the field of cultural production provides a useful model for looking at the dialectical relationship between the literary margin and mainstream in 1960s Egypt.[1] The field consists of a network of objective relations between positions of occupants, agents and institutions. These positions are defined by their present and potential situation in the structure of the distribution of power (capital, in this case literary recognition and success), the possession of which governs access to the specific profits at stake in the field. Field is a more inclusive concept than market and therefore better suited to the mapping of Egypt's avant-gardists, for it suggests hierarchy and status as well as the commercial relations between buyers and sellers and therefore becomes the arena of a struggle for legitimation. It is an open concept emphasizing the social, rather than the merely intellectual, conditions of struggle that shape cultural production. Positions in the field are defined by their relation to other positions: domination in the case of the literary establishment (the Ministry of Culture, its journals and publishing houses and its Writers' Union: 'the curators of culture'), and subordination in the case of avant-garde 1960s writers ('the creators of culture').

Action within this field is both generated and regulated by what Bourdieu terms 'habitus', a kind of cultural matrix consisting of a set of overriding internalized dispositions. Habitus is not innate, rather it is the result of the internalization, mainly unconscious, of the objective chances common to members of a particular status group or class (for our purposes, this group comprises young avant-garde writers in 1960s Egypt). While the fact that their literary action can be located within the framework of a group does not necessarily mean that those involved constituted a school or a specific trend. Nevertheless, habitus does set structural limits for action by developing internalized dispositions of what is possible or unlikely for a particular group in a stratified environment ('structured

1 I would like to thank Richard Jacquemond for being the first to suggest that I explore Bourdieu's work in 1994 after attending a paper I gave at Aix-en-Provence University. Jacquemond has since published an excellent and expansive work on the field of modern Egyptian literature, *Entre Scribes et Écrivains*, Paris: Sindbad, Actes Sud, 2003.

structures'). At the same time, habitus also generates perceptions, aspirations and practices that correspond to this socialization ('structuring structures').[2] In other words, habitus regulates aspirations and expectations in relation to the probabilities of success common to members of the same group for a particular behaviour. At the heart of habitus lies the issue of power which in this case resides with those who control the definition of cultural capital and the distribution of cultural resources through which hierarchies are constituted, that is, the Egyptian cultural establishment and its apparatus. The group consists of avant-garde 1960s writers, the particular behaviour aspired to is the publication of their literary work and the action generated by the limitations of habitus is the journal *Gallery 68* (1968–71).

Bourdieu tends to merge expectations and aspirations, claiming a high correlation between subjective hopes and objective chances. He focuses on habitus as a means of leading individuals to a submission to the established order and an acceptance to act within the conditions of their existence. In 1960s Egypt, however, the action necessitated by habitus was more a means to overcome the established literary order rather than to submit to it. This might still be explained within the broader framework of Bourdieu's theory: habitus is substantially formed by 'primary' socialization, in this case more than a decade of state control of the Egyptian literary field, yet it has the capacity to be affected by 'secondary' socialization. Although Bourdieu offers no clarity on the dynamics of the relation between the two, elsewhere he concedes that the relatively permanent set of dispositions that is habitus comes into tension when it confronts objective conditions different from those in which it was originally generated. Particularly during times of crisis, the immediate adjustment of habitus to field is disrupted, creating the conditions for change rather than reproduction. For 1960s avant-garde writers, this 'secondary' socialization and crisis point was the devastating 1967 defeat by Israel which jolted them into more severe action/reaction against the literary status quo.

Gallery 68: its position in the literary field

Bourdieu identifies three different types of strategy within a field: conservation, exercised by those holding dominant positions; succession, exercised by those attempting to access dominant positions, generally new entrants to the field; and subversion, exercised by those who challenge the dominant group's legitimacy to define standards in the field and who expect to gain little from the dominant groups.[3] The strategies of succession and subversion become somewhat blurred in the Egyptian literary field of the 1960s. While succession was clearly practiced by many writers adhering to established norms and techniques in order to gain

2 Pierre Bourdieu, *The Field of Cultural Production* (1993), p. 64.

3 P. Bourdieu, 'The Peculiar History of Scientific Reason', *Sociological Forum*, Vol. 6, no. 1, March 1991, p. 17.

access to dominant positions ultimately controlled by the Ministry of Culture, those exercising subversion strategies, including many *Gallery 68* writers, might over time graduate to succession strategies or run both strategies simultaneously. Here, the essential difference between expectation and aspiration comes into play: avant-garde 1960s writers might not expect the dominant group to yield much, but they might still aspire to dominant positions. The crucial point is that their succession strategy would not make use of the expedient shortcut of imitation for they refused to compromise their aesthetics. The combination of succession and subversion strategies is demonstrated in their much-touted call for an independent National Union of Writers; this would provide a secure environment for a true literary democracy in which experimental writers would have the opportunity to win some cultural capital in the field. The failure of this dream necessitated alternative action, hence the launch of *Gallery 68*.

The position of *Gallery 68* within the Egyptian literary field was not only relative to the contemporary literary establishment; by implication, its position also cut vertically through time, for its relation to the establishment was necessarily to some extent defined by its relation to the literary heritage. Contrary to the heated claims of some contemporary critics, the sixties generation did not brand itself the enemy of literary tradition. In keeping with the recognition that its current literary convictions might develop into a different literary future, *Gallery 68* also acknowledged its link to past literary generations. Issue seven's statement of clarification emphatically denied that *Gallery 68* stood in opposition to everything that had gone before. Such a stance would have been pointless in any case since much literary renewal had already taken place within established forums such as *al-Masā'* (Tonight, 1956–) and *al-Majalla* (The Journal, 1957–71) and was simply being confirmed and magnified through *Gallery 68*. The journal's impatience to convey this fundamental point is revealed in its rare display of a more exaggerated tone, reminiscent of the manifestos of *al-Bashīr* (The Herald, 1948–50) and *al-Taṭawwur* (Development, 1940):

> Those who have lost their mental faculties, they alone are the ones who wish for a fight or who try to destroy mummified corpses. There is no doubt that the mental hospitals are crowded with the enemies of Napoleon Bonaparte, Louis XVI and Katherine II.[4]

The majority of writers brought together in *Gallery 68* were quite willing to acknowledge that past literary generations had produced important work. Yusrī Khamīs wrote of the need to understand experimentation within its historical framework, in order to dispel inter-generational friction.[5] Amal Dunqul too wrote

4 Editorial to *Gallery 68*, no. 7, Oct. 1969.

5 Yusrī Khamīs' reply to questionnaire, 'Hākadhā Yatakallamu al-Udabā' al-Shabāb', *al-Ṭalī'a*, Sept. 1969.

fondly and respectfully of past generations of writers, and made his demands of the future, not the past.[6] The young writers, poets and artists who used to gather in *Café Riche* welcomed Naguib Mahfouz's and Yūsuf Idrīs' visits to sit with them, and a number of them enjoyed warm personal relationships with Yaḥyā Ḥaqqī, who nevertheless preferred to sit around the corner at *La Place*.[7] Ḥaqqī included several brief articles discussing the experimentation of *Gallery 68* in *al-Majalla* between the years 1968 and 1970, and, when Shukrī 'Ayyād presented a more negative view of *Gallery 68*,[8] Ḥaqqī personally asked Ibrāhīm Manṣūr to pen a response.[9]

Naguib Mahfouz in particular provided a link between the establishment and fringe. On Fridays, he would hold a literary 'salon' at *Casino Opera*, after which he would go to *Nādī al-Qiṣṣa* (The Writing Club), then later he would retire to *Café Riche* where the young avant-gardists gathered.[10] Here he would listen paternally rather than participate actively, and his few comments were always encouraging and constructive, never negative.[11] Both Aḥmad Hāshim al-Sharīf and Ibrāhīm Fatḥī, regular participants in the Friday literary 'salon', later published books of their discussions with Naguib Mahfouz, in which the fond respect their generation felt for Mahfouz is apparent.[12] Yet at the same time al-Sharīf pointed out that, although Mahfouz was able to explore his subject matter on different levels and from different perspectives, still his was 'a single subject-matter and a single style'.[13] Al-Sharīf chides those who exaggerate Mahfouz's literary talent during the 1960s 'for purely political reasons' at the expense of more talented writers like Yūsuf al-Shārūnī and Idwār al-Kharrāṭ.[14] Therefore, despite an admiration and fond regard for Mahfouz, *Gallery 68* did not include any of his work, partly because of his well-established status and partly because the journal did not deem him experimental enough. *Gallery 68* wanted the past to make room for the present: 'We felt that we belonged to the same field, but we wanted to be independent. We did not want to make concessions to belong to the establishment'.[15] For these

6 A. Dunqul's reply to questionnaire, ibid.

7 Bahā' Ṭāhir, taped interview, Cairo, 1 May 1996.

8 *al-Majalla*, June 1969, pp. 94–5.

9 Ibrāhīm Manṣūr, taped interview, Cairo, 3 May 1996.

10 J. al-Ghīṭānī, taped interview, Cairo, 30 April 1996.

11 Na'īm 'Aṭiyya, taped interview, Cairo, 28 April 1996. Corroborated in A. H. al-Sharīf, *Naguib Mahfouz: Muḥāwarāt Qabl Nobel* (1989), p. 122.

12 The influence of Mahfouz and Ḥaqqī and the respect felt for them is demonstrated by the fact that others attending the Friday literary 'salon' were also to write books about them in the future. For example, Na'īm 'Aṭiyya wrote a book on Yaḥyā Ḥaqqī (1978); Ibrāhīm Fatḥī (1977) and Muḥammad Ibrāhīm Mabrūk (n.d.) both wrote books on Naguib Mahfouz; Ghālī Shukrī wrote two books on Naguib Mahfouz (1964 and 1988); and Jamāl al-Ghīṭānī edited and introduced a book of Mahfouz's memoirs (1980).

13 A. H. al-Sharīf, op. cit. (1989), p. 121.

14 Ibid., pp. 128–9.

15 B. Ṭāhir, taped interview, Cairo, 1 May 1996.

sixties writers, Egypt's new position now required them to adopt a new literary position outside the establishment but without cutting themselves off entirely from their literary tradition.

In the very first issue of *Gallery 68*, one of the editors, Ḥasan Sulaymān, affirmed that art should 'express our reality and our future whilst retaining links to the past'.[16] Sulaymān's view of the ideal artistic position of the *68* generation was remarkably subtle for one of the editors in the first issue of an avant-garde journal: 'Art expresses the tension between past and present. It is not a dividing line between them'.[17] Another editor, Ghālib Halasā, was downright conservative in his acknowledgement of the continuing link to the past: 'Traditions are part of the framework from which the artist communicates his experience to the recipient. Although he may reject some of them, he remains within the framework'.[18] Halasā went so far as to give tradition equal weighting to language; he considered both as necessary media through which the artist could generalize his experience to reach the public.[19] (The *Iḍā'a* (Illumination) group of poets would later challenge such preconceived views of language in the 1970s.)

The extent of the *68* generation's link to the past was, however, open to debate on the pages of *Gallery 68*, as well as in a number of other literary journals at the time. *Gallery 68*'s special issue, the selection of short stories representing new trends, included Muḥammad Ḥāfiẓ Rajab, famous for his declaration 'we are a generation without masters (*naḥnu jīl bi-lā asātidha*)', alongside 'Abd al-Ḥakīm Qāsim who adopted a much more moderate stance, admitting, 'I do not believe that I am fundamentally different from Ṭaha Ḥusayn, Tawfīq al-Ḥakīm, Naguib Mahfouz, Yūsuf Idrīs or Yaḥyā Ḥaqqī. I am an extension of them, created by them. I carry them in my blood'.[20] Qāsim went so far as to concede Lūwīs 'Awaḍ's judgement that the *Gallery 68* generation of writers did not constitute a new literary school, but not on the grounds that he objected to the narrow connotation of 'school', as did most of *Gallery 68*'s contributors. Rather, he believed simply that his generation's work naturally bore similarities to that of the older generation since they shared the same concerns and were tortured by similar crises and contradictions.[21] Shafīq Maqqār too stressed that artists are linked by universal concerns, in particular 'the mother of all problems, the gift of life'. He drew a direct parallel between Jamāl al-Ghīṭānī's *Awrāq Shābb 'āsha mundhu Alf 'Ām* (Memoirs of a Young Man who Lived One Thousand Years Ago, 1969) and Muḥammad al-Muwayliḥi's *Ḥadīth 'Īsā Ibn Hisham* (The Story of 'Īsā Ibn Hishām, 1907), not only in its expression of alienation, but also in its form and language.

16 Ḥasan Sulaymān, untitled, *Gallery 68*, no. 1, April–May 1968, p. 32.

17 Ibid.

18 Ghālib Halasā, 'Mulāḥaẓāt Ḥawla Difā' 'an al-Ghumūḍ', *Gallery 68*, no. 3, July 1968, p. 76.

19 Ibid.

20 'Abd al-Ḥakīm Qāsim's reply to questionnaire, 'Hākadhā Yatakallamu al-Udabā' al-Shabāb', *al-Ṭalī'a*, Sept. 1969.

21 Ibid.

In fact, Maqqār was so convinced of the strength of the link to the literary heritage that he went so far as to assert that the only difference between ancient cave scribblers and modern artists lay in the evolution of 'dexterity' and 'capability'.[22]

While on the surface, antagonism repeatedly flared up between the *Gallery 68* generation and longer established writers, with greater hostility generally felt among the established writers,[23] in reality the gulf between them was not that great. After the publication of *Gallery 68*'s short story selection, the critic Luṭfī al-Khūlī, writing in the daily *al-Ahrām* (The Pyramids, 1876–), refuted the idea of the recent birth of the short story, stating that the new was nothing more than a continuation of the old.[24] This view was both upheld and attacked in the subsequent issue of *Gallery 68*, proving the journal's sincere desire to act as an open forum for debate. Ibrāhīm Fatḥī upbraided al-Khūlī, trying to make him identify with the position of the *Gallery 68* generation by deeming the first generation of socialist realists to which al-Khūlī belonged a 'generation without masters' too, in the sense that they 'learnt much and rejected much from the previous heritage'.[25] Yet given this moderate interpretation of what a 'generation without masters' actually means, Fatḥī and al-Khūlī do not appear to be fundamentally at odds. It is simply that al-Khūlī defined birth as having *no* links to the past, while Fatḥī defined birth as having *some* links to the past, but being overwhelmingly new. Fatḥī is essentially admitting that all literary activity is to a greater or lesser extent part of a continuum.

Shafīq Maqqār in the same issue took an openly more objective stance, placing the work of the *Gallery 68* writers in a broader context and recognizing the ceaseless avant-garde dynamic. Although he was himself writing experimental stories at the time and had published one in *Gallery 68*, as one of the more mature contributors (aged 43) he rejected *Gallery 68*'s over-zealous suggestion that the short story was perhaps being born for the first time:

> Rather, let us say that it is blossoming, or that it is passing through a phase of revitalization, or that it is developing and passing through the familiar stage of rebellion, renewal and discovery . . . there is no writer who creates without a heritage to support him, inspire him, and encourage him, even in the deepest hours of his rebellion.[26]

22 Shafīq Maqqār, ''An al-Jadīd wa-l-Qadīm wa-Mā Bayna Bayna', *Gallery 68*, no. 7, Oct. 1969, pp. 93–5.

23 Experimental writers were branded existentialists, nihilists, communists or reactionaries at various times (see B. Ṭāhir's introduction to his novel *Khālatī Ṣafiyya wa-l-Dayr*) in an attempt by those exercising Bourdieu's conservative strategy to undermine them and retain their own grip on cultural capital.

24 Cited in Ibrāhīm Fatḥī, 'Ba'ḍ al-Masā'il al-'Āmma fī al-Naqd', *Gallery 68*, no. 7, Oct. 1969, p. 65.

25 Ibid.

26 Sh. Maqqār, ''An al-Jadīd wa-l-Qadīm wa-Mā Bayna Bayna', *Gallery 68*, no. 7, Oct. 1969, p. 95.

The perspective gained from *Gallery 68* as a whole is that, while admitting that the literary phenomena it presented had not occurred in a vacuum, independent of the literary past or future, it nevertheless occupied a special status within literary history. While it admitted that the process of renewal in Egyptian fiction had been ceaseless since its inception, nevertheless 'the fingers of one hand are enough, more than enough, to count the number of those who turned around the *Weltanschauung* (*ru'ya*) of the short story'.[27] Bahā' Ṭāhir testifies to the fact that *Gallery 68* gave expression to writers and poets who badly needed it, but he believes that to call it a 'turning point' is an exaggeration. Since modernist trends had not only existed but been published throughout the 1960s, in small quantities, one can see Ṭāhir's point. However, by uniting such trends for maximum impact, *Gallery 68* did send ripples across the stagnating literary scene, giving fresh impetus to the short story in particular. One can therefore conclude that it aided and epitomized a cultural turn which was already in slow motion when it emerged. It was a launch pad rather than a turning point, allowing certain modernist writers to gather momentum instead of grinding to a slow halt; it acted as an accelerator rather than a steering wheel, for it made no attempt to propagate a specific ideology. *Gallery 68*'s claim to mark a departure was therefore not a conceit, for the unique historical moment of disillusionment, uncertainty and anger following the 1967 defeat made it the natural springboard for the collective launch of a new era in literary experimentation.

With regard to poetry, *Gallery 68* was open to new currents, but since the energies of the sixties generation were focused on the short story, this is what monopolized the journal's pages. *Gallery 68* did not therefore mark a departure for poetry in the way that it did for the short story, since new voices did not gather the volume or momentum needed to take off in a similar way. In any case, the general attitude of 'life first, aesthetics second'[28] was not sufficiently new to warrant the attention accorded new developments in the short story. Muḥammad Ṣāliḥ, himself a young poet in the 1960s who published in *Gallery 68*, believes that the June defeat hampered poetic progress: 'With the defeat, the old image of the poet as an omniscient prophet and spokesman of the tribe collapsed. It took long years to overcome this and discover a different formulation for writing and escaping the crisis'.[29] It was not until a decade later that the groups *Aṣwāt* (Voices) and *Iḍā'a 77* (Illumination 77) inspired by the endeavour of *Gallery 68*, though disagreeing with much of its approach, marked a radical departure for poetry.

Within the medium of the avant-garde journal itself, *Gallery 68* marked a significant departure. On a practical level, *Gallery 68* took pride in its journalistic medium, rather than viewing it as a utilitarian platform for a literary or political ideology. Ibrāhīm Manṣūr, a journalist and the energy behind the publication

27 Editorial to *Gallery 68*, no. 7, Oct. 1969.

28 Y. Khamīs, taped interview, Cairo, 26 April 1996.

29 Muḥammad Ṣāliḥ, taped interview, Cairo, 27 April 1996.

process, stressed the importance of journalistic expertise in coordinating and presenting material. The aesthetics of the journal, under the supervision of the artist Ḥasan Sulaymān, were deemed important enough to incur significant expense. Artwork was reproduced well in colour, high quality paper was used and the journal's novel appearance (it was twice as wide as it was long) was innovative and made it instantly recognizable. This novel presentation obviously made an impact, for *Rūz al-Yūsuf* (Rose al-Yūsuf, 1925–) made specific mention of *Gallery 68* as 'a new journal read sideways rather than lengthways'.[30] In terms of approach, for those launching an experimental journal to do so without rhetoric, using only occasional brief introductions, but nevertheless trying to implicate the reader in what was written, was radical in the context of the time. Moreover, *Gallery 68*'s willingness to introduce conflicting opinions encouraged more open debate, as opposed to the polarized standpoints of previous avant-garde journals. *Gallery 68*'s relative openness, and the high number of talented writers involved as a result, may in part account for its resounding impact, among the narrow literary elite at least, but by extension, the results of this impact would in turn filter down eventually into the literary mainstream. Hence Manṣūr concludes without too much exaggeration: 'They [*al-Taṭawwur* and *al-Bashīr*] were a wave, but *Gallery* was the ocean'.[31]

Gallery 68: a political act?

Bourdieu stresses that the boundaries between fields are blurred and this holds true for the Egyptian literary and political fields. *Gallery 68*'s objective of helping to build a 'new liberal, democratic, socialist nation'[32] indicates that literature remained closely bound up with politics. The fact that the literary norms against which sixties writers rebelled were largely supported and propagated by the various organs of the Ministry of Culture meant that *Gallery 68* was by implication a political act, at least to a certain extent. Moreover, the links of 'legitimate' writers to the regime, necessitated by the internal structure of the literary field, meant that the older generation of established writers was necessarily associated with those responsible for the June 1967 defeat, even if not directly implicated. Ibrāhīm Manṣūr, probably the most energetic force behind the publication of *Gallery 68*, affirms that the June defeat sparked the launch of the journal: 'We did not feel that we were responsible for the defeat. . . . We felt that the time had come for our voice to be heard'.[33] 'Abd al-Raḥmān Abū 'Awf, commenting in 1969, believed that new developments in the Egyptian short story were a spontaneous response by a young generation of writers to the June defeat.[34]

30 *Rūz al-Yūsuf*, 17 June 1968, p. 54.
31 I. Manṣūr, taped interview, Cairo, 3 May 1996.
32 Editorial to *Gallery 68*, no. 1, April–May 1968.
33 I. Manṣūr, taped interview, Cairo, 1 May 1996.
34 'Abd al-Raḥmān Abū 'Awf, 'al-Baḥth 'an Ṭarīq Jadīd li-l-Qiṣṣa al-Miṣriyya al-Qaṣīra', *al-Hilāl*, Aug. 1969.

While this is true, it is not the whole picture. The new literary sensibility was not the exclusive property of the young generation and it was more than a spontaneous response to the defeat. As Bourdieu writes, the changes which take place in the field of limited production are in principal 'largely independent of the external changes which appear to determine them because they accompany them chronologically', although this coincidence does play a part in their ultimate success.[35] In fact, early manifestations of the new sensibility in Egypt were glimpsed as early as the 1940s.[36] Although many perceived *Gallery 68* as a political act, Manṣūr insists that the defeat was 'only a triggering point,' that the journal was intended to express a literary phenomenon and took care to distance itself from politics.[37] Jamīl 'Aṭiyya Ibrāhīm, one of the more active members of the editorial committee, also insists 'We did not support a single political view'.[38] This is true in comparison with the overt political stances of the groups of young Marxist writers gathered around journals in the 1940s and 1950s.[39] However, the nature of the concerns of intellectuals in 1968 meant that in any journal identifying itself with 'today's generation', political considerations necessarily lurked beneath the surface. Muḥammad Ṣāliḥ, a young poet in the 1960s who published in *Gallery 68*, admits that 'the most serious concerns of our generation were inevitably political and social'.[40] One can generalize that all those involved in *Gallery 68* veered to the left and were thus regarded with suspicion by the establishment, proof of the homologous link between the Egyptian political and literary fields. This is a natural result of habitus which makes actors display similar dispositions across fields. 'We were all in one way or another leftist writers, even those who weren't Marxists'.[41] Yet, like their literary positions, 'their politics shared the same common laws, but the branches were very different'.[42] The left in fact consisted of various different tendencies, united by their opposition to Zionism, imperialism, capitalism, hackneyed romanticism and hackneyed realism. All agreed that survival depended on surmounting the military, political, social and intellectual repercussions of the 1967 defeat.

While *Gallery 68* was therefore politically aware, and politically positioned in a general leftist sense, it was not a direct reflection of this politics; Ibrāhīm Manṣūr observes, 'You had to read between the lines to find it'.[43] Ḥasan Sulaymān, one of the founding editors of *Gallery 68*, warned that while art may

35 P. Bourdieu, *The Rules of Art* (1996), pp. 252–3; also *The Field of Cultural Production* (1993), pp. 56, 187.

36 Idwār al-Kharrāṭ, *al-Ḥassāsiyya al-Jadīda: Maqālat fī al-Ẓāhirat al-Qiṣaṣiyya* (1993), p. 7.

37 I. Manṣūr, taped interview, Cairo, 1 May 1996.

38 Jamīl 'Aṭiyya Ibrāhīm, taped interview, Cairo, 30 April 1996.

39 See Rif'at al-Sa'īd, *al-Ṣiḥāfa al-Yasāriyya fī Miṣr*, Vol. 1 1925–48 (1974), Vol. 2 1950–2 (n.d.).

40 M. Ṣāliḥ, taped interview, Cairo, 27 April 1996.

41 B. Ṭāhir, taped interview, Cairo, 1 May 1996.

42 Ghālī Shukrī, taped interview, Cairo, 3 May 1996.

43 I. Manṣūr, taped interview, Cairo, 3 May 1996.

play a political role, art serving a *direct* political purpose is usually artificial, and 'persistence in creating this kind of art will lead to the strangulation of art as a whole'.[44] Overt political comment in *Gallery 68* is in fact extremely rare and deliberated with care. At the very outset, Aḥmad Mursī carefully identified the journal's stance:

> Although *Gallery 68* is not a political journal, it believes that if it succeeds in discovering the truth of that which stirs the wings of the writers, poets and artists of today's generation, then it will have fulfilled its pledge to itself to participate in the battle for freedom and progress.[45]

With hindsight, it is clear that no intellectual was in fact persecuted under Nasser directly for his literature or art, only for his politics.[46] Jamīl 'Aṭiyya Ibrāhīm even speaks of a slight relaxation in government cultural policy in the wake of the June defeat: 'We did not face any danger'.[47] Without the benefit of hindsight, however, uncertainty prevailed and no one was yet sure whether the government would choose to pursue a harder or a more conciliatory cultural policy in the wake of the defeat. As a sympathizer observing from the fringes of the *68* gathering, Na'īm 'Aṭiyya affirms that launching *Gallery 68* 'was a very courageous action'.[48] Ibrāhīm Manṣūr too testifies, 'Many of us were interrogated about why we were involved in the journal. One issue was delayed for three months by the authorities'.[49] Several of *Gallery 68*'s editors had already spent time in prison: Ibrāhīm Manṣūr had been arrested in 1953, 1956 and 1960; Ghālib Halasā, Sayyid Ḥijāb, Sa'd 'Abd al-Wahhāb, Mīlād 'Abd al-Sayyid and 'Abd al-Ḥakīm Qāsim had all been arrested in 1959. Some of the most prominent new writers of the 1960s were arrested in 1966 and imprisoned for a number of months; among them were those who went on to contribute to *Gallery 68*, most of whom in fact shared the same cell:[50] Jamāl al-Ghīṭānī, Sabry Hafez, Yaḥyā al-Ṭāhir 'Abd Allāh, Ghālī Shukrī, Ghālib Halasā, Ibrāhīm Fatḥī, 'Abd al-Raḥmān al-Abnūdī and Sayyid Ḥijāb.[51] So in pursuing its objective of winning positive interest from the establishment, *Gallery 68* was careful to steer a middle course between antagonistic confrontation and compromising its independence.

44 Ḥ. Sulaymān, untitled, *Gallery 68*, no. 1, April–May 1968, p. 30.

45 Editorial to *Gallery 68*, no. 1, April–May 1968.

46 I. Manṣūr and B.' Ṭāhir, taped interviews, Cairo, 1 May 1996. Marina Stagh confirms this in her interviews with writers active during the Nasser era, *The Limits of Freedom of Speech* (1993).

47 J. A. Ibrāhīm, taped interview, Cairo, 30 April 1996.

48 N. 'Aṭiyya, taped interview, Cairo, 28 April 1996.

49 I. Manṣūr, taped interview, Cairo, 1 May 1996.

50 Gh. Shukrī, *Min al-Arshīf al-Sirrī li-l-Thaqāfa al-Miṣriyya* (1975), p. 96.

51 J. al-Ghīṭānī, taped interview, Cairo, 30 April 1996. In fact, Yaḥyā al-Ṭāhir 'Abd Allāh remained in hiding until he was finally arrested in April 1967, introduction to Yaḥyā al-Ṭāhir 'Abd Allāh, *al-Kitābāt al-Kāmila* (1983), p. 5.

Two officials of the Ministry of Culture gave *Gallery 68* unconditional support: Suhayr al-Qalamāwī placed a full page advertisement for six Ministry of Culture-sponsored journals, and Sa'd al-Dīn Wahba contributed financially and enabled *Gallery 68* to distribute in other Arab countries using official channels.[52] To conclude that *Gallery 68* represented an intermediate stage between state and independent publication (i.e., the independent non-periodic journals of the 1970s and later) and that they were 'forced to negotiate conditions with the authorities' on the basis of this, as Jacquemond does,[53] is not altogether fair. The circumstances for this kind of publication become easier as the autonomization process progresses[54] (as it did in Egypt of the 1970s and 1980s), so one can accept the attempts of pioneering efforts to see how much they can extract from the authorities without compromise. Indeed, *Gallery 68* took care to maintain its distance from the Ministry of Culture by restricting all dealings with Qalamāwī and Wahba to the telephone or post. It also gained credibility by refusing conditions attached to Yūsuf al-Sibā'ī's offers:

> We went to him very proud, crossing our legs and speaking to him man to man. He was astonished. We told him that we accepted no supervision from him at all. He tried to attach some of his officials to us but we refused. . . . He was very angry but told us afterwards that he would try to help us. Through Idwār [al-Kharrāṭ] he gave us a cheque for L.E. 150, and we got it without any condition.[55]

In fact, Yūsuf al-Sibā'ī withdrew his offer of repeat payments when *Gallery 68* refused to apologize for a comment published.[56] *Gallery 68*'s strong belief in the need to retain political and literary independence led it to refuse the offer of *Dār al-Thaqāfa*, a private publishing house run by communists, to finance the journal and split the profits.[57] Yusrī Khamīs still displays the view prevalent among young writers at this time: 'You cannot trust these institutions. You have to find your own way'.[58] Bahā' Ṭāhir echoed these sentiments when he spoke admiringly of fellow young writers in the *Café Riche* gathering who were unemployed and yet still refused the opportunity to receive a wage from the Ministry of Culture.[59] In *Gallery 68*'s very few editorial intrusions, one of the points most emphasized

52 J. A. Ibrāhīm, taped interview, Cairo, 30 April 1996.

53 R. Jacquemond, *Entre Scribes et Écrivains* (2003), p. 99.

54 P. Bourdieu, *The Field of Cultural Production* (1993), p. 63.

55 J. A. Ibrāhīm, taped interview, Cairo, 30 April 1996.

56 Sabry Hafez criticized the enforced change of title for a collection by Yūsuf al-Shārūnī in his article 'al-Uqṣūṣat al-Miṣriyya wa-l-Ḥadātha', *Gallery 68*, Oct. 1969, no. 7.

57 I. Manṣūr, taped interview, Cairo, 1 May 1996.

58 Y. Khamīs, taped interview, Cairo, 26 April 1996.

59 B. Ṭāhir, taped interview, Cairo, 1 May 1996.

was the desire to remain independent: 'We have not had and could not have a model belief of any kind. *68* is not surrealist or existential or Marxist'.[60]

Some critics, even generally supportive ones, were frustrated by *Gallery 68*'s refusal to promote a specific intellectual stance. Sāmī Khashaba believed that a clear statement of policy from the journal would enable its writers to act as 'a buttress for the political battle and solid troops in every battle'.[61] Suhayr al-Qalamāwī made the same point about the younger generation of writers in general. While they might share a similar anger and world view, they had not mapped out what exactly they hoped to achieve through this.[62] On the other hand, subsequent avant-gardes have been quick to upbraid the sixties generation for what they perceive as its overt political engagement.

The truth is that *Gallery 68* remained intentionally neutral, both politically and literarily, as far as neutrality is ever possible in a project requiring editors to exercise their own judgement. Moreover, as writers, most *Gallery 68* contributors, whilst politically driven and inspired, in fact shied away from direct political comment in their literature. Instead, they aimed to achieve progress through their oft-repeated aim of getting at 'the truth', a truth which was acknowledged as fluid and, as such, was not and could not be closely defined. They believed that brutal honesty in their writing, with whatever new stylistic and technical departures this entailed, was enough to shake up their readership and eventually to effect literary change. Yet the political scene had been central in the formation of their habitus, their whole worldview, and this inevitably impacted the development of their new literary styles and techniques. Thus, they attached most importance to literary renewal, yet this could not occur in splendid isolation; it required engagement with society and its politics, though not necessarily in the direct and transparent fashion of the prevailing wave of 'committed' literature.[63]

Gallery 68: in pursuit of truth and progress

What then was the purpose of *Gallery 68*, if not to propagate a particular literary or political doctrine or ideology? Why did *Gallery 68* emphasize so strongly its desire to be 'an open field, wide ranging and clashing?'[64] The answer lies in the higher purpose *Gallery 68* conceived for itself of helping to search out truth. Although Kharrāṭ himself admitted that this aim was difficult, dangerous and

60 Editorial to *Gallery 68*, no. 8, Feb. 1971.

61 Ibid.

62 Suhayr al-Qalamāwī's analysis in 'Hākadhā Yatakallamu al-Udabā' al-Shabāb', *al-Ṭalī'a*, Sept. 1969, p. 66.

63 The underlying importance of politics for sixties writers is evidenced by the fact that some of them now criticize nineties writers precisely for their political indifference (e.g. B. Ṭāhir, taped interview, Cairo, 1 May 1996). Moreover, those writers actively defending the freedom of speech in Egypt today and challenging government control of the Writers' Union are largely the same ones who struggled for an independent union of writers in the late 1960s and early 1970s, rather than the new generation.

64 Editorial to *Gallery 68*, no. 8, Feb. 1971.

over ambitious to the point of being almost meaningless, it was nevertheless necessary.[65] In practice, as the journal itself admitted, the only way for it to make a meaningful contribution to this search was to present sincerely, but inevitably subjectively, the truth of its writers' own situation:

> *68* should be a true and sincere forum of exploration, a theatre of experimentation through which may pass . . . those who are able to penetrate distress to see the truth of it, *our* truth, in all its beauty and ugliness . . . and to speak about it [my italics].[66]

Since their truth was revealed implicitly through their work, *Gallery 68*'s main purpose was to act as a publication outlet, rather than as a platform for manifesto-like propaganda directly aimed at dictating absolute truths. In fact, narrative fiction had legitimized itself through presenting itself as part of the discourse of truth ever since the cultural renaissance (*nahḍa*), so in reality most writers, whether avant-garde or reactionary, appeared engaged in a kind of rewriting of Egypt's description. Indeed, those who first introduced realism in Egypt began by translating the term using derivatives of 'truth' (*haqīqa*).[67] Yet in the 1960s and especially after the June 1967 defeat, the truth of Egypt's situation had changed, particularly in the eyes of the younger generation, and they felt that the way in which it was expressed should also change. *Gallery 68* wanted 'to show the reader that it was the reactionaries who were writing in a rhetorical way without presenting anything inside, just rhetorical language, and that this kind of language should be dropped'.[68] The weakness of the Arab press in general at this time, against which *Gallery 68* reacted, was observed unforgivingly by Jacques Berque:

> If . . . we examine the innumerable pieces of writing which take up so much space in Arab periodicals in the form of reports, essays, and debate, we are impressed by the many weaknesses. . . . It arrogates to itself a normative function, handing down its verdicts quite arbitrarily.[69]

What *Gallery 68* aimed at was a kind of Sartrian utopia of a convergence between literary truth and social truth,[70] a literature that was both pure and

65 Editorial to *Gallery 68*, no. 8, Feb. 1971.

66 Ibid.

67 R. Jacquemond, *Entre Scribes et Écrivains* (2003), p. 114.

68 J. A. Ibrāhīm, taped interview, Cairo, 30 April 1996.

69 Jacques Berque, *Cultural Expression in Arab Society Today* (1978), p. 231.

70 R. Jacquemond points out that Jean-Paul Sartre's *Qu'est-ce que la Littérature?* appeared in Cairo in Arabic translation in 1961 with much ensuing debate in the journal *al-Ādāb*; and in 1967, during a fortnight's visit to Cairo, Sartre lectured to a packed hall. R. Jacquemond, op. cit. (2003), p. 125. In fact, the nascent essay had originally been introduced to Arabic readers by Ṭaha Ḥusayn in an advance review in *al-Kātib al-Miṣrī*, Vol. 6, no. 21, June 1947, pp. 9–21. Cited in Verena Klemm, 'Different Notions of Commitment (*iltizām*) and Committed Literature (*al-adab al-multazim*) in the Literary Circles of the Mashriq', *Arabic and Middle Eastern Literatures*, Vol. 3, no. 1, 2000, p. 51.

engaged, but without the latter encroaching on the former and subordinating creativity to politics. There was no hidden agenda behind *Gallery 68*; it was simply 'something spontaneous . . . a special reaction of writers to the moment . . . a fundamental beautiful reaction'.[71] Such an outlet for this reaction was necessary because writers still had to deal with editors and sub-editors of mainly nationalized journals, and although Nasser did not persecute writers directly for their literary work, editors themselves exercised censorship, out of fear if not guided by directives; 'both literary and non-literary magazines were very suspicious of the young generation'.[72]

Even Yaḥyā Ḥaqqī at *al-Majalla* had to balance his sympathy for young writers with his responsibility to keep his journal out of trouble with the censor. In an issue devoted to the short story (August 1966), he was careful to make prominent mention of the wonderful changes brought about by the Revolution, and he published the potentially provocative new stories side by side with more conservative critical commentary. Shaheen writes that Ḥaqqī, in his editorial to this special issue, 'blames the young generation of short story writers for being out of harmony with society (of course, the new society of the Revolution). He urges them to respond to the new patterns of life (brought about by the Revolution) with new modes of realism instead of those of surrealism and the absurd which they were actually employing'.[73] When read closely, however, it is clear that Ḥaqqī does not 'blame' the writers. While he makes a point of expressing displeasure at the gloomy society they depict, nowhere does he write that the experience which motivates such writing is not genuine; and while he does indeed hope 'to revive the realist school in a contemporary framework which reflects Egypt,'[74] this could be interpreted as requiring Egyptian society itself to change first. Nevertheless, Ḥaqqī's approach is certainly more conservative than one might have expected: he revealed that *al-Majalla*'s criteria for choosing its avant-gardists was that they had already been published in other journals, and he trivialized the whole issue with his opening remark that *al-Majalla* purposely chose August for this special number, since the scorching heat inclined readers to prefer lighter material.[75] Moreover, that his opening editorial should have praised Tharwat Abāẓa's conservative journal *al-Qiṣṣa* (The Story, 1964–5) as an outlet for avant-garde trends indicates just how desperately short of outlets such trends were.

Naguib Mahfouz identified the popularity of the short story as partly responsible for the dilemma of short story writers, since publishers were inundated with more stories than they could cope with.[76] Bahā' Ṭāhir relates that many young

71 Y. Khamīs, taped interview, Cairo, 26 April 1996.

72 B. Ṭāhir, taped interview, Cairo, 1 May 1996.

73 Mohammed Shaheen, introduction to *The Modern Arabic Short Story: Shahrazad Returns* (1989).

74 Editorial to *al-Majalla*, Aug. 1966.

75 Ibid.

76 *al-Hilāl*, Aug. 1969 (special issue on the short story).

writers would sit in *Café Riche*, discussing who had and who had not managed to publish, for 'at that time, there were so many writers, so many people trying to publish'.[77] Frustration had led some writers to try to publish by raising or borrowing the necessary money themselves through various schemes. Bahā' Ṭāhir, for example, tried to raise money for publication costs by selling copies in advance. In return for payment, he issued friends with receipts to be exchanged for his book when it materialized. But the scheme came to nothing as he could not gather enough receipts to cover the cost of publication.[78] Statistics testify to the difficulties faced by new young writers: although 38 per cent of books published during 1961–7 were by newcomers to the market, well over half never published another fictional work. This was a much lower rate of success than in the 1950s.[79] Moreover, Corm found that in 1967 itself 50 per cent of novels published were by the same five established writers.[80]

With regard to poetry too, the opportunities for publishing new innovative work within Egypt were limited after the cultural right's campaign against 'the new poetry' in the mid-1960s: Shukrī reflects grimly on the naivety of himself and others for believing that talented new poets would be encouraged to publish because the Poetry Committee included the likes of Ṣalāḥ 'Abd al-Ṣabūr and had officially recognized many more modern poets such as 'Abd al-Mu'ṭī Ḥijāzī, Muḥammad 'Afīfī Maṭar and 'Abd al-Wahhāb al-Bayyātī.[81] In reality, the cultural climate was still dominated by the right, as was demonstrated by the mass arrests in October 1966. Ibrāhīm Fatḥī tells of new young writers 'scraping their way along stony soil' while conventional literature, much of it reflecting the views of those controlling the commercial market, 'has managed to penetrate the spiked fences of publication'.[82]

However, it was not so much that new experimental currents could find *no* outlet at all. In addition to the oral outlet of literary salons (*nadawāt, jalasāt* and *ḥalaqāt*), and publication opportunities provided by 'Abd al-Fattāḥ al-Jamal at *al-Masā'* and Yaḥyā Ḥaqqī at *al-Majalla*, several writers had been able to publish in more liberal Beirut journals like *al-Ādāb* (The Literary Arts, 1953–) and *Ḥiwār* (Dialogue, 1962–7?). Rather, *Gallery 68* was needed because uniting these experimental currents within a single outlet inside Egypt would magnify their impact and thus win recognition for the fact that a new literary phenomenon had emerged. For, as Ḥaqqī had acknowledged two years earlier, they were 'experiencing the torment of someone who is shouting in a valley and not even an echo

77 B. Ṭāhir, taped interview, Cairo, 1 May 1996.

78 Ibid.

79 M. Stagh, op. cit. (1993), pp. 50–5.

80 Yūsuf al-Sibā'ī, Ṭaha Ḥusāyn, Iḥsān 'Abd al-Qaddūs, 'Abd al-Ḥalīm 'Abd Allāh and Naguib Mahfouz. Youssef Corm, 'L'Édition Égyptienne en 1967', *Travaux et Jours*, April–June 1968, no. 27, pp. 25–49. Cited in M. Stagh, op. cit. (1993), p. 51.

81 Gh. Shukrī, *Min al-Arshīf al-Sirrī li-l-Thaqāfa al-Miṣriyya* (1975), p. 90.

82 I. Fatḥī, 'Malāmiḥ Mushtaraka fī al-Intāj al-Qiṣaṣī al-Jadīd', *Gallery 68*, no. 6, April 1969, p. 111.

replies'.[83] *Gallery 68*'s collective strategy to win attention was particularly apparent in special issue six, the selection of experimental short stories. The selection was intended as 'an affirmation and establishment of this contemporary generation which is standing at a turning point in our culture'. It was submitted as proof that contemporary literary experimentation was significant, 'a necessity for life itself,' not merely a passing fashion 'as the traditionalists and conservatives like to say'.[84]

That *Gallery 68* considered this literature a life necessity shows that it was not a nihilistic journal intending the negation of life as some critics accused. Rather it served some kind of social purpose, in both an individual and broader context. Certainly, *68*'s contributors gained personal catharsis from their work – Ḥasan Sulaymān wrote, 'We only live on paper. Our only real victory is on paper'[85] while Kharrāṭ wrote of *Gallery 68* as a collective attempt 'to grasp salvation through art'.[86] However, had the purpose been restricted to the purely personal, they would not have felt the need to launch their journal as widely as possible. While they realized that *Gallery 68* itself could not reach a wide readership, they urged journalists to write about them in the mass media and went to considerable expense to place advertisements in *al-Ahrām* to publicize each issue.[87] So while Kharrāṭ admitted to 'our burning desire to withdraw into ourselves in this ocean of ugliness and evil,'[88] this was only half the picture. Whilst looking inside themselves for their truth, the literary manifestation of this truth was intended to be shared more broadly, to celebrate 'the determination to confirm our pride, no matter how shattered', and hope, however faint, in the possibility of sincerity, justice, love and the durability of life.[89] For the writer 'is in the ideal position to motivate this society'.[90] Na'īm 'Aṭiyya describes *Gallery 68* as 'serious . . . something soothing,' designed 'to raise the spirit of the people through the tool which they respected very much'.[91] More than just a negative rejection of the past, *Gallery 68* was a constructive approach to the future. Yaḥyā Ḥaqqī actually concluded that the rising generation of writers was more serious about its art and more aware of its role in serving the nation than the previous generation.[92] The work of *68*'s contributors was not intended to alienate them; rather, they were already alienated and their work strove for reintegration into a better future.

83 Editorial to *al-Majalla*, Aug. 1966 (special issue on avant-garde writers).

84 Editorial to *Gallery 68*, no. 6, April 1969.

85 Ḥ. Sulaymān, 'Ilāh wa-Ṭifl wa-Samkarī', *Gallery 68*, no. 5, Feb. 1969, p. 6.

86 Editorial to *Gallery 68*, no. 8, Feb. 1971.

87 J. A. Ibrāhīm, taped interview, Cairo, 30 April 1996.

88 Editorial to *Gallery 68*, no. 8, Feb. 1971.

89 Ibid.

90 B. Ṭāhir speaking in *Ughniya fī al-Manfā*, a film directed by J. A. Ibrāhīm, Geneva, 1995.

91 N. 'Aṭiyya, taped interview, Cairo, 28 April 1996.

92 Editorial to *al-Majalla*, Aug. 1966 (special issue on the avant-garde short story).

Therefore, while *Gallery 68* was not socially involved in the sense that its literature and art were a straight-forward reflection of society – many of its critical articles attacked the continuing prevalence of socialist realism – it still carried a social function that extended to the public at large. Ḥasan Sulaymān believed that 'art can always transform the inner vision of the artist into an external awareness influencing social change'.[93] Ghālib Halasā corroborated this view when he described art as 'the greatest and most effective source of knowledge, not because it imparts the experience of others, but because it clarifies the public's own experiences for them. . . . The task of art is to reveal a deep order to the apparent chaos of the world'.[94] Therefore, despite the alienation felt by many of *68*'s contributors and the unfamiliar nature of much of their work, there was some agreement that 'the value of an artist depends on the extent of his link to the public'.[95] Yet any social function could be effected without resorting to overt manifestos, since the work published in *Gallery 68* would speak for itself through some kind of emotional or intellectual rapprochement: 'sound art has the ability to influence everyone in different ways'.[96]

Gallery 68 was accused from time to time of having a Zionist or American imperialist agenda, but in fact those involved showed a deep patriotism and concern for Egypt, although the manifestation of this concern was unforgiving. It was through *Gallery 68* that the *68* generation could expose 'the essence of the wounded nation, the essence of its tormented, confused brothers roving in the labyrinth, the essence of the harsh face of the truth'.[97] It was determined to show that while the regime might have been defeated, the Egyptian people could still rise up from the ashes. One young poet to publish in *Gallery 68* reveals, 'As a result of the defeat, we lost many of our dreams, dreams of the rise of the nation. There is no doubt that the effect of this was destructive for Egyptian creative artists who had sung day and night about the nation and national dreams'.[98] The reaction of *68*'s contributors was to attempt 'to change the course of culture, to change the concept of culture, . . . to create . . . a literature which would encourage the reader to think about his language, his formulations, his structures'.[99] In this way, *Gallery 68* compacted optimism for a new and better future in an attempt to reconstruct the confidence of young writers and intellectuals. It aimed to restore cultural credibility by publishing the work of those writers sincerely attempting to cut through to the truth of their situation, to expose a genuine perspective on Egypt's changed reality. Kharrāṭ explained, '*68* tried . . . to be the other face, ardent and intimate, of our life, our yearnings and our endeavours, the

93 Ḥ. Sulaymān, untitled, *Gallery 68*, no. 1, April–May 1968, p. 32.
94 Gh. Halasā, 'Mulāḥaẓāt Ḥawla Difā' 'an al-Ghumūḍ', *Gallery 68*, July 1968, no. 3, p. 77.
95 Ḥ. Sulaymān, untitled, *Gallery 68*, no. 1, April–May 1968, p. 31.
96 Ibid.
97 Editorial to *Gallery 68*, no. 8, Feb. 1971.
98 M. Ṣāliḥ, taped interview, Cairo, 27 April 1996.
99 B. Ṭāhir speaking in *Ughniya fī al-Manfā*, a film directed by J. A. Ibrāhīm, Geneva, 1995.

face which reveals itself, appearing new and strange, but it was always there, hidden, rooted behind many masks'.[100] And if Egyptian culture and literature, in particular the short story, could be regenerated, why not Egypt itself? Bahā' Ṭāhir firmly links social transition to cultural transition, lamenting that while great men of the past such as Qāsim Amīn and Sa'd Zaghlūl had recognized this, Nasser and Sadat had not.[101] He himself was even to dedicate one of his novels to Egypt.[102]

While *68*'s contributors were generally aware of international fermentation in the sixties – of student uprisings in France, the Greens in Germany and the Beatniks in America – yet *Gallery 68* arose solely out of concern for Egypt and Egyptian culture.[103] It was a celebration of indigenous Egyptian literature in its newest forms, not simply a gathering of foreign modernist tendencies imported wholesale from the West, as those accusing it of Zionism or imperialism believed.[104] On the contrary, *Gallery 68* aimed 'to show that the sensibility of the age has reached us here [in Egypt] and that it has fertile seeds here . . . of originality and individuality'.[105] Bahā' Ṭāhir asserts that it was the previous generation of writers [better 'a previous phase of literature', for some of the writers he mentions were still continuing to experiment in the 1960s and 1970s] who had looked to the western model to inspire their work. This enabled Ṭāhir's own generation to take as its starting point an indigenous model. Ṭāhir also pointed out that although several of the younger writers had read classics like Dostoyevsky and Balzac, often in translation, few of them were widely read in more contemporary western modernist literature at that stage, nor indeed were many of them at that stage proficient enough in a foreign language to access such literature,[106] with the notable exception of Idwār al-Kharrāṭ whom Bahā' Ṭāhir describes as 'a special case'.[107] Jamīl 'Aṭiyya Ibrāhīm reveals that Kharrāṭ was always encouraging the younger writers to read modernist authors like Alain Robbe-Grillet.[108]

The unfamiliarity of foreign and highly modernist work of the type advocated by Kharrāṭ, some of which he translated for *Gallery 68*, would naturally seem

100 Editorial to *Gallery 68*, no. 8, Feb. 1971.

101 Ibid.

102 *Khālatī Ṣafiyya wa-l-Dayr*. Other contributors also dedicated work to Egypt, for example, the poet 'Izzat 'Āmir dedicated his first collection of poetry (1971) to Egypt.

103 I. Manṣūr, taped interview, Cairo, 1 May 1996; J. A. Ibrāhīm, taped interview, Cairo, 30 April 1996; and Y. Khamīs, taped interview, Cairo, 26 April 1996.

104 Even some respected critics saw new developments in the short story as imported directly from the West. For example Mahmoud Manzalaoui, *Arabic Writing Today: The Short Story* (1968), p. 21.

105 Editorial to *Gallery 68*, no. 6, April 1968.

106 J. A. Ibrāhīm, taped interview, Cairo, 30 April 1996; and I. Manṣūr, taped interview, Cairo, 3 May 1996.

107 B. Ṭāhir, taped interview, Cairo, 1 May 1996. NB Other contributors to *Gallery 68* who had a good knowledge of western European and American authors and critics at this early stage were Ghālib Halasā, Ghālī Shukrī and Sabry Hafez.

108 J. A. Ibrāhīm, taped interview, Cairo, 30 April 1996.

baffling at first. For those already set in their views on literature, such an alien and confusing intrusion would naturally provoke dismissive criticism in some quarters and, in a few exceptional cases, heated attacks. Consider, for example, the opinion of Mahfouz, who was sympathetic to the experimentation of young writers in the 1960s, but who was forced to admit even two decades later:

> I read Robbe-Grillet and find that a crime has taken place . . . There is a murdered person, but I don't know whether the murder actually happened or not. Fine, but why these riddles? . . . It seems to me that this is not art, this is despair of art.[109]

He failed to recognize that despair of art (or rather, the prevailing concept of art) can lead to the regeneration of art.

Kharrāṭ was in fact responsible for most of the foreign translated literature in *Gallery 68*, which proved especially valuable in the context of the time. Political and financial considerations raised by the June defeat prompted the Ministry of Culture to withdraw its subsidization of translation projects. As a result, the supply of affordable foreign novels which had been rising since the mid-1950s, with a record high in the first half of 1967, dried up within only a few months of the June defeat.[110] Ḥaqqī, in an editorial to *al-Majalla* a year after the defeat, drew attention to the low number of and delay in imported books.[111] Yet at the same time as providing this valuable perspective from abroad, *Gallery 68* did not lose focus on its primary concern – Egyptian literature. In fact, translated literature occupied only 16 per cent of each issue on average, even excluding issue 6 from the calculation since this was devoted in its entirety to the contemporary Egyptian short story. Moreover, the broad variety of countries covered by these translations, from America to India, proves that the journal's aim was to broaden the horizons of readers and writers rather than to encourage them to become disciples of modern Western culture.

Gallery 68: clique or open society?

In summing up the 1960s ideal, Riyāḍ al-Rayyis writes, 'It is the trend which calls for the mutual tolerance of all intellectual, artistic and literary experience without limits or restraints. It is the trend which screams in the face of extremism in its various religious, cultural and political forms'.[112] This description of tolerance is diametrically opposed to much of the establishment criticism surrounding the young avant-gardists in the contemporary mainstream press. Yet one of *Gallery*

109 Naguib Mahfouz, in A. H. al-Sharīf, op. cit. (1989), p. 31.
110 M. Stagh, op. cit. (1993), p. 53.
111 Editorial to *al-Majalla*, June 1968.
112 Riyāḍ al-Rayyis, *al-Fatra al-Ḥarija: Naqd fī Adab al-Sittīnāt* (1992), p. 14.

68's main objectives was indeed to remain open to all perspectives, and within certain parameters it remained faithful to this ideal. One initial proviso is that these various perspectives were focused overwhelmingly on the short story, and while poetry and some modern art were also published and discussed, drama and the novel were to a large extent sidelined. *Gallery 68* was the brainchild of a core group of about 10 writers and artists, but in practice it embraced a much wider circle of intellectuals, with over 60 writers, poets, artists and critics publishing in its 8 issues. This support base was both broader and looser than had been the case with the previous avant-garde journals, *al-Taṭawwur* and *al-Bashīr*. *Gallery 68* published six Iraqi short story writers, one Palestinian and several Alexandrians and Egyptian provincials, most of whom mailed their contributions. Moreover, the Cairene gatherings of young writers who used to meet in 'Abd al-Fattāḥ al-Jamal's literary 'salon' at *Café Sphinx* and Naguib Mahfouz's Friday morning literary 'salon' at *Casino Opera*, moving afterwards to *Café Riche* where *Gallery 68* was born, included several writers from provincial Egypt, among them Amal Dunqul, Yaḥyā al-Ṭāhir 'Abd Allāh, 'Abd al-Raḥmān al-Abnūdī and 'Abd al-Ḥakīm Qāsim.[113]

This mix of backgrounds was a relatively new feature on the literary scene, for it was only in the late 1940s, when young men from the provinces started to go to Cairo to study, that provincials truly began to brush with cultural life which was, and still is, overwhelmingly centred in Cairo. Perhaps this mix of backgrounds in part explains the appeal of *Gallery 68* among serious young would-be writers and poets throughout Egypt. In this respect, *Gallery 68* remains unique; even in *Iḍā'a 77*, most of its poets were conversely linked by their non-Cairene backgrounds. Although the 1970s saw various attempts to integrate provincial writers into the broader Egyptian literary scene, most notably through a Union of Writers, these attempts relied on conditions stipulated by the cultural authorities; as a result, many disenchanted young writers refused to cooperate.[114] Over time, provincial writers no longer had the same opportunity to come to Cairo at all as accommodation grew more expensive and jobs more scarce. What emerged at the end of the 1970s was 'the Offset Revolution' (*thawrat al-masṭar*), a new cheap means of independent printing using a stencil which resulted in a flood of avant-garde journals in the late 1970s and 1980s. These factors may in part explain why these subsequent journals, often regionally based, were more prone to cliquedom than *Gallery 68* had been.

In *Gallery 68*'s first issue, the artist–editor Ḥasan Sulaymān, stressed the need to retain artistic individuality, despite the group action of publishing a journal, for 'art results from the rebellion of outstanding individuals'.[115] Jamīl 'Aṭiyya

113 J. al-Ghīṭānī, taped interview, Cairo, 30 April 1996.

114 Heated debate about the merits and flaws of the Union of Writers took place on the pages of *al-Ṭalī'a's* literary supplement between Dec. 1975 and Feb. 1976. See ch. 6.

115 Ḥ. Sulaymān, untitled, *Gallery 68*, no. 1, April–May 1968, pp. 30–1.

Ibrāhīm, one of the founding editors, insists that the journal was not the mouthpiece of a specific clique pursuing its own experimental trend, 'We were a gathering of different points of view, a gathering of good writers from all trends. . . . The measure was good writing, even if it was reactionary writing'.[116] Ghālī Shukrī too stresses that literature was published primarily for its high quality, not just because it was experimental, although he admits that 'most of the contributors were radicals'.[117]

However, since one of the criteria for accepting new work was that an institutional journal would not accept it,[118] although it had to be of high quality for *Gallery 68* to accept it, the obvious conclusion to draw is that either such work was too experimental for the established market, or that *Gallery 68* had its own peculiar definition of high quality, or probably a bit of both. Ḥasan Sulaymān pointed out in the first issue that a generation linked by a common human experience usually gives rise to unity of thought, which in turn produces correlated views of art.[119] And since *Gallery 68* could not represent all sixties writers, poets and artists, given its limited resources, space and lifespan, those whom it did publish were naturally linked by the common denominator of editorial approval. In practice, therefore, these writers, poets and artists shared a sympathy, differing in degree, to the kind of literature and art which they deemed to express their contemporary situation. Since Egypt's and hence their situation had changed, it was natural that they should wish to experiment with new styles in order to express this changed situation, thus giving rise to much diversity within the general current. So *Gallery 68* acted as an umbrella for various, more or less diverse, but generally modernist trends, with a definite predilection for the experimental.

This role was especially apparent in issue six, a special issue which drew together a selection of contemporary Egyptian short stories representative of various trends. The works selected were chosen to reflect 'the greatest possible variety, diversity and novelty,' rather than being what *Gallery 68* considered to represent the best work of the best writers.[120] Moreover, the selection was followed by two controversial critical studies with which *Gallery 68* itself disagreed, but which were included for their serious opinions and to provoke debate.[121] Māhir Shafīq Farīd, who had a critical commentary and a translation turned down by *Gallery 68*, believes that it was 'to some extent a clique. . . . While it was open to other views, there was a solid consensus of opinion'.[122] Na'īm 'Aṭiyya too believes that his stories were rejected for publication in the special selection since

116 J. A. Ibrāhīm, taped interview, Cairo, 30 April 1996.

117 Gh. Shukrī, taped interview, Cairo, 3 May 1996.

118 B. Ṭāhir, taped interview, Cairo, 1 May 1996. NB Special issue no. 6, a selection of contemporary Egyptian short stories, was obviously an exception.

119 Ḥ. Sulaymān, untitled, *Gallery 68*, no. 1, April–May 1968, pp. 30–1.

120 *Editorial* to *Gallery 68*, no. 6, April 1969.

121 Ibid.

122 Māhir Shafīq Farīd, taped interview, Cairo, 30 April 1996.

he was only a fringe participant in the *Café Riche* gathering, while most of the main participants had their own short stories to publish.[123] However, selection necessarily involves subjective judgement, and at least one of the editors admits to the possibility of some bias towards the inner circle of friends.[124] For example, all of the short story writers on the editorial committee of special issue six included stories of their own. A certain degree of solidarity is, however, a natural rather than a negative feature of fringe literary activity: 'We were not a public service. We were a group of friends from different trends'.[125] Bahā' Ṭāhir stresses this latter disclaimer, 'a clique of friends, yes; a clique of writers, no'.[126]

This view is borne out by Sāmī Khashaba writing in *al-Ādāb*. While welcoming the emergence of *Gallery 68*, he nevertheless criticized it for representing only one group among 'today's generation' and for failing to define itself clearly in its opening editorial. He believed *68* should link itself to clear concepts of social and intellectual development and enter into open debate with the old established viewpoints. He accused the journal's editors of refusing to shoulder these responsibilities and wrote, 'they raise the banner of an intellectual truce and fear the debate, yet they are the ones who suppose themselves rebels against the old fetters'. Khashaba traced *68*'s 'strange stance' to two motives: a preference for personal ties over intellectual ties, and a desire for intellectual neutrality and objectivity. Khashaba's article was one of the most detailed and well-balanced, and in detecting both of these motives, he implicitly recognized the ambivalent nature of his criticisms. In fact, he himself advised in the same article that reliance on definite positions was dangerous, for it led to reliance on the weak foundation of slogans.[127] It was exactly this kind of polarization that *Gallery 68* was striving to avoid. A desire to publish their own work notwithstanding, *Gallery 68*'s editors still aimed to remain open and honest in their journal's content.

Just how much variety *Gallery 68* supported – within the bounds of modernism – remained a controversial issue. Bourdieu points out that the practices of the members of the same group are always more harmonized than the agents know or wish.[128] Sabry Hafez complained in issue seven that every story in special issue six was simply a variant of the same Kafkaesqe trend, and that some works had only been included as a result of 'entrenched interests and personal whims'. Hafez challenged: 'What in God's name do the works of Khalīl Kalfat, Ibrāhīm Manṣūr, Ibrāhīm 'Abd al-'Āṭī and Jamīl 'Aṭiyya represent of the reality of the Egyptian short story today?' Hafez also dismissed Ibrāhīm Fatḥī's balanced study

123 N. 'Aṭiyya, taped interview, Cairo, 28 April 1996.

124 J. A. Ibrāhīm, taped interview, Cairo, 30 April 1996.

125 Ibid.

126 B. Ṭāhir, taped interview, Cairo, 1 May 1996.

127 Sāmī Khashaba, 'al-Nash'a al-Thaqāfiyya fī-l-Waṭan al-'Arabī', *al-Ādāb*, July 1968. Yet, more than a year later, Khashaba still wrote disapprovingly about the lack of unity in *Gallery 68*'s editorial style, 'al-Nash'a al-Thaqāfiyya fī-l-Waṭan al-'Arabī', *al-Ādāb*, Dec. 1969.

128 P. Bourdieu, *The Rules of Art* (1996).

of the previous issue on the grounds that it was 'full of gaps and generalizations and avoided serious penetrating discussion'. He accused Fatḥī of using obscure and meaningless phrases, 'crumbs that had fallen from the table of the medical lexicon',[129] and of cowardice in failing to be personal in his criticism. Fatḥī did indeed become more personal in his criticism. He compared Ghālī Shukrī, whom he criticized for deeming abstraction to be the only means to progress, to a diver in a bowl of soup. Yet he considered Hafez even worse – namedropping European writers while knowing virtually nothing about them, contradicting himself in different articles and stringing together terms he had stumbled upon into useless sentences. Yet he did admit to the value of Hafez's statistics on the short story.[130] The very fact that *Gallery 68* was willing to print such diverse views (also remembering that the three writers criticized by Hafez were all current or former members of the actual editorial committee) points to the sincerity of its attempt to present a fair picture of contemporary experimental currents and not simply to indulge a clique of friends.

Gallery 68's attempt at impartiality within the whirlpool of experimental currents is reflected in its considered use of terminology. 'The new generation' (*al-jīl al-jadīd*), by now an age-discriminating cliché, tended generally to be avoided in favour of more meaningful temporal categorization such as 'today's generation' (*jīl al-yawm*), 'the contemporary generation' (*al-jīl al-mu'āṣir*) or 'the 68 generation' (*jīl 68*) which suggest groupings based primarily on shared experience rather than date of birth. What is referred to as 'new' is this (sociological rather than biological) generation's view of art.[131] One critic used 'the 68 generation' interchangeably with 'the spiritural generation' (*al-jīl al-rūḥī*) to encompass broadly those short story writers who were trying to make sense of the same burning questions, having been sparked into new creative activity by the June defeat.[132] In fact, the image of *Gallery 68* as a group of anarchic young rebels was a calculated exaggeration spread by opponents within the establishment. *Gallery 68* actually took a mature responsible approach to publicizing the new experimental literary currents. 'The whole editorial board read all the material' and everything published was decided by a democratic vote among the editorial board of each issue.[133] Māhir Shafīq Farīd tells of a mocking commentary on *Gallery 68*, written in the form of an internal monologue, which he submitted for publication. Idwār al-Kharrāṭ agreed that some of his criticisms were worth making, but asked him to rewrite it, since certain comments could expose the journal to libel.[134] But that this was not the result of personal exclusion from

129 Sabry Hafez, 'al-Uqṣūṣa al-Miṣriyya wa-l-Ḥadātha', *Gallery 68*, no. 7, Oct. 1969, p. 84.

130 I. Fatḥī, 'Ba'ḍ al-Masā'il al-'Āmma fī al-Naqd', *Gallery* 68, no. 7, Oct. 1969, p. 68.

131 Editorial to *Gallery 68,* no. 6, April 1969.

132 Jalāl al-'Asharī, 'al-Qiṣṣa al-Qaṣīra min al-Azma ilā al-Qaḍiyya ', *al-Fikr al-Mu'āṣir*, June 1969.

133 I. Manṣūr, taped interview, Cairo, 1 May 1996.

134 M. Sh. Farīd, taped interview, Cairo, 30 April 1996.

some kind of clique is proved by the fact that *Gallery 68* was perfectly prepared to publish material critical of it, as well as quality work sent by post, where virtually nothing was known about the author.[135]

Part of the reason for the journal's more responsible approach and recognition of the need to keep its pages open to other new blood may be that the core group whose names appeared on the cover of the first issue were more mature than those typically involved in other Egyptian avant-garde journals such as *al-Taṭawwur* or *Iḍā'a 77*. None was under 30 years of age (although Muḥammad Ibrāhīm Mabrūk was only 26 when he became involved in *Gallery 68*'s editorial process a year later). That the range of ages found in *Gallery 68* is wider than one might expect in a markedly avant-garde journal is indicative of the fact that while writers in their twenties may hold a greater stake in literary experimentation, they do not have a monopoly on it. The involvement of some older or well-established figures may also be seen as part of a conscious objective to ensure that the journal receive serious critical appraisal. Ibrāhīm Manṣūr admits, 'Idwār [al-Kharrāṭ] was much older than us. We took him on as we thought he would be useful to get through to Yūsuf al-Sibā'ī [Secretary-General for Culture]. We needed protection actually; during Nasser's time people were really frightened'.[136] This last point about a latent fear is important in understanding why *Gallery 68* was more radical and rebellious in the context of the time than it perhaps appears with the benefit of hindsight.

Gallery 68 can be regarded as a sort of mother-figure to avant-garde activity, harbouring among its experimental content material of a more radical rebellious nature, without declaring *itself* as a radical rebellion. As such it demonstrated a development from the more inflexible antagonism of previous avant-garde journals such as *al-Fajr al-Jadīd* (The New Dawn, 1945–6) and *al-Taṭawwur*.[137] This attempt at a more objective stance was reflected in the strikingly small amount of overt editorial intrusion. The opening editorial was only thirteen lines long, and no other editorial was published until the sixth issue. Instead, *Gallery 68* published a brief disclaimer on the back cover of its second issue:

> What *Majallat 68* publishes does not necessarily express the view of the editorial committee. The journal does not originate out of a closed group and is not restricted to the writers themselves. Rather, as every avant-garde or new experiment, it opens its pages in a complete and true welcome of all that is produced by new writers who explore a difficult road. In this, it does not stipulate a particular point of view, stance or

135 For example, poems in no. 4 (Nov. 1968) sent by Ṭarrād al-Kubaysī in Iraq and Tharwat al-Baḥr in Alexandria; stories in no. 3 (July 1968) and no. 7 (Oct. 1969) sent by Yūsuf al-Qiṭṭ in Dimyāṭ.

136 I. Manṣūr, taped interview, Cairo, 1 May 1996.

137 *al-Bashīr* (The Herald), whose license was taken over by a group of experimental writers 1948–50, was more open to differing forms, techniques and ideas.

intellectual or artistic school as long as it is original and expresses the climate of new writing in our nation, is in touch with the thoughts and sentiments of our country's intellectuals and writers, and springs from the creative source which we believe will never dwindle in this nation.

We must look to the actual choice of content to reveal the agenda of *Gallery 68*. The brief opening editorial by Aḥmad Mursī had avoided the fiery arrogance of the manifestos of *al-Fajr al-Jadīd* and *al-Taṭawwur*. Mursī took a cautiously optimistic view of Egypt's gloomy position, likening the June defeat to the pains of childbirth, a heavy labour which would result ultimately in the birth of a 'new liberal, democratic, socialist nation'.[138] As more issues were published and its impact began to be felt, *Gallery 68*'s confidence grew and we find a similar childbirth analogy a year later: 'the short story in Egypt has not died, perhaps it is being born, born for the first time after the traumas of a painful childbirth'.[139] Yet this confidence was motivated more by enthusiasm and optimism than by pure arrogance, for the same introduction praised a whole list of more established writers and admitted to their continuing importance in the future as well as the present. Rather than pronouncing itself the final truth in a long legacy of deficient cultural tradition as some of its critics alleged,[140] *Gallery 68* took a more realistic view of the limitations of its role which it defined as 'to place a humble brick in the palace of the new liberal, democratic, socialist nation'.[141]

The debate stirred up by the special issue (no. 6) comprising a selection of contemporary Egyptian short stories and two critical articles forced *Gallery 68* to define its position more tangibly, in the face of criticism that the journal lacked direction and was run by nihilists.[142] The editorial to issue seven (Oct. 1969) therefore presented the first real collective statement of opinion, akin to a manifesto but less dogmatic and rigid, drafted by Idwār al-Kharrāṭ and signed '68'. One might accuse *Gallery 68* of succumbing to common avant-garde hubris, since its collective statement deemed the journal the mark of a whole new epoch, rather than just one aspect of the generation struggle. Yet the statement actually steered markedly clear of narrow distinctions and sweeping generalizations. Synchronous with the assertion of *Gallery 68*'s epoch-making significance came a reminder that no single chronological period or generation holds a monopoly on literary renewal. For literary renewal 'is not a matter of a new generation facing an old generation; it is in fact a matter of an entire age dying, together with its concepts, values and relationships, and a new age being born, the concepts, values

138 Editorial to *Gallery 68*, no. 1, April–May 1968.
139 Editorial to *Gallery 68*, no. 6, April 1969.
140 For example, Luṭfī al-Khūlī, *al-Ṭalī'a*, Sept. 1969, p. 83.
141 Editorial to *Gallery 68*, no. 1, April–May 1968.
142 J. A. Ibrāhīm, taped interview, Cairo, 30 April 1996.

and relationships of which are not yet defined'.[143] The fact that *Gallery 68* resisted the temptation to dictate the values of the new age, describing them instead as 'not yet defined', makes it a turning point within the broader historical context. It places the journal at the beginning of a continuing wave of literary renewal and predicts its inspirational role for further literary experimentation in the 1970s and 1980s.

Gallery 68's attempt to balance the instinct towards introverted group solidarity, born of the need for self-defence, with a conscious effort to remain an open and evolving literary forum is also revealed in the statement of clarification. Narrow and outmoded criticism of *Gallery 68* sparked by the special issue of selected stories stimulated a hot riposte. Critics were described as literary 'brokers, midwives and hair stylists' and told that 'no artist, especially not the artist with a new outlook experimenting with new expression, needs the intervention of anyone, and he especially doesn't need their advice'. Yet the same editorial admitted that 'much of the sincere criticism directed against us was justified'. The keyword here is 'sincere', for while *Gallery 68* recognized the need for a healthy critical movement that was prepared to consider new literary trends on their own merits, it refused to acknowledge a distorted criticism that judged new trends using the criteria applied to past literary trends. The editorial scathingly pointed out that 'the judgement of avant-garde and experimental works of literature will never come from the literary Stone Ages'.[144]

The statement of clarification upholds the notion of *Gallery 68*, not as a closed clique, but as a mother-figure encouraging existing avant-garde tendencies. *Gallery 68* stands apart from other avant-garde journals, both past and future, whose manifestos were much more egocentric and uncompromising, thus proving that 'there was nothing called 'group 68' (*majmūʿat 68*); it was a movement, a current'.[145] The beginning of the editorial does indeed dwell on *Gallery 68*'s impact on the literary scene, printing numerous quotations in praise of itself. However, this self-celebration was to a large extent included to demonstrate to critical officials in the Ministry of Culture that *Gallery 68* could not be suppressed without anyone noticing. Moreover, *Gallery 68* balanced the praise with a warning that the sudden celebration of the short story was still superficial, the result of excitement and the wish to celebrate something Egyptian, rather than true comprehension of contemporary literary trends. The journal warned young writers not to become static in style, declaring 'we are still dissatisfied'.[146]

The sincerity of this desire to develop is apparent in *Gallery 68*'s assumption of complete responsibility for its development. It was published initially at significant personal expense to the individuals involved. Yet there is only fleeting mention of financial difficulties, since it recognized that 'the successive financial

143 Editorial to *Gallery 68*, no. 7, Oct. 1969.
144 Ibid.
145 I. Manṣūr, taped interview, Cairo, 3 May 1996.
146 Editorial to *Gallery 68*, no. 7, Oct. 1969.

crises that *68* has faced since its emergence are no excuse or justification for it falling short of fulfilling all for which it was published'.[147] This willingness to remain open to sincere criticism was important in stimulating general debate that was constructive rather than hopelessly polarized, and that was therefore able to have a more lasting impact on literary developments over the next decade.

The impression given is that *Gallery 68* added up to more than just a passing clique of writers; for by resisting the temptation to disavow the past completely and deny the future by publishing an absolute doctrine, the journal maintained a slight but crucial distance from its editors and contributors, at the same time providing a forum for their individual views and beliefs. The precarious balance between group and individual is most obvious, significantly, in the final editorial. The journal continued after a gap of 16 months with an editorial signed by Idwār al-Kharrāṭ rather than by '*68*'. Although the editorial refers to 'the generation of *68*,' a term which blurs any distinctions between age groups and between new and old, and uses 'we' and 'our' throughout, it is subtitled 'a very personal point of view'. This concurs with Kharrāṭ's conviction that '*68*'s most serious error would be to give herself a manifesto, to adopt an attitude, to publish a doctrine'. The journal's only commitment should be 'the search for . . . the terrible beauty of the truth, and sincerity in this search'. Yet the possession of this ultimate truth is subtly denied to any single group or generation in recognition of the restless avant-garde dynamic: 'We wish to open our pages to fervent and strange experiments of a battered but obstinate generation, risking its neck – artistically – for the sake of what it deems to be *its* truth and *its* art' (my italics, as opposed to *the* truth and *the* art). For truth is not absolute, but ever elusive, 'the daughter of adventure, exploration and elements that stand between darkness and light'.[148] This loyalty to the quest for their notion of truth was the common bond which united the individual contributors.

Gallery 68: mission accomplished

A few of those involved in *Gallery 68* recognized the transitory nature of their avant-garde adventure. The journal peaked with issues six and seven in which were published the special selection of short stories and the ensuing debate. The modernist trends featured in *Gallery 68* had now truly made an impact and the relative positions of some sixties writers in the literary field were changing as they became more successful in the struggle to gain specific and symbolic cultural capital and legitimacy. One established critic complained, 'Why do they shout when their names resound in the newspapers and on the radio and television?'[149] In fact, the attention *68*'s contributors now commanded in established

147 Editorial to *Gallery 68*, no. 7, Oct. 1969.
148 Editorial to *Gallery 68*, no. 8, Feb. 1971.
149 Dialogue between Aḥmad Ḥijāzī and Lūwīs 'Awaḍ in *Ṣabāḥ al-Khayr*. Quoted in 'Hākadhā Yatakallamu al-Udabā' al-Shabāb', *al-Ṭalī'a*, Sept. 1969, p. 21.

media did take the wind out of *Gallery 68*'s sails. Jamīl 'Aṭiyya Ibrāhīm admits, 'Our writing had been accepted by the institutional magazines . . . There was no need to continue; we were established writers'.[150] In a sense then, they became victims of the attention they craved: 'a little magazine, when it becomes too successful, loses the freedom of spirit which having nothing to lose bestows'.[151]

Thus financial difficulty was not the primary cause behind the disappearance of *Gallery 68*, despite several financial crises. The journal never paid for itself, and in its early days it was financed largely by the personal contributions of those writers directly involved with it. It had also received money from the sale of artwork donated by supportive painters, as well as contributions from sympathetic intellectuals, including Naguib Mahfouz, Yaḥyā Ḥaqqī, Sa'd al-Dīn Wahba and Suhayr al-Qalamāwī. *Gallery 68* was, however, expensive to produce, since great attention was paid to its presentation. But on facing bankruptcy towards the end of 1968, Badr al-Dīb was persuaded to print it at *al-Jumhūriyya's* (The Republic, 1953–) presses with the promise of future payment.[152] Manṣūr therefore admits, 'We could have continued publishing. It was not a financial problem'.[153]

The real cause of *Gallery 68*'s disappearance was that many of its writers believed that it had fulfilled its role. New trends in writing had been acknowledged, albeit often critically, and Manṣūr makes the point that morale had been raised among *68*'s contributors; they had demonstrated that in 1967 'it was the government and the regime that was defeated, not us'. As a result, there was a shortage of suitable material for publication in *Gallery 68*; 'people felt that they had done enough, that they had said what they wanted to say'.[154] Since its editors were now able to find regular outlets in institutional journals, their need for *Gallery 68* was less urgent and they had less to publish in it. Jamīl 'Aṭiyya Ibrāhīm admits, 'We stopped because we didn't have enough material to publish . . . We had nothing more that was new. . . . There were no new writers such as those who appeared at the end of the seventies'.[155]

It may be, however, that this last point was a symptom rather than a cause of *Gallery 68*'s disappearance. Certainly Kharrāṭ always remained hopeful of new development and insisted on the continuing need for the journal as an outlet for work that appeared strange and was therefore still unacceptable to institutional journals. Kharrāṭ firmly believed that *Gallery 68* should continue as an ever evolving theatre for experimental literature, as opposed to fading out as it won

150 J. A. Ibrāhīm, taped interview, Cairo, 30 April 1996.

151 F. Pollak, 'Landing in Little Magazines – Capturing a Trend', *Arizona Quarterly*, Summer 1963, Vol. 19, no. 2, p. 105.

152 *Gallery 68* paid Badr al-Dīb L.E. 50 and owed him a substantial amount which they never paid. He tried to sue them, but the case came to nothing. J. A. Ibrāhīm, taped interview, Cairo, 30 April 1996.

153 I. Manṣūr, taped interview, Cairo, 1 May 1996.

154 Ibid.

155 J. A. Ibrāhīm, taped interview, Cairo, 30 April 1996.

attention from the establishment. For this was the only way to adhere to its principle of claiming no absolute ideology or doctrine for the short story. This is why Kharrāṭ tried to keep *Gallery 68* alive, publishing another issue in February 1971 after a gap of a year and four months. His personal editorial entitled 'Why *68*? And why was it necessary to continue?' recognized that 'avant-gardism and renewal is not a wish, it is a cruel necessity'.[156] Ibrāhīm Manṣūr, one of four original editors to remain to the very end, comments 'Maybe Idwār thought this magazine could go on for ever. This kind of magazine does not go on for ever'.[157] As Bourdieu's model shows, unlike those occupying the dominant positions in the literary field who are strongly homogenous, those in the 'dominated groups, whose unity is essentially oppositional, tend to fly apart when they achieve recognition'.[158]

It is clear that Kharrāṭ too recognized this, although he felt compelled to strive for his ideal, for at the same time as announcing plans for forthcoming issues, he warned that continuation would be difficult, ending his editorial ominously with the question, 'What shall we do?'. Without *Gallery 68*, he despaired of experimental writers finding an outlet for such work, concluding that 'the overwhelming likelihood is that we shall not be able to'.[159] He was correct, for in the same year that Kharrāṭ tried to revitalize *Gallery 68*, seven institutional literary journals were closed, and cultural conditions continued to deteriorate throughout the 1970s. Many writers actually left Egypt, including *Gallery 68* contributors Jamīl 'Aṭiyya Ibrāhīm, Ibrāhīm Manṣūr, Bahā' Ṭāhir, Ghālī Shukrī and 'Abd al-Ḥakīm Qāsim. In fact, other similarly avant-garde journals, inspired by the model of *Gallery 68*, did not emerge until the end of the 1970s.

Therefore, instead of continuing as the forum in which various avant-gardes fought their battles and crystallized, *Gallery 68* would in practice be reduced to its very own avant-garde: the position in which it became static, the position the short story had reached by the time *Gallery 68* ceased in 1971. This is exactly what Kharrāṭ predicted when he acknowledged the impossibility of *Gallery 68* attaining *the* truth. Realistically, he admitted that the most they could do was to present *their* truth,[160] although he believed the former ideal to be necessary and remained faithful to it. Thus *Gallery 68* did indeed live up to Shafīq Maqqār's description of it in the penultimate issue as an example of 'the eternal old story, the story of rebellion, novelty and originality – a rebellion which will soon revert to the inheritance . . . when a new wave of rebellion and a more novel view, more contemporary with its time, comes along'.[161] In one way then, sixties writers did

156 Editorial to *Gallery 68*, no. 8, Feb. 1971.
157 I. Manṣūr, taped interview, Cairo, 1 May 1996.
158 P. Bourdieu, *The Field of Cultural Production* (1993), p. 66.
159 Editorial to *Gallery 68*, no. 8, Feb. 1971.
160 Ibid.
161 Sh. Maqqār, ' 'An al-Jadīd wa-l-Qadīm wa-Mā Bayna Bayna', *Gallery 68*, Oct. 1969, no. 7, p. 95.

indeed capture the logic of Bourdieu's model of reproduction of the established order in the sense that their aesthetics was gradually assimilated into the literary mainstream; as their grip on symbolic and specific cultural capital increased, newcomers emerged to take up the position of subordinates and pursue their literary struggle from the margins. While the actors may have changed, the fundamental structure of the literary field endured. As Bourdieu concludes, while actors in a field may contest the legitimacy of the rewards, by engaging in field competition they unintentionally and necessarily end up reproducing the structure of fields.[162]

162 P. Bourdieu, *The Rules of Art* (1996).

5

THE SIXTIES GENERATION IN SEARCH OF A SPECIFIC LITERARY IDENTITY

> In the creative experience, man is himself only insofar as he moves beyond what he is. His identity is a dialectic between what he is and what he is becoming . . . To put it another way, identity is less an inheritance than a creation.
>
> (Adūnīs[1])

In order to understand fully the literary works of a period, it is necessary to reconstruct the mood of the age by placing works within the context of the most potent debates of their time; works should not be viewed independently of the surrounding cultural field to which they are dialectically related. This chapter therefore examines the literary controversies fuelled by the sixties generation, controversies which were taken up by subsequent journals and remain relevant today, for the structure of the literary field has endured and reproduced itself. Debate raged around three main issues. First, the extent of Western influence in the new literature was questioned as hostile critics levelled accusations of blind imitation and stirred up fears over encroaching foreign cultural hegemony. Second, the issue of new versus old – a fear of the Egyptian and Arab cultural heritage being lost through a consuming lust for novelty and innovation – was inevitably raised as the younger generation attempted to stamp its own identity onto its literary works. Third, controversy arose over the relevance of the new modernist forms and techniques in comparison with the immediate popularity and obvious application of 'committed' socialist realist works – so widespread in the 1950s and 1960s – to the contemporary Egyptian social and political scene. However, we shall see that what really emerged in the short story of the sixties generation was a new kind of realism, still very much in tune with its surrounding society, a realism that would evolve further in the subsequent novels of this generation. A fourth area of controversy was poetry, although the poetry of this generation was generally not as radical a departure as their short story. Hence

1 Adūnīs ('Alī Aḥmad Sa'īd), *The Pages of Day and* Night, trans. Samuel Hazo (1994), p. 108.

debates over poetry (at least, the poetry written by the sixties generation in Egypt) were neither as widespread nor as fierce as they were over the short story in the 1960s. Norms of poetic taste had already been strongly challenged by more experimental work emerging on the pages of *Shi'r* (Poetry, 1957–64, 1967–70) in Beirut.

Although these areas of contention centre on points which had been cause for greater or lesser debate since the early stages of the *nahḍa* (the Arab intellectual 'awakening') up to a century earlier, it was in the 1960s that controversy flared up to an unprecedented extent. Fundamentally driven by the search for a specific literary identity and the desire for truth and progress, the sixties generation unleashed a storm of talent as it attempted to navigate the rocky route towards new literary forms and techniques that could express the malaise of the times. It is important to stress here that the notion of a shared identity in no way negates the possibility of plurality within this identity; the sixties generation demonstrated a variety of standpoints in the debates outlined in this chapter. As one Arab writer has explained, a nuanced understanding of identity can refer to 'the sharing of essential elements that define the character and orientation of people and affirm their common needs, interests, and goals with reference to joint action. At the same time it recognizes the importance of differences'.[2] After an introductory section examining the key axes of controversy as a whole, this chapter will examine each of the above controversies in turn in an attempt to re-assess the general attitude struck by the sixties generation as it sought to assert its own literary identity and jockey for position in the Egyptian literary field.

As we have seen in Chapter 4, sixties writers – in general, at least – were not guilty of what we might call 'strategic essentialism', that is, invoking binary oppositions such as new–old, modern–traditional or Arab–Western. One might even posit that it was the rear-guard, in an attempt to perpetuate their domination of the literary field and exclude the avant-garde, who stirred up and exploited the notion of such polarization, for it provided them with a focal point of opposition from which to launch an easy and obvious defence. Established writers and critics raised the spectre of Egyptian cultural dislocation at the hands of a Western-influenced avant-garde. The most dismissive critics identified Western influences with the forces of imperial domination. At worst, they were exaggerated into a Zionist plot, indicating the suspicion and fury that permeated these politically fraught times. Although extreme, it is possible to understand the roots of this critical stance and therefore to empathize with it: Western literary influence was linked to the power structures perpetuated by European imperialism on the grounds that both the practical and ideological aspects of cultural globalization are ultimately powered by an imperial dynamic of influence, dissemination and hegemony. Yet, by implying that the modernist techniques employed and the alienation pervading the new literature were purely imported, critics were compounding the very

2 Ḥalīm Barakat, *The Arab World: Society, Culture and State* (1993), p. 32.

cultural imperialism that they believed themselves to be challenging. This is because, with notable exceptions, it eluded most critics that the new techniques did not have to be viewed solely as derivatives of a dominant West; the influences of Western writers could be processed and expressed in a new literature that was both original and relevant to Egyptian society. Renowned poet, novelist and short story writer Jabrā Ibrāhīm Jabrā bears witness to the relevance of new Western influences (such as Eliot and Mayakovsky), which had an established legacy in the free verse poetry of the 1950s and 1960s, to Arab reality as people tried to come to terms with the loss of Palestine and encroaching Zionism:

> Suddenly, with the shock and the bitterness, young people all over the Arab world not only saw things in a new light but had to express them in a new way... taking Western innovations in their stride in a struggle for a freer imagination.[3]

After all, the understanding of a text across cultures is always an interpretative transformation through which it may assume a different set of meanings determined by the horizons of the recipient's historical and individual situation: a process of re-creation rather than simple reproduction.[4] In brief, a self-confident Egyptian literature should be able to derive inspiration from Western literature without exposing its writers to accusations of blind Europhilia.

Rather than simply pandering to the West, some sixties writers were in fact actively looking further back into their own heritage for inspiration: Yaḥyā al-Ṭāhir 'Abd Allāh drew upon popular village lore while Jamāl al-Ghīṭānī drew upon Middle Eastern history and legend. Popular lore and legend, as a distinctive feature of Egyptian local and national culture, were collective forms giving expression to a specific Egyptian identity. The inclusion of such material in the work of sixties writers interrogates the assumptions of rational linear narrative and encloses it within an indigenous metatext that focuses attention on the pre-colonial culture. One might therefore judge it to convey a new kind of reconstructed realism. Frantz Fanon's model of post-colonial culture might interpret the inclusion of such material in contemporary narrative as a desire 'to shrink away from that Western culture in which they all risk being swamped' and 'renew contact once more with the oldest and most pre-colonial springs of their people'.[5] This reading tallies with the at times obsessive attempts of many Egyptian writers in the 1950s and 1960s to locate their work within a continuum of indigenous

3 Jabrā Ibrāhīm Jabrā, 'The Rebels, the Committed and the Others', in Issa J. Boullata (ed.) *Critical Perspectives on Modern Arabic Literature* (1980), p. 193. Originally published in *Middle East Forum*, Vol. 43, no. 1, 1967, pp. 19–32.

4 See Verena Klemm's useful discussion on cross-cultural translation in V. Klemm, 'Literary Commitment Approached through Reception Theory', in B. Gruendler and V. Klemm (eds) *Understanding Near Eastern Literatures* (2000), pp. 145–8.

5 Frantz Fanon, *The Wretched of the Earth* (1967), pp. 168–9.

Egyptian literature, in a way that is indeed reminiscent of Spivak's 'strategic essentialism'[6] inasmuch as certain signifiers of indigenous culture were favoured as a strategy for resisting the perceived tsunami of global culture. One aspect of this was the insistence on indigenous precursors (like the shadow play or folk story) as the true roots of modern literary forms such as the play or short story. For the sixties generation represented in *Gallery 68* (1968–71), however, the desire to renew contacts with their ancient cultural roots was not the reverse function of a desire to spurn the influences of Western culture. Both could act as equally legitimate sources of literary inspiration. Indeed, over time, the insular idea of a specifically Egyptian literature based on a shared Egyptian and Arab identity and heritage has rapidly become an unsustainable myth, given the possibilities thrown up by the increasing globalization of communications.

So sixties writers cannot be said to have looked towards Western models while neglecting indigenous models. Nor can their position be deemed one of new versus old in any extreme binary sense; for, as well as drawing upon their own distant heritage, some writers, at least – and several more, over time – acknowledged that even their immediate predecessors played some sort of role within a literary continuum. In other words, the literary identity of these sixties writers was palimpsestic in that, despite attempts to break from the literary past, their own experience – and hence their experimentation – was necessarily imbued with traces of that past. In fact, no act of resistance can occur in isolation from the dominant discourse in which its language and conceptual categories are conceived.[7]

On a more general level, Foucault has argued that the author is unable to be the originator of meaning; rather, he is a variable and complex function of discourse, while the various competing discourses are always a function of the power of those who control the discourse to determine knowledge and truth.[8] In other words, the author is in a dialectical relationship with the system of power – in this case the cultural and hence also political establishments – and cannot act in splendid isolation. His identity is formed through being addressed by and related to these others.[9] Just as sixties writers sought to propound their own specific literary identity before the cultural establishment, so also was their self-image to some extent influenced by the image of them constructed *by* the cultural establishment as it objectified them within the identifying system of power relations. The image of them as radically new – whether deemed positive or negative – was welcomed by the writers themselves, probably even nurtured, at least at first. Yet calling experimental writers the 'new' or 'young' generation branded them as

6 See Gayatri Chakravorty Spivak, 'Subaltern Studies: Deconstructing Historiography,' in Ranajit Guha and G. C. Spivak (eds) *Selected Subaltern Studies* (1988), pp. 1–32.

7 See Spivak's development of this idea in G. C. Spivak, 'Can the Subaltern Speak?', *Wedge*, nos. 7–8, Winter/Spring 1985, pp. 120–30.

8 Michel Foucault, 'What is an Author?', trans. Josué V. Harari, in Josué V. Harari, *Textual Strategies: Perspectives in Post-Structural Criticism* (1980), pp. 158–9.

9 Johnathan D. Culler, *The Pursuit of Signs: Semiotics, Literature, Deconstruction* (1981), p. 33.

immature in relation to dominant established writers whose literary achievements were thus implicitly constructed as superior. What sixties writers themselves wished to emphasize as 'new' was their literature, not themselves. Rather than 'immature' or even 'promising', they saw their work as a distinctive literary departure that was more relevant to Egypt's changing position. Moreover, this was a literature that could equally well be produced by not-so-new writers who were able to span generations by remaining creative and innovative, for example Idwār al-Kharrāṭ and Yūsuf al-Shārūnī.

Highly relevant to sixties writers is Jameson's claim that third world texts inevitably act as national allegories. Jameson believes that this is particularly the case when the textual form develops out of 'predominantly Western machineries of representation, such as the novel', or, for our purposes, the short story.[10] Jameson's rationale is that private experience is not separated off from the public domain in third world countries in the way that capitalism has ensured in the developed world. Although the label 'third world' is questionable, one might still generalize that the story of private individual destiny is therefore naturally the story of the embattled society as a whole. This would endow the seemingly self-indulgent individual psychological studies and flights into fantasy, with which so many of their short stories were concerned, with a new kind of realist – even populist – relevance, contrary to common critical perception.

It is with regard to this aspect of giving expression to a new sensibility borne of and reflecting Egypt's changing reality that the literature of sixties writers can be located within a 'new versus old' debate. In practice, this boiled down to a father–son antithesis, which was a popular theme in many of their short stories, rather than a rejection of the Arabic literary heritage per se, as the most hostile critics claimed. The kind of literature 'approved of' by the literary establishment tended to display broadly similar and predictable traits, creating a degree of homogeneity which served to represent and consolidate the interests of those holding dominant positions in the field of literature and culture. Thus, in defining themselves, sixties writers tended to perceive the previous (literary rather than strictly biological) generation as the Other, rather than holding up the West as the Other. This antithesis heightened their self-awareness and helped to define their sense of identity, expressed at its most extreme in Muḥammad Ḥāfiẓ Rajab's now-famous claim, 'We are a generation without masters'.[11]

In other words, patterns of 'filiation' (heritage or descent) as a primary factor in literary production were being supplanted by patterns of 'affiliation' (identification through culture rather than descent), which naturally included identification with the expression of some Western writers alongside elements from Egyptian and Arab culture. This identification was exercised with a greater or lesser degree

10 Frederic Jameson, 'Third World Literature in the Era of Multinational Capital', *Social Text*, 15, 1986, p. 67.

11 Muḥammad Ḥāfiẓ Rajab, *al-Jumhūriyya*, 3 Oct. 1963, p. 13.

of discernment.[12] However, the comments of some contemporary Egyptian critics reveal that they themselves perceived this process of affiliation as no more than an alternative process of filiation in which the role of the father figure had simply shifted from the Arab to the Western writer. Even though some more progressive and encouraging critics deemed this perceived shift a positive development, the judgement remains a distortion of literary reality. This is exemplified in the comments of critics such as Sabry Hafez and Suhayr al-Qalamāwī who praised certain writers for 'almost' mastering the style of Hemingway, Kafka or Robbe-Grillet (see the following section), rather than recognizing the Egyptian writers in question as trying to forge their own new styles out of these Western influences. By bandying about the names of Western writers as figures to be lived up to or mastered, it was these critics – and not necessarily the writers themselves – who were actually responsible for invoking the hegemonic power of a dominant Western culture. The literature of sixties writers needed to be judged by its distinctiveness and specific concerns rather than its provenance in or ability to match up to European or American culture.

Rather than focusing on either Western cultural hegemony or, indeed, an at times artificial harking back to the Egyptian literary heritage, it is perhaps more accurate to identify the beginnings of a more transcultural process in which the emphasis should be placed on Egyptian responses to, not imitation of, modern Western literary forms and techniques. As some sixties writers themselves pointed out, this process had already begun among previous generations of Egyptian writers who had read and absorbed Western works, many of them French, English and Russian texts already in Arabic translation. Sixties writer Bahā' Ṭāhir, now a prominent novelist, asserts that it was because previous generations had absorbed Western models for the short story that his generation had been able to draw on an indigenous model.[13] Eventually, the processes of influence, inspiration and imitation would become more syncretic with the translation of many works of sixties writers into English and other languages. Remarkably, this very possibility was pointed out by the Minister for Culture in the early 1960s, 'Abd al-Qādir Ḥātim, in a public lecture with an apparently post-colonial agenda of initiating cultural revolution to shore up a socialist society. While calling for intellectuals to uphold their cultural tradition, Ḥātim also encouraged them to open up to foreign cultures, 'interacting with them without fear...or vanity' and exporting Egyptian culture at the same time.[14] In other words, a dialectical relationship with the West could both empower the Egyptian literary scene and, ultimately, begin to exert its own influence on global culture.

12 See Edward Said, *The World, the Text, and the Critic* (1983), pp. 174–5.

13 Bahā' Ṭāhir, taped interview, Cairo, 1 May 1996.

14 In Lūwīs 'Awaḍ, *al-Thawra wa-l-Adab* (1967), pp. 167–75. Cited in A. Isstaif, 'Forging a New Self, Embracing the Other: Modern Arabic Critical Theory and the West – Luwīs 'Awaḍ', *Arabic and Middle Eastern Literatures*, Vol. 5, no. 2, 2002, p. 164.

As such, it had the power to liberate Egyptian writers from both Western and Arab forms of cultural oppression. So, while the effects of the powerful Western centres of global culture are plainly present in many sixties writers, the ultimate endgame is proving to be the interpenetration of Western, Arab and Egyptian elements. This has occurred in varying proportions and with varying degrees of success and may be perceived in some of the sixties writers who today dominate the Egyptian literary scene (e.g. Jamāl al-Ghīṭānī, Idwār al-Kharrāṭ, Bahā' Ṭāhir and Sun' Allāh Ibrāhīm).

Thus the literary identity sought by avant-garde sixties short story writers was effected through the embryonic phases of a growing cultural syncretism, not to be confused with cultural homogenization which, in this context, was far more likely to arise from protecting the status quo. This process might be associated with Homi Bhabha's 'third space of enunciation', a contradictory and ambivalent space in which cultural identity emerges.[15] It is in this liminal space that sixties writers were able to forge a new identity through a constant process of engagement involving both contestation and appropriation. If the literary dynamics at play are viewed through such a framework, then the kind of cultural purity hotly sought and claimed by certain Egyptian critics and writers cannot exist. While cultural difference still operates, it does so from within an empowering hybridity through which a more international culture is forged. This hybridity does not deny the existence of imbalance and inequality which inevitably exists in any cross-cultural exchange. It certainly does not imply a wholesale process of transculturation, nor does it aim to dislocate Egyptian culture from its temporal, spatial, geographical and linguistic context and replace it with a globalized textual concept. Quite the opposite, in fact: this notion of hybridity has the potential to challenge the assumption of Western domination.

Thus the sixties generation might be read as offering an amalgamation of three models of resistance in their quest to establish their own literary identity. First, a national Egyptian culture and pre-colonial literary tradition were asserted through the incorporation of myth, legend and historical material from the distant Egyptian and Arab past (anti-colonial discourse); second, the hybrid nature of their literature contested the very basis of imperialist pretensions of cultural superiority (counter discursive practices); and third, the rejection of the literary practices of the immediate Arab past and the emergence of a new realism challenged the social, political and literary status quo, while the creation of their own independent journal gave them a certain autonomy from the greater field of power (anti-establishment).

Nevertheless, in the sense that the literature to emerge did so in a symbolic liminal space, it cannot be held up as a wholesale break with the Egyptian and Arab literary heritage any more than it can be said to have shaped its identity independent of Western literary influences. Yet the end result can be recognized

15 Homi Bhabha, *The Location of Culture* (1994), p. 37.

as a distinct literary departure. It is the points of contention – the debates of the time – outlined in this chapter that reveal the areas around which the specific literary identity of the sixties generation was shaped.

Western infiltration

Controversy regarding Western influences, which many critics were quick to read into the kind of new literature featured in *Gallery 68*, can be separated into two issues. First, to what extent did the *68* generation draw on Western authors? – that is, where did writers fall along the scale of imitation to inspiration to innovation? And, second, how relevant were 'Western' modernist techniques to an Egyptian or Arab experience?

The sense of alienation expressed by sixties writers was one of the main causes of controversy regarding the new literature. Some critics viewed it as an import from the imperialist West of no relevance to Egyptian society.[16] Others viewed it as a genuinely Egyptian dilemma,[17] though this dilemma was itself frequently attributed to the effects of Western imperialism. Writing in *Gallery 68*, Halasā explained that the sense of alienation simply sprang from the inability to fulfil oneself within one's own sphere of life, whatever and wherever that might be.[18] However, he was later forced to explain his views in response to harsh criticism of him for having failed to relate alienation directly to imperialism. Halasā's critics insisted that one had to rise above alienation and fight imperialism,[19] clearly showing that the prevailing literary mood was still utilitarian; literature should actively contribute to, rather than simply give expression to, society. That Halasā, whose socialist credentials were beyond doubt, should be criticized for neglecting the struggle against imperialism simply because he had written sympathetically about aspects of alienation demonstrates how deep suspicion about the new approach to literature ran in some quarters and how simplistic a postcolonial critique was being batted about on the Egyptian literary scene.

Typical of such critics was Shukrī 'Ayyād, the influential editor of *al-Majalla*, who described contemporary Egyptian literature as a war industry and made it clear that true literature was 'created in the trenches'. He insisted that the techniques required to create such a literature could not be imported since they derived from a specifically Arab and Egyptian situation. Such literature, which was apparently arriving in *al-Majalla*'s postbag in increasing quantities, combined deep internal with precise external observation to express the spirit of patience and endurance displayed by the fighter at the front with Israel. 'Ayyad condemned

16 For example, 'Abd al-Mun'im 'Abd al-Ḥalīm al-Hawwārī, *al-Ṭalī'a*, Feb. 1970, p. 156.

17 For example, Shafīq Maqqār, ''An al-Jadīd wa-l-Qadīm wa-Mā Bayna Bayna', *Gallery 68*, no. 7, Oct. 1969, p. 97.

18 Ghālib Halasā, 'al-Adab al-Jadīd: Malāmiḥ wa-Ittijāhāt', *Gallery 68*, no. 6, April 1969, pp. 116–17.

19 Gh. Halasā, ''An al-Falsafa wa-'Ilm al-Jamāl', *Gallery 68*, no. 7, Oct. 1969, pp. 70–2.

contemporary experimentation for its incomprehensible confusion and obscurity which he believed arose less from a mistrust of established values and more from a vague imitation of Western modernist trends.[20]

Linking the new literature directly to the names of Western writers became a popular critical practice. 'Ayyād, in an article intended to prove that *Gallery 68*'s special selection of short stories had contributed nothing really new, identified Kharrāṭ's style as that of Henry James and the existentialists, Sulaymān Fayyāḍ's style as that of Hemingway or Steinbeck and the style of Ibrāhīm 'Abd al-'Āṭī and Ibrāhīm Manṣūr as a contrived and ridiculous derivation of Libedinsky.[21] Even sympathetic critics joined in the intellectual game of focusing their critical apparatus on points of comparison with Western literature. Writing in *Gallery 68* itself, both Hafez and Halasā deemed the influence of Hemingway strong enough to constitute an entire trend within the new literature. Halasā wrote that many sixties writers had adopted only the external features of Hemingway's difficult style: short sentences and the observation of man's outer features and movements, so that their world became no more than sectors and lines. He suspected that this external orientation indicated a desire to escape from critical Arab issues. However, he identified the *Gallery 68* contributors Sulaymān Fayyāḍ, Yaḥyā al-Ṭāhir 'Abd Allāh and Muḥammad al-Bisāṭī as exceptional in penetrating to the true core of this style. He praised the new trend for its objectivity, for avoiding the prevalent tendency to confuse the characters' opinions with those of the writer and for abolishing linguistic and emotional exaggeration and digression.[22] Hafez, on the other hand, identified Hemingway's objective yet tragic view of modern man as one of the new trends neglected by *Gallery 68*'s special selection of short stories.[23]

For Hafez, the literature showcased in *Gallery 68* was heavily biased towards the Kafkaesque. Yet he did not entirely rule out the possibility of innovation derived from this foreign influence, rather than simply imitation, for he described the trend as 'a step beyond the Kafkaesque... It blends Kafka's poetic expression with the intellectual content and artistic style of alienation literature'.[24] There is doubtless much truth in this assessment; Kafka had cropped up in several literary journals before *Gallery 68*,[25] and the latter had itself published an Arabic translation of Kafka's *Beim Bau der chinesischen Mauer* (translated into English

20 Sh. 'Ayyād, 'Adab al-Khandaq', *al-Majalla*, May 1970, pp. 2–3.

21 Shukrī 'Ayyād, 'al-Qiṣṣa al-Miṣriyya al-Mu'āṣira: 'Adad Khāṣṣ fī Majallat *Gallery 68*, April 1969', *al-Majalla*, June 1969, pp. 94–7. NB Ibrāhīm Manṣūr, in the interviews recorded in his book *al-Izdiwāj al-Thaqāfī wa-Azmat al-Mu'āraḍa al-Miṣriyya* (1981), in fact revealed a wariness of European cultural domination.

22 Gh. Halasā, 'al-Adab al-Jadīd: Malāmiḥ wa-Ittijāhāt', *Gallery 68*, no. 6, April 1969, pp. 118–19.

23 S. Hafez, 'al-Uqṣūṣa al-Miṣriyya wa-l-Ḥadātha', *Gallery* 68, no. 7, Oct. 1969, p. 86.

24 Sabry Hafez, 'al-Uqṣūṣa al-Miṣriyya wa-l-Ḥadātha', *Gallery 68*, no. 7, Oct. 1969, pp. 84–6.

25 Of particular and recent relevance was Aḥmad 'Iṣām al-Dīn's critical article on existentialist elements in Kafka's fiction, *al-Qiṣṣa*, Aug. 1965.

as 'The Great Wall of China') in issue four, alongside an extremely elementary effort at a comparative study of Kafka, Gogol and Nathaniel West.[26] However, Hafez's insistence in reading various complex Western influences into the new literature – which apparently also derived elements ranging from Camus to Saul Bellow, as well as demonstrating a generally false understanding of Hemingway's view of sex and violence and his style of linking the eye and object directly – appears unnecessary and strained. Hafez does little more than identify the element of alienation in the stories, and one feels that the emphasis should be on the writer's own personal experience and experiment, rather than on what he may (or may not) have derived from foreign authors.

Looking to the West for inspiration was not, of course, a new phenomenon in the 1960s. Even as 'Ayyād criticized young writers for chasing after translations and belittling their own culture, he pointed out that it was the older generation who had dropped them in 'the ocean of international culture', vulnerable to being swept away by international cultural currents.[27] It was more that the kinds of influences now infiltrating the literary scene were perceived as negative and detrimental to Egypt's recovery. Older established writers were reluctant to condone the influence of Western modernist writers on the rising generation, despite having themselves been influenced by Maupassant and Chekhov.[28] Typical of this ambivalent attitude towards Western influence was Aḥmad Ḥasan's advice to young writers, printed in one of the Ministry of Culture's journals:

> I would advise our young people to immerse themselves in as much Western literature as they want that is termed 'classical, 'romantic' and 'realistic'. Everything else thereafter is a mess. Such things should be avoided, since they represent the beginnings of decline.[29]

At worst, Western influences were exaggerated into an open attack on the Arabic language.[30] Khashaba felt it necessary, in a Beirut journal, to defend

26 The article is by Idrīs Bey (trans. Shawqī Fahīm). The first point of comparison between Kafka and Gogol is that Kafka's Gregor Samsa (*Die Verwandlung*) and Gogol's Korolev (*Korolev*) wake up in the same place at the same time – in bed in the early morning [This is not so unusual!], and it is apparently 'no coincidence' that it is also in the morning that Kafka's Josef K. (*Der Prozess*) is arrested, and moreover while he is getting out of bed. The comparison is stretched yet further to include Nathaniel West, for it is also in the morning, and indeed after he has got out of bed, that Simpson (*The Day of the Locust*) puts his hands in cold water to wake them up. *Gallery 68*, no. 4, Nov. 1968, p. 26.

27 Sh. 'Ayyād's analysis in 'Hākadhā Yatakallamu al-Udabā' al-Shabāb fī al-Waṭan al-'Arabī', *al-Ṭalī'a*, Dec. 1969, pp. 74–5.

28 Jalāl al-'Asharī, 'al-Qiṣṣa al-Qaṣīra min al-Azma ilā al-Qaḍiyya', *al-Fikr al-Mu'āṣir*, June 1969.

29 Aḥmad Ḥasan, *al-Thaqāfa*, Jan. 1976. Cited in Roger Allen, 'Egyptian Drama and Fiction in the 1970s', *Edebiyat*, Vol. 1, no. 2, 1976, p. 228.

30 For example, Tharwat Abāẓa, in his introduction to Aḥmad Hāshim al-Sharīf's first collection (1966), wrote of the linguistic terrorism of some young writers, and believed that many stories could not be considered to belong to the Arabic language.

Gallery 68 against such criticisms,[31] although elsewhere he admitted that much innovative work was hampered by the mechanical application of imported trends.[32] Hafez too, in a panel discussion shortly after the appearance of *Gallery 68*, firmly equated new developments in narrative technique with the adoption of foreign civilization and a disregard for the present Arab reality.[33] Even Naguib Mahfouz, whose paternal encouragement of *68*'s experimentation earned him much respect among the journal's contributors, later spoke of the 'tragedy' of Egyptian literature turning so heavily to the West, insisting that 'rationality must play its role in ordering the artistic work'.[34] While Mahfouz allowed that temporary loss of rationality might occur, he was adamant that, even in his experimental works like *Khammārat al-Qiṭṭ al-Aswad* (The Black Cat Tavern, 1968), a meaning could still be extracted.[35] He admitted in 1988, 'I no longer write using symbols and parallels. Rather, I write directly, for matters have become clear'.[36] This prompted *Gallery 68* contributor Aḥmad Hāshim al-Sharīf himself to look back negatively on sixties experimentation, telling Mahfouz,

> You escaped from the trap and left young writers in it.... You led young writers astray for, like you, they immersed themselves in new forms. ... But because they were in the formative period, they perished in the domain of form.[37]

Elsewhere, however, al-Sharīf was more confident of the validity of the new forms, affirming that, while they were reminiscent of Joyce, Kafka or Robbe-Grillet, 'there is no doubt that they result from circumstances experienced by the new generation'.[38]

Few critics even broached the possibility of Egyptian writers forging a new literature of their own which could actually contribute to, rather than simply take from, international cultural currents. Ghālī Shukrī was one exception. While sceptical about the positive benefits of Western influence on the previous literary

31 Sāmī Khashaba, 'al-Nash'a al-Thaqāfiyya fī al-Waṭan al-'Arabī', *al-Ādāb*, Dec. 1969.

32 S. Khashaba's analysis in 'Hākadhā Yatakallamu al-Udabā' al-Shabāb', *al-Ṭalī'a*, Sept. 1969, p. 63.

33 S. Hafez in *al-Majalla's* panel discussion on the contemporary situation in Arabic fiction, *al-Majalla*, June 1968, p. 9.

34 Naguib Mahfouz, in a 1988 interview conducted by Aḥmad Hāshim al-Sharīf, *Naguib Mahfouz: Muḥāwarāt Qabl Nobel* (1989), p. 31.

35 Mahfouz's style had been described, in 1971, as even more obscure than that of Alain Robbe-Grillet by the young critic and *Gallery 68* contributor Ghālī Shukri. Gh. Shukrī, *Ṣirā' al-Ajyāl* (1971), p. 147.

36 N. Mahfouz, in a 1988 interview conducted by A. H. al-Sharīf, *Naguib Mahfouz: Muḥāwarāt Qabl Nobel* (1989), p. 101.

37 A. H. al-Sharīf, Ibid., p. 32.

38 A. H. al-Sharīf's response to questionnaire in Muḥammad al-Rāwī, *Udabā' al-Jīl Yataḥaddathūna* (1982), p. 33.

generation,[39] he had faith in the ability of sixties writers to subjugate foreign forms to local experience to reflect Egypt's own problems and he recognized that the new 'abstract trend' embraced features common to the age, whether East or West, North or South.[40] It was this last attitude which 'Ayyād vehemently rejected when he upbraided young writers for deluding themselves that Egyptian concerns produced the same literary results as European concerns.[41] Yet Shukrī was subtle enough to regret that many among Egypt's new generation were unaware that their own sense of loss differed from that of their contemporaries in Europe and America. He pessimistically perceived the Western sense of loss to be the product of a developed civilization constantly surpassing itself as opposed to a backward civilization regressing further.[42]

In fact, the alienation felt and expressed by many of *Gallery 68*'s contributors was fundamentally different from the kind of existentialism that had wielded so much influence in Europe. In an era of defeat and in which many sixties writers had experienced imprisonment, the focus was on society's alienation from the individual rather than vice versa. *Gallery 68*'s contributors remained deeply concerned with reality; their alienation did not seek to sever ties to life, but to reject old ties while striving for new ones. Khashaba has pointed out that existentialism reached the sixties generation through the translation of works of literature rather than philosophy, and, unlike existentialist philosophy, existentialist literature has a powerful human presence. It was the basic image of normal men crushed in an intolerable world to which *Gallery 68*'s contributors related, not simply escapism and death as some critics concluded.[43] Therefore, while the sixties generation could be influenced by existential literature, they were not themselves existentialist.

While it is often more practical and of greater general interest to deal with the new literary phenomenon as a collective, those making the pronouncements did not always put sufficient emphasis on, or even admit to, the generalized nature of their discussion. While much of the new literature clearly betrayed elements of Western modernism, a good proportion of *68*'s writers were still at an early stage in their development and were not yet familiar enough with Western literary techniques to justify some of the charges levelled against them. In many cases, the critics, especially some of those contributing to *Gallery 68* itself – such as Ghālib Halasā, Sabry Hafez and Ghālī Shukrī, in addition of course to writer/critic Idwār al-Kharrāṭ – were more familiar with Western literature than the writers themselves.

39 Ghālī Shukrī, *Muḥāwarāt al-Yawm* (1980), p. 146.

40 Gh. Shukrī, *al-'Anqā' al-Jadīda: Ṣirā' al-Ajyāl fī al-Adab al-Mu'āṣir* (1977), p. 153.

41 Sh. 'Ayyād's analysis in 'Hākadhā Yatakallamu al-Udabā' al-Shabāb fī al-Waṭan al-'Arabī', *al-Ṭalī'a*, Dec. 1969, p. 75.

42 Gh. Shukrī, *Dhikrāyāt al-Jīl al-Ḍā'i'*. Cited in Sh. 'Ayyād, 'Hādhā al-Jīl al-Ḍā'i' ', in Ḥusayn Mahrān (ed.) *Ghālī Shukrī, Dhākirat al-Jīl al-Ḍā'i'* (1996), p. 40.

43 S. Khashaba, 'Jīl al-Sittīnāt fī al-Riwāya al-Miṣriyya', *Fuṣūl*, Vol. 2, no. 2, Jan.–March 1982, p. 121.

It is therefore unsurprising that they made connections between the Egyptian and foreign works they had read. As many of *68*'s contributors continued to read foreign works, encouraged especially by Kharrāṭ, the importance of absorbing Western techniques alongside the Arab heritage and integrating both into the writer's unique personal literary development was generally recognized. Mehrez sums up their position as follows:

> The sixties generation were not the alienated intellectuals of the first half of the century, torn between their indigenous reality and the Western model…: having distanced themselves from the European model and the slogans of the dominant ideology, they focused their attention on what to represent and how to represent it.[44]

This stance naturally opened them up to experimentation and innovation – and the subsequent backlash.

Some Arab intellectuals acknowledged that the young Egyptian writer was beginning to synthesize his general reading, of the Arab literary heritage as well as Lorca, Hemingway or Gorky, into something individual to him.[45] A decade later, *Gallery 68* contributor Jamīl 'Aṭiyya Ibrāhīm was able to state confidently, 'I personally am neither fearful of, nor crushed before, European civilization. For I belong to a nation with its own established and continuous civilization'. The case of Jamīl Ibrāhīm demonstrates one of the effects of self-exile during the Sadat years: having lived in Europe for several years, Jamīl Ibrāhīm admitted that he had been 'distorted': he could neither assimilate to the culture in which he found himself, nor could he go back to how he was before.[46] What Jamīl Ibrāhīm is actually describing approximates a syncretic approach to literary creativity, the product of an in-between space in which the writer absorbs various influences, then integrates them to forge his own personal creative path.

The success of the best of *68*'s writers in maturing towards integration rather than imitation is demonstrated in Suhayr al-Qalamāwī's comments on Majīd Ṭūbyā. In her introduction to Ṭūbyā's first collection (1967), she praised his stories for reflecting 'some of the currents of the modern novel in France which some short story writers are imitating but which I have not encountered in Arabic with this degree of success'.[47] Remarking on Ṭūbyā's work a decade later, she intimated that the Western model once aspired to had been uniquely integrated and in fact surpassed: Ṭūbyā confronts reality, 'exploding realistic meanings, not

44 Samia Mehrez, introduction to 'Abd al-Ḥakīm Qāsim, *Rites of Assent* (1995).

45 For example, Palestinian poet Mu'īn Basīsū's analysis in 'Hākadhā Yatakallamu al-Udabā' al-Shabāb', *al-Ṭalī'a*, Sept. 1969, pp. 80–1.

46 I. Manṣūr, Interview with Jamīl 'Aṭiyya Ibrāhīm in Basel, *al-Safīr* (Beirut), 31 May 1981, in I. Manṣūr, *al-Izdiwāj al- Thaqāfī wa-Azmat al-Mu'āraḍa al-Miṣriyya* (1981), pp. 115–23.

47 Suhayr al-Qalamāwī, introduction to Majīd Ṭūbyā, *Fustuk yasilu ilā al-Qamar* (1967).

in a monotonous and silly way as some Western writers do, but in a way that is deep, majestic and spiritual, as our literature should be'.[48] This kind of development among *68*'s contributors went some way towards attaining the aspiration of an international literature outlined by Shafīq Maqqār in *Gallery 68*. Unlike Ghālī Shukrī, whose notion of an international literature was based on the idea of a certain unity derived from global historical and sociological parallels,[49] Maqqār's understanding of international literature was akin to Goethe's concept of *Weltliteratur*. He implied that the best work of *68*'s contributors might eventually take its place as part of a wider international literary heritage. Rather than venture a judgement on the relative merits of 'Eastern' or 'Western' literature, or even 'old' or 'new' literature, Maqqār adopted a more general stance which might, at best, be considered broad-minded and diplomatic, and at worst, vague and over-idealistic. Maqqār described the process of literary development as merging the best of the old with the best of the new to become part of the international literary heritage. Creative works in one language soon become available in other languages, so that the only criterion for becoming part of the heritage is literary merit. Maqqār dodged the obvious question about how one judges literary merit, stating simply 'the components and measures of this merit are well-known and widespread'.[50] Bahā' Ṭāhir too spoke about the importance of Egyptian literature reaching Europe and becoming part of world literature.[51]

Shukrī 'Ayyād, on the other hand, claimed that talk of an international literature was deceptive and artificially based on a desire for unity. But it was really the type of internationality perceived by Ghālī Shukrī that 'Ayyād rejected, for he accepted that literature could attain internationality by being loyal to the principles of truth, justice and good. Ra'ūf Naẓmī, writing in *Gallery 68*, also rejected Shukrī's notion of internationality based on shared civilizational concerns, as expressed in his landmark book *Shi'ru-nā al-Ḥadīth ilā Ayn?* (Our Modern Poetry: Where to?). Naẓmī held that man's frame of reference remained confined to the concerns of the society and relationships around him.[52] While 'Ayyād agreed with Maqqār's notion of universally respected values for literature, he did not project this notion into a future world heritage as Maqqār had done, nor did he believe it to apply to contemporary experimentation in Egyptian literature which he deemed overwhelmingly confused and obscure.[53] However, some of the best work of those experimenting at that time is now gaining international recognition. Al-Qalamāwī's praise of Ṭūbyā can now be applied to several of

48 S. al-Qalamāwī, cited on back cover of M. Ṭūbyā's *Ghurfat al-Muṣādafa al-Arḍiyya* (1978).

49 Gh. Shukrī, *al-'Anqā' al-Jadīda: Ṣirā' al-Ajyāl fī al-Adab al-Mu'āṣir* (1977), pp. 6–8.

50 Sh. Maqqār, ''An al-Jadīd wa-l-Qadīm wa-Mā Bayna Bayna', *Gallery 68*, no. 7, Oct. 1969, p. 94.

51 B. Ṭāhir speaking in *Ughniya fī al-Manfā*, a film directed by J. A. Ibrāhīm, Geneva, 1995. Significantly, Ṭāhir's work has since been reviewed in the American journal *World Literature Today*: Vol. 77, no. 1, April–June 2003, p. 158; Vol. 71, no. 1, Jan–March 1997, p. 216.

52 Ra'ūf Naẓmī,' 'An *Shi'ru-nā al-Ḥadīth ilā Ayn?*', *Gallery 68*, no. 5, Feb. 1969, p. 65.

53 Sh. 'Ayyād, 'Adab al-Khandaq', *al-Majalla*, May 1970, pp. 2–3.

68's contributors whose works are being integrated into a wider world literature as they are selected for translation.[54] One of the ultimate symbols of such integration was the dominant status of sixties writers in the Egyptian delegation sent to the 2004 Frankfurt Book Festival which specifically showcased Arab writers.[55]

'New' versus 'Old'

The reverse side to the accusation of imitating Western literature was the charge that sixties writers were ignorant of their own Arab literary heritage. Four years after *Gallery 68*'s closure, Tharwat Abāẓa, a prolific novelist and Sadat's cultural henchman, gave the following assessment:

> There has been a tendency among men of letters to turn away from their own authentic heritage and look to foreign literature alone. . . . For a long time, the press has been dominated by a group of people whose major goal has been to destroy our heritage.[56]

Abāẓa himself was editor of both *al-Qiṣṣa* and *al-Idhā'a wa-l-Tilīvizyūn* as well as heading *al-Ahrām*'s literary section at this time, and one might conclude instead that the cultural press was dominated by conservative men of letters such as himself.

Similar concern about the neglect of the Arab heritage was voiced in a more balanced way by Suhayr al-Qalamāwī. Commenting on *al-Ṭalī'a*'s survey of young writers, one third of whom were contributors to *Gallery 68*, al-Qalamāwī surmised that no writer's interest extended back before the 1930s. She also voiced a suspicion that their knowledge of certain writers and philosophers derived from secondary sources.[57] Al-Qalamāwī's concerns were echoed by both Rashād Rushdī[58] and Lūwīs 'Awaḍ, who added that many young writers appeared

54 Among *Gallery 68*'s contributors to have had short stories published in English translation are Yaḥyā al-Ṭāhir 'Abd Allāh, Ibrāhīm Aṣlān, Jamīl 'Aṭiyya Ibrāhīm, Na'īm 'Aṭiyya, Muḥammad al-Bisāṭī, Sulaymān Fayyāḍ, Jamāl al-Ghīṭānī, Ghālib Halasā, Shafīq Maqqār, 'Abd al-Ḥakīm Qāsim, Muḥammad Ḥāfiẓ Rajab, Yūsuf al-Shārūnī, Bahā' Ṭāhir, Fu'ād al-Takarlī and Majīd Ṭūbyā. Moreover, several contributors now have whole novels published in English translation, including Idwār al-Kharrāṭ, Jamīl 'Aṭiyya Ibrāhīm, Jamāl al-Ghīṭānī, 'Abd al-Ḥakīm Qāsim, Bahā' Ṭāhir, Majīd Ṭūbyā and Sulaymān Fayyāḍ.

55 For example, Idwār al-Kharrāṭ and Jamāl al-Ghīṭānī. Significantly, Bahā' Ṭāhir refused his position in the delegation on the grounds that the government-directed selection process was unsound.

56 Tharwat Abāẓa, *al-Idhā'a wa-l-Tilīvizyūn*, 6 Dec. 1995. Cited in R. Allen, 'Egyptian Drama and Fiction in the 1970s', *Edebiyat*, Vol. 1, no. 2, 1976, p. 226.

57 S. al-Qalamāwī's analysis in 'Hākadhā Yatakallamu al-Udabā' al-Shabāb', *al-Ṭalī'a*, Sept. 1969, pp. 66–7.

58 Rashād Rushdī's analysis in 'Hākadhā Yatakallamu al-Udabā' al-Shabāb fī al-Waṭan al-'Arabī', *al-Ṭalī'a*, Dec. 1969, p. 77.

unaware even of Naguib Mahfouz's contemporaries.[59] These concerns may, however, have been overstated, for the phrasing of *al-Ṭalīʿa*'s questionnaire upon which they based their comments required writers to mention who had actually influenced their work most, not with whose work they were familiar. That the early Arab literary heritage in particular received scant mention simply indicates that this was not a high priority; it does not necessarily show that the writers were badly read. Khashaba in fact perceived the rediscovery of Egypt's cultural roots, through abundant reading, to be the primary influence on the sixties generation.[60] It was not that young writers were hostile to the role played by the Arab literary heritage but, rather, that time had moved on and a new literature had evolved, more relevant to Egypt's contemporary concerns. Naturally then, they would be unlikely to elaborate on the literature of past generations in a limited questionnaire.

What *68*'s contributors did deem of continuing relevance to their contemporary situation was the popular heritage. Yet drawing on the rich stock of legend and folklore was itself a technique gleaned in part from foreign literature, which had done the same with its own cultural roots. Again, the diversity within *Gallery 68* is apparent in the varying degrees of importance different writers attached to legend, myth and folklore and the diverse ways in which these were incorporated into their stories.[61] Both Hafez and Halasā numbered the utilization of folklore, myth and legend among the five new literary trends identified in their *Gallery 68* articles.[62] Hafez did not elaborate, but Halasā expounded his overwhelmingly negative view.

In his analysis of folklorists, Halasā slipped into over-generalization, which was precisely the accusation he levelled against folklorists. He wrote that renewed interest in folklore sprang from 'a search for romanticism', a belief that all good qualities arise in the countryside and that the city is the seat of corruption. This kind of simplistic polarized vision can be traced back to much of the literature written earlier in the century, but Halasā endowed the folklorist strain with dangerous racist elements in their pursuit of Egyptianism. He believed it ridiculous that the murderers, highwaymen and dervishes of popular tales should be refined into heroes fighting against imperialism and feudalism. Even worse were those folklorists who regarded the workings of the external world as parallel expressions of the spirit of Isis, believing that the more spontaneous art was, the closer it was to the latent spirit. While Halasā agreed that folklore was worthy of examination, he perceived it as a sociological rather than an aesthetical

59 L. 'Awaḍ's analysis in 'Hākadhā Yatakallamu al-Udabā' al-Shabāb', *al-Ṭalīʿa*, Sept. 1969, p. 76.

60 S. Khashaba, 'Jīl al-Sittīniyyāt fī al-Riwāya al-Miṣriyya', *Fuṣūl*, Vol. 2, no. 2, Jan.–March 1982, p. 122.

61 See also the brief comment on this trait in the 'Socialist Realism and Commitment' section of this chapter, p. 156.

62 S. Hafez, 'al-Uqṣūṣa al-Miṣriyya wa-l-Ḥadātha', *Gallery 68*, no. 7, Oct. 1969, p. 86; and Gh. Halasā, 'al-Adab al-Jadīd: Malāmiḥ wa-Ittijāhāt', *Gallery 68*, no. 6, April 1969, pp. 117–18.

phenomenon. He deplored what he termed the 'exaggerated appreciation of the artistic value of the popular arts, adding meanings and nuances that could not possibly have occurred in the mind of the popular artist'.[63]

Halasā had begun his article prudently, denouncing himself as an expert, warning against polarized distinctions and stressing that not all writers fell into the trends he identified, while other writers might fall into more than one. Yet in his discussion of folklore, he succumbed to the unscientific type of critique that he deplored in others. Not only did Halasā generalize about the intentions of folklorists, but, even worse, he failed to distinguish between the writer's use of elements from the popular heritage (with the intention of creating something new out of it) and the critic's often over-zealous analysis of the popular heritage (with the intention of discovering/creating something new in it). However, Halasā's attitude cannot be dismissed as just another conservative viewpoint among those regressive critics refusing to credit the folk arts with literary value. For by 1969, the tables had truly turned and folk arts had become the darling of the establishment. A chair for folk studies had for some time been in existence at Cairo University and the Ministry of Culture had even launched a specialist journal devoted to the folk arts, *al-Funūn al-Sha'biyya* (The Folk Arts, 1965–71). Thus Halasā's remarks were in fact going against the grain, and it is precisely this attitude of questioning the accepted which characterized *Gallery 68*. It is no surprise to find that Halasā's article aroused a storm of protest, with his remarks on the racism of Egyptian folklorists providing ammunition for those determined to see *Gallery 68* as the friend of Western imperialism. But, true to its aim of presenting all views and remaining open to debate, *Gallery 68* had itself published the kind of folkloric material Halasā attacked in the form of Sayyid Ḥijāb's detailed analyses of the rhythms of folk songs. In any case, as a forum for debate not propaganda, *Gallery 68* had taken care in its editorial to distance the journal from the views expressed in Halasā's article.[64]

In terms of sixties writers' attitude to their Arab literary heritage, all *Gallery 68* contributors who participated in *al-Ṭalī'a*'s survey of young writers acknowledged its value. Where the new–old debate raged fiercest was over the relationship of the sixties generation to its immediate literary predecessors. Ghālī Shukrī had written of this generational struggle in inflammatory terms, using war imagery: 'a new generation has surprised the literary movement by invading the arena of the short story, armed with modern youthful experience... The new generation has all but murdered traditional structure'.[65] But probably the most famous exposé of a clash of generations appeared as early as 1963 in the national press:

> Yesterday I shouted: O great ones, O masters! We are great, and masters too, make way! But they barred the way in my face. I have not uttered my words for nothing. They said that they were only ink on blotting

63 Gh. Halasā, ibid.

64 Editorial to *Gallery 68*, no. 6, April 1969.

65 Gh. Shukrī, *Ṣirā' al-Ajyāl* (1971), p. 111.

> paper. The truth is that we are writing what no one before us has written. No one has discovered the treasure that we have discovered. They have not seen the glitter of diamonds that we have seen.[66]

In reality, both Shukrī's and Rajab's statements were exceptionally radical rather than broadly representative. In fact, the critic, Ibrāhīm Fatḥī, was taken to task by a fellow member of the sixties generation – Hafez – for apparently accepting Rajab's controversial declaration, 'We are a generation without masters', in a study accompanying *Gallery 68*'s special short story selection. Hafez insisted that most modernist Egyptian trends were a continuation of old trends.[67] In fact, Fatḥī had merely emphasized that the contemporary short story was more than just an extension of past literary trends, whilst acknowledging that artistic revolutions can never completely sever ties to the past.[68]

Despite disagreement on the surface, most of *68*'s contributors were fundamentally in agreement that the present, however new and different, had been born of the past. But the shades of nuance within this general attitude give an indication of the complexities at risk of homogenization by the umbrella term 'sixties generation'. Khashaba distinguished between the 'rebellion' of some of the sixties generation's older writers, such as Rajab, and the 'disagreement' of younger writers such as Yaḥyā al-Ṭāhir 'Abd Allāh. The older writers felt true horror at the campaign against the communists and found the key to their rebellion in Western absurdism. Since younger writers were relatively remote from that horror, instead of rebelling as enemies, they disagreed as sons, and their rejection of conventional expression was more instinctive than contrived.[69] Khashaba's analysis goes some way to explaining varying attitudes but it is too prescriptive. While many writers among the sixties generation were repelled by the horror of the suppression of communists in the late 1950s and early 1960s, this was a horror shared by many writers among previous literary generations and cannot therefore be held responsible for antagonism between the generations. As for taking refuge in Western absurdism, this over-emphasizes one aspect of sixties literature and diverts attention from the fact that writers were reflecting Egyptian and Arab reality – as they perceived it. Moreover, Rajab himself claimed to have been totally uninfluenced by Western literature, having read next to none. In any case, Rajab was an extreme example of the rebel.

66 Muḥammad Ḥāfiẓ Rajab, *al-Jumhūriyya*, 3 Oct. 1963, p. 13.

67 S. Hafez, 'al-Uqṣūṣa al-Miṣriyya wa-l-Ḥadātha', *Gallery 68*, no. 7, Oct. 1969, p. 86.

68 Ibrāhīm Fatḥī, 'Malāmiḥ Mushtaraka fī al-Intāj al-Qiṣaṣī al-Jadīd', *Gallery 68*, no. 6, April 1969, pp. 111–12.

69 Conversation between S. Khashaba and Yūsuf Abū Rayya, in Yūsuf Abū Rayya, 'Mādha Baqiya min Yaḥyā?', *Khaṭwa*, no. 3, n. d. 1981? (special issue commemmorating Yaḥyā al-Ṭāhir 'Abd Allāh), p. 54.

It may be that some young writers were provoked to a more radical stance by the patronizing pronouncements of established men of letters, who were often unwilling or unable to judge new work on its own merits. Maḥmūd Taymur, for example, voiced his attitude towards new writers thus:

> I follow what they produce, but I whisper in their ears that exceeding the proper bounds is an infringement and I hope they will moderate the tendency to renewal and abstraction. I myself believe, and I hope every new writer also believes, that the creative man of letters is a mirror of life, a mirror of society.[70]

Tawfīq al-Ḥakīm too advised young writers – perhaps wisely – that they must allow themselves to be directed by the 'leading lights' before graduating to a more independent phase.[71] *Gallery 68* contributor Aḥmad Hāshim al-Sharīf later complained of 'official men of letters and their disciples opposing the new generation and inundating it with various accusations: exaggeration, obscurity, subjectivism and linguistic ignorance'.[72] This inter-generational antagonism is exemplified in an exchange between Shukrī 'Ayyād and Ghālī Shukrī. In response to the latter's complaints about the older generation monopolizing the cultural apparatus, 'Ayyād indignantly accused him of indulging in 'diseased self-pity' and reminded young writers that they should be grateful to the political authorities for allowing their elders to supervise the writers' grant scheme.[73]

While many established writers complained of the younger generation dismissing the work of previous generations without having read widely enough, the same might be said of the former dismissing the younger generation without having given their works a thorough perusal. The critic Sayyid Ḥāmid al-Nassāj recognized the younger generation of writers, intellectuals and critics as 'oppressed... for it is required to defend itself for a crime it has not committed... Those who accuse the new generation do not follow what it writes . . .'[74] Ibrāhīm Fatḥī complained in *Gallery 68* of the establishment's reluctance to publish new writers.[75] Ghālī Shukrī echoed these criticisms,[76] and indeed *al-Ṭalī'a*'s survey of young writers revealed an overwhelming dissatisfaction with the existing publication apparatus. It was not so much that sixties writers objected to the literary

70 Maḥmūd Ṭaymūr, in Rashīd al-Dhawwādī, *Aḥādīth fī al-Adab* (1986), pp. 118–19.

71 Tawfīq al-Ḥakīm, in Muḥammad Shalabī, *Ma' Ruwwād al-Fikr wa-l-Fann* (1982), p. 67. Shalabī's book is a collection of interviews conducted in the 1970s.

72 A. H. al-Sharīf, in M. al-Rāwī, *Udabā' al-Jīl* (1982), p. 33.

73 Gh. Shukrī, *Dhikrāyāt al-Jīl al-Ḍā'i'*. Cited in Sh. 'Ayyād, 'Hādhā al-Jīl al-Ḍā'i' ', in Ḥ. Mahrān (ed.) *Ghālī Shukrī: Dhākirat al-Jīl al-Ḍā'i'* (1996), p. 40.

74 Sayyid Ḥāmid al-Nassāj, in M. al-Rāwī, *Udabā' al-Jīl* (1982), p. 17.

75 I. Fatḥī, 'Malāmiḥ Mushtaraka fī al-Intāj al-Qiṣaṣī al-Jadīd', *Gallery 68*, no. 6, April 1969, p. 111.

76 Gh. Shukrī, *Dhikrāyāt al-Jīl al-Ḍā'i'*. Cited in Sh. 'Ayyād, 'Hādhā al-Jīl al-Ḍā'i' ', in Ḥ. Mahrān (ed.) *Ghālī Shukrī: Dhākirat al-Jīl al-Ḍā'i'* (1996), p. 40.

contribution of established writers; rather, they opposed what they perceived as the previous generation's unrelenting monopoly over the cultural apparatus. Aḥmad Hāshim al-Sharīf described the new generation as growing up 'distant from...the media which was monopolized by a group of official literary men. This is why the new generation started shouting in the sixties, demanding its right to express its existence'.[77]

To some extent, and perhaps inevitably, these claims of a publication crisis were exaggerated. Shukrī 'Ayyād responded in *al-Majalla*, stating that many works by young writers had in fact been published, criticized and discussed alongside traditional literary currents, and that the remarkable phenomenon of the past few years was that the literary far left had at last been able to reach the public.[78] Up to a point, 'Ayyād was justified – *al-Majalla* had itself published 4 of the 15 stories in *Gallery 68*'s special selection. Moreover, an anthology of stories selected for English translation included five *Gallery 68* writers with a foreword by the Egyptian Minister for Culture himself – and this already in 1968.[79] Khashaba too rejected the notion of publication crisis,[80] although he admitted that cultural institutions were obstructed by backwardness and bureaucracy, and generally lacked interest in proliferating specialist material, forcing some writers to publish in Beirut. Yet he believed that young writers themselves exacerbated the problem by failing to crystallize into distinct intellectual groups which would enable each group's most talented members to be put forward for publication.[81] This is in fact what *Gallery 68* intended to achieve, although it did not wish to define itself specifically and risk suffocating in its own intellectualism.

The views expressed by 'Ayyād and Khashaba were broadly representative. Al-Sayyid Yass, writing in *al-Kātib* (The Writer, 1961–80), echoed 'Ayyād's rejection of a publication crisis, pointing out that only 5 of the 30 writers in *al-Ṭalī'a*'s survey of young writers remained unpublished.[82] Yūsuf Idrīs testified to hypocrisy on both sides of the debate but basically thought that new writers were receiving a great deal of attention from the literary establishment.[83]

77 A. H. al-Sharīf, in M. al-Rāwī, *Udabā' al-Jīl* (1982), p. 33.

78 Sh. 'Ayyād, 'al-Qiṣṣa al-Miṣriyya al-Mu'āṣira: 'Adad Khāṣṣ fī Majallat *68*, April 1969', *al-Majalla*, June 1969, p. 94.

79 Idwār al-Kharrāṭ, Ghālib Halasā, Sulaymān Fayyāḍ, Majīd Ṭūbyā and Muḥammad Ḥāfiẓ Rajab, in Mahmoud al-Manzalaoui, *Arabic Writing Today* (1968).

80 *Dār al-Kātib al-'Arabī*'s new series *Kitābāt Jadīda* (New Writings) was intended principally to publish the work of young writers; *al-Jumhūriyya* newspaper published a story weekly and had until recently done so daily; *al-Masā', al-Majalla, Ṣabāḥ al-Khayr, Rūz al-Yūsuf, Ākhar Sā'a*, and *al-Idhā'a wa-l-Tilīvizyūn* all regularly published stories; and *Nādī al-Qiṣṣa*, despite its shortcomings, still played host to literary activity. S. Khashaba, 'al-Nash'a al-Thaqāfiyya fī al-Waṭan al-'Arabī', *al-Ādāb*, Dec. 1969, pp. 58–61.

81 S. Khashaba's analysis in 'Hākadhā Yatakallamu al-Udabā' al-Shabāb', *al-Ṭalī'a*, Sept. 1969, p. 65.

82 al-Sayyid Yass, 'al-Shahādāt al-Wāqi'iyya li-l-Udabā' al-Shabāb', *al-Kātib*, Nov. 1969.

83 Yūsuf Idrīs, 'Sū' Tashkhīs li-Amrāḍ al-Ḥaraka al-Thaqāfiyya fī Miṣr', *al-Masā'*, 16 Aug. 1982.

Both Badr al-Dīb and Fārūq Khūrshīd actually complained of a surplus of stories by immature young writers, even in the culturally lean years of the 1970s, and Khūrshīd confirmed, 'In our day, our elders would never allow us to publish our first attempts'.[84] Suhayr al-Qalamāwī, Mahfouz, Yass and Hafez all believed that it was poor quality that ultimately prevented a work from being published.[85]

Yet one must beware of tainting all young writers with the same brush. There were clearly those published whose work did not merit such attention, and part of the problem was that, with so many young writers competing for limited space, some would succumb to writing what the editorial boards might favour. The result of this would be that – in general – the more experimental innovators would indeed be the ones to lose out. Hafez, in a panel discussion, had in fact raised the issue of publishers' inability to understand new literary forms.[86] Moreover, al-Qalamāwī, Mahfouz, and Hafez all admitted to difficulties posed by obstacles in the cultural system, with al-Qalamāwī testifying to the financial and bureaucratic anarchy that reigned in the publication apparatus.[87] Mahfouz went further, offering strong criticism of government policy when he excused the unpalatable nature of some new literature by comparing the writer's situation to that of 'someone who wants to burn candles in a sealed room full of carbon dioxide. The problem is not with the candles but with the atmosphere which puts out the candles'.[88]

It is clear that 'the new literature' continued to spark abundant talk of a crisis in the short story but that this notion of a crisis actually entangled four separate strands. The perception of the crisis varied dramatically between different writers and critics, often according to their literary age and experience, but the main interpretations may be reduced to the following:

1 quality works of new literature were being produced but encountered a hostile publishing establishment;
2 there were few quality works being produced, a view that implied a somewhat negative approach to much of the new literature;

84 Badr al-Dīb and Fārūq Khūrshīd, *al-Kātib*, Nov. 1975. Cited in R. Allen, 'Egyptian Drama and Fiction in the 1970s', *Edebiyat*, Vol. 1, no. 2, 1976, pp. 229–30.

85 N. Mahfouz, in R. al-Dhawwādī, *Aḥādīth fī al-Adab* (1986), p. 35; S. al-Qalamāwī's analysis in 'Hākadhā Yatakallamu al-Udabā' al-Shabāb', *al-Ṭalī'a*, Sept. 1969, p. 67; al-Sayyid Yass, 'al-Shahādāt al-Wāqi'iyya li-l-Udabā' al-Shabāb', *al-Kātib*, Nov. 1969; S. Hafez, 'Naẓra fī Ba'ḍ Majmū'āt 1968 al-Qiṣaṣiyya', *al-Majalla*, March 1969, p. 62.

86 S. Hafez in *al-Majalla*'s panel discussion on the contemporary situation in Arabic fiction, *al-Majalla*, June 1968, p. 10.

87 S. al-Qalamāwī's analysis in 'Hākadhā Yatakallamu al-Udabā' al-Shabāb', *al-Ṭalī'a*, Sept. 1969, p. 67.

88 N. Mahfouz, in A. H. al-Sharīf, *Naguib Mahfouz: Muḥāwarāt Qabl Nobel* (1989), p. 33.

3 writers of new literature were being accorded too much attention at the expense of other more worthy writers;
4 censorship of the new literature was hampering literary development. Indeed, *Gallery 68* had its own run-in with the censor[89] and *Gallery 68* contributor Ghālī Shukrī's book about the generation clash was massacred by the censor.[90]

Others intellectuals, while allowing to differing degrees that the cultural scene had its shortcomings, believed that to talk of a crisis was an exaggeration (but they still talked about it anyway!).

Some kind of clash of generations was an inevitable result of the introduction of radically new styles and techniques. *Al-Ṭalī'a* in fact recognized this and made a point of welcoming the clash as a positive and natural factor in the evolution of literary taste.[91] The antagonism between generations was, however, exacerbated by the media tendency to oversimplify and exaggerate. A discussion between Aḥmad Ḥijāzī and Lūwīs 'Awaḍ, recorded in *Ṣabāḥ al-Khayr* was given exaggeratedly negative subtitles, which could serve only to inflame debate. Among them were the following: 'The literature of the young is neither serious nor profound', 'It is not a generation struggle but an attempt to destroy the Greats' and 'I shall not write about them for I have more important work to do'. Yet the body of dialogue showed Lūwīs 'Awaḍ, at least, to be more sympathetic towards young writers, regarding them as rising talents on their way to maturity;[92] and, elsewhere, 'Awaḍ had been at pains to distinguish between the pretentious minority and the genuine majority of young writers.[93] Likewise, interviews tended to favour a confrontational line of questioning. Take for example Rashīd al-Dhawwādī's simplistic, 'Are you a supporter of the literature of the old or the young?'.[94]

In fact, *Gallery 68* encouraged writers to regard such superficial categorization with a more discerning eye. For example, a translated article on Kafka, Gogol and

89 *Gallery 68*'s license was revoked after the third issue, apparently owing to an article rebelling against grammatical rules. Khashaba took a bleak view of the effects of this censorship, concluding that it had served to increase the negative and cliquey attitude of *Gallery 68* to the extent that it was lost intellectually forever. S. Khashaba, 'al-Nash'a al-Thaqāfiyya fī al-Waṭan al-'Arabī', *al-Ādāb*, Dec. 1969.

90 Shukrī's *Ṣirā' al-Ajyāl* (1971) was missing the last three chapters, the introduction and half of the title. The complete book was not published for another six years, and then in Beirut not Cairo. Gh. Shukrī, *al-'Anqā' al-Jadīda: Ṣirā' al-Ajyāl* (1977), p. 10.

91 'Taqārīr al-Shahr: al-Adab', *al-Ṭalī'a*, June 1968.

92 'Abd al-Ḥakīm Qāsim complained about *Ṣabāḥ al-Khayr*'s portrayal of the discussion in his response to *al-Ṭalī'a*'s questionnaire, 'Hākadhā Yatakallamu al-Udabā' al-Shabāb', *al-Ṭalī'a*, Sept. 1969, p. 21.

93 L. 'Awaḍ's analysis in 'Hākadhā Yatakallamu al-Udabā' al-Shabāb', *al-Ṭalī'a*, Sept. 1969, p. 69.

94 R. al-Dhawwādī, *Aḥādīth fī al-Adab* (1986), p. 118. This book is a collection of interviews with Egyptian writers, conducted in the early 1980s.

Nathaniel West, despite glaring shortcomings, reminded readers that there was no simple delineation between new and old: while a modern writer like Kafka was deemed old in terms of content and technique, a writer 'from the previous age' like Gogol might in fact be viewed as modern.[95] Moreover, sixties writers' insistence on the validity and novelty of their own new forms and techniques did not presuppose a hostility towards older writers. When we examine those of the twenty-nine young short story writers surveyed by *al-Ṭalīʻa* who told of their feelings of anger, we discover that this anger was not necessarily directed at the older generation of writers. Both ʻAbd al-Ḥakīm Qāsim and Aḥmad Hāshim al-Sharīf wrote of their anger at their unfruitful relationship with their own generation. Artist and *Gallery 68* editor Ḥasan Sulaymān, writing in 1980 with hindsight, lamented the fact that calls for generational equality had shifted the role of support from established men of letters to the financial power of governments or large organizations.[96] Indeed, during the Conference of Young Writers in December 1969, we find many young writers apparently coexisting amicably with older writers on committees headed by established men of letters. No wonder that Muḥammad al-Rāwī was prompted to wonder, 'Is this crisis – the struggle between generations – real or artifical?'. In fact, al-Rāwī's own interviews with Egyptian writers revealed that while the new was firm about its points of departure, it still embraced the old.[97] There are questions as to how close to the establishment the writers dealt with by al-Rāwī were, but we can still surmise that the generational conflict was, at times, overstated.

Acknowledging the contribution of past literary generations, however, did not mean acceptance of traditional structures, and *68*'s writers were keen to assert their independence. Some of those most aware of the work of past generations, like Majīd Ṭūbyā, Ibrāhīm Manṣūr and Aḥmad Hāshim al-Sharīf, were also those to reject traditional structures most resoundingly. This desire for independence, to start afresh and deal with Egypt's changed reality, was expressed most clearly in an article by the young writer Khalīl Kalfat, significantly using an image from the Western heritage:

> The stables of Aegeus, in which the filth of the long history of all forms of slavery had accumulated, were waiting for the arrival of Hercules carrying the broom of history. Hercules is agitating at the heart of a new young stormy spirit that is dawning in Egypt.[98]

The main difference between the new generation and its predecessor has been defined by Luṭfī al-Khūlī as follows: the previous generation had started in the

95 Idrīs Bey (trans. Shawqi Fahim), 'Kafka, Gogol and Nathaniel West', *Gallery 68*, no. 4, Nov. 1968.
96 Ḥasan Sulaymān, *Ḥurriyyat al-Fannān*, p. 17.
97 M. al-Rāwī's interviews, conducted in the journal *al-Miṣbāḥ* in the early 1980s, were collected into a book: *Udabāʼ al-Jīl* (1982).
98 Khalīl Kalfat, 'Mulāḥaẓāt Ḥawla Kuttāb *68*', *Gallery 68*, no. 7, Oct. 1969, p. 80.

political arena and turned to literature as an indirect means of opposition. Content therefore dominated over form and technique, and their literature was 'more action than expression'. Conversely, the sixties generation had been born into the literary field and drawn ever closer to the political one. Therefore, while they agreed on the unity of form and content, the new generation's technique dominated over the actual message, and their literature was 'more expression than action'.[99] This is, of course, an oversimplification, but one can generalize that *68*'s contributors laid more emphasis on expression. In fact, much of the difference between the generations can be reduced to this lowest common denominator. It was natural that *68*'s contributors should share many of the previous generation's fears and concerns, since both were products of the same historical continuum; the basic point of difference lay in the way in which these concerns were expressed. Yet this difference was significant enough to shift the emphasis from Laṭīfa al-Zayyāt and Luṭfī al-Khūlī's descriptions of the new generation as an extension of forties and fifties writers[100] onto the new generation as a departure from its predecessors. Probably the most flagrant departure over which feelings ran highest was the changing attitude towards – or, more specifically, the changing modes of expression of – socialist realism and commitment.

Socialist realism and commitment

Debate about 'commitment' (*al-iltizām*) and 'socialist realism' (*al-wāqi'iyya al-ishtirākiyya*) continued to thrive in the mid-1960s with the release of many leftist intellectuals from prison; and with the 1967 defeat, nationalist feelings and burning anger endowed the term *iltizām* with an increasingly militant and anti-Israeli interpretation in many quarters. Judging from the responses to *al-Ṭalī'a*'s survey of sixties writers, many shared the concerns of the committed writers of the 1950s. While stressing the fact that literary creativity had moved on, calling the previous generation 'emaciated ghosts',[101] Aḥmad Hāshim al-Sharīf identified his generation's experience of the 1967 defeat with the previous generation's experience of the 1948 defeat.[102] And 'Abd al-Ḥakīm Qāsim told of a visit he paid Yūsuf Idrīs at *al-Jumhūriyya*, discovering to his surprise that Idrīs was a kindred spirit, tortured by similar crises and contradictions.[103] However, Yūsuf Idrīs himself

99 L. al-Khūlī's analysis in 'Hākadhā Yatakallamu al-Udabā' al-Shabāb', *al-Ṭalī'a*, Sept. 1969, p. 84.

100 Laṭīfa al-Zayyāt's and L. al-Khūlī's analyses in 'Hākadhā Yatakallamu al-Udabā' al-Shabāb', *al-Ṭalī'a*, Sept. 1969.

101 A. H. al-Sharīf's response to *al-Ṭalī'a's* questionnaire, 'Hākadhā Yatakallamu al-Udabā' al-Shabāb', *al-Ṭalī'a*, Sept. 1969.

102 A. H. al-Sharīf, response to questionnaire, M. al-Rāwī, *Udabā' al-Jīl* (1982), p. 33.

103 'Abd al-Ḥakīm Qāsim's response to *al-Ṭalī'a's* questionnaire, 'Hākadhā Yatakallamu al-Udabā' al-Shabāb', *al-Ṭalī'a*, Sept. 1969.

allegedly confided his opinion of short story writers of the sixties generation to Yūsuf Abū Rayya as follows:

> I alone am the best writer in the world . . . The source of the deviation that occurred [in the short story in the sixties] is that they wrote about tragic heroes. The Egyptian reader does not like this kind of writing, for his mood is not tragic . . . Therefore they have accused me of casting my shadow over two generations in the story, but what fault is it of mine if the writer cannot see inside himself?[104]

It is clear that, despite some similarities, the modernist developments encouraged through *Gallery 68* marked a true departure from the generation of Yūsuf Idrīs. After more than a decade's domination of socialist realist and committed literature, the focus of *Gallery 68*'s contributors on portraying the individual rather than society at large and employing modernist techniques, disruptive to the familiar view of external reality, naturally provoked a good deal of hostile reaction.

The new literary forms and techniques which were gaining currency, particularly among those who were to contribute to *Gallery 68*, forced critics into either reinterpreting or defending entrenched definitions of the now generally accepted and ubiquitous terms: 'commitment' and 'socialist realism'. Part of the problem was that commitment, in Egypt at least, had become generally synonymous with a direct style of socialist realism. Yet the sixties generation's abandonment of the old transparent socialist realism sprang from their disillusionment, despair and frustration at their own powerlessness in the face of the establishment, feelings which had actually arisen out of a sense of commitment to society and the nation, and to truth. Underlying their negative portrayal of contemporary reality was a hope for the future. However, for *Gallery 68*'s contributors, the prevailing thought systems of socialism and Marxism had lost their power to authenticate or sanction the literary work. One can generalize that *68*'s contributors were leftists, but their leftism – in general – evolved as much out of their own experience of reality, culminating in the 1967 defeat at the hands of the 'new imperialism', as from a pure and specific intellectual commitment. This did not mean that they as individuals necessarily rejected socialism or Marxism, nor even that they necessarily condemned approaching the literary work through a specifically socialist or Marxist worldview. It was simply that these beliefs were no longer considered prescriptive for literature because, in their view, literature arose from interaction with reality rather than the purely mimetic reflection of a particular reality. As *Gallery 68* critic Ibrahīm Fatḥī subsequently concluded, 'they sought to redefine

104 Conversation between Y. Idrīs and Y. Abū Rayya, in Y. Abū Rayya, 'Mādhā Baqiya min Yaḥyā?', *Khaṭwa*, no. 3, n.d. 1981? (special issue commemmorating Yaḥyā al-Ṭāhir 'Abd Allāh), pp. 51–2.

reality away from both the right and the old left which had become part of the establishment'.[105]

Gallery 68 provided a crucial forum for further development of the debate, particularly given the reluctance of official organs to publish Marxist critique. The key exchanges were between Ghālib Halasā and Ibrāhīm Fatḥī (who had been blacklisted from publication since 1967), and Ra'ūf Naẓmī and Ghālī Shukrī, and these appeared alongside the kind of literature that had stirred the debate. Ghālī Shukrī, writing in *Gallery 68*, frankly advocated a Marxist cultural revolution and, elsewhere, he had described socialism as 'the system of freedom, progress and peace'.[106] Yet he remained highly critical of socialist realism. He stressed that the artistic and literary world was neither a supplement to nor a reflection of the philosophical and political worlds. Rather, it was an equal, able to discover its own unique laws whilst retaining the right to interact with the latter worlds and their struggles.[107] Keen to stir debate, *Gallery 68* published Shukrī's article – uncompromisingly entitled 'We have Bidden Farewell to Zdanov for the Last Time' – alongside Ra'ūf Naẓmī's challenge to which Shukrī was responding. Naẓmī insisted that socialism had to be every poet's point of departure, believing that the poet was obliged to fight alongside the masses to conquer imperialist exploitation.[108] The debate was not as black and white as it had been in the 1950s, for Shukrī and Naẓmī had many socialist beliefs in common. In fact, they had shared a cell, together with others, after being imprisoned for their beliefs in 1966. What Shukrī disagreed with was Naẓmī taking Zdanov's teachings as his point of departure, for these constituted a Stalinist approach to literature, 'a gross simplification of the Marxist theory of art'. Shukrī understood the Marxist theory to centre on man's relationship with nature, in which the social struggle represented merely one phase; civilization was the content of poetry, and society was only one element of civilization.[109]

Ghālib Halasā, whose own strong socialist credentials were well known, was another fierce critic of socialist realist critique. He upbraided critics like Maḥmūd Amīn al-'Ālim for failing to define the nature of the relationship between art and philosophy, seeing only philosophy in art. He censured al-'Ālim's recent criticism (in the high profile *al-Ahrām*) of alienation in Jamāl al-Ghīṭānī's work, accusing al-'Ālim of focusing on the sentiments expressed in a literary work instead of on the aesthetics of that work. Halasā warned of the dangers of such partisan critique: 'Any serious critical movement with an agenda has the power to create or kill a literary movement in its entirety'.[110] In fact, al-'Ālim did eventually

105 Hala Ḥalīm, 'Ibrāhīm Fatḥī: Curbstone Critic', *al-Ahram Weekly*, no. 602, 5–11 Sept. 2002. Online. Available HTTP: http://weekly.ahram.org.eg/2002/602/profile.htm

106 Gh. Shukrī, *Shi'ru-nā al-Ḥadīth ilā Ayn?* (1968), p. 215.

107 Gh. Shukrī, 'Wadda'-nā Zdanov ilā Ghayr Raj'a', *Gallery 68*, no. 5, Feb. 1969, pp. 67–70.

108 R. Naẓmī, ' 'An *Shi'ru-nā al-Ḥadīth ilā Ayn?*', *Gallery 68*, no. 5, Feb. 1969, p. 65.

109 Gh. Shukrī, 'Wadda'-nā Zdanov ilā Ghayr Raj'a', *Gallery 68*, Feb. 1969, pp. 67–70.

110 Gh. Halasā, 'al-Adab al-Jadīd: Malāmiḥ wa-Ittijāhāt', *Gallery 68*, no. 6, April 1969, p. 124.

modify his critical stance to admit the importance of an aesthetical evaluation of the literary work.[111] Yet Halasā fell into the widespread habit of criticizing other critics and calling for more rigorous critical analysis without actually constructively entering into theoretical debate. His follow-up article in *Gallery 68*, 'On Philosophy and Aesthetics', did not live up to its title, being largely a reiteration of his previous article on new literary trends. Only 1 of the 10 pages tackled the title subject, explaining weakly that literature or criticism based directly on ideology was wrong because the subordination of reality to theory led to extremism. Yet, even more so than Shukrī, Halasā employed a socialist lexicon and political argumentation to make his point. Like Shukrī, he criticized the Stalinist approach, but unlike Shukrī, his argumentation was rather analogous and vague. For example, he argued that, in politics, the subordination of reality to theoretical principles resulted in a police state controlling previously democratic institutions and that this had been Stalin's mistake. While Halasā insisted that the aesthetics of a literary work was of greater relevance than whether a work was judged under the Stalinist approach as regressive or progressive, his proof was tenuous: he simply pointed out that the latter evaluation must be flawed since Einstein's theory of relativity was dismissed as regressive but later found to be true and therefore progressive. As in his previous article, Halasā pleaded lack of space and promised to deal with the relationship between philosophy and aesthetics in future articles[112] (which did not, however, materialize within the framework of *Gallery 68*).

Halasā's critique may be viewed in a more positive light if one allows that his overtly political terminology might have been calculated to appeal to the supporters of socialist realism whom he was trying to persuade, that space was indeed limited, and that a simple approach to aesthetics might have had more effect at this early stage. That the latter disclaimer was to some extent true is indicated by the fact that Khalīl Kalfat too, in a special insertion in his *Gallery 68* article entitled 'The Story of Aesthetics', ventured a few of his own brief and extremely simple observations about what constituted aesthetics, a term that was gaining in popularity. Kalfat merely noted that aesthetics was not static, that philosophy, politics and ideology were 'not far removed from it' and that, like other sciences, it could have different classes: 'the proletariat has a Marxist aesthetics while international imperialism has a bourgeois aesthetics'.[113] A decade later in the avant-garde journal launched by the poets of the Illumination group (*Iḍā'a 77*), the term 'aesthetics' (*'ilm al-jamāl*) was to be bandied about tirelessly.

111 This is outlined in the introduction to the 1989 edition of his seminal work *Fī al-Thaqāfa al-Miṣriyya* (First edition 1955) which became the Marxist manifesto for literary criticism. See Maḥmūd Ghanayim, 'Maḥmūd Amīn al-'Ālim: Between Politics and Literary Criticism', *Poetics Today*, Vol. 15, no. 2, Summer 1994, pp. 321–38.

112 Gh. Halasā, ''An al-Falsafa wa-'Ilm al-Jamāl', *Gallery 68*, no. 7, Oct. 1969.

113 Kh. Kalfat, 'Mulāḥaẓāt Ḥawla Kuttāb *68*', *Gallery 68*, no. 7, Oct. 1969, pp. 77–8.

Ibrāhīm Fatḥī succeeded in making more impressive use of the space afforded him in *Gallery 68*. Fatḥī's refutation of the excesses of socialist realism was more logical than that of Halasā, and he was clearer in isolating various components of the socialist realist approach. Fatḥī argued that all artists viewed reality through a theory, whether consciously or subconsciously, and that the artist should not have to strive to rid himself of an ideological perspective any more than he should seek to adhere to one. This contrasted starkly with the convictions of artist Ḥasan Sulaymān who insisted that for the artist to penetrate to the truth of reality, he needed to be free from preconceived rigid thought patterns.[114] At first glance, Halasā too appeared to advocate such cleansing and, indeed, Fatḥī accused Halasā of robbing the artist of his right to view reality through a specific philosophical theory, and of writing about aesthetics as if it were physics or chemistry. Like Kalfat, Fatḥī regarded aesthetics as a more fluid science which could not be viewed in isolation from general social and intellectual trends. However, Halasā too had allowed that ideology might influence one's aesthetics; what he had disputed was that aesthetics be replaced by politics and philosophy and applied directly to the literary work.[115] In short, the disagreement between Halasā and Fatḥī was simply a matter of emphasis: Halasā emphasized the technical aspects of aesthetics while Fatḥī emphasized its intellectual aspects. But as for Halasā's declaration that a work should be judged only on its 'artistic excellence and absence of manifest treachery', Fatḥī rightly questioned the logic of giving up socialist realist critique for such woolly concepts.[116]

It was not so much the portrayal of working class realities with which *Gallery 68*'s contributors disagreed; it was the static socialist realist approach to this portrayal. In fact, both Ghālib Halasā and Sabry Hafez, writing in *Gallery 68*, identified a new kind of socialist realism as one of the principal trends of the new literature. Hafez stressed that its development from the simplistic leftist literature of the 1950s made it 'almost a new trend',[117] and Halasā offered a new broad definition of this trend: socialist realism is practiced by the artist whose thoughts and outlook are formed by commitment to the nation; he is able to rise above alienation in order to portray it; socialist realism does not have definitive features but recognizes that all sound styles are able to express human experience.[118] This looser definition meant that the new socialist realism could incorporate all the other trends and styles. Halasā therefore believed it was able in theory to absorb reality more completely than other trends, although it had not yet evolved

114 Ḥ. Sulaymān, untitled, *Gallery 68*, no. 1, April-May 1968, p. 29. This was reiterated later in his book *Ḥurriyyat al-Fannān*, pp. 14–16.

115 Gh. Halasā, ''An al-Falsafa wa-'Ilm al-Jamāl', *Gallery 68*, no. 7, Oct. 1969, p. 82.

116 I. Fatḥī, 'Ba'ḍ al-Masā'il al-'Āmma fī al-Naqd', *Gallery 68*, no. 7, Oct. 1969. NB In 1967, Fatḥī had found himself blacklisted from publication owing to his Marxist views. Thus *Gallery 68* was a vital forum for furthering the debate over Marxism and aesthetics.

117 S. Hafez, 'al-Uqṣūṣa al-Miṣriyya wa-l-Ḥadātha', *Gallery 68*, no. 7, Oct. 1969, p. 85.

118 Gh. Halasā, 'al-Adab al-Jadīd: Malāmiḥ wa-Ittijāhāt', *Gallery 68*, no. 6, April 1969.

sufficiently to supersede other trends in this. So, while the ideological link to former socialist realism remained, *Gallery 68* contributors like Sulaymān Fayyāḍ and 'Abd al-Ḥakīm Qāsim had reached far beyond the idea of the exemplary hero. They illuminated all aspects of the human soul, negative as well as positive, and social problems were raised as a framework for more universal human issues. Their stories relied on situations rather than events, incorporating opaque symbols in an enlightening rather than obscure way. They rid socialist realism of its lyrical remnants, its inflexibly realistic treatment of events and its 'ridiculous devotion to the people'.[119] Hence the relevance of the seemingly contradictory description of Sulaymān Fayyāḍ as 'one of the avant-garde among committed Arab story writers'.[120]

Muḥammad al-Bisāṭī too appears to have developed a more experimental kind of socialist realism dating from the *Gallery 68* period. His first collection *al-Kibār wa-l-Ṣighār* (The Old and The Young/The Great and The Insignificant, written 1960–1, published 1968) was closer to the straight forward socialist realism prevalent in the 1950s. *Gallery 68*, in its second issue, published one of the stories from this collection alongside an article by Ghālib Halasā offering his constructive criticism of the collection. That al-Bisāṭī's story, which was more conservative than those of many other *Gallery 68* contributors, should be accorded so much attention so early on in *Gallery 68*'s life stresses that much of the new literature retained a concern for working class realities and was a valid development from the old, but without resorting to 'the stony heroes of artificial socialist realism'.[121] At the same time, the inclusion of al-Bisāṭī's work provided an opportunity to appreciate and distinguish between different levels of avant-garde activity within the same generation. Al-Bisāṭī succeeded in diversifying his literary world in issues six and seven of *Gallery 68*, and his second collection *Ḥadīth min al-Ṭābiq al-Thālith* (Conversation from the Third Floor, 1970) was much more innovative than his first. The influential role of al-Bisāṭī's work was later recognized in the avant-garde journal *Miṣriyya* in the 1980s.[122]

This 'reinterpretation' of socialist realism does not mean that *Gallery 68* did not also witness a more radical reaction against the former socialist realism. Halasā actually identified a reaction against socialist realism as one of five principal trends in the new literature: the politically disillusioned writer saw the world as ridiculous, and responded to every artistic idea and stance with mockery and ridicule. Halasā disapproved of this arrogant trend, which he believed regarded itself as the only source of great literature, and warned that 'contempt alone cannot be transformed into art'. He described this negative reaction as 'the

119 Gh. Halasā, 'al-Adab al-Jadīd: Malāmiḥ wa-Ittijāhāt', *Gallery 68*, no. 6, April 1969.

120 From the back cover of Sulaymān Fayyāḍ's *Wafāt 'Āmil Maṭba'a* (1984).

121 Gh. Halasā, '*al-Kibār wa-l-Ṣighār*', *Gallery 68*, no. 2, June 1968, p. 43.

122 See for example, Muḥammad Kashīk's ''Alāmāt al-Taḥdīth fī al-Qiṣṣa al-Miṣriyya al-Qaṣīra', *Miṣriyya*, no. 6, Jan. 1984, p. 23.

poorest of the new literary trends with the least to contribute, but it is the most radical of them and shouts the loudest'. Halasā regarded the stories of Ibrāhīm Manṣūr and Ibrāhīm 'Abd al-'Āṭī as representative of this trend, for they were characterized by mockery of the socialist realist lexicon, rapid transferral from an alienated view of the world to joking and defamation, and concentration on human spontaneity to try to portray a natural person rather than a steadfast revolutionary.[123]

By identifying new socialist realism first of the five new trends, by deeming it able to absorb all the other trends and hence more able to comprehend reality, and by characterizing another of the new trends only negatively, as a reaction against socialist realism instead of positively on its own merits, Halasā has indicated to what extent social and political ideology still loomed large for many critics as well as writers. While Halasā stressed that art should not be a mere vehicle for politics or morals, he still believed that 'all great literature is progressive and serves the human cause' and he was well known for his own passionate belief in socialism. The objections raised to Halasā's article indicate that even his stance was perceived by some as a betrayal rather than a revision of socialist principles. In fact, that many critics and writers continued to advocate a belief in the strong social and political role of literature is indicated by the conference of young writers at the end of 1969. The opening manifesto advised young writers to resist 'diseased indulgence in subjectivity' and the closing recommendations stressed that the writer's work should demonstrate commitment to socialism since this reflected the reality of contemporary society. The conference also concluded that writers should be more actively involved in the war with Israel. In fact, the conference was intentionally held in the eastern province of al-Zaqāziq in order to be near the bullets at the Eastern front. Writers were advised to visit the battle front and to undertake their avant-garde role within the framework of war committees.[124]

Indeed, the view that literature should be directly socially and politically involved was surprisingly entrenched. While the 1967 defeat shocked *68*'s contributors in general into moving further away from the prevalent style of socialist realism and commitment, it prompted others to advocate this kind of overt political commitment even more strongly. The strength of feeling was demonstrated by 'Abd al-'Azīz al-Ahwānī who, writing in *al-Kātib*, cast doubt on the relevance of the art of fiction itself on the grounds that it depleted the ranks of political writers. He considered fiction to be mere escapism and a poor substitute for reality, even where he deemed the style realistic.[125] Indeed Yaḥyā Ḥaqqī was moved to publish a defence of fiction in *al-Majalla*, lamenting the fact that fiction had

123 Gh. Halasā, 'al-Adab al-Jadīd: Malāmiḥ wa-Ittijāhāt', *Gallery 68*, no. 6, April 1969.

124 Reports on the First Conference of Young Writers, al-Zaqāziq, 4–8 Dec. 1969, *al-Kātib*, Jan. 1970 and *al-Majalla*, Jan. 1970.

125 'Abd al-'Azīz al-Ahwānī, 'al-Siyāsa wa-Fann al-Qiṣṣa', *al-Kātib*, Dec. 1967, pp. 7–9.

gained connotations of distortion and deception, since it was the truth factor which distinguished it from non-fiction. He complained of the sad situation where serious, intelligent, virile men were not supposed to read stories, and where it was no longer enough to be a mere writer, one also had to be a social reformer. This attitude was attributed to the reader's refusal to face up to harsh realities in the lives of others. While non-fiction enabled the flat absorption of facts, fiction enabled the reader to empathize more completely with his fellow men, to penetrate from the surface to the depths of the human psyche. Ḥaqqī's article concluded that the task of literature was to provoke questions, not to answer them, for answers do not endure.[126] This accorded with *Gallery 68*'s aim of stirring up debate and searching for the truth, whilst recognizing that an ultimate truth cannot be attained because contemporary reality does not endure.

Nevertheless, the prevalence of the negative view of fiction which Ḥaqqī condemned is indicated by the difficulties encountered in convincing *al-Ṭalīʻa* to launch a literary supplement. A minority within *al-Ṭalīʻa*, including Laṭīfa al-Zayyāt, Luṭfī al-Khūlī and Ghālī Shukrī, had pressed for a literary supplement from its very beginning in 1965, but were opposed by the majority led by ʻAbd al-Rāziq Ḥasan. The minority had been allowed to publish critical articles on art and literature, but only as socio-cultural phenomena with political significance. The majority within *al-Ṭalīʻa* had maintained that literary matters that did not contribute directly to the struggle for socialism were of little interest.[127] For example, an article praising the modernist techniques of *Gallery 68* contributors Ibrāhīm Aṣlān, Yaḥyā al-Ṭāhir ʻAbd Allāh, Majīd Ṭūbyā, Muḥammad al-Bisāṭī and Jamāl al-Ghīṭānī began with the qualifying remark that contemporary literary endeavours were evaluated by 'the truth of our bloody struggle against Zionist and American aggression, and against other social relationships which were to blame for the 5th of June defeat'.[128] *Al-Ṭalīʻa* did not in fact launch a literary supplement until 1972,[129] and even two years later, *al-Ṭalīʻa's* panel discussion on the crisis of Egyptian culture in 1974 might have be mistaken for a discourse on the merits of socialism.[130]

Part of the problem was that socialist realist critique, although it existed alongside socialist realist literature, had arisen independent of such literature. Ibrāhīm Fatḥī wrote that, in Egypt, the rise of socialist realist critique actually preceded the rise of socialist realist literature, having sprung from the victory of socialist realism on the world stage and its association with several famous writers.[131]

126 Yaḥyā Ḥaqqī, 'al-Adab al-Qiṣaṣī al-Yawma', *al-Majalla*, June 1970. Ḥaqqī took this from a contemporary article in the *Times Literary Supplement* by Richard Hughes.

127 *al-Ṭalīʻa*, Jan. 1972, pp. 147–8.

128 'Ẓilāl Azmat 5 Yūniyū wa-l-Qiṣṣa al-Qaṣīra al-Miṣriyya', *al-Ṭalīʻa*, March 1971.

129 *al-Ṭalīʻa*, Jan. 1972, pp. 147–8.

130 *al-Ṭalīʻa*, Dec. 1974, pp. 147–56.

131 I. Fatḥī, 'al-Wāqiʻiyya al-Ishtirākiyya', *al-Thaqāfa*, July 1964.

Writing in *Gallery 68*, Fatḥī admitted that socialist realism had succeeded in 'saving the artist from the abyss of sickly subjectivism', but he complained that 'the critical lexicon which served this school when it was active has become general property'.[132] As such, many critics applied socialist realist critique even to that literature to which it was obviously irrelevant.

For example, soon after *Gallery 68*'s special selection of short stories and the ensuing survey of young writers in *al-Ṭalīʻa*, 'Abd al-Munʻim 'Abd al-Ḥalīm al-Hawwārī, in a letter to *al-Ṭalīʻa*, attacked obscurity in much of the new literature for failing to serve the aims of the nation. He concluded that the world which such work portrayed was lifted from European literature and was only relevant for a capitalist society with a high literacy rate. Apart from the fact that the literacy rate is of no relevance, given that 'obscure' or difficult literature is read primarily by the intellectual elite in any society, al-Hawwārī was also ignoring the fact that reality could be just as complex in a socialist society as in a capitalist one. Al-Hawwārī also attributed the obscurity of new forms and techniques to lack of courage, as if this were a shameful discovery.[133] However, many writers frankly – one might even say courageously – admitted to their fear. For example, of the stories published in the subsequent issue of *Gallery 68*, Ghālib Halasā's was actually entitled 'Fear', while Yūsuf al-Shārūnī clearly showed that his protagonist was wholly motivated by fear, drawing attention to this fact by ending with a one-line postscript which had not appeared in the previous version of this story: 'I fear, therefore I do not exist'.[134]

Likewise, in the same issue of *al-Ṭalīʻa*, the Palestinian writer Taysīr Zubaydī categorically stated that for literature to be of value, it must be committed, and that society had no room for indulgences like art for art's sake or surrealist work. Zubaydī rejected the notion that the depression of writers resulted from the difficulties they faced, and he attributed it instead to their weak ties to social reality.[135] Naturally, however, this all depended on what one perceived as social reality. Such critique was simply not applicable to much of the new literature, and it is clear that the prevailing literary norms which *Gallery 68* challenged were deeply entrenched. Indeed, even a decade later, the experimental poetry journal *Iḍā'a 77* was at pains to point out to critics that the fossilized concept of socialist realism had outlived its usefulness.[136]

True to its aim of remaining open to debate, *Gallery 68* itself included an alternative view, questioning the social relevance of the new literature. Like Zubaydī, the young writer and critic Khalīl Kalfat also stressed the overwhelming

132 I. Fatḥī, 'Baʻḍ al-Masā'il al-'Āmma fī al-Naqd', *Gallery 68*, no. 7, Oct. 1969, pp. 64–5.

133 'Abd al-Munʻim 'Abd al-Ḥalīm al-Hawwārī, letter to *al-Ṭalīʻa*, Jan. 1970, pp. 155–6.

134 Yūsuf al-Shārūnī, *Lamaḥāt min Ḥayāt Mawjūd 'Abd al-Mawjūd, wa-Mulāḥaẓātāni, Gallery 68*, no. 8, Feb. 1971, p. 57.

135 Taysīr Zubaydī, letter to *al-Ṭalīʻa*, Jan. 1970, pp. 157–8.

136 *Iḍā'a 77*, July 1979, no. 5, pp. 148–51.

importance of the writer's link to society, and surmised that those included in *Gallery 68*'s special selection 'are not – in general – close to social life in Egypt; they do not generally associate with it; they do not – in general – believe in it'. Fortunately, Kalfat stressed his remarks as a generalization, but he still went on to betray remnants of the uncompromising approach that had come to characterize socialist realist critique in the 1950s. While Kalfat praised Ibrāhīm Aṣlān's contribution to *Gallery 68*'s selection as an 'exploration of bravery' depicting 'the hero of our times', and Muḥammad al-Bisāṭī's contribution for its realistic portrayal of living events, he criticized Bahā' Ṭāhir's contribution for being unrealistic. Kalfat held the view that 'reality is neither strange nor obscure; it is as clear as the sun!'.[137] In comparison with many of *Gallery 68*'s contributors, Kalfat's perspective on reality was limited. All *Gallery 68*'s contributors agreed on the need to portray the reality of Egyptian society; it was simply that some of the different ways of expressing the different experiences and perspectives of this reality were more personal or more strange than others, and were therefore less favoured to win broad appeal. In fact, Bahā' Ṭāhir's *al-Khuṭūba* (The Betrothal), the story Kalfat criticized as remote from reality, was a strong comment on reality – a violent protest against the human condition. Yet Ṭāhir achieved this by subverting realistic material into an unrealistic nightmare, smashing the calm surface of normality with outbursts of horror.

It was probably the element of alienation in the new literature which aroused most controversy, with many intellectuals unsure whether to deny or recognize it, and in the latter case, whether to regard it as a positive or negative development. Halasā wrote that the many attacks against alienation from both the left and right were more political than artistic: while the right's objections were founded on the morals of dying social groups, the left believed that the writer should be linked to the struggle of the masses and so could not be alienated.[138] Ibrāhīm Fatḥī clearly felt the need to defend the alienation of sixties writers. He stressed that behind their severance of old ties to life lay the hope that new and better ties could be constructed – passive indulgence in alienation was rare.[139] Here again, *Gallery 68* presented various views. Both Halasā and Kalfat distinguished between two types of alienation. Halasā identified a comprehensive passive alienation devoid of any attempt to overcome the crisis (as in the work of Ibrāhīm Manṣūr and Ibrāhīm 'Abd al-'Āṭī among others), and a more objective alienation which respected the outlook of the alienated character, but was not without a hint of possibility. This latter type he deemed best exemplified in the work of Bahā' Ṭāhir.[140] Kalfat on the other hand criticized Bahā' Ṭāhir's *al-Khuṭūba* for demonstrating what he

137 Kh. Kalfat, 'Mulāḥaẓāt Ḥawla Kuttāb *68*', *Gallery 68*, no. 7, Oct. 1969.

138 Gh. Halasā, 'al-Adab al-Jadīd: Malāmiḥ wa-Ittijāhāt', *Gallery 68*, no. 6, April 1969, p. 116.

139 I. Fatḥī, 'Malāmiḥ Mushtaraka fī al-Intāj al-Qiṣaṣī al-Jadīd', *Gallery 68*, no. 6, April 1969, pp. 113–14.

140 Gh. Halasā, 'al-Adab al-Jadīd: Malāmiḥ wa-Ittijāhāt', *Gallery 68*, no. 6, April 1969, pp. 116–17.

regarded as the unrealistic type of alienation rather than the realistic type. This latter 'useful' type reflected reality through real-life characters and events, as demonstrated in the contributions of Muḥammad al-Bisāṭī (*Ḥadīth min al-Ṭābiq al-Thālith*) and Ibrāhīm Aṣlān (*Fī Jiwār Rajul Ḍarīr*).[141]

Fundamentally though, Kalfat concurred with Fatḥī that alienation could play a positive role; he was simply less convinced that all the stories of *Gallery 68*'s special selection demonstrated this. A decade younger than Fatḥī, his perception of this role was more radical and aggressive. While he admitted to the social fact of alienation, he criticized those artists who betook themselves and their art to the fringes of society as suffering from an incurable social anaemia which stunted their literary growth. For the power of alienation lay in its ability to provoke positive action. The artist should 'focus his talent on the principal forms of alienation, meaning the oppressed masses whose response to alienation is revolt'.[142] Shafīq Maqqār, writing in the same issue of *Gallery 68*, pointed out that alienation was considered synonymous with treachery. More so than Kalfat, Maqqār emphasized the positive role of alienation, stating that what concerned *68*'s writers was really 'the gift of life', although this might be expressed through alienation. While Kalfat tolerated alienation for its potential to lead to revolt, Maqqār took a more constructive view, harmonizing the two states: the act of revolt necessarily alienates the artist. Alienation does not mean isolation, rather it brings the artist closer to life, for he is searching for ties to society that will ensure a less-stifling future.[143]

So, not only did *Gallery 68*'s contributors challenge the prevailing view of commitment, but also the prevailing view of realism. For what *Gallery 68*'s contributors were committed to was the honest portrayal of their reality, and it is this attempt to portray reality that is the basic tenet of realism. However, as no two people agree as to what precisely reality is, realism has come to have an evaluative or merely personal meaning. Realism does not have to be a coherent literary school but, in Egypt, its identification with socialist principles had resulted in the notion of truth being fossilized into a specific interpretation. Confusion was compounded by the fact that realism, as well as being thought of as a school of literature with a socialist agenda, was also held to be a particular artistic style which expressed reality in a mimetic and 'objective' way. So realism, as well as dictating the content of a literary work, also dictated the way in which the content was dealt with. In other words, it was not enough to be a realist (whatever the different parties perceived this reality to be), one had to be a 'realistic' realist. It was in recognition of the confusion over realism that *Gallery 68* included an extract from a study of realism by F. D. Klingender, translated by Ibrāhīm Fatḥī, in its second issue. This was an attempt to question

141 Kh. Kalfat, 'Mulāḥaẓāt Ḥawla Kuttāb *68*', *Gallery 68*, October 1969, no. 7, p. 75.
142 Ibid., p. 77.
143 Sh. Maqqār, ''An al-Jadīd wa-l-Qadīm wa-Mā Bayna Bayna', *Gallery 68*, no. 7, Oct. 1969, p. 97.

the lethargic and imprecise acceptance of realism and to encourage more discerning critical evaluation of what realism could mean. Fatḥī's endeavour won grudging praise for *Gallery 68* from Aḥmad 'Abd al-Mu'ṭī Ḥijāzī in *Rūz al-Yūsuf*.[144]

While *Gallery 68*'s contributors rejected the accumulated baggage that had made ***R***ealism into a static concept, they did not reject ***r***ealism per se, for their greatest common aim was to portray reality truthfully. But for them, since truth was not absolute, the text remained open and contained multiple layers of meaning, instead of fulfilling a preconceived mission. For them, realism did not simply mean the reflection of external realities, since this yielded only a two-dimensional view; it also meant the portrayal of internal realities, both conscious and subconscious. Writers asserted their freedom to stretch the bounds of actual reality to create or approximate a new broader reality, a step beyond even three-dimensional reality into a fourth dimension as it were. Chronological time, the logical progression of events and the notion of a plot ceased to be important. Ghālī Shukrī pointed out that 'the abstract . . . is a metaphorical withdrawal from reality . . . but at the same time, it is the bowels of this reality'.[145]

Moreover, the inclusion of material from folklore and legend in some of their stories also interrogated the assumptions of rational linear narrative. Shukrī 'Ayyād later identified the tendency among young writers to 'draw some strength . . . from the obscure forces treasured in the huge mass of the people' as a possible cause of conflict between older and younger generations: whereas writers of the older generation attempted to awaken the population from its superstitions, the younger generation used it to flavour their writing.[146] Yet, rather than consigning such narrative to indulgent flights into the realms of fantasy, it might be held up as focusing on the Egyptian reality of a pre-colonial culture. In fact, the inclusion of material from the popular heritage had been positively encouraged by advocators of a socialist literature,[147] for it affirmed the writer's connection to the masses and disavowed any rigid or prescriptive split between high and low culture.

The achievement of *Gallery 68*'s contributors in extending the bounds of the short story to capture the true nature of their reality was acknowledged by the next generation of avant-garde writers in the early 1980s. Maḥmūd al-Ḥusaynī,

144 Aḥmad 'Abd al-Mu'ṭī Ḥijāzī, *Rūz al-Yūsuf*, 17 June 1968, p. 54.

145 Gh. Shukrī, *al-'Anqā' al-Jadīda* (1977), p. 154.

146 Sh. 'Ayyād, 'On Criticism and Creativity', in Ferial Ghazoul and Barbara Harlow (eds) *The View from Within* (1994), p. 204. Originally published in *Alif*, no. 4, 1984.

147 Folk literature was at the centre of Lūwīs 'Awaḍ's views on socialist literature, as outlined in two articles entitled 'Fī al-Thaqāfa al-Ishtirākiyya'. These were reprinted in L. 'Awaḍ, *al-Thawra wa-l-Adab* (1967). Cited in A. Isstaif, 'Forging an New Self, Embracing the Other: Modern Arabic Critical Theory and the West – Lūwīs 'Awaḍ', *Arabic and Middle Eastern Literatures*, Vol. 5, no. 2, 2002, p. 164.

writing in Muḥammad Ibrāhīm Mabrūk's independent journal *al-Nadīm*, recognized that the new literature of the sixties generation which was termed absurdist or surrealist was in fact 'of the essence of realism from start to finish . . . We have gone as far as [to conclude that] absurdist literature is more truthful than realism'.[148] Likewise, Muḥammad Kashīk, writing in the avant-garde journal *Miṣriyya*, singled out Ibrāhīm Aṣlān, Yaḥyā al-Ṭāhir 'Abd Allāh, Muḥammad Ḥāfiẓ Rajab and Muḥammad al-Bisāṭī, all of whom had contributed to *Gallery 68*, as exemplary in the 1960s literary rebellion: 'They exposed the counterfeit reality, the cracked structure'.[149] Even a resolute Marxist critic like Maḥmūd Amīn al-'Ālim eventually recognized that

> The notion of literature as a social product does not exclude the vision, the inspiration, the creativity, or the novelty that distinguishes its creation, nor its specific characteristics, which differ from the general consciousness and from the characteristics of reality itself.[150]

The point of departure in the 1960s, then, was that the text was no longer an imitation or reflection of a general reality, but a dialogue with reality. This may help to explain the negative response to and misunderstanding of new literary forms and techniques among many critics who had become used to the committed socialist realist literature of the previous decade. What was important was that *Gallery 68*'s contributors had asserted their freedom to choose: in the very first issue of *Gallery 68*, Ḥasan Sulaymān had expressed his wish to reopen debate about commitment and the artist's lost freedom and individuality, warning that the artist had reached 'a kind of slavery'.[151] Jabrā, writing in 1967, summed up the experimental writer's dilemma perfectly:

> A rebel cannot become, in Lenin's words, a 'professional revolutionary' – a term many committed writers like to apply to themselves – because it is in the essence of his rebellion to be unique and unpredictable in thought and language. The language of the committed authors, on the other hand, though pretty strong, tends to get stereotyped: it has already developed a readily recognizable lexicon of its own, like a professional

148 Maḥmūd al-Ḥusaynī, 'Malāmiḥ al-Wāqi'iyya fī Adab al-lā-Ma'qūl', *al-Nadīm*, no. 3, March 1982, p. 36.

149 M. Kashīk, ''Alāmāt al-Taḥdīth fī al-Qiṣṣa al-Miṣriyya al-Qaṣīra', *Miṣriyya*, no. 6, Jan. 1984, p. 22.

150 Maḥmūd Amīn al-'Ālim, in the 1989 edition of his 1955 book, co-written with 'Abd al-'Aẓīm Anīs, *Fī al-Thaqāfa al-Miṣriyya*, p. 209. Cited in M. Ghanayim, 'Maḥmūd Amīn al-'Ālim: Between Politics and Literary Criticism', *Poetics Today*, Vol. 15, no. 2, Summer 1994, p. 331.

151 Ḥ. Sulaymān, untitled, *Gallery 68*, no. 1, April–May 1968, p. 29.

> jargon. Their thought has become more or less equally predictable. Rebellion is based on a moral and philosophical attitude adopted by an individual who finally aspires to effect a change in the lives of men as individuals.[152]

This emphasis on the freedom of the writer to mediate an individual interpretation of reality, as both the basis for and the underlying message of literature, was closer to the original Sartrian concept of *littérature engagée* from which *iltizām* (commitment) as a literary term was coined by Ṭaha Ḥusayn in the late 1940s.[153] Nevertheless, while focusing on the individual's interpretation of his reality, sixties writers still firmly believed that art should carry a social function. Idwār al-Kharrāṭ, for example, has described his writing as 'a weapon to bring about change,'[154] and Yaḥyā al-Ṭāhir 'Abd Allāh later declared, 'My ultimate pleasure . . . is rebellion and provoking the stagnant population into motion'.[155] Of the twenty-nine young writers who responded to *al-Ṭalī'a's* survey, only *Gallery 68* contributor Māhir Shafīq Farīd stressed that he wrote for the god of art alone; the vast majority of those surveyed wrote out of a sense of commitment to the nation, expressed in a variety of ways and with varying degrees of subtlety.

Respect for freedom of choice and variation were what characterized *Gallery 68*. Writers were encouraged to develop their own personal artistic and intellectual stances, consisting of a tangle of influences – new and old, Eastern and Western – resulting in the emergence of various and at times conflicting attitudes and artistic tendencies. This freer approach was reflected in the fact that *Gallery 68* itself refused to present a manifesto setting out its views as absolute truths. The broader and more tolerant attitude is summed up by the words of one of *Gallery 68*'s founders and editors:

> It is both unreasonable and unacceptable, after this people has presented throughout history all these refined artistic creations...for us then to come and try...to impose on them specific kinds of artistic creativity, then accuse them of ignorance and backwardness if they do not cooperate with us.[156]

152 J. I. Jabrā, 'The Rebels, the Committed and the Others', in I. J. Boullata (ed.) *Critical Perspectives on Modern Arabic Literature* (1980), p. 195. Originally published in *Middle East Forum*, Vol. 43, no. 1, 1967, pp. 19–32.

153 V. Klemm, 'Literary Commitment Approached through Reception Theory', in B. Gruendler and V. Klemm (eds) *Understanding Near Eastern Literatures* (2000), p. 149.

154 Amal Amireh, 'Edwar al-Kharrāṭ and the Modernist Revolution in the Egyptian Novel', *al-Jadīd*, July 1996, p. 13.

155 Yaḥyā al-Ṭāhir 'Abd Allāh in an interview with Samīr Gharīb, *al-Mustaqbal al-'Arabī*, n.d. Cited in Yaḥyā al-Ṭāhir 'Abd Allāh, *al-Kitābāt al-Kāmila*, p. 490.

156 Interview with J. A. Ibrāhīm, in I. Manṣūr, *al-Izdiwāj al Thaqāfī wa-Azmat al-Mu'āraḍa al-Miṣriyya*, p. 116.

Gallery 68 and poetry

While the aesthetic paradigms set in place by the sixties generation in the short story in essence continued to endure, albeit with new life breathed into them by subsequent avant-gardists, poetic norms underwent more radical change post-*Gallery 68* in the 1970s and beyond. By the late 1960s, major poetic innovations in both form and content had already taken place on the pages of the journal *Shi'r* in Beirut: the monopoly of the monorhyme poem had been broken by continuing experimentation in free verse and the introduction of the prose poem. The *Shi'r* poets focused on linguistic renewal and emphasized the poem's mythical and spiritual dimension while deemphasizing its political role.[157] Egyptian poetry of the late 1960s was still based overwhelming on the foot (*taf'īla*) and retained the notion of the poet as spokesperson for his society. It was the subsequent generation of the so-called 'seventies poets', clustered mainly around the groups *Iḍā'a 77* and *Aṣwāt*, that introduced radical changes in form, content and language.[158] From this, it may be inferred that creative excitement was greater for the short story at this time than it was for poetry, and this was certainly true for those who initiated *Gallery 68*.[159] Of the core group of nine editors (those billed as editors for at least three of *Gallery 68*'s eight issues), only Sayyid Ḥijāb, Aḥmad Mursī (also a painter) and Yusrī Khamīs were poets; the others were all concerned primarily with prose fiction at this time. Hence I have chosen to concentrate overwhelmingly on the short story and devote only this brief space to poetry.

There were no studies of the actual poems published in *Gallery 68*, as there were of the short stories, and the few critical articles concerning modern poetry (*al-shi'r al-ḥadīth*) were more debate than constructive analysis. They consisted of two exchanges – the first between Shafīq Majallī and Ghālib Halasā concerning the issue of obscurity, and the second between Ra'ūf Naẓmī and Ghālī Shukrī broadly concerning the role of modern poetry. The defence of obscurity by Shafīq Majallī, an assistant professor of English at Cairo University, was sweeping and arrogant, as one might expect in an early number of an avant-garde journal. However, the firmness and logic of the brief response of one of the editors, Ghālib Halasā, in the following issue demonstrates that *Gallery 68* was keen to stir up debate rather than advocate Majallī's view. Naẓmī and Shukrī's exchange was longer and more involved and thus more progressive.

157 See Ed de Moor, 'The Rise and Fall of the Review *Shi'r*' and Francesca M. Corrao, '*Shi'r*: Poetics in Progress'. Both in *Quaderni Di Studi Arabī*, no. 18, 2000, pp. 85–104.

158 See S. Mehrez, 'Experimentation and the Institution: The Case of *Iḍā'a 77* and *Aṣwāt*'. In F. J. Ghazoul and B. Harlow (eds) *The View from Within* (1994). See also *Alif*, no. 11, 1991 (special issue on 'Poetic Experimentation in Egypt since the Seventies').

159 Poems occupied only 12.5 per cent of *Gallery 68*, while short stories occupied 49 per cent of the journal, and the total number of contributing poets was 22 as opposed to 36 short story writers. Moreover, studies of poetry only occupied half as much space as studies of prose literature.

Majallī began with a hasty and simplistic definition of genuine obscurity: that emanating from profound poems as opposed to that emanating from second-rate poems. Rather than interrogating this poetic obscurity, he glossed over it as the natural result of a more complex modern way of life. Instead of making a constructive effort to dispel misunderstandings about modern poetry, Majallī was satisfied that English poetry had already proved the validity of poetic obscurity in what rang out as a simplistic invocation of European cultural hegemony. Those who remained sceptical he accused of ignorance and intellectual laziness for preferring to bask in the 'sense of great satisfaction, glowing intelligence and poetic sensitivity' provided by the predictable traditional Arabic poem. Majallī also ventured other sweeping judgements: second-rate poets 'should be banned from writing poetry'; pre-Islamic poetry is entirely predictable whereas modern poetry is complex; and the experiences expressed by poetry are more elevated, profound and complicated than those of prose.[160] This latter pronouncement was echoed in the opening editorial of *Iḍā'a 77* (the next substantial avant-garde journal to follow *Gallery 68*) when it declared poetry 'the most creative and present' of genres.[161] However, both journals in subsequent issues distanced themselves from this breed of arrogance.[162]

Gallery 68 editor Ghālib Halasā's reproach of Majallī appeared at first to defend what both men referred to as 'traditional poetry'. Halasā pointed out that tradition was of particular importance for poetry since the genealogy of poetry in Arabic was longer than that of the short story. He regarded tradition to be as fundamental to the framework of poetry as language itself, through which the subjective experience was generalized for public consumption.[163] During the following decade, the poets of *Iḍā'a 77* were to reject this view of poetry: while they acknowledged tradition in their experiment inasmuch as they recognized themselves as 'an original link' in the chain of poetic evolution,[164] language for them was used primariliy to reinforce rather than to mediate the unique poetic experience. The comprehension of the public, while hoped for, was not a priority. It is clear, however, that Halasā's primary intention here was simply to attack dismissive generalizations (which in Majallī's case happened to be about traditional poetry) and to advocate a more rigorous approach to criticism in general.

The insistence on a more rigorous and precise critical approach was reiterated by Ra'ūf Naẓmī in *Gallery 68*'s second exchange concerning modern poetry. Naẓmī's criticism of Ghālī Shukrī's latest book *Shi'ru-nā al-Ḥadīth ilā Ayn?*, published a few months earlier, recognized the validity of Shukrī's opinions but

160 Shafīq Majallī, 'Difā' 'an al-Ghumūḍ', *Gallery 68*, no. 2, June 1968.

161 Opening editorial to *Iḍā'a 77*, July 1977.

162 *Iḍā'a 77*, Dec. 1977, p. 81 and Gh. Halasā in 'Mulāḥaẓāt Ḥawla Difā' 'an al-Ghumūḍ', *Gallery 68*, no. 3, July 1968.

163 Gh. Halasā, 'Mulāḥaẓāt Ḥawla Difā' 'an al-Ghumūḍ', *Gallery 68*, no. 3, July 1968, p. 76.

164 Editorial to *Iḍā'a 77*, no. 2, Dec. 1977.

demanded a stricter research method. Naẓmī called for more concrete definition of categories and terminology, improved organization, a more scientific basis of analysis and more comprehensive footnotes and bibliography. However, Naẓmī's real disagreement with Shukrī might be regarded as a matter of commitment, for he added that for poetry to be of high quality, it must maintain strong ties to the struggle of the masses, and every poet must make socialism his point of departure.[165] The late 1960s had seen the publication of two books on Palestinian resistance poetry by Ghassān Kanafānī and their impact was profound in the despondent atmosphere following the 1967 defeat. Many critics shared Kanafānī's views that certain Palestinian poets practiced a model aesthetics of commitment and that all Arab poets should demonstrate a clear sense of social responsibility.[166] The impact of the defeat on Egyptian poetry of the late 1960s is clear in the testimonial of 'Abd al-Raḥmān al-Abnūdī, a contributor to *Gallery 68*,

> my voice did not find free expression until the 1967 defeat . . . Now that the military authorities had been humiliated, I could raise my voice and sing as I wanted. I went back to my nationally oriented poetry with even greater force.[167]

It was this kind of political protest poetry that the poets of *Iḍā'a* associated with the 1960s and vehemently rejected; Ghālī Shukrī, in his response to Naẓmī, also rejected such overt politics. While remaining a dedicated Marxist, Shukrī – like the poets of *Iḍā'a 77* a decade later – considered form and content inseparable. Politics was only related to poetry inasmuch as the poem related to a poet's experience, and politics might be part of that experience. Ideally, poetry should relate to the Arab individual and Arab society in general (rather than to a partisan cause) and combine this with aesthetic renewal; certainly a poem should not be judged by its politics. Like Majallī, but in a more sensitive and precise way, Shukrī too perceived a special place for poetry among literary genres: man's relationship to poetry is more fundamental than with other genres, for poetry's essential musical rhythms rise above social change like 'an eternal prayer'.[168]

The exchange between Naẓmī and Shukrī avoided exaggerated and personal criticism and was a landmark for mature and quality debate about the critical methodology needed to approach contemporary poetry. In fact, Shukrī's *Shi'ru-nā al-Ḥadīth ilā Ayn?*, the book under discussion, reached its third edition in 1991 and the exchange between Naẓmī and Shukrī was republished in an edited volume

165 R. Naẓmī, ''An *Shi'ru-nā al-Ḥadīth ilā Ayn*?', *Gallery 68*, no. 5, Feb. 1969.

166 See S. Hafez, 'Shi'r al-Ma'sāh fī al-Arāḍī al-Muḥtalla', *al-Ādāb*, Vol. 17, no. 3, 1969, p. 70.

167 'Our Revolution', Interview with 'Abd al-Raḥmān al-Abnūdī conducted by Youssef Rakha, *al-Ahram Weekly*, no. 595, 18–24 July 2002. Online. Available HTTP: http://weekly.ahram.org.eg/2002/595/sc15.htm

168 Gh. Shukrī, 'Wadda'-nā Zdanov ilā Ghayr Raj'a', *Gallery 68*, no. 5, Feb. 1969.

in the late 1990s, together with the text of a panel discussion about the book which took place in Cairo in the early 1990s and involved contemporary poets like Aḥmad al-Shahāwī, Muḥammad Sulaymān and ʻAbd al-Munʻim Ramaḍān.[169]

Another level of poetic interest in *Gallery 68* was demonstrated by Sayyid Ḥijāb's studies of folk songs as poetry. This may be viewed in the context of growing interest in folk literature over the preceding decade rather than as a radical innovation. Ḥijāb analysed the folk songs almost to breaking point as he revealed the complex implications of various rhythms. He wrote of the creative *fallāḥ*

> swimming in the whirlpool of a deep daze . . . (which) composes its rhythms and evokes hidden portraits from the subconscious as the artist spontaneously abandons himself to his turbulent experience. With the same spontaneity, he abandons his tongue to the rhythms and images hidden in his soul.[170]

This was exactly the type of analysis that Halasā, a fellow editor of *Gallery 68*, deplored in a later issue,[171] proving *Gallery 68*'s willingness to incorporate varying views – a quality which later came under criticism from the poets of *Iḍā'a 77* who believed in the promotion of a homogenous poetics if true progress was to be made.[172]

Yet Ḥijāb's studies reflected a fellow editor, Ḥasan Sulaymān's, hope that any distinction between high art and popular art would eventually be destroyed. Sulaymān stressed that there was no disgrace in expressing an experience or emotion in a simple way, for it was sincerity that was important.[173] While many critics were by this stage willing to take folk literature seriously on its own merits, it was rarer to advocate the destruction of any distinction between high and popular culture. Ḥijāb suggested that Egyptian poetry would benefit if cultivated poets were willing to learn from anonymous folk poets. In particular, he advocated the use of various metres within the same poem, insisting that the poet had the capacity to construct thousands of new metres.[174] *Gallery 68*'s contributing poets, among them Amal Dunqul, were in fact beginning to put this into practice, suspending and varying their poetic metres. Ḥijāb's desire to break the domination of the mono-metric poem was not new, having been introduced in Egypt as early as the 1940s by Lūwīs ʻAwaḍ in his introduction to *Plutoland* and entrenched over the previous decade in the Beirut journal *Shiʻr*, but Ḥijāb was to help stretch poetic experimentation to new horizons in years to follow.

169 Ḥ. Mahrān (ed.) *Ghālī Shukrī: Dhākirat al-Jīl al-Ḍā'iʻ* (1996).
170 S. Ḥijāb, 'Thalātha Īqāʻāt wa-Takwīn', *Gallery 68*, no. 3, July 1968, p. 8.
171 Gh. Halasā, 'al-Adab al-Jadīd: Malāmiḥ wa-Ittijāhāt', *Gallery 68*, no. 6, April 1969, pp. 117–18.
172 Opening editorial to *Iḍā'a 77*, July 1977.
173 Ḥ. Sulaymān, untitled, *Gallery 68*, no. 1, April–May 1968.
174 S. Ḥijāb, ''An al-Īqāʻ wa-l-Takwīn: Qirā'a Naqdiyya li-Ashʻār Fūlklūr', *Gallery 68*, no. 4, Nov. 1968.

Ḥijāb himself wrote in the colloquial and published poems in *Gallery 68* alongside other colloquial poets such as 'Abd al-Raḥmān al-Abnūdī with whom he shared a flat, Usāma al-Ghuzūlī and Muḥammad Sayf. Ḥijāb revealed, 'We poets of Egyptian dialect felt that we were doing something new, freeing the literary life that had been locked up in classical Arabic'.[175] Muḥammad Sayf later confirmed, 'I am part of a new generation, rising today in the land of Egypt' and he dedicated his first collection, not published until 1977, 'to a new generation'.[176] Colloquial Egyptian poets, including many who did not contribute to *Gallery 68* – such as Fu'ād Ḥaddād, Ṣalāḥ Jahīn, Fu'ād Qa'ūd and Maḥmūd al-Shādhilī – had been active on the literary scene for several years, and both Ḥijāb and al-Abnūdī had already published collections before the launch of *Gallery 68*. Nevertheless, the journal still played a valuable nurturing role, giving poets the freedom in which to develop; Ḥijāb testified, 'once read, the periodical is thrown away, and soon the reader has forgotten it. Publishing poetry in a book that can be kept by the reader is a much heavier responsibility'. Yet it is also clear from Ḥijāb's testimony that the avant-garde dynamic was shifting, for Ḥijāb revealed that, by the end of the 1960s, their colloquial poetry was infiltrating the establishment. He admitted, 'In choosing to write in the Egyptian dialect, we were trying to reject the sophistication of snobbish intellectuals and to reach the simple people. Now it was the snobbish intellectuals who made much of our books. Something was wrong'.[177]

Reaching readers was of obvious importance to poets writing in the colloquial. The intention of Ḥijāb, who had composed his first poems in classical Arabic, was to express, share and illuminate the world of the ordinary *fallāḥ*, and he confessed, 'I realized my efforts were not understood by the victims themselves . . . To hell with the dead language!'.[178] Yet that the colloquial was more than just a tool to reach the masses was affirmed by fellow *Gallery 68* contributor Muḥammad Sayf. He called it 'a dictionary of life and human activity . . . [through which] we are trying to build a new palace in the history of art and literature'.[179] Their poetry helped to rebuild bridges between oral and literary cultures.

Gallery 68 also interacted with Iraqi poets, featuring poems by Ṭarrād al-Kubaysī and Ḥāmid al-Maṭba'ī (owner of the Iraqi journal *al-Kalima*); it even inspired the launch of a poetry journal in Iraq in 1969: *Shi'r 69*.[180] *Gallery 68* poet and editor Yusrī Khamīs, writing in the mid-1960s, had affirmed the Iraqi poet

175 Sayed Hegab (Sayyid Ḥijāb), *A New Egyptian: The Autobiography of a Young Arab* (1971), p. 144.

176 Introduction to Muḥammad Sayf's first collection, *Ghinā'iyyāt* (1977), p. 8.

177 S. Hegab, *A New Egyptian: The Autobiography of a Young Arab*, pp. 150–2.

178 Ibid., p. 119.

179 Introduction to M. Sayf, *Ghinā'iyyāt* (1977), pp. 3–4. It was in this collection that Sayf's *Gallery 68* poem, *al-Khandaq*, was finally published.

180 This is reported in the editorial to *Gallery 68*, no. 7, Oct. 1969.

'Abd al-Wahhāb al-Bayyātī as 'the true model for the poet for whom renewal is spontaneous, natural and indeed inevitable'.[181] Therefore, despite the fact that al-Bayyātī was an established poet by the time *Gallery 68* was launched, having published more than ten collections of poetry by 1968, his poems were still included in four of the journal's eight issues, and several of *Gallery 68*'s contributors were to write books or articles about him.[182]

Several of *Gallery 68*'s contributors continued to participate in poetic activity at the fringe in the 1970s and 1980s, after *Gallery 68* itself had come to an end. The most influential were probably Sayyid Ḥijāb and Idwār al-Kharrāṭ, both editors of *Gallery 68*, and Muḥammad 'Afīfī Maṭar. It was at poetry readings organized by Sayyid Ḥijāb in the early 1970s that many of the poets of the *Iḍā'a 77* and *Aṣwāt* groups first met one another.[183] Despite the fact that the poets in these groups write in the classical language (Mājid Yūsuf is a notable exception), they have remained supportive of colloquial poetry – *Iḍā'a* published nine colloquial poets including Sayyid Ḥijāb. Ḥijāb's poetry also appeared in the independent journals *al-Naddāha* (The Caller, n.d. 1979?) and *Khaṭwa* (A Step, 1980–5), the latter devoting a 25-page supplement to his poems.[184] More recently, there is evidence of the literary scene having shifted once more with young Egyptian avant-garde colloquial poets like 'Umar Ṭāhir having little time for the colloquial poets of the 1960s and 1970s. The now household names of Sayyid Ḥijāb and 'Abd al-Raḥmān al-Abnūdī stand accused of being overly political and dependent on their image, such that their poems have become consumer products.[185]

Gallery 68 editor Idwār al-Kharrāṭ was especially interested in poetic experimentation in the 1970s and 1980s. He has been singled out by Rif'at Sallām, one time *Iḍā'a* poet, as an exemplary critic of contemporary poetry, writing about the actual poem rather than about the self, ideology or external rules.[186] Kharrāṭ himself contributed to *Iḍā'a 77* a detailed and lengthy study of a collection by Ḥilmī Sālim in the mid-1980s. As well as encouraging young poets personally, he has published several books of criticism of modern poetry and began publishing his own poetry in the 1990s.

Also of great influence in the decades to follow *Gallery 68* was Muḥammad 'Afīfī Maṭar. He contributed only one poem to *Gallery 68* since his efforts were

181 Yusrī Khamīs, *al-Qāfila* (Cairo University), June 1966. Cited in 'Adnān Ḥaqqī (ed.) *Rabī 'al-Ḥayāh fī Mamlakat Allāh*, pp. 18–19.

182 For example, Shawqī Khamīs and Ṭarrād al-Kubaysī have published monographs about him; Khalīl Kalfat has published a detailed study of him in three parts in *al-Ādāb*; Sabry Hafez, Shawqī Khamīs and Ghālī Shukrī have contributed to edited volumes about him.

183 S. Mehrez, 'Experimentation and the Institution', *Alif*, no. 11, 1991, p. 120.

184 *Khaṭwa*, no. 7, July 1985.

185 Rania Khallaf, 'Of jeans and self-belief', *al-Ahram Weekly*, no. 730, 17–23 Feb. 2005. Online. Available HTTP: http://weekly.ahram.org.eg/2005/730/cu2.htm

186 Rif'at Sallām, 'Bībliyūghrāfiyyat Shu'arā' al-Sab'īniyyāt fī Misr', *Alif*, no. 11, 1991, p. 183.

concentrated on his own experimental poetry journal *Sanābil* (Ears of Corn, 1969–71), based in Kafr al-Shaykh, but Bahā' Ṭāhir testifies to how well liked and respected he was among those involved in *68*.[187] Maṭar in fact retained this loyalty from new fringe participants in the decades to follow. While *Iḍā'a* criticized *Sanābil* alongside *Gallery 68* in its opening editorial – the former for its links to the authorities and the latter for its lack of homogeneity – it published a critical study of a collection by Maṭar and dedicated a poem to him in its second issue. And when *Iḍā'a* poet Rif'at Sallām criticized poets of the 1960s, he added the proviso 'with the exception of Maṭar of course'.[188] A special issue of *Alif* (no. 11, 1991), the comparative poetics journal, on poetic experimentation in the 1970s was actually dedicated to Maṭar.

The poet most published in *Gallery 68* was 'Izzat 'Āmir, an engineering student 'discovered' by *Gallery 68*. It was 'Āmir's first collection – with a commentary by *Gallery 68* contributor Ibrāhīm Fatḥī – that was chosen to launch the series of *Kuttāb al-Ghad* (Tomorrow's Writers) in 1971. The *Iḍā'a* poets would later criticize *Kuttāb al-Ghad*, alongside *Gallery 68* and *Sanābil*, as narrow and conservative. The introduction to 'Amir's collection, however, insisted that 'this series is published by men of letters who belong to neither a single intellectual school, nor a single artistic school... nor even a single generation'. The journal of *Kuttāb al-Ghad* did describe the group as 'a social and cultural alliance... working to destroy the old world of imperialist greed, Zionist expansion and capitalist exploitation'. But while it stressed the writer's responsibility to reach the public and insisted that art should be socially effective, it criticized direct propaganda in art. Art should be innovative rather than overtly socialist, for 'artistic commitment means exploring virgin soil'. Like *Iḍā'a* after it, *Kuttāb al-Ghad* also complained about poetry 'weighed down by spurious slogans'.[189] 'Āmir became a founding editor of the independent journal *Adab al-Ghad* (Tomorrow's Literature, 1983–4) in the early 1980s, and also published stories in *al-Nadīm* (al-Nadīm, 1980–5), the Alexandria-based journal of former *Gallery 68* editor Muḥammad Ibrāhīm Mabrūk.

Others of *Gallery 68*'s poets also continued to participate at the fringe to varying degrees, contributing to several independent non-periodic journals in the 1970s and 1980s.[190] But it was the poets of *Iḍā'a 77* and *Aṣwāt* who marked the most radical departure for poetry. The former published through their journal

187 B. Ṭāhir, taped interview, Cairo, 1 May 1996.

188 R. Sallām, op. cit. (1991), *Alif*, no. 11, 1991, p. 183.

189 Introduction to the first book in the *Kuttāb al-Ghad* series, 'Izzat 'Āmir's *Madkhal ilā al-Ḥadā'iq al-Ṭāghūriyya* (1971).

190 For example, Usāma al-Ghuzūlī contributed to *al-Thaqāfat al-Jadīda, al-Fikr al-Mu'āṣir, Adab al-Ghad, Khaṭwa* and *al-Nadīm*; Muḥammad Ṣāliḥ to *al-Fikr al-Mu'āṣir, Adab al-Ghad* and *Khaṭwa*; al-Abnūdī to *al-Thaqāfa al-Waṭaniyya*; Muḥammad Sayf to *Khaṭwa*, and Fatḥī Farghalī and Amal Dunqul to *al-Thaqāfa al-Jadīda* and *al-Fikr al-Mu'āṣir*.

Iḍā'a 77, which ran to 14 issues over the course of a decade, while *Aṣwāt* clubbed together to publish one another's collections before issuing the one and only number of their journal *al-Kitāba al-Sawdā'* (Black Writing, 1988). While some *Gallery 68* contributors such as Idwār al-Kharrāṭ, Sabry Hafez and Sayyid Ḥijāb were supportive of and enthusiastic about the new experimentation of these poets, others have been more reluctant to welcome it. Ibrāhīm Manṣūr and Ghālī Shukrī, for example, dismiss them as imitators of Adūnīs and Muḥammad 'Afīfī Maṭar. Manṣūr argues that their work does not represent a comprehensive new outlook, while Shukrī categorically declared, 'there is no one after Amal Dunqul'.[191]

Dunqul was published in *Gallery 68*'s opening issue, but was already reasonably well known and the publication of his first collection the following year propelled him to the forefront of the literary mainstream with its clear political engagement apparent immediately in the title, *al-Bukā' bayna Yaday Zarqā' al-Yamāma* (Crying in front of Zarqā' al-Yamāma, 1969). Dunqul articulated the basic difference between his generation and its predecessors, Ṣalāḥ 'Abd al-Ṣabūr and 'Abd al-Mu'ṭī Ḥijāzī, as follows: 'Their generation was the generation of victories... we were the generation of defeats'. While the former believed the poet belonged to an international heritage, his generation, which had to fight a new kind of cultural and economic imperialism, relied on the Arab heritage. And while the former had tried to bring the language closer to the colloquial, his generation tried to forge a new language that was 'neither the old classical nor the cheap colloquial'. Unlike *Gallery 68* editors Sayyid Ḥijāb and Ḥasan Sulaymān who affirmed the value of simplicity, Dunqul considered simplicity of rhythm, structure and idea inconsistent with the complexity of the modern world, although he stressed that he was not a defender of the metric poem.[192]

Like Shukrī, Dunqul affirmed the point insisted on by *Iḍā'a 77* – that to separate content from form was like 'an eye without vision, a tongue without speech' – but he declared that 'this uproar over form and content has given rise to a group of confused poets'.[193] For Dunqul's concept of language was less radical; to him, words were 'the vessel for thoughts... words have no special magic other than what they gain from the context'.[194] The ongoing debate over language shows that the issue of obscurity brought up in *Gallery 68* was one that endured. In years to come, Dunqul asked exasperatedly why promising poets had 'hurried behind the fog of Adūnīs', loading their poetry with obscurity.[195] Dunqul classed himself together with poets such as 'Abd al-Mu'ṭī Ḥijāzī, believing that true poetry must

191 I. Manṣūr and Gh. Shukrī, taped joint interview, Cairo, 3 May 1996.

192 Interview with Amal Dunqul conducted by Jihād Fāḍil, *al-Ḥawādith* (Beirut), March 1983.

193 Interview with Amal Dunqul conducted by 'Abd al-Ilāh Ṣā'igh, *al-Thaqāfa* (Iraq), Yr. 7, no. 1. Reprinted in Anīs Dunqul (ed.) *Aḥādīth Amal Dunqul* (1992), pp. 57, 60.

194 Interview with Amal Dunqul conducted by Ṭal'at Shanā'a, *al-Ra'y* (Jordan), 30 July 1982. Reprinted in Anīs Dunqul, op. cit. (1992), p. 117.

195 Interview with Amal Dunqul conducted by 'Abd al-Ilāh Ṣā'igh, in Anīs Dunqul (ed.) op. cit. (1992), p. 60.

act as a weapon and should therefore reveal an intelligible social stance, but it is clear that he did not deem his poetry overly direct, as the rising avant-garde poets of the 1970s claimed: 'As for the charge of directness, I laugh at it sometimes. Until recently I was accused of obscurity'. Dunqul was careful not to show himself against obscurity *per se* – that is, when it was born of a genuine poetic thought or image and simply required reader effort to penetrate it. However, he wrote off pretentious obscurity as 'poetic opportunism', explaining: 'I am against obscurity when it is born of an unclear image in the poet's mind, such that he resorts to linguistic games through which he hides his inability to penetrate to the meaning…'.[196] It is in this considered context that we should read his claim, 'I like Adūnīs, but I do not respect the disciples of Adūnīs (*al-Adūnīsiyyīn*)'.[197]

The poet Ḥilmī Sālim, a founder member of *Iḍā'a 77*, launched a vehement attack against Dunqul, attempting to discredit the latter's pronouncements on obscurity and 'Adūnīsism' through an exaggerated counter-offensive which polarized Dunqul's arguments, making him appear more reactionary. Sālim dismissed Dunqul's attempts to define obscurity as critically unsound and concluded that it was direct poetry such as Dunqul's that should instead be labelled 'opportunistic'. Such poetry, Sālim claimed, was incapable of changing anything since it indulged the whims of the public, diffusing their inner anger. Sālim took particular offence to the charges of 'Adūnīsism and imitation' levelled against many new poets in the 1970s and those of *Iḍā'a 77* in particular. He sarcastically praised Dunqul for having refrained from also accusing Adūnīs (whom Dunqul had in fact defended) and the so-called *Adūnīsiyyin* of co-operating with Israel and imperialism and betraying the nation.[198]

This controversy points to the fact that, unlike the short story, the generation struggle surrounding Egyptian poetry was fought out more in the decade following *Gallery 68* and with the so-called sixties poets often appearing as the rearguard. One time *Iḍā'a* poet Rif'at Sallām complained that the sixties poetic ideal, exemplified by Dunqul and others, had become so much the critical measure that a poem's success lay in it 'confirming the poetic moment of the sixties and abridging all subsequent moments in it'. He criticized 'the sixties poem' as familiar, listless and in harmony with the world.[199] By contrast, experimental poets in Egypt in the 1970s marvelled at the complexity of Adūnīs' elevated language. In the opening issue of the *Aṣwāt* group's journal, the poet 'Abd al-Mun'im Ramaḍān revealed, 'At the end of the sixties we were small, looking more to the

196 Interview with Amal Dunqul conducted by Y. Abū Rayya, *al Kurrāsa al-Thaqāfiyya*, no. 1, June 1979, pp. 37–8.

197 Ibid, p. 38. This statement was also made in an interview with Amal Dunqul conducted by Nabīl Sulaymān, supplement to *al-Thawra* (Syria), 12 May 1975. Reprinted in Anīs Dunqul, op. cit. (1992), p. 103.

198 Ḥilmī Sālim, 'Dunquliyyūn wa-Adūnīsiyyūn', *al-Kurrāsa al-Thaqāfiyya*, no. 2, March 1980, pp. 6–7.

199 R. Sallām, op. cit. (1991), pp. 181–2.

past... At that time, slogans were tying up our dreams in sealed packages'. He rejoiced that they had finally overcome 'the fairytale of the accusation of Adūnīsism . . . It is wonderful that we greet Adūnīs and embrace him'.[200] *Iḍā'a* published two poems and an editorial to Amal Dunqul, praising him for 'injecting hot new blood into the body of the Egyptian poem', saving it from stagnating and fading out.[201] One must remember, however, that this praise was accorded him as a tribute directly after his death. In reality, there were fundamental differences between the *Iḍā'a* poets and Dunqul, as indicated by the coinage of the opposing categories *Dunquliyyūn* and *Adūnīsiyyūn* (Duqulists and Adūnīsites).

Gallery 68 did not therefore mark as radical departure for poetry as it did for the short story. As early as 1973, in a special feature on poetic experimentation in Egypt published in *al-Ṭalī'a*, only three of the nine poets featured had contributed to *Gallery 68* (Yusrī Khamīs, Muḥammad Mihrān al-Sayyid and Muḥammad 'Afīfī Maṭar). And significantly, it was the three *Gallery 68* contributors who were singled out as bridging the gap between new voices and established ones, rather than being actually representative of the new generation like the other six poets.[202] It was in the 1970s that poets thoroughly smashed the boundaries of the *taf'īla*, the boundaries between fantasy and a blemished reality, and the boundaries between form and content, all at the same time, to take poetic experience to a wholly new dimension. The continuing avant-garde dynamic is clearly at play in Rif'at Sallām's image of poets in the 1970s 'destroying the walls of the paternal barrier towards crucial horizons of Egyptian freedom'.[203] Nevertheless, *Gallery 68* had been a step on the way. Having criticized *Gallery 68* in the heat of its opening manifesto, *Iḍā'a 77* later conceded the valuable contribution made by the journal.[204] And today, *Iḍā'a* poet Jamāl al-Qaṣṣāṣ confirms that *Gallery 68*, together with Maṭar's *Sanābil*, had a direct practical influence on poetic experimentation, through their initiative if not their poetics, for they inspired him and fellow poets to launch journals to crystallize and refine their own experiments.[205] Even Ḥilmī Sālim now acknowledges the talent of Dunqul, who was perhaps the best example of *Gallery 68*'s poetic ideal of a blend between aesthetic renewal and engagement with society and its politics. Having launched such a harsh attack on Dunqul, Sālim's recent words are indicative of the maturation of the avant-garde cycle:

> I (together with many of my generation) at the beginning of my poetic life adopted a negative stance towards Dunqul's poetry, accusing it of

200 'Abd al-Mun'im Ramaḍān, 'Ziyārat Rāqiṣ al-Bālīh', *al-Kitabat al-Sawda*', 1988, pp. 31–3.
201 *Iḍā'a 77*, no. 10, April 1983.
202 'al-Tajriba al-Shi'riyya al-Miṣriyya: al-Tawāṣul lā al-Inqiṭā'', *al-Ṭalī'a*, April 1973.
203 R. Sallām, op. cit. (1991), p. 183.
204 *Iḍā'a 77*, no. 2, Dec. 1977, p. 80.
205 Jamāl al-Qaṣṣāṣ, taped interview, Cairo, 4 Nov. 1994.

directness and impassioned clamour. However, as my perspective has broadened, I have come to see that poetry is multifarious and I have begun to understand that the artistic beauty in Dunqul's poetry does not obliterate the intellectual vision, nor does the intellectual vision encroach on the artistic beauty.[206]

206 Ḥilmī Sālim, 'Amal Dunqul Kawwana "Jamāhīriyya" bi-Shi'ri-hi al-Ṣādiq', *al-Ḥayāh*, 25 April 2003. Online. Available HTTP: http://www.jehat.com/ar/amal/page-8–2.htm

6

THE ESTABLISHMENT OF A NEW LITERARY PARADIGM

The 1970s and beyond

Despite much argument about whether the *68* phenomenon might be categorized into trends, how this might be done and whether the literature had any value in any case, there was nevertheless general agreement on the fact that something new had emerged, hence the term 'the new literature' (*al-adab al-jadīd*) abounded in the cultural press of the late 1960s. Yet it was not just a new literary phenomenon that *Gallery 68* helped to entrench, but a whole new literary dynamic propelled by an autonomous sub-field of non-periodic avant-garde journals. Understanding the evolution of the Egyptian literary field of the 1970s, 1980s and 1990s necessitates, even more than before, an appreciation of the pivotal role of the struggle between avant-gardists and those holding fast to the status quo. The root of the struggle was, as ever, the definition of legitimacy in the literary field but the avant-garde weapon, the journal, had now blossomed into an ever regenerating stream as the *Gallery 68* paradigm took hold.

This chapter looks first at how the marginal position of *Gallery 68* and its writers began to change and filter through into the literary establishment. This occurred initially through the resounding responses to *Gallery 68* in the contemporary mainstream press, which confirmed the emergence of a new literary phenomenon. As some sixties avant-gardists won ever more symbolic capital (recognition and prestige), their position in the Egyptian literary field shifted from the margin towards the mainstream, leaving space and reason for others to take on the literary struggle from the margins. Moreover, with the cultural establishment under Sadat flexing its muscles over the literary field during the 1970s, the incentive and need for new platforms from which to launch literary campaigns against established traditions grew more intense. This chapter explores how, from the late 1970s, experimental Egyptian writers confronted this cultural challenge by launching a whole stream of non-periodic avant-garde journals, along the lines brought to their attention and practiced so successfully by *Gallery 68*. This forum for expression became a truly established part of the Egyptian literary scene and a crucial part of Egypt's literary dynamic. These journals are examined as an autonomous sub-field (within the greater literary field), showing certain common features and focal points that cut across what were often very different aesthetics. This chapter then maps out the struggle for legitimacy – for public recognition and/or critical acclaim – as it was understood, experienced and realized by this autonomous sub-field, concluding with the perceptible canonization of sixties writers as life at the literary margins passed to others.

'Sixties' writers: shifting positions in the literary field?

Although special issues of *al-Qiṣṣa* (The Story, 1964–5) and *al-Majalla* (The Journal, 1957–71) devoted to the avant-garde short story in Egypt had appeared before *Gallery 68* (in June 1965 and Aug. 1966 respectively) and were recognized at the time as 'a birth certificate for this generation',[1] they were hampered by conservative critique and by their one-off nature. Their real use was in preparing the literary scene for the launch of *Gallery 68* and, in fact, one-third of the stories in both collections were by future contributors to it. Although it could not rival the distribution infrastructure and subscriptions of the Ministry of Culture's journals, *Gallery 68* provided a dedicated outlet for avant-garde activity, while the momentum achieved by the rapid succession of the first three issues (April–May, June, July 1968) helped to magnify the impact of the new literary phenomenon. Na'īm 'Aṭiyya, a more mature and recognized writer on the periphery of the *Café Riche* gathering, remembers that 'as soon as they published the first issue, they were very respected', both by those within and outside the cultural establishment. He recalls that after the first issue, several well-known writers presented work for publication in *Gallery 68*, but were rejected on the grounds that they were either already established or not experimental enough.[2]

Already by mid-1968, *Gallery 68* had made waves on the literary scene, receiving attention in the national press, not only in the cultural periodicals, but also in the daily and weekly press, with the overwhelming majority of comment and reaction focusing on the short story. *Al-Ṭalī'a* (The Avant-Garde, 1965–77) and *al-Majalla* were among the quickest to recognize the potential gathered in *Gallery 68*, while *Rūz al-Yūsuf* remained more sceptical. *Gallery 68* also drew attention in Iraq and Lebanon, aided by established distribution channels accessed through Sa'd al-Dīn Wahba. Both Ibrāhīm Manṣūr and Jamīl 'Aṭiyya Ibrāhīm, who managed *Gallery 68*'s correspondence, testify to the large number of letters received from the Arab world. Manṣūr admits, 'None of us expected this reaction actually, especially in the Arab world'[3] while Ibrāhīm asserts, 'we had more readers in Iraq than in Egypt'.[4] Even when the natural nostalgic exaggeration of those who were themselves active in the movement is taken out of the equation, the evidence still indicates that *Gallery 68* did in fact make an impact in Iraq. In the

1 'Taqārīr al-Shahr: al-Adab', *al-Ṭalī'a*, June 1968.
2 Na'īm 'Aṭiyya, taped interview, Cairo, 28 April 1996.
3 Ibrāhīm Manṣūr, taped interview, Cairo, 1 May 1996.
4 Jamīl 'Aṭiyya Ibrāhīm, taped interview, Cairo, 30 April 1996.

course of its eight issues, five Iraqi writers and poets were published[5] and 1969 saw the birth of Fāḍil al-'Azzāwī's *Shi'r 69* (Poetry 69, 1969) in Iraq, clearly inspired by the endeavour of *Gallery 68*, although banned after only four issues. In Beirut too, *Gallery 68* received almost immediate attention, with a glowing reception in *Shi'r* (Poetry, 1957–64, 1967–70) and a more cautious welcome in *al-Adab* (The Literary Arts, 1953–), but which was nevertheless enthusiastically entitled 'The Cultural Renaissance in the Arab Nation'.[6]

Given the literary explosion after 1967, with dozens of short story writers trying to make themselves heard,[7] *Gallery 68* played an important role in selecting some of the higher quality – or at least more innovatory and interesting – work in amongst the piles of 'new literature' under production at the time. Sifting new work and gathering it into a single outlet facilitated the critical process and helped even contemporaries to distinguish between new and old-style work. Evidence of this clarifying role is provided by the reception accorded *Gallery 68* in *al-Ṭalī'a* and *Shi'r*. *Al-Ṭalī'a* noted *Gallery 68*'s value in its 'embodiment of some of the new outlooks which have not yet crystallized in the main work of this generation, outlooks which distinguish between avant-garde and conservative traditional trends among writers of the same generation'. *Al-Ṭalī'a* also praised several of *Gallery 68*'s contributors for exceptionally managing to avoid imitation, 'the greatest fault of emerging literary generations'.[8] *Shi'r* was even more enthusiastic about *Gallery 68* as the bright spot of its literary generation. It began by referring to new young writers as badly read and preoccupied with the entertainment media, but singled out *Gallery 68* as 'that which astounds and brings joy . . . Their writings are characterized by the fact that they go beyond the ranting rabble, beyond tradition and simplicity'.[9]

Rather than singling out *Gallery 68* as the good amongst the bad, Aḥmad 'Abd al-Mu'ṭī Ḥijāzī in *Rūz al-Yūsuf* (Rose al-Yūsuf, 1925–) singled out the odd contribution to *Gallery 68* as the good amongst the bad. He resorted to scathing personal criticism of those involved in *68*: 'They used to sit in the café, taking it in turns to read their poems and stories, complaining about critics, publishers and editors. Resentment reached its peak in them, and they cursed all who preceded them.'

5 Ṭarrād al-Kubaysī sent a poem to *Gallery 68* (no. 4, Nov. 1968) and went on to publish several books on poetry and culture, as well as being commissioned by the Iraqi Ministry of Culture in the 1980s to write a book on the philosophy of President Saddam Hussein; Ḥāmid al-Maṭba'ī also sent a poem to *Gallery 68* (no. 7, Oct. 1969) – he was owner of the journal *al-Kalima* and went on to publish numerous books on the history of Iraq and Iraqi culture; Fu'ād al-Takarlī contributed a short story to *Gallery 68* (no. 3, July 1968), his first to be published for several years and his first ever in an Egyptian journal; 'Abd Allāh 'Abd al-Raziq contributed a short story to *Gallery 68* (no. 7, Oct. 1969); poems by 'Abd al-Wahhāb al-Bayyātī were reprinted in *Gallery 68* (no. 1, April–May 1968; no. 5, Feb. 1969; no. 8, Feb. 1971).

6 Sāmī Khashaba, 'al-Nash'a al-Thaqāfiyya fī-l-Waṭan al-'Arabī', *al-Ādāb*, July 1968.

7 Yūsuf al-Shārūnī, *Dirāsāt fī al-Qiṣṣa al-Qaṣīra* (1989), pp. 99–100.

8 'Taqārīr al-Shahr: al-Adab', *al-Ṭalī'a*, June 1968.

9 *Shi'r* (Beirut), Spring 1968, pp. 150–3.

In Ḥijāzī, one glimpses the kind of establishment conservative who opposed *Gallery 68*, especially in his disapproving description of their meetings as a cycle of reading, discussion, resentment and alcohol. Yet at least these writers were now being discussed, and even Ḥijāzī summoned up a grudging respect for the fact that their dream of publishing a journal had rapidly become a reality, and he accepted that *68*'s contributors might be 'modestly talented' and not just 'adventurers'.[10] Moreover, even negative criticism of a literary work implies a recognition of its value, since it has been deemed worthy of legitimate discourse. In other words, the polemic of dominant players in the field endows the challengers with participant status, while at the same time affirming their own legitimacy.[11]

Yet even praise and encouragement in the mainstream press might be perceived negatively, as may be seen from the reaction to Badr al-Dīb's enthusiastic comments in *al-Jumhūriyya* (The Republic, 1953–): while Ibrāhīm Fatḥī praised Badr al-Dīb's objective discussion,[12] Khalīl Kalfat criticized him for addressing new writers as if they were a united body. It may be that Kalfat feared recognition would ebb away creative momentum and artistic individuality, for he wrote of Badr al-Dīb trying 'to calm their alarm, assuage their pride and curb the defiance of their rashness and exaggerations'.[13] Kalfat in fact represents the more radical avant-garde spirit: young (aged twenty-four in 1968) and hot-headed; the fact that *Gallery 68* included his article alongside the comments of more mature critics such as Maqqār (two decades his senior) is a clear indication of *Gallery 68*'s sincere and fundamental desire to stir up debate.

Conflicting critical response to the new literature was a strong feature of *Gallery 68* and something which marked it out as a force to be reckoned with. Critical articles by Ibrāhīm Fatḥī and Ghālib Halasā, published alongside the special issue selection of short stories, fulfilled *Gallery 68*'s aim of opening discussion, and debate raged in five more articles in the following issue: Ghālib Halasā defended his analysis of the new literature; Ibrāhīm Fatḥī and Khalīl Kalfat contributed articles criticizing Halasā; Sabry Hafez criticized both Halasā and Fatḥī and took a generally dimmer view of the special issue's short story selection and Shafīq Maqqār stayed on the fringes of the debate, contributing an encouraging and – with the exception of his moralistic comments on Sulaymān Fayyāḍ's work – balanced analysis.

Gallery 68's special selection of short stories illustrating new points of departure provoked much debate on the broader literary scene. The more guarded approach is exemplified by Shukrī 'Ayyād's detailed report in *al-Majalla*. 'Ayyād acknowledged only three of the contributors, Jamāl al-Ghīṭānī, Khalīl Kalfat and Yaḥyā al-Ṭāhir 'Abd Allāh, as demonstrating completely new trends, but stressed

10 Aḥmad 'Abd al-Mu'ṭī Ḥijāzī, 'Mughāmarat *68*', *Rūz al-Yūsuf*, 17 June 1968, p. 54.
11 Pierre Bourdieu, *The Field of Cultural Production* (1993), pp. 35–6.
12 Ibrāhīm Fatḥī, 'Ba'ḍ al-Masā'il al-'Āmma fī al-Naqd', *Gallery 68*, no. 7, Oct. 1969, p. 64.
13 Khalīl Kalfat, 'Mulāḥaẓāt Ḥawla Kuttāb *68*', *Gallery 68*, no. 7, Oct. 1969, p. 73.

that this did not represent a revolution in narrative style. Significantly, what struck him as most valuable was what he identified as a new regional trend bearing the characteristics of its local environment, as represented in the works of Khalīl Kalfat and Yaḥyā al-Ṭāhir 'Abd Allāh. Probably the most radical and unfamiliar of the material featured were the stark absurdist stories of Ibrāhīm Manṣūr and Ibrāhīm 'Abd al-'Āṭī. Having already been criticized by Halasā in *Gallery 68* itself,[14] 'Ayyad dismissed them as obscene, gossipy and contrived, posing the classic reactionary question, 'can this really be called art?'.[15] Interestingly, 'Ayyād's predilections appear to have corresponded broadly to subsequent reality. The local village setting introduced by Yaḥyā al-Ṭāhir 'Abd Allāh retained its value, and other *Gallery 68* contributors such as Bahā' Ṭāhir and 'Abd al-Ḥakīm Qāsim would explore it with much success. Meanwhile, little more fictional work was in fact seen from either Ibrāhīm Manṣūr or Ibrāhīm 'Abd al-'Āṭī.

While critics might have dismissed the avant-garde hubris of the short story being born for the first time, they nevertheless acknowledged the talent of some of *68*'s contributors. 'Ayyād was especially impressed by Kharrāṭ's contribution, although he believed that neither Kharrāṭ nor Sulaymān Fayyāḍ – who were the oldest writers included in the selection – had demonstrated any fundamental development in style in their *Gallery 68* stories. Shafīq Maqqār also deemed Kharrāṭ's and Yūsuf al-Shārūnī's *Gallery 68* work superior. Significantly, both Kharrāṭ and Shārūnī had started experimenting much earlier than other contributors. It was therefore natural that most other contributors had not yet reached their full potential, and this was in fact pointed out in *Gallery 68* itself by Kalfat, Hafez and Maqqār, all of whom still looked to the future for the new to truly surpass itself and break decisively from what had gone before.

The more positive and discerning critique was exemplified by Jalāl al-'Asharī writing in *al-Fikr al-Mu'āṣir* (Contemporary Thought, 1965–71), who announced to readers that *Gallery 68* had confirmed that there was a new literary phenomenon to be reckoned with. Al-'Asharī recognized 'the new literature' as a complex phenomenon with many different strands, rather than seeing it as an umbrella term for all abstract and alienated literature. Half of the writers named by al-'Asharī as the leaders of the 'youthful squadron' in literature had contributed stories to *Gallery 68*'s special selection two months earlier, with Jamāl al-Ghīṭānī singled out for special praise even at this early stage. Like *al-Ṭalī'a*, al-'Asharī in *al-Fikr al-Mu'āṣir* also stressed that the styles of most of these writers had not yet crystallized and so he did not attempt to categorize them. He realized that most were linked negatively by their search for new expression

14 Ghālib Halasā, 'al-Adab al-Jadīd: Malāmiḥ wa-Ittijāhāt', *Gallery 68*, no. 6, April 1969, pp. 121–2.
15 Shukrī 'Ayyād, 'al-Qiṣṣa al-Miṣriyya al-Mu'āṣira: 'Adad Khāṣṣ fī Majallat *Gallery 68*, April 1969', *al-Majalla*, June 1969, pp. 94–7.

rather than positively by a particular style of expression and gave a balanced assessment of what he termed 'the *68* generation':

> They are not a movement; they are a phenomenon. They do not constitute a revolt, but rather an upsurge. They are not a torrential current, but they are a new breeze... Although they are really a mass of individuals, not members of a single body,... it is a mass whose aims meet in a single belief without strangling the individual aim.[16]

Al-'Asharī concluded by predicting that the short story would witness a revolution in form equal to the recent revolution in poetic form. *Al-Ṭalī'a* too, while it did not seek to portray *Gallery 68* as an immediate literary revolution, nevertheless recognized its potential to extend influence into the future, describing it as 'a point of departure for experimentation in our country'.[17]

The truth of this assessment is demonstrated by various developments over the subsequent two years, which hint at *Gallery 68*'s impact on the official literary scene. The two series *Kitāb al-Ṭalī'a* (The Avant-Garde Book) and *Kitāb al-Thaqāfa al-Jadīda* (The New Culture Book) were launched; *al-Akhbār* (The News, 1952–) started a literary supplement; and after *Gallery 68*'s special selection of short stories in April 1969, special issues devoted to the short story or young writers were published by *al-Hilāl* (The Crescent Moon, 1892–) and *al-Majalla*, both in August 1969, and *al-Ṭalī'a* in September 1969. The latter also established an actual literary supplement in 1972, with a short story in every issue. Significantly, *al-Majalla's* editorial to its August 1969 special issue on the short story demonstrated a much more serious approach towards it than had the editorial to its August 1966 special issue. While the earlier issue had all but dismissed the avant-garde stories as light relief for readers during the hot summer month of August,[18] the 1969 issue wrote of the short story penetrating to the human core and posing the reader with a pertinent challenge, thus warranting a special issue despite other serious contemporary world events such as landing on the moon.[19] And while the earlier issue had given the impression (in the accompanying critique as well as in the editorial) that the stories on display were somehow freak, significantly, the 1969 editorial acknowledged that a completely changed concept of the short story had indeed taken root over the course of the previous decade.

As well as the resounding impact effected by *Gallery 68* in the mainstream press and the subsequent more positive interest in 'the new literature' (*al-adab*

16 Jalāl al-'Asharī, 'al-Qiṣṣa al-Qaṣīra min al-Azma ilā al-Qaḍiyya', *al-Fikr al-Mu'āṣir*, June 1969, pp. 62–8.

17 'Taqārīr al-Shahr: al-Adab', *al-Ṭalī'a*, June 1968.

18 Editorial to *al-Majalla*, Aug. 1966.

19 Editorial to *al-Majalla*, Aug. 1969.

al-jadīd), there is tangible evidence that the writers themselves were beginning to penetrate the literary establishment. In fact, the extent to which the new literature had penetrated the literary scene led Aḥmad Bahjat to complain in *al-Ahrām* (The Pyramids, 1876–) that the short story was being taken over by new young writers, and that established writers as well as the dozens of young winners of *Nādī al-Qiṣṣa* (The Writing Club) competitions were losing out.[20] That the attention accorded new literature surged with the publication of *Gallery 68* is affirmed in *Nādī al-Qiṣṣa*, which stated in July 1970 that the literary press had concerned itself for more than two years (note that *Gallery 68* had begun just over two years previously) with the new literature, young writers and the generation struggle. Indeed, the extent of the response is indicated by *Nādī al-Qiṣṣa's* fatigued remark that there appeared to be more fuss about the new literature than there was actual literature and that certain new writers had more to say than did their work.[21]

Gallery 68 furnished young writers with a valuable alternative to *Nādī al-Qiṣṣa*. Yusrī Khamīs, Ibrāhīm Manṣūr and Muḥammad Ṣāliḥ all deemed *Nādī al-Qiṣṣa* too official to be of great importance for literary progress,[22] despite its support of some more innovatory work – *Gallery 68* contributors Aḥmad Hāshim al-Sharīf and Muḥammad Ḥāfiẓ Rajab had both won *Nādī al-Qiṣṣa* competitions. Sāmī Khashaba too admitted to its many shortcomings[23] while Jamāl al-Ghīṭānī bluntly described it as 'mummified'.[24] *Al-Ṭalī'a* also recognized that while *Nādī al-Qiṣṣa* had supported a long line of new writers, it rarely embraced wholly new experimentation or outlooks as *Gallery 68* did. *Nādī al-Qiṣṣa* basically favoured stories which adhered to models prevailing in the 1940s and 1950s, as opposed to *Gallery 68* whose 'most important distinguishing factor is the attempt to steer prevailing literary experience down a new road'.[25] Yet *Nādī al-Qiṣṣa* journal itself bore the impact of the new literary momentum when new young blood was injected into the editorial board, such that nearly half the board comprised *Gallery 68* contributors in 1970.[26] This led to *Nādī al-Qiṣṣa's* publication of more modernist and experimental works, both translated and Egyptian, including several by contributors to *Gallery 68*.[27]

20 Aḥmad Bahjat, *al-Ahrām*, Nov. 1969. Cited in S. Khashaba, 'al-Nash'a al-Thaqāfiyya fī-l-Waṭan al-'Arabī', *al-Ādāb*, Dec. 1969.

21 Editorial to *Nādī al-Qiṣṣa*, July 1970.

22 Yusrī Khamīs, taped interview, Cairo, 26 April 1996; I. Manṣūr, taped interview, Cairo, 1 May 1996; and Muḥammad Ṣāliḥ, taped interview, Cairo, 27 April 1996.

23 S. Khashaba, 'al-Nash'a al-Thaqāfiyya fī-l-Waṭan al-'Arabī', *al-Ādāb*, Dec. 1969.

24 Jamāl al-Ghīṭānī's response to *al-Ṭalī'a*'s questionnaire 'Hākadhā Yatakallamu al-Udabā' al-Shabāb fī al-Waṭan al-'Arabī', *al-Ṭalī'a*, Sept. 1969.

25 'Taqārīr al-Shahr', *al-Ṭalī'a*, June 1968.

26 Among the nine members of *Nādī al-Qiṣṣa's* editorial board were Idwār al-Kharrāṭ, Bahā' Ṭāhir, 'Abd al-Ḥakīm Qāsim and Sulaymān Fayyāḍ.

27 Some of the improvements effected in *Nādī al-Qiṣṣa* were noted by Maḥmūd 'Abd al-Rāziq, 'Damā' Jadīda fī Nādī al-Qiṣṣa', *Nādī al-Qiṣṣa*, June 1970, pp. 68–72.

The increasing attention accorded young writers culminated in the First Conference for Young Writers, organized by the Youth Secretariat of the United Arab Republic in December 1969. The conference represented an attempt by the establishment to incorporate the younger generation of writers, although it is difficult to assess how genuine this attempt really was, or how successful. Writing in *al-Majalla*, Hafez at least reported that the conference had treated young writers as part of the greater whole, and that their views on various issues had been made clear.[28] ʻAlī Muṣṭafā Amīn, writing in *al-Kātib*, agreed that the conference had yielded important results. Nine committees were set up for the different genres and media, headed by established men of letters, including Yūsuf Idrīs (short story), Fārūq Khurshid (novel) and Ṣalāḥ ʻAbd al-Ṣabūr (poetry), and presided over by Naguib Mahfouz. The concerns of writers in the provinces were not neglected, with over sixty preparatory conferences held throughout Egypt to choose representatives, and over 1000 entries gathered from all over Egypt for the literary competitions. Problems of publication, censorship and lack of translation were all raised, and committee members agreed on many worthy recommendations to improve opportunities for young writers, such as extension of the grants scheme (*tafarrugh*) and the foundation of an independent writers' union. Naturally the conference also had many shortcomings, including a lack of attention to journalism, questionable criteria for the election of some committees and representatives, and the absence of several worthy young writers. Nevertheless, some of those who had contributed to *Gallery 68* were elected to the secretariat of governorate representatives for the implementation of the conference's recommendations, including Ibrāhīm Fatḥī (Cairo), Muḥammad Ḥāfiẓ Rajab (Alexandria) and Muḥammad ʻAfīfī Maṭar (Kafr al-Shaykh).[29]

The 1970s, however, witnessed a spiralling culture setback and the optimistic recommendations of the Conference for Young Writers did not translate into positive action. Not only was the Ministry of Culture, at which most of the recommendations had been directed, not officially represented at the conference, but the advent of Sadat a year later meant that the more experimental writers were all but thrown back to square one. *Gallery 68* editor Muḥammad Ibrāhīm Mabrūk concluded bitterly that once the celebrations welcoming the more creative innovative writers of the 1960s alongside popular established writers were over, the former found themselves isolated – they had merely been the stars of the show, not hosting the show as they had imagined.[30]

28 Sabry Hafez, 'Ḥawla Mu'tamar al-Udabā' al-Shubbān', *al-Majalla*, Jan. 1970, pp. 51.

29 ʻAlī Muṣṭafā Amīn, 'al-Mu'tamar al-Awwal li-l-Udabā' al-Shubbān, *al-Kātib*, Jan. 1970, pp. 118–23.

30 Muḥammad Ibrāhīm Mabrūk, 'Zaman al-Kataba ya'ful wa-Azminat al-Kuttāb tajī' ', *al-Nadīm*, no. 2, Feb. 1982, p. 7.

While government funding for literature and the arts decreased, government intervention increased, beginning with the closure of most state literary and cultural journals in 1971 and continuing with the dismissal of over 100 writers and journalists in February 1973. Shukrī described this as 'a massacre undertaken by the apparatus of the cultural counter revolution'.[31] As well as *Gallery 68* contributors like Ibrāhīm Manṣūr, Amal Dunqul, Jamāl al-Ghīṭānī and Ṣāfī Nāz Kāẓim, prominent established leaders of Egyptian culture such as Lūwīs 'Awaḍ, Luṭfī al-Khūlī, Yūsuf Idrīs and Aḥmad 'Abd al-Mu'ṭī Ḥijāzī were also dismissed.

The repressive conditions and limited opportunities in Egypt prompted several of *Gallery 68*'s most talented contributors to leave, just at the time when they might have concretized their impact and thoroughly penetrated the Egyptian literary scene.[32] The critic Mohammed Shaheen expressed regret for 'the unfortunate circumstances surrounding the [short story] *genre* at a time which was supposed to be the high season of its growth and development'.[33] One writer remembers, 'people did not read at that time. Most good writers and poets were out of Egypt, and it was no use publishing anything.'[34] Al-Sayyid Abū al-Najā too confirmed that there was little opportunity for writers to practice their talents in Egypt.[35] *Al-Ṭalī'a* also testified to the detrimental effects of the emigration of Egyptian writers,[36] and Stagh devotes a whole chapter of her work on the freedom of speech at this time to 'The Flight to Beirut, Damascus and Baghdad'. The flight on paper was naturally greater than the flight in person. Stagh necessarily limits her statistics to book publication, but, were the number of articles, short stories and poems published in journals outside Egypt also included, the evidence for a serious migration of Egyptian talent would be even more compelling.

Gallery 68's successors: entrenchment of the paradigm

The above tale of success followed by suffocation demonstrates the fluidity of the objective relations between the positions of occupants, agents and institutions in Bourdieu's 'field' of cultural production. Here, all three of the strategies identified by Bourdieu as operative in the field – conservation, succession and subversion – come into play. Sixties writers were beginning to succeed to institutionally

31 Ghālī Shukrī, *Min al-Arshīf al-Sirrī li-l-Thaqāfa al-Miṣriyya* (1975), p. 106.

32 Among *Gallery 68*'s contributors to leave Egypt over the next decade were 'Abd al-Ḥakīm Qāsim, Bahā' Ṭāhir, Jamīl 'Aṭiyya Ibrāhīm, Aḥmad Mursī, Ghālī Shukrī, Muḥammad al-Bisāṭī, Muḥammad Maqqār and Sabry Hafez.

33 M. Shaheen, *The Modern Arabic Short Story: Shahrazad Returns* (1989), p. 2.

34 Interview with Ibrāhīm 'Abd al-Majīd conducted by Marina Stagh, Cairo, May 1991, in M. Stagh, *The Limits of Freedom of Speech* (1993), p. 243.

35 Interview with Sayyid Abū al-Najā conducted by Muḥammad Shalabī, in M. Shalabī, *Ma' Ruwwād al-Fikr wa-l-Fann* (1982), p. 33.

36 Shams al-Dīn Mūsā, 'Malāmiḥ al-Thaqāfa al-Miṣriyya bayna al-Qiṭā'ayn al-'Āmm wa-l-Khāṣṣ', *al-Ṭalī'a*, Oct. 1975, pp. 160–5.

recognized positions, rather than merely subverting dominant norms from the margins. However, the establishment's strategy of conservation through domination made succession ever more difficult as Sadat tightened his grip on the cultural apparatus, resulting in the polarization of the field; for players in the field (whether individuals or institutions) are defined by their relation to one another (whether this be opposition or alliance). In other words, the behaviour of any player in the field is a product of the forces impinging on it from other players in the field. In Egypt of the 1970s and 1980s, the forces of state domination compelled experimental activity to concentrate heavily inside its own relatively autonomous sub-field, where struggling writers – some of them former *Gallery 68* contributors – had little alternative but to set up their own publication outlets in their bid for specific cultural capital.[37] Strategies are highly dependent on the rules and tools of conflict within each field; in the Egyptian literary field, for those seeking autonomy, the tool was the independent journal and the rule was the non-periodic publication of it to circumvent issues of licensing and censorship.

Thus numerous unofficial independent journals invaded the literary scene in the late 1970s and early 1980s,[38] not only in Cairo and Alexandria, but with feverish enthusiasm in the Egyptian provinces.[39] The new phenomena of photocopiers and stencils meant that the journals could be produced more cheaply and easily, thus increasing the autonomy of this literary sub-field of restricted production. Unlike licensed journals or publications for the commercial market driven by a heteronomous principle bowing to concerns in the economic and political fields, these small independent journals enjoyed the freedom of having nothing to lose in their own autonomous sub-field. Idwār al-Kharrāṭ once commented, 'I am certain that what could be written by Egyptian writers if the famous three taboos – religion, sex and to a lesser extent politics – were lifted, is a

37 Indeed, over time, opening editorials often stressed their concern for increased publication outlets more than they did their insistence on having broken with tradition. See, for example, the modest 'manifesto' penned by Muntaṣar al-Qaffāsh and others, *Qiṣṣa*, no. 1, Aug. 1986.

38 Although the censorship of books had been abolished in December 1976, it was still practiced. The following year, however, Fu'ād Ḥijāzī won a test-case over the publication of his novel *Sujanā' li-Kull al-'Uṣūr* in Manṣūra. This gave rise to *thawrat al-masṭar* (the stencil revolution), with other writers following Ḥijāzī's example and printing their books, generally by the cheaper offset method. Journals still required a license, but editors could circumvent the law by publishing non-periodically as books.

39 For example, *Nahār* (Day) was launched in Daqhaliyya in 1983, edited by 'Abd al-Wahhāb 'Alī, 'Abd al-'Āl Sa'd and Riḍā 'Aṭiyya; *al-Shams al-Jadīda* (The New Sun) was launched in al-Zaqāziq in 1984, edited by 'Abd al-Mun'im 'Abd al-Qādir and Zahrān Salāma. *Ruwwād* (Pioneers) was published by the literary club of Dimyāṭ in the early 1980s (*al-Hilāl* reviewed its fourth issue in April 1983, p. 128). NB Such regional initiatives had been pre-empted by Muḥammad 'Afīfī Maṭar's *Sanābil* (Ears of Corn, 1969–72), published – and officially approved – in Kafr al-Shaykh. It was out of innovative activity in Kafr al-Shaykh that 'Alī Qindīl, Aḥmad Samāḥa, 'Alī 'Afīfī, Jamāl al-Qaṣṣāṣ and others emerged. Another early initiative was *Adab al-Jamāhīr* (The Literature of the Masses), published in the early 1970s by a group of writers in Manṣūra. It has not been possible to track down reliable precise dates for these initiatives.

fantastic vision',[40] and it is precisely in these independent non-periodic journals that we catch occasional glimpses of this vision. And so the kind of cultural renewal sponsored by *Gallery 68* continued, using the same vehicle, the independent non-periodic journal, modelled so well by *Gallery 68*.

According to Bourdieu, as the autonomizing process advances, it becomes easier to occupy the position of producer without requiring the same properties that had to be in place to produce the position in the first place.[41] In other words, in Egypt, as the notion of combating established literary norms through publishing one's work in non-periodic journals took hold and became more commonplace during the late 1970s and 1980s, successive newcomers trying their hand in this autonomous sub-field could dispense with the kinds of sacrifices and breaks required from their predecessors. This further indicates the ground-breaking position of *Gallery 68* and its lasting, if seemingly indirect, influence as a journal.

Evidence of the respect felt for the *Gallery 68* model is indicated by an attempt to revive *Gallery 68* itself. Forty two artists took part in an exhibition in Cairo's Atelier in June and July 1975 to muster both financial and moral support for the journal's resurrection. Painter and short story writer 'Izz al-Dīn Najīb described the attempt as the one positive event on the art scene which was being dominated by the Spring Exhibition, to which he referred disdainfully as a tourist market. He added that 'the need for *68* as an independent platform for writers is even more pressing now than it was then',[42] evidencing the deep impression made by *Gallery 68*. Although the journal was not ultimately revived, the exhibition still represented a valuable result of *Gallery 68*'s impact, rather than just a failed attempt at continuation. Time had moved on and neither Ibrāhīm Manṣūr nor Jamīl 'Aṭiyya Ibrāhīm, two former dynamos of *68*'s production, were involved.[43] Moreover, its one time editor-in-chief Aḥmad Mursī, himself a talented and innovative artist, had emigrated to the United States the previous year. Nevertheless, the attempt was a development. *Gallery 68* had originally sold artwork to help finance the journal,[44] and had included art in the journal. As well as dedicating a few pages in each issue to good quality reproduction of artwork, it had also published brief studies of avant-garde art by Aḥmad Mursī and Idwār al-Kharrāṭ. 'Izz al-Dīn Najīb commented that the attempt by artists to revive *Gallery 68* confirmed their worthiness of space in the journal and represented

40 Interview with Idwār al-Kharrāṭ conducted by M. Stagh, Cairo, May 1991, in M. Stagh, op. cit. (1993), p. 124.

41 P. Bourdieu, op. cit. (1993), p. 63.

42 'Izz al-Dīn Najīb, 'al-Fann al-Tashkīlī', *al-Ṭalī'a*, Aug. 1975.

43 Jamīl Ibrāhīm does not even remember the attempt (taped interview, Cairo, 30 April 1996), while Ibrāhīm Manṣūr was not enthusiastic for *Gallery 68*'s revival since he believed it had already achieved its aims (taped interview, Cairo, 1 May 1996).

44 Even Naguib Mahfouz donated a painting (N. 'Aṭiyya, taped interview, Cairo, 28 April 1996).

a step towards founding an independent journal dedicated to art.[45] Such initiatives did indeed materialize, for example with the series *Āfāq 79* (Horizons 79) in 1979, launched by the painter, critic and latterly also novelist Maḥmūd Baqshīsh, and 'Izz al-Dīn Najīb's own launch of *al-Kalima* (The Word, 1978?).[46] While *Gallery 68*'s time had passed, other independent journals following its example – though not necessarily its editorial or literary principles – provided oases of literary creativity and debate in Sadat's cultural wasteland. A few even bore echoes of the former's title: *Shi'r 69* in Iraq, *Iḍā'a 77* (Illumination 77, 1977–88), *Kāmīrā 79* (Camera 79, 1979–?) and the series *Āfāq 79*.

While the launch of these journals may be seen as positive action under difficult circumstances, what actually united them was a culture of negation. Mutual opposition to a domineering cultural policy and its prevalent literary norms bred a certain supportive solidarity within the autonomous sub-field that these journals were creating. Thus, despite their sometimes differing views on aesthetics and poetics, non-periodic journals did share some common denominators, most obviously: the debates around which they focused. While their attitudes on some of these may have varied, the actual talking points of the day were largely the same, the four main ones being: the appalling cultural crisis; the desperate need for an independent union of writers; the role of politics in literary endeavours; and their avowed openness to at least acknowledge the existence of different aesthetic views. Examining these common focal points helps us to reconstruct the mood of the age, in isolation from which the literary works themselves cannot fully be understood, for their meaning is linked to the surrounding literary field to which they dialectically related in space and time. In Bourdieu terminology, position-takings (i.e., literary works) cannot be considered independently of the actual positions which they manifest.[47]

A united stand against the cultural crisis

Unsurprisingly, since it constituted one of their main *raisons d'être*, the surrounding cultural crisis was the subject of ubiquitous complaint in these journals. Ḥasan Ḥanafī, writing in *Kitābāt*, took a typically bitter view, asserting that the crisis of Egyptian culture was worse than ever before and that, apart from a small group of writers, creativity had died out, and with it the spirit of the nation.[48] *Al-Ghad* (Tomorrow, 1953, 1959, 1985–6) asked one thousand Egyptians for their views on culture and concluded that the cultural outlook was overwhelmingly

45 'Izz al-Dīn Najīb, 'al-Fann al-Tashkīlī', *al-Ṭalī'a*, Aug. 1975.

46 I have only been able to locate one copy of *al-Kalima* (no. 2, April 1978), but it is unlikely that the journal (comprising only eight pages) was extant much before or after this date. Najīb, in his late thirties, devoted this issue to criticizing the Artists' Union and exposing establishment corruption.

47 P. Bourdieu, *The Field of Cultural Production* (1993), p. 32. Bourdieu emphasizes that one should not have to choose between an internal reading or an external analysis of a work.

48 Ḥasan Ḥanafī, *Kitābāt*, no. 4, March 1980, pp. 15–16.

negative.[49] Both *al-Nadīm* (al-Nadīm, 1980–5) and *al-Thaqāfa al-Jadīda* (The New Culture, 1976) complained of Egyptian culture being led by 'corpses'.[50] And Muḥammad 'Abd al-'Āl al-Fīl's *Abjadiyyāt* (Elementary Truths, 1980) actually carried the subtitle 'About the Crisis of Culture and Creativity in Egypt'. Talk of a crisis proliferated to the extent that *Mawqif* (Stance, 1981–?) actually felt compelled to begin its opening editorial with the disclaimer: 'We know that the [cultural] arena…has had sharp experience of the term "crisis" in its many different aspects, meanings and embodiments.' *Mawqif* itself then joined the ranks of those protesting for 'the release of serious thoughts and opinions from their imposed isolation'.[51] This echoed the sentiments of *Kitābāt* (Writings, 1979–84) a year earlier when it described the non-periodic journal's aim as 'to dismantle the blockade placed around a culture that is being isolated'.[52] Yet conversely, this imposed isolation – and the resulting concentration of creative activity in independent journals – actually encouraged the margin to blossom as never before as its own dynamic literary movement. One of *Gallery 68*'s founders and editors later acknowledged, 'What saved us actually was that we were rejected by the market…the margin was characterized by honesty, sincerity'.[53]

Naturally, the flight of intellectuals met with recriminations from some of those remaining in Egypt. Some regarded the flight as a cause of the cultural crisis rather than a symptom of it, convinced that writers and intellectuals should stay to fight their corner and improve the situation, and those active at the fringe were particularly vocal. *Al-Thaqāfa al-Waṭaniyya* (The National Culture, 1980–1), for example, accused those who emigrated of giving up their nationalist patriotic ambitions in favour of selfish ones. It warned intellectuals against attempts to fragment them, 'preying on them one after the other to the advantage of American–Zionist designs'.[54] *Al-Kurrāsa al-Thaqāfiyya* (The Cultural Notebook, 1979–80) too bewailed the self-exile of so many writers, at the same time criticizing the passivity of many of those remaining.[55] *Miṣriyya* (Egyptian, 1979?–86) accused those who fled to Arab oil countries of hypocrisy since the regimes there also practiced repression.[56] It blamed the search for financial gain, not only for luring Egyptian writers abroad, but also for luring them from the provinces to Cairo.[57] *Al-Nadīm* was passionately critical, accusing writers of running away instead of solving Egypt's problems on her own soil. Its editor, former *Gallery 68* editorial board member Muḥammad Ibrāhīm Mabrūk, even criticized publication abroad,

49 *Al-Ghad* (III), no. 1, 1985 (no month).
50 Opening editorial to *al-Thaqāfa al-Jadīda*, 1976, and M. I. Mabrūk, op. cit. (1982), p. 2.
51 Opening editorial to *Mawqif*, no. 1, Jan. 1981.
52 Editorial to *Kitābāt*, no. 4, March 1980.
53 I. Manṣūr, taped interview, Cairo, 1 May 1996.
54 Editorial to *al-Thaqāfa al-Waṭaniyya*, no. 2, Jan. 1981.
55 Editorial to *al-Kurrāsa al-Thaqāfiyya*, no. 2, March 1980.
56 Editorial to *Miṣriyya*, no. 4, April 1981.
57 'Azmat al-Thaqāfa al-Miṣriyya', signed *Miṣriyya*, *Miṣriyya*, no. 1, n.d. (1979?).

believing that writers should 'insist on the vital link with their readers' by creating their own independent outlets in Egypt – as he had done by founding *al-Nadīm*. He described moving abroad, both in person and on paper, as 'heavy bleeding' and called those who did so 'mercenaries'.[58] One must remember, however, that work published abroad, especially in Beirut, could find its way to Cairo, and was often reprinted in Cairo at a later stage. Nonetheless, for much of the 1970s and 1980s, it was only the non-periodic journals, the successors to the *Gallery 68* paradigm, that kept the life blood of creativity pumping around the Egyptian literary scene.

There was a certain solidarity perceptible among these fringe journals as they embraced one another in opposition to the cultural establishment. *Kitābāt*, for example, in March 1980, welcomed the proliferation of independent non-periodic journals as intellectuals rallied into democratic groups, and urged greater interaction between them. It made a point, however, of ruling out amalgamation into a single journal, preferring instead that the various journals deal with related subjects,[59] which would naturally favour diversity and spawn more fertile debate. *Kitābāt* itself took steps to facilitate this by beginning to devote each issue to a particular subject.[60] Poet Ḥilmī Sālim's *Kāf Nūn* (K. N., 1977–80)[61] also made a conscious decision to devote each issue to a single subject, with one issue wholly devoted to encouraging Murād Munīr's newly founded drama group *Jamā'at al-Masraḥ al-Miṣrī* (The Egyptian Drama Group, 1978–84) and its avant-garde drama pamphlet *al-Masākhīṭ* (The Idols, n.d.).[62] *Mawqif* too expressed its aim of interacting with other independent non-periodic journals 'to break that hard shell behind which the crisis hides'.[63] In general, however, the coordination of subject matter between journals did not occur. The very nature of such journals – unpredictability of publication dates, limited edition and poor distribution – made formal interaction difficult. Amjad Rayyān, who was himself heavily involved in such publications, concluded that they 'only obey the law of the jungle'.[64]

A more practical means of solidarity and interaction was simply to include news of 'fellow' independent journals, a widespread practice by which journals recognized and encouraged the strengths and interests of others.[65] Even breakaway

58 M. I. Mabrūk, op. cit. (1982).

59 Editorial to *Kitābāt*, no. 4, March 1980.

60 Starting with *Kitābāt*, no. 6, Aug. 1982.

61 This name is probably a play on the verb 'to be' in the imperative, which is what the two letters spell, since the journal aimed to bring into being a new literature. Neither the first nor the last issues of *Kāf Nūn* are dated, but according to Jamāl al-Qaṣṣāṣ, it first appeared in Dec. 1977 and ran until 1980 (taped interview, Cairo, 4 Nov. 1994). All issues were handwritten.

62 *Kāf Nūn*, no. 5, n.d. (1979?) NB Given that *Kāf Nūn* was never more than nineteen pages long, each issue could only usefully deal with a single subject in any case.

63 Opening editorial to *Mawqif*, no. 1, Jan. 1981.

64 Amjad Rayyān, 'Les Revues Non-Periodiques dans les Années 70', *Bulletin du CEDEJ*, 1er semestre 1989, pp. 117–21.

65 For example, *Kitābāt* (no. 5, n.d. (1981?) pp. 10–11) welcomed *al-Ru'ya* (Viewpoint), launched by the group *al-Ru'ya al-Jadīda* (The New Viewpoint) to introduce a new alternative concept of

journals demonstrated remarkable cooperation. *Kitābāt*, despite being launched by the poet Rif'at Sallām after he had failed to persuade *Iḍā'a 77* to adopt a more politically militant editorial policy,[66] remained on good terms with *Iḍā'a*. The latter even published a note of encouragement and welcome to *Kitābāt*, which included among its four other editors three *Iḍā'a* poets: Maḥmūd Nasīm, Jamāl al-Qaṣṣāṣ and Walīd Munīr; and *Kitābāt's* special issue on Egyptian poets of the 1970s featured six of the eight poets of *Jama'at Iḍā'a 77*.[67] Other journals were also associated with *Iḍā'a*: Ḥilmī Sālim's *Kāf Nūn* was actually published by *Iḍā'a*. Its launch coincided with *Iḍā'a*'s second issue[68] and its six issues demonstrated *Iḍā'a*'s interest in other cultural forms such as art and drama. Poet Amjad Rayyān's *al-Kurrāsa al-Thaqāfiyya* too was linked to *Iḍā'a* – nearly all its editorial board were *Iḍā'a* poets and, applying a strategy of magnification for impact, its publication was timed to coincide with *Iḍā'a*.[69] There was also healthy exchange between the poets of *Iḍā'a 77* and the *Aṣwāt* (Voices) group through their joint poetry readings and debates, both in Cairo and the provinces.[70]

The fact that so many of the same names crop up in several different journals indicates that some degree of interaction was achieved and it is significant to note how many of these names are now well known at the heart of the literary establishment. Among those most active at the margins in the 1970s and 1980s – in other words, those who might be seen as both casualties and heroes of the cultural crisis – were: 'Izz al-Dīn Najīb, Mājid Yūsuf, Amjad Rayyān, Aḥmad Rayyān, Yūsuf Abū Rayya, Maḥmūd Baqshīsh, Maḥmūd 'Abd al-Wahhāb, Ḥilmī Sālim, Rif'at Sallām, Muḥammad Khalaf, Muḥammad Hishām (mainly for his translations), Muḥammad Kashīk, Aḥmad al-Nashshār, Maḥmūd al-Wirdānī and Muḥammad al-Makhzanjī. Several former contributors to *Gallery 68* also remained active in this movement of independent literary journals, in particular Yaḥyā al-Ṭāhir 'Abd Allāh (before his death in 1981), Idwār al-Kharrāṭ, Ibrāhīm Fatḥī, 'Izzat 'Āmir, Usāma al-Ghuzūlī and Muḥammad Ibrāhīm Mabrūk.

film into the Egyptian cinema, while criticizing *al-Sīnimā al-'Arabīyya* (The Arab Cinema) for losing its innovative approach to become a mere review. Eventually, *Kitābāt* (no. 9, Nov. 1984) decided to dedicate a special section to looking specifically at non-periodic journals, but this turned out to be the last issue. *Miṣriyya*, in its opening editorial, n.d. (1979?), greeted *Iḍā'a 77, al-Naddāha, Āfāq 79, Kitābāt, al-Fajr* and *Bānūrāmā*, even adding that it hoped the latter would surpass *Miṣriyya* itself.

66 Samia Mehrez, 'Experimentation and the Institution', *Alif*, no. 11, 1991, ft.7.

67 *Kitābāt*, no. 7, Jan. 1983.

68 Jamāl al-Qaṣṣāṣ, taped interview, Cairo, 4 Nov. 1994.

69 Of the four members of *al-Kurrāsa al-Thaqāfiyya*'s editorial board, Amjad Rayyān, Ḥasan Ṭilib and Muḥammad Khalaf were *Iḍā'a* poets; the last was Sayyid Sa'īd. Its two issues (June 1979, March 1980) coincided with nos. 5 and 6 of *Iḍā'a*, which were much more meagre than usual.

70 The *Aṣwāt* poets published collections of poetry but did not actually publish their journal, *al-Kitāba al-Sawdā'* (Black Writing) until 1988. Only one issue of it ever appeared.

Lobbying for an independent union of writers

Since these non-periodic journals by their very nature provided an alternative to the official cultural apparatus, it was natural that the main rallying point between them was the call for a democratic platform for writers, and lobbying for an independent union of writers provided a focal point of the struggle for power/legitimacy. What is at stake in the literary field is 'the power to impose the dominant definition of the writer and therefore to delimit the population of those entitled to take part in the struggle to define the writer'.[71] Hence the importance among avant-gardists for the union to be democratic, leaving it open for them to propagate their own definitions of legitimacy in the field; likewise, the vested interest of those already in dominant positions to conserve their dominance by restricting membership of the union.

Although the *Majlis al-Sha'b* (The National Assembly) eventually decided to found a writers' union in June 1975, more than five years after the recommendation of the Conference for Young Writers in December 1969, it was not the independent, democratic union for which writers had been hoping, and the bill had been passed into law without any consultation with writers. *Al-Ṭalī'a* took the lead in the ensuing debate, publishing detailed criticisms of the Union in November 1975. This provoked a flurry of letters offering additional critical observations in the next three issues. The major flaws in the Union of Writers were as follows: the temporary committee set up to consider applications for membership of the Union was too closely affiliated to the Ministry of Culture – three of its five members were Sa'd al-Dīn Wahba (First Undersecretary of State for Culture), Tharwat Abāẓa (cultural editor of *al-Ahrām*) and 'Abd al-'Azīz al-Dasūqī (editor of *al-Thaqāfa*); and the Ministry of Culture ultimately had total control over the Union's actions and decisions. Since the frequently ambiguous small print had not been debated with writers and intellectuals before the bill was passed into law, there was much room for conflicting interpretation of the Union's powers. For example, membership was conditional on the applicant being reputable and noteworthy (*ḥasan al-sīra, maḥmūd al-sum'a*). Moreover, debate of religious and political issues 'contrary to public good order' was banned, as was gambling and drinking spirits. In fact, the law included six articles outlining disciplinary procedures against members. *Al-Ṭalī'a* commented that 'this law takes from writers and hardly gives them a thing'.[72] The heat of the debate reached the point where both Fārūq 'Abd al-Qādir in *al-Ṭalī'a* and 'Abd al-'Azīz al-Dasūqī in *al-Thaqāfa* accused one another not only of lying, but also of being responsible for the 1967 defeat.[73] Unsurprisingly, *al-Ṭalī'a* incurred the wrath of

71 P. Bourdieu, *The Field of Cultural Production* (1993), p. 42.

72 Fārūq 'Abd al-Qādir, 'Ittiḥād al-Kuttāb', *al-Ṭalī'a*, Nov. 1975, p. 138.

73 'Abd al-'Azīz al-Dasūqī, 'Sū' al-Fahm wa-Sū' al-Khalaq', *al-Thaqāfa*, Dec. 1975. Fārūq 'Abd al-Qādir, 'Ta'liq', *al-Ṭalī'a*, Jan. 1976, pp. 171–2.

the regime and was forced to close in January 1977 when members of its editorial board were imprisoned.[74]

Although most intellectuals agreed that the Union needed reform, opinions differed as to whether this should be attempted from within or without. While remaining highly critical of the Union, ʻAbd al-Munʻim Ṭalīma[75] pointed out that it gave writers a legitimate legal framework within which to continue the fight for a more democratic union. Fārūq ʻAbd al-Qādir and ʻIzz al-Dīn Najīb also encouraged writers to cooperate with the Union to ensure a common rallying point and avoid isolation.[76] The group of writers calling itself *Jamʻiyyat Kuttāb al-Ghad* (The Society of Tomorrow's Writers), on the other hand, represented the most extreme opposition. Led by the critic Ibrāhīm Fatḥī, a former *Gallery 68* contributor, this group was the organ of the Egyptian Communist Workers' Party and dozens of its members had been arrested in January 1975 in a mass government crackdown on the leftist opposition. Predictably, it dismissed the Union outright, perceiving it as a bureaucratic sub-division of the Ministry of Culture – more of a syndicate (*niqāba*) than a true union (*ittiḥād*) – and heaped blame on those writers attempting to join the Union under the pretence of changing it from the inside.[77]

Ultimately, the Union failed to rally writers: while some rejected it outright, others who sought to join had their applications refused. The rule stating that a writer should have at least some kind of publication record (*intāj malḥūẓ*) worked against provincial writers who did not have the same opportunities to publish as those based in Cairo or Alexandria,[78] while the rule requiring a writer to be reputable and noteworthy could exclude just about anyone. *Gallery 68* founder and editor Jamīl ʻAṭiyya Ibrāhīm, for example, had his application rejected, despite having published in at least six journals, both in Egypt and abroad, as well as broadcasting for the cultural station Programme Two.[79] Naturally, the fear was that any unregulated expansion of the set of people enjoying a legitimate right to pronounce on literary matters could alter dominant norms of taste and style, and this would pose a threat to those determined to safeguard their dominant positions in the field. As a result, many protestors rallied around their own independent cultural journals rather than around the Union. In fact, *al-Ṭalīʻa*, in

74 Opening editorial to *al-Ṭalīʻa*, no. 1, May 1984, when it was revived briefly as a non-periodic journal for four issues.

75 NB Ṭalīma is also variously referred to under the transliteration Ṭulayma and Ṭillīma.

76 ʻIttiḥād al-Kuttāb: al-Munāqasha Mustamirra', *al-Ṭalīʻa*, Dec. 1975.

77 Ibid.

78 For example, Al-Sayyid Saʻd Māḍī, a member of the literary club of Damanhūr, protested against the Union's neglect of provincial writers in a letter to *al-Ṭalīʻa*, Dec. 1975, pp. 176–7. Meanwhile, Qāsim Musʻad ʻAlīwa observed that, although cultural meetings and festivals were held in various provinces, their custodians tended to cultivate a cultural feudalism which kept out young writers and their revolutionary slogans. *al-Ṭalīʻa*, Jan. 1976, pp. 169–71.

79 J. A. Ibrāhīm, letter to *al-Ṭalīʻa*, Feb. 1976, pp. 176–7.

which anti-Union strategy was much debated, was itself relaunched as a non-periodic journal in the mid-1980s, siding with the margin (the autonomous sub-field) against the literary establishment. The fuss kicked up by and about the Union is neatly summed up by *Gallery 68* editor Muḥammad Ibrāhīm Mabrūk who, remembering the resounding debate about the Union in the Egyptian press, cynically identified its most active member as the typewriter.[80]

Thus, immediately from the opening editorial of *Iḍā'a 77*, the earliest and most high profile non-periodic journal of the 1970s, the call for an independent democratic union of writers continued unabated. One of the most vocal in its criticism of the existing Union of Writers was *Kitābāt*, founded in 1979 by the *Iḍā'a* poet Rifʿat Sallām after a disagreement over the editorial policy of *Iḍā'a 77*. Even more strongly than *Iḍā'a, Kitābāt* declared its aim of 'working towards the realization of a national democratic union of writers and artists', adding that 'this is the responsibility from which there is no escape'. The opening editorial declared its aim of providing democratic intellectuals with a rallying point, around which an alternative culture could crystallize.[81] The second editorial further elaborated the aim of creating 'an independent national democratic union of writers' and, unlike *Iḍā'a 77*, acknowledged the need to create slogans as a powerful rallying force.[82] Amjad Rayyān's *al-Kurrāsa al-Thaqāfiyya* also stressed its aim of 'helping to create a cultural front for nationalist democratic writers and intellectuals' and it regarded the publication of independent literary journals as 'an effective step on the hard road to a democratic union of writers'.[83] The rights of the Union of Artists were also championed by the independent journals. For example, 'Izz al-Dīn Najīb dedicated a whole issue of his journal *al-Kalima*, founded after the closure of *al-Ṭalīʿa* in 1977, to harsh criticism of the existing Union. The opening article was entitled 'The Petty Dictator' and referred to the Ministry of Culture official in charge of the Union.[84] Likewise, the opening issue of Ḥilmī Sālim's *Kāf Nūn* was dedicated to opinions on the Union by the artists 'Izz al-Dīn Najīb, Maḥmūd Baqshīsh and 'Ādil al-Sīwī.[85]

The angry indignation of those opting out of the Union of Writers was eloquently expressed by *Gallery 68* contributor Muḥammad Ibrāhīm Mabrūk when he wrote in his own independent journal *al-Nadīm*,

> Why prevent intellectuals and creative artists from meeting in the forms they organize in their complete freedom in order to discuss their creations and problems without previously ordained areas of exclusion?...

80 M. I. Mabrūk, op. cit. (1982), p. 9.
81 Opening editorial to *Kitābāt*, no. 1, May 1979.
82 Editorial to *Kitābāt*, no. 2, June 1979.
83 Editorial to *al-Kurrāsa al-Thaqāfiyya*, no. 2, March 1980.
84 *al-Kalima*, no. 2, April 1978.
85 *Kāf Nūn*, no. 1, n.d. (Dec. 1977).

> the acceptance of any banned areas is tantamount to accepting that the peasant be banned from agriculture, the craftsman from his craft, and the sun from rising.

By this time (1982), however, the familiarity and general adoption of the call for 'an independent democratic union of writers' prompted Mabrūk to concede that it had become no more than a meaningless slogan.[86] Yet even in the mid-1990s, echoes of the familiar call persisted. The opening editorial of the non-periodic journal *Bashīr* (Herald, 1994–5?), for example, was entitled, 'For the Sake of Establishing a Democratic Cultural Platform'.[87] In other words, the desire for and talk of a free and independent rallying point still remained, although programmatic plans of action to secure the dream failed to materialize. Even today, Jamāl al-Ghīṭānī – who resigned from the union alongside fellow *Gallery 68* contributor Bahā' Ṭāhir owing to its close ties with the Ministry of Culture – talks of secret plans to establish an alternative writers' union.[88]

Political stance

These wranglings over a democratic independent union of writers furnish an excellent example of the intersection of the literary field and the larger system of political power. Indeed, *Kitābāt's* notion of a writers' union in the 1980s was even more overtly political than that which had been envisaged by young writers in 1969. Its desired union was perceived as 'the first step towards achieving the realization of Egypt – socialist Egypt, democratic Egypt, civilized Egypt'. It would counter Zionist cultural forms and restore writers' political rights.[89] However, for some of *Gallery 68's* successors, the notion of state intervention in the proposed union became increasing anathema. *Al-Thaqāfa al-Waṭaniyya* and *Miṣriyya* in particular demonstrated a shift in attitude from *Gallery 68* in their criticism of those leftist intellectuals who believed the state should nurture cultural activity. Both journals loathed the notion of state intervention in culture, and accused leftist intellectuals of hypocrisy – reproaching the authorities while, at the same time, hoping for their support, through *tafarrugh* grants for example. *Gallery 68* contributors Idwār al-Kharrāṭ and Sulaymān Fayyāḍ were among those singled out for criticism.[90]

While criticism of Egypt's cultural crisis, the desire to challenge dominant cultural values held responsible for the general cultural crisis and the call for a

86 M. I. Mabrūk, op. cit. (1982), pp. 7–8.

87 Opening editorial to *Bashīr*, no. 1, May 1994.

88 Rania Khallaf, 'A Questionable Reincarnation', *al-Ahram Weekly*, no. 737, 7–13 April 2005. Online. Available HTTP: http://weekly.ahram.org.eg/2005/737/cu1.htm

89 Editorial to *Kitābāt*, no. 2, June 1979.

90 Editorial to *Miṣriyya*, no. 4, April 1981; and Ṣalāḥ 'Īsā, 'Ta'līq 'alā al-Taḥqīq: al-Kahana wa-l-Jallādhūn', *al-Thaqāfa al-Waṭaniyya*, no. 2, Jan. 1981.

nationalist democratic platform for writers acted as the principal common denominators between the non-periodic journals to follow *Gallery 68*, a very general political stance can also be identified. For example, anti-Zionist and anti-imperialist sentiments ran high in the autonomous avant-garde sub-field, exacerbated by the move towards the normalization of relations with Israel in the late 1970s. The extent of political comment varied considerably according to the role each journal perceived for itself. *Kitābāt*, for example, broke from *Iḍā'a 77* after Sadat's visit to Jerusalem in 1978 prompted Rif'at Sallām to adopt a more militant stance. Direct political comment, critical of all aspects of Zionism and highlighting the Palestinian plight, featured heavily in *Kitābāt*'s nine issues. *Miṣriyya* too was overtly anti both America and Israel, to the extent that actual literature was eventually replaced by direct articles on various political, social and religious matters.[91] Meanwhile, *al-Thaqāfa al-Waṭaniyya* bitterly reproached the Egyptian intelligentsia for 'dancing on the class staircase,...and fighting American imperialism while adopting its way of thinking and living, believing deep down in its superiority in everything'.[92] *Mawqif* devoted a large proportion of its first (and probably only) issue to articles condemning Zionism and exposing the Palestinian tragedy. It even published a petition for readers to sign and return, opposing plans for Israel to receive water from the Nile.[93] Even *Iḍā'a 77*, notwithstanding its scathing objection to politics dressed up as literature, demonstrated its concern for political realities. As well as declaring support on several occasions for arrested poets in various Arab countries, a whole issue was focused on the Beirut tragedy and Zionist aggression.[94] It is clear that, in general, the desire to somehow couple the two imperatives of political engagement and literary renewal remained strong in the avant-garde sub-field.

Foreign literature featured but rarely in these independent non-periodic journals. This is probably because, given state control of the publishing industry and the stagnation of official culture at this time, concentrating on exposing Egypt's own creativity was the priority. The lack of Western literature in translation may also in part have been a backlash against Sadat's friendly relations with America which had fostered peace with Israel. *Kitābāt*, one of those most militantly anti-imperialist, was strikingly devoid of both translated literature and studies of non-Arab literature or culture, apart from a damning analysis of Zionist fiction in the 1982 issue.[95] In fact, one of the only references to Western culture was negative – a criticism of those who immersed themselves in Western modes of

91 *Miṣriyya*'s ninth (and final?) issue in Oct. 1986 featured only one poem and no short stories, despite being the longest issue, comprising over 100 pages.

92 Ṣ. 'Īsā, op. cit. (1981). Written by the editor, this piece is much more provocative than the editorial but is tucked away at the back of the journal as the penultimate item.

93 *Mawqif*, no. 1, Jan. 1981.

94 *Iḍā'a 77*, no. 9, Jan. 1983.

95 Aḥmad 'Umar Shāhīn, *Kitābāt*, no. 6, Aug. 1982, pp. 62–70.

literary criticism.[96] *Al-Ghad*, in its opening editorial, had also scathingly referred to Western art as mere escapism.[97] The only foreign interest *al-Thaqāfa al-Waṭaniyya* showed was in Russian culture, remaining true to its socialist and anti-American sentiments.[98] *Miṣriyya* too, as its name implied, focused exclusively on Egyptian literature, with the occasional foray into broader Arab culture – its sole foreign literature was a very brief look at modern Spanish poetry.[99]

In general though, the lack of foreign literature can be attributed to the fact that Egyptian creativity was particularly fertile at the fringe at this time. Poetry had found a whole new momentum with the emergence of *Aṣwāt* and *Iḍā'a 77* – only two of the fifty-six poets published by the latter were non-Arab. Short story writers, meanwhile, could look to indigenous examples of modernist forms and techniques, such as those published in *Gallery 68*. The inclusion of foreign literature – a low priority – was therefore to some extent linked to space availability. Unsurprisingly, shorter journals such as *Kāf Nūn, al-Kalima* and *al-Naddāha* (The Caller, 1979) all fewer than twenty pages long, were completely devoid of foreign literature. *Al-Kurrāsa al-Thaqāfiyya* (after no. 1), *al-Nadīm* (no. 3), *al-Thaqāfa al-Jadīda* and *al-Fikr al-Mu'āṣir* (Contemporary Thought, 1978–81?), all of which ranged from 100 to over 300 pages in length, included some translated literature and the latter two journals, which were bulkiest, also published studies of foreign literature. In particular, a growing interest in Latin American writers is perceptible among non-periodic journals in the 1980s.

Avowed openness

Despite this reluctance to engage with Western literature, an extraordinary common feature of these independent avant-garde journals was their avowed openness towards other points of view, claiming to have listened to, digested and rejected the bad whilst retaining the good. This openness can be perceived in their attitude towards their literary heritage and, so they alleged, in their editorial policy, albeit within certain parameters.

These avant-gardists' position in the main was not to deny their actual literary heritage as such. Rather, it was to insist on the possibility – indeed, the necessity – of the further evolution of this heritage, by relegating dominant norms of taste and style to this heritage and introducing their own new literary forms and techniques

96 Editorial to *Kitābāt*, no. 7, Jan. 1983.

97 Opening editorial to *Al-Ghad* (III), no. 1, 1985.

98 *al-Thaqāfa al-Waṭaniyya*, no. 1, Jan. 1980; and no. 2, Jan. 1981 (final issue).

99 Muḥammad al-Shaḥḥāt, 'Riḥla ma' al-Shi'r al-Isbānī al-Mu'āṣir', *Miṣriyya*, no. 2, n.d. (1980?), pp. 27–9.

to become contemporary or future currency. Bourdieu describes this literary dynamic thus:

> It is the continuous creation of the battle between those who have made their names [*fait date*] and are struggling to stay in view and those who cannot make their own names without relegating to the past the established figures, whose interest lies in freezing the movement of time, fixing the state of the field forever. On the one side are the dominant figures, who want continuity, identity, reproduction; on the other, the newcomers, who seek discontinuity, rupture, difference, revolution. To 'make one's name' [*fait date*] means making one's mark, achieving recognition (in both senses) of one's *difference* from other producers, especially the most consecrated of them; at the same time, it means *creating a new position* beyond the positions presently occupied, ahead of them, in the avant-garde. To introduce difference is to produce time.... As the newcomers come into existence...they necessarily push back into the past the consecrated producers with whom they are compared, 'dating' their products and the taste of those who remain attached to them.[100]

Like *Gallery 68*, most subsequent non-periodic journals were quite prepared to acknowledge that their experiments had not sprung from a vacuum, that the literary heritage had played an important role. *Abjadiyyāt* dedicated its entire first issue to a critical historical account of Egypt's cultural development, on the grounds that the present could only be a product of the past.[101] Even *Iḍā'a 77*, while affirming the novelty of its poetry, admitted that its initiative was wholly precedented. Yet avant-garde arrogance was perceptible in *Iḍā'a*'s view of itself as remedying the shortcomings of previous initiatives, claiming to 'seek to complete all serious independent endeavours in this field'.[102] In fact, *Iḍā'a*'s hasty dismissal of previous initiatives by *Gallery 68, Sanābil* (Ears of Corn, 1969–72) and *Kuttāb al-Ghad* in its opening editorial was softened in the next issue by its inclusion of a letter from the artist 'Ādil al-Sīwī defending these enterprises. The second editorial was also more conciliatory, stressing *Iḍā'a*'s debt to the literary heritage – Egyptian, Arab and international: 'no earth nor sky can delimit our heritage'.[103]

100 P. Bourdieu, *The Field of Cultural Production* (1993), pp. 106–7.

101 *Abjadiyyāt*, no. 1, April 1980.

102 Opening editorial to *Iḍā'a 77*, July 1977. NB Hala Ḥalīm translates this as 'a *continuation* of *many other* serious independent endeavours in this field' (my italics), *Alif*, no. 11, 1991, p. 100. However, the original Arabic betrays a more arrogant nuance: 'the completion/perfection of all attempts' (*istikmal li-kull al-muḥāwalāt*). Interestingly, in a response to criticism of its arrogance in a letter published in issue 2, *Iḍā'a* used the word 'completion / perfection' (*istikmal*) only in conjunction with 'continuation' (*istimrār* or *tawāṣul*).

103 Editorial to *Iḍā'a 77*, no. 2, Dec. 1977.

As Bourdieu points out, 'one never observes either total submission…or an absolute break – and a break with the preceding generation (fathers) is often supported by a return to the traditions of the next generation back (grandfathers)'.[104] Indeed the *Aṣwāt* group of experimental poets provide a good example of this tendency. They acknowledged their cultural legacy indirectly by publishing other bygone revolutionary initiatives in the first and only issue of their journal, *al-Kitāba al-Sawdā'* (Black Writing, 1988). In it they included a chapter from Ṭaha Ḥusayn's hugely controversial book from the 1920s *Fī al-Shi'r al-Jāhilī* (On Pre-Islamic Poetry, 1926), as well as poems by Jūrj Ḥunayn and artwork by Ramsīs Yūnān, both of whom had been active in the *Jamā'at al-Fann wa-l-Ḥurriyya* (Society of Art and Freedom) and its journal *al-Taṭawwur* in the late 1930s and early 1940s.

Also like *Gallery 68*, other non-periodic journals avowed their intention to remain open to the views of others and to encourage critical dialogue. *Al-Kurrāsa al-Thaqāfiyya* welcomed diversity and controversy as the natural means to progress, and its editorial tone was more intimate and informal than that of other journals. *Mawqif* too, in its opening editorial, stressed the value of debate, inviting all Egyptian writers to participate in future issues. Like *Gallery 68*, it stressed that the views published in the journal were not necessarily those of the editorial board.[105] Although *Kāf Nūn* also declared itself 'open to every revolutionary pen', its extreme brevity (only eight pages for the first four issues) made this impossible.[106] *Al-Thaqāfa al-Jadīda*, in which a large proportion of those published had contributed to *Gallery 68*, took a more seasoned approach. While affirming its intention 'to bring to light all serious literary and artistic trends' in its 200 pages, it recognized the inevitable subjectivity of selection.[107] *Iḍā'a 77*, though often accused of arrogant introversion, affirmed in its opening editorial, 'as socialists, we do not consider ourselves the keepers of Egyptian culture', recognizing that 'the cultural scene is not devoid of genuine and original endeavours other than our own'.[108] As well as intending to publish some such endeavours, it hoped for dialogue 'with those who disagree with us before those who agree'.[109] *Iḍā'a* was indeed mindful of these intentions, for it was willing to publish several letters critical of it and 54 per cent of the journal's poems were by outsiders.

Unlike *Gallery 68*, however, some journals believed at the same time that each individual journal should be marked by a clear cohesive view of literature in order for it to make a true impact. *Iḍā'a* criticized *Gallery 68* for its lack of

104 P. Bourdieu, *The Field of Cultural Production* (1993), p. 58.

105 Opening editorial to *Mawqif*, no. 1, Jan. 1981. This appears to have been the first and only issue of *Mawqif*, giving it no opportunity to fulfil this intention.

106 Opening editorial to *Kāf Nūn*, no. 1, n.d. (Dec. 1977).

107 Opening editorial to *al-Thaqāfa al-Jadīda*, no. 1, 1976. Like *Mawqif*, it seems that *al-Thaqāfa al-Jadīda* did not publish any further issues.

108 Opening editorial to *Iḍā'a 77*, no. 1, July 1977.

109 Editorial to *Iḍā'a 77*, no. 2, Dec. 1977.

homogeneity and failure to promote a single view or theory of culture, thus 'making room for bigmouth imposters'.[110] Ironically, while *Gallery 68*'s openness and avoidance of an absolutist position might be considered one of its strengths, *Iḍā'a* held it responsible for the journal's termination (although this was contradicted in the following issue when termination was blamed on excessive introversion).[111] *Kitābāt* too emphasized the need for a clear position and criticized *al-Fikr al-Mu'āṣir*, which incidentally included a high proportion of *Gallery 68* contributors, for its lack of homogeneity.[112] *Kitābāt's* smarter ninth issue, when its subtitle changed from booklet (*kurrāsa*) to magazine (*majalla*), introduced a new section dedicated to communicating the journal's stance, taking pride in its lack of neutrality.[113] *Khaṭwa* (A Step, 1980–5) too advocated a clear united stance, declaring in her fifth issue: 'we believe the time has come to bring this hidden internal outlook into the open, to expose it sincerely and directly'. It then unequivocally announced its support for a realist critical method based on Marxist aesthetics,[114] and subsequent issues continued the discussions of realism.

Several journals attempted to evolve their production over time, improving their internal organization and presentation, and clarifying their objectives, as had *Gallery 68* to some extent after issue six. Among those to develop were *Kitābāt, Miṣriyya, Khaṭwa, al-Nadīm* and *Iḍā'a 77*, but such independent journals, by their very nature, would not ransom their short life spans with slick professionalism and soon faded out. *Iḍā'a*, exceptionally, continued for a decade, but it remained amateur and sincere, producing only fourteen issues with intervals ranging from 3 months to 3 years, and bulk varying from 7 to 58 pages.

The struggle for legitimacy: canonization begins

The structure of the literary field is determined by the struggle to monopolize the definition of legitimacy within the field and hence to secure a dominant position. This struggle is located in the space between two poles: consecrated literature enshrined by establishment institutions and avant-garde literature; popular approval from the consumer masses has no significant influence on the definition of legitimacy in this space. The former consecrated literature dominates the field of production and the market, having built up both economic capital (book sales, etc.) and symbolic capital (recognition and prestige) over time, and naturally it wishes to conserve its domination. It is rare for those newcomers to the literary field who practice and pander to prevailing tastes to win actual consecration

110 Opening editorial to *Iḍā'a 77*, no. 1, July 1977.
111 *Iḍā'a 77*, no. 2, Dec. 1977, p. 81.
112 *Kitābāt*, no. 3, Aug. 1979, p. 14.
113 Editorial to *Kitābāt*, no. 9, Nov. 1984. Ironically, this turned out to be the final issue.
114 'al-Manhaj al-Wāqi'ī: Li-Mādhā? wa-Kayfa?' (in place of editorial), *Khaṭwa*, no. 5, Dec. 1983, pp. 2–3.

(symbolic capital), although they might enjoy speedy commercial success (economic capital) and a fleeting consecration of sorts since those in dominant positions tend to praise those who confirm their domination by imitating their style. The avant-garde, on the other hand, consists largely (though rarely wholly) of newcomers who, conversely, seek to win recognition (symbolic capital) precisely by asserting their difference from the prevailing norms.[115]

When dealing with the struggle for legitimacy, it is necessary to recognize that different players in the field perceive success in different ways, resulting in a double hierarchy. One hierarchy is temporally dominant and operates according to a heteronomous principle by which success is measured in establishment terms (book sales, honours, appointments, etc.). The other hierarchy projects into the future and operates according to an autonomous principle by which success is equated with specific literary prestige (in other words, the only criterion for legitimacy for these writers is to be recognized by those whom they themselves recognize).[116] In this instance, success with the public is regarded with suspicion and deemed to indicate an interest in the economic and political profits secured by this success.[117] Adherence to this autonomous hierarchy based on disinterestedness (in economic and political successes within the broader field of power) can, paradoxically, furnish the writer with eventual economic and political success over time and thus transpose him into the heteronomous hierarchy, without this necessarily being a conscious move. Ultimately, many of the sixties writers featured in *Gallery 68* did indeed amass enough symbolic capital for their positions in the Egyptian literary field (and hence the positions of those around them) to change as the process of canonization began.

The following paragraphs consider two principal aspects of the struggle for legitimacy: public recognition and critical acclaim. How did the non-periodic journal interact with the public from its position outside the establishment and its institutions? Did it even wish to do so? Was popularity perceived as desirable capital and, if so, how successful could this avant-garde position be at capturing it? What importance did these journals attach to critical acclaim? How successful were the journals in winning critical attention, let alone positive acclaim? Were critics even equipped to evaluate new work which might flout or negate prevailing literary norms?

115 P. Bourdieu, *The Field of Cultural Production* (1993), p. 83. In fact, Bourdieu (p. 187) further subdivides the struggle in the French literary field. Not only does he identify a struggle between pure and commercial sub-fields over the legitimate principal of domination, he also mentions the struggle between the consecrated avant-garde and the new avant-garde; in the case of sixties Egypt, however, the consecrated avant-garde was itself enjoying more commercial success, although without necessarily becoming commercial.

116 Ibid., pp. 37–8.

117 Of course, even within the dominant pole of the literary field operating according to a heteronomous principle, there is an intellectual snobbery against the popular successes of detective stories, romantic love stories and the like.

It seems unlikely that non-periodic journals, independent of institutional support as they were, were actually able to reach a significant proportion of the reading public. Even *Gallery 68*, which had partial access to the distribution apparatus of the Ministry of Culture, never sold out, despite a limited issue of less than 3000 copies.[118] It is important, however, to bear in mind that a single copy could serve more than one individual, for example by being read aloud in cafés. One critic affirmed, 'With the publication of *Gallery 68*, littérateurs of the far left have been able for the first time in the history of our modern Arabic literature to forge a way through to the reading public and to interact with traditional literary currents'.[119] Shukrī 'Ayyād too judged that in 1969 the literary left had, remarkably, succeeded at last in reaching its public.[120] Yet the introduction of modernist techniques inevitably erected a barrier between the writer and the broader reading public. Shukrī 'Ayyād himself recognized this with hindsight, although he attributed the barrier to the writer having lost concern for the social impact of his work: 'This has gradually been dropped in the last thirty years or so. Literary people now write for themselves to be read by each other, if anyone. There is no feeling at all of obligation to reach the less fortunate layers of the Egyptian public.'[121]

Gallery 68's social concern was very much apparent, despite the unusual modernist forms and techniques through which it was expressed. Bahā' Ṭāhir speaks for most contributors when he comments that, although he makes no artistic concessions to appeal to or reach the public, nevertheless the public remains 'my major concern'.[122] The separation between the writer or poet and the broader reading public was exacerbated by some subsequent independent journals modelled on the example, if not the editorial or literary principles, of *Gallery 68*. This did not necessarily result from a theorized position (as was the case with *Iḍa'a 77*), but from the practical conditions in which they were forced to publish as the autonomy of their sub-field increased. While *Iḍā'a 77* was too impenetrable for the broader reading public, although it wielded considerable influence within a certain elite, other journals were too fleeting (e.g. *al-Thaqāfa al-Waṭaniyya* and *al-Thaqāfa al-Jadīda*), too bitter (e.g. *al-Nadīm*) – or it was simply that few independent journals could equal the polished presentation of *Gallery 68*

118 Jamīl 'Aṭiyya Ibrāhīm admits that they circulated propaganda that the first issue had sold out, and indeed, this did appear to be the case at first. Unsold issues were, however, returned by the distributor after a few months (taped interview, Cairo, 30 April 1996). Interestingly, Na'īm 'Aṭiyya remains convinced that the first issue sold out completely (taped interview, Cairo, 28 April 1996).

119 Roger Allen (ed.) *Modern Arabic Literature* (1987), p. 185.

120 Sh. 'Ayyād, 'al-Qiṣṣa al-Qaṣīra al-Mu'āṣira: 'Adad Khāṣṣ fī Majallat *Gallery 68*', *al-Majalla*, April 1969, p. 94.

121 Sh. 'Ayyād, taped interview, Cairo, 29 April 1996. NB Shukrī 'Ayyād launched a new non-periodic journal in 1996, *al-Nidā'*, 'to regain this link between the writer and his broader public'. *Al-Nidā'* was to publish periodically as soon as 'Ayyād obtained the 200 partners needed to fulfil the licensing requirements.

122 Bahā' Ṭāhir, taped interview, Cairo, 1 May 1996.

or access the same sophisticated distribution apparatus. In addition, the shock force of *Gallery 68*'s historical moment following the 1967 defeat by Israel could not be matched. Of course, none of these observations need necessarily cast aspersions on the literature published in these later journals.

The work of poets like the *Iḍā'a 77* group has been described as 'a slap in the face for public taste'.[123] One time *Iḍā'a 77* poet Rif'at Sallām actually agreed with this view and stressed that being easily accessible to or pleasing the public was not a priority for *Iḍā'a 77*.[124] *Iḍā'a* valued its link to the public in terms of the ability to give refined expression to popular desires, not in terms of size of readership.[125] Yet, paradoxically, the success of *Iḍā'a* poets in expressing popular desires was necessarily judged by their own peer group in accordance with the autonomous principle of the avant-garde sub-field. In fact, it was exactly this situation that prompted *Gallery 68* editor Ḥasan Sulaymān to clarify in 1980 that 'the task of art, most emphatically, must not be confined to a narrow circle of colleagues, for the artist does not create for the sake of this circle'.[126] In later years and in the light of heavy criticism, *Iḍā'a* became more defensive about its links to the public, admitting that 'there is no genuine art without a public'. It apportioned some of the blame for the lack of public interest in its poetry to the social, political and cultural conditions which shaped the reading public, since the poets themselves could not be expected to sacrifice aesthetic quality for the sake of accessibility.[127]

Other non-periodic journals were, like *Gallery 68*, more ostensibly concerned with reaching readers. In *Kitābāt* for example, Rijā'ī al-Mīrghanī criticized *Iḍā'a*'s lack of regard for readers;[128] and 'Izz al-Dīn Najīb's *al-Kalima* called for greater public involvement in art to destroy the cycle of isolation between the artist and society.[129] *Al-Ghad* placed exceptional importance on the link between literature and the public – culture was deemed a basic necessity and equated with a loaf of bread.[130] The group's immediate aim of fostering a progressive national culture was but a step towards its ultimate goal of ensuring that 'no Arab is unable to eat, be educated or live'.[131] *Al-Kurrāsa al-Thaqāfiyya* too testified to its

123 Rajā' al-Naqqāsh, 'Mādhā turīdūna Ayyuhā al-Shu'arā'', *al-Muṣawwar*, 30 Sept. 1977.

124 Rif'at Sallām, 'Bībliyūghrāfiyyat Shu'arā' al-Sab'īniyyāt fī Miṣr', *Alif*, no. 11, 1991, p. 182–4.

125 Opening editorial to *Iḍā'a 77*, no. 1, July 1977.

126 Ḥasan Sulaymān, *Ḥurriyyat al-Fannān*, p. 18.

127 Editorial to *Iḍā'a 77*, no. 14, Nov. 1988. The introduction to the collected volume of all fourteen issues of *Iḍā'a 77*, published in 1994, also stressed the group's links to its public and its interaction with Egyptian cultural life.

128 Rijā'ī al-Mīrghanī, '*Iḍā'a 77* wa-Tajribatu-hā al-Jamāliyya', *Kitābāt*, no. 8, 1984 (no month), pp. 62, 107.

129 Back cover of *al-Kalima*, no. 2, April 1978.

130 'Alf Muwāṭin Yaqūlūna Ra'ya-hum fī al-Fikr wa-l-Fann wa-l-Thaqāfa', *al-Ghad* (III), no. 1, 1985 (no month).

131 Ḥasan Fu'ād, 'al-Fann fī Sabīl al-Ḥayāh', opening editorial to *al-Ghad* (III), no. 1, 1985 (no month).

concern to be publicly accessible when it described itself as 'a very ordinary and very simple call to all readers in Egypt and the Arab nation' and reminded readers that it was 'published by you and for you'.[132] At any rate, given the high price of books,[133] such independent journals and pamphlets were at least more accessible financially to the reading public.[134]

Nevertheless, the impact of non-periodic journals, including *Gallery 68*, was necessarily limited – mainly to other producers but, more importantly in terms of long-term impact, to younger would-be producers. *Gallery 68* contributor Māhir Shafīq Farīd, who became an established literary critic and academic at Cairo University, is surprised by how much influence such journals did in fact wield among certain groups. He judges,

> I would not underestimate the impact they [non-periodic journals] have had upon a certain number of the young generation, upon other writers, and upon new critics as well... But they have hardly affected the reading public. ... The influence is real, but it is very limited.[135]

Shukrī 'Ayyād, conversely, actually views the whole phenomenon of non-periodic journals in the 1970s and 1980s as negative on the grounds that it increased the separation between intellectuals and the public.[136] Yet this misses the whole point of such journals – most were a workshop for producers not consumers, designed to effect their literary, cultural and intellectual development.

The avant-garde nature of the work of writers involved in such journals was inevitably of limited appeal. One of *Gallery 68*'s founders and editors, Jamīl 'Aṭiyya Ibrāhīm, conceded a decade after its final issue: 'After continuous thought over long years, I admit my complete failure, my inability to reach the public in the broad sense of the word'. Although Ibrāhīm himself came from a lower class family and bore a deep concern for the plight of the ordinary man, he acknowledged that those whom he addressed through his literature shared formative years similar to his own; 'I have absolutely no ambition to reach the

132 Opening editorial to *al-Kurrāsa al-Thaqāfiyya*, no. 1, June 1979.

133 Complaints that the high price of books kept them out of reach were voiced several times in *al-Ṭalī'a*. For example, S. Khashaba's analysis of 'Hākadhā Yatakallamu al-Udabā' al-Shabāb', *al-Ṭalī'a*, Sept. 1969; Maḥmūd Diyāb in 'Nadwat *al-Ṭalī'a*', *al-Ṭalī'a*, Dec. 1974; Shams al-Dīn Mūsā, 'Malāmiḥ al-Thaqāfa al-Miṣriyya bayna al-Qiṭā'ayn al-'Āmm wa-l-Khāṣṣ', *al-Ṭalī'a*, Oct. 1975; and 'Jumhūr 75: Mādhā Qara'a? Hal Hiya Bidāya Ḥiqba Jadīda?', *al-Ṭalī'a*, Feb. 1976.

134 The following dates and costs are based on the first issue: *al-Thaqāfa al-Jadīda*, 1976 (200 pages) cost 30 piastres; *Iḍā'a 77*, 1977 (28 pages) cost 10 piastres; *Kāf Nūn*, 1977 (8 pages, hand-written) cost 3 piastres; *al-Naddāha*, 1979 (16 pages) cost 5 piastres; *al-Kurrāsa al-Thaqāfiyya*, 1979 (54 pages) cost 10 piastres; *Miṣriyya*, 1979? (48 pages) cost 20 piastres; *Abjadiyyāt*, 1980 (30 pages) cost 25 piastres; *al-Nadīm*, 1981 (69 pages) cost 25 piastres.

135 Māhir Shafīq Farīd, taped interview, Cairo, 30 April 1996.

136 Sh. 'Ayyād, taped interview, Cairo, 29 April 1996.

popular masses, for I recognize my total inability to reach or connect to them... my modes of expression bear no relation to the masses'.[137] One must also bear in mind that several more innovative writers, including Jamīl 'Aṭiyya Ibrāhīm, were living outside Egypt and so were already physically, let alone intellectually, removed from their potential public.

A few of *Gallery 68*'s contributors were able to gain a somewhat broader appeal, for example 'Abd al-Raḥmān al-Abnūdī and Sayyid Ḥijāb who composed poetry in the colloquial, and Yaḥyā al-Ṭāhir 'Abd Allāh and 'Abd al-Ḥakīm Qāsim who wrote, amongst other things, about everyday life in Upper Egyptian villages. Even Yaḥyā al-Ṭāhir 'Abd Allāh, however, realistically recognized the weakness of the literary medium, 'I found that the people whom I wrote about could not read my work... Therefore I believe that speech is better...'.[138] Many of his stories had in fact been memorized and told to villagers in Karnak and Qana long before he moved to Cairo and published them as books.[139] 'Abd al-Ḥakīm Qāsim, on the other hand, actually declared his ability to reach the masses of peasants by writing both about them and for them,[140] but this was certainly a delusion. Even the 'public' of *Gallery 68*'s more accessible contributors was only broad in a relative sense – it was still only a minority of the reading public, which was in any case only about 250,000 strong.[141]

The problem was fuelled by the dominant positions in the literary field, working on the heteronomous principle of success – for example, the ascendancy of the mass media was widely held to be responsible for plundering the potential readership while lowering the general level of taste. During the course of *Gallery 68*'s eight issues, this concern was mentioned by all of *al-Majalla, al-Ṭalī'a* and *al-Kātib*,[142] as well as being mentioned at the First Conference for Young Writers in 1969; and after experiencing the cultural stagnation of the 1970s, the detrimental effects of mass media distractions became even clearer.

137 Interview with J. A. Ibrāhīm conducted by I. Manṣūr, in I. Manṣūr, *al-Izdiwāj al-Thaqāfī wa-Azma al-Mu'āraḍa al-Miṣriyya* (1981), pp. 115–16.

138 Interview with Yaḥyā al-Ṭāhir 'Abd Allāh conducted by Samīr Gharīb, *al-Mustaqbal al-'Arabī*, n.d, in Yaḥyā al-Ṭāhir 'Abd Allāh, *al-Kitābāt al-Kāmila* (1983), p. 491.

139 Introduction to Y. 'Abd Allāh, op. cit. (1983), p. 5.

140 Interview with 'Abd al-Ḥakīm Qāsim conducted by I. Manṣūr, in I. Manṣūr, o. c. (1981), p. 117.

141 This statistic is supplied by S. Khashaba in his analysis of 'Hākadhā Yatakallamuna al-Udabā' al-Shabāb', *al-Ṭalī'a*, Sept. 1969, pp. 63–64. NB According to a 1972 UNESCO-sponsored study, the illiteracy rate in 1960 was 70.3 per cent. Writing in 1969, Khashaba gave the illiteracy rate as 80 per cent. While one would have expected the illiteracy rate to have fallen, not risen, by the time of Khashaba's analysis, it is possible that the UNESCO figure was exaggerated since the study was conducted by Majdī Wahba who was at the time Undersecretary at the Egyptian Ministry of Culture. In any case, one would expect the actual reading public to be much smaller than the literate public and as such, Khashaba's figure of 250,000 seems justified.

142 See for example: S. Khashaba's comments in *al-Ṭalī'a*, Sept. 1969, p. 65; Mu'īn Basīsū's comments in *al-Ṭalī'a*, Dec. 1969, p. 80; Editorial to *al-Majalla*, Aug. 1969; *al-Kātib*, Jan. 1970, p. 122 and Dec. 1972, pp. 112–16.

Yūsuf al-Shārūnī noted that 'although their [short stories in the sixties] writers recognized a broader public, it was a public that did not read. That was because of the mass media....[143] Meanwhile, Naguib Mahfouz was led to conclude that 'literature is one of the values which has disappeared', since the predominance of television had relegated literature to the elite.[144] Kharrāṭ demonstrated the same concern, but from a more positive, possibly over-idealistic, perspective: the new sensibility's incorporation of multiple layers of meaning into the text was an attempt to tear readers away from the television, since 'the text only exists with the positive participation and creation of the reader'.[145]

This increasing tendency for dominant positions in the literary field to bind themselves up with the field of economic power is evidenced in the growing commercialization of 'literary' writings in the media and a general recognition of cultural stagnation. Of course, those enjoying commercial success were always able to justify it as popular success by packaging it in the more respectable guise of a populist mission. Yet even the Minister for Culture himself, Yūsuf al-Sibā'ī, admitted that Arab (though not specifically Egyptian) thought had grown dim, although he insisted that the source flame was still present.[146] Ironically, of course, the source flames had positioned themselves within the sub-field of non-periodic journals, autonomous of his domain, in order to combat the literary norms upheld by his Ministry of Culture institutions. Other literary figures were more outspoken: Ghālī Shukrī wrote that under Yūsuf al-Sibā'ī, 'the chosen entourage of rotting corpses and remains had progressed to positions of direct responsibility in Ministry of Culture establishments'.[147] And the Egyptian woman writer Salwā Bakr, writing in the Beirut journal *al-Miṣbāḥ* in the mid-1970s, unequivocally declared that 'whoever respects his mind would not resort to reading the journals of the Egyptian Ministry of Culture'.[148] This is consistent with Bourdieu's model of the cultural field, for which he claims that the players involved, in extreme cases, have nothing whatsoever in common except their mutual struggle to impose their own definition of legitimacy within the field. Bourdieu concludes that 'there are few fields (other than the field of power itself) in which the antagonism between the occupants of the polar positions is more total'.[149]

143 Y. al-Shārūnī, *Dirāsāt fī al-Qiṣṣa al-Qaṣīra* (1989), p. 99.

144 Interview with Naguib Mahfouz, in Aḥmad Hāshim al-Sharīf, *Naguib Mahfouz: Muḥāwarāt Qabl al-Nobel* (1989), p. 15.

145 I. al-Kharrāṭ, *al-Ḥassāsiyya al-Jadīda* (1993), p. 344.

146 Yūsuf al-Sibā'ī, in M. Shalabī, op. cit. (1982), p. 233.

147 Gh. Shukrī, *Min al-Arshīf al-Sirrī li-l-Thaqāfa al-Miṣriyya* (1975), p. 109.

148 Salwā Bakr. Cited in Muḥammad al-Rāwī, *Udabā' al-Jīl Yatahaddathūna* (1982), p. 24. NB Salwā Bakr had been a frequent visitor in the beginning to the *Café Riche* gatherings around which *Gallery 68* had crystallized (N. 'Aṭiyya, taped interview, Cairo, 28 April 1996).

149 P. Bourdieu, *The Field of Cultural Production* (1993), p. 46.

Recognizing this encroachment of the fields of economic and political power on the dominant pole of the literary field, some blamed oil money for corrupting talent, not only by tempting writers abroad,[150] but by dictating what they published in the Egyptian press itself. The poet and journalist Aḥmad al-Shahāwī complains that editors have been loathe to publish work on sex, politics and religion, often because their journals are distributed in Saudi Arabia. He explains bitterly, 'that means that I, as an Egyptian, publishing for Egyptians in an Egyptian paper, cannot write something because of Saudi Arabia . . . the matter is a type of hypocrisy, a type of cheap flattery of the country in which the journal can be sold at a higher price'.[151] Abū Bakr al-Saqqāf, writing in *al-Ghad* in the mid-1980s, held oil money responsible for the fact that 'intellectuals have at best become bureaucrats and at worst brokers in a disfigured cultural market'.[152] And *Gallery 68* contributing poet Amal Dunqul also complained that Arab culture had become the puppet of rich Arab markets in the Gulf.[153]

Former *Gallery 68* editor, Muḥammad Ibrāhīm Mabrūk, was one of the harshest critics of Egyptian culture in the 1970s and 1980s. He likened Egypt's cultural institutions to 'wax museums' and wrote bitterly, in his own independent journal *al-Nadīm*, of the domination of the official cultural press by those who 'fill space without being able to leave any impression on that tyrannical silence'. The only way talented writers could publish in the official arena was by succumbing to compromise and presenting work 'with no taste, colour, or smell'.[154] This cultural strait-jacket effectively stayed the forward momentum of Egyptian literary experimentation in the early 1970s, hampering interaction both between the serious writer and the broader reading public, but also among the elite of serious intellectuals themselves since many emigrated abroad. In fact, a survey of 'this generation's littérateurs' (*udabā' al-jīl*) by Muḥammad al-Rāwī, disconcertingly revealed that, even in the 1980s, Yaḥyā Ḥaqqī, Yūsuf Idrīs and Naguib Mahfouz remained the focal point of most young writers.[155]

This does not, however, mean that *Gallery 68*'s contributors had failed to impact the Egyptian literary scene. Already at the beginning of the 1970s, Ghālī Shukrī had felt able to write that it was a number of short story writers from 'the sixties generation' who, notwithstanding their varying styles, techniques and talents, represented 'the literary phenomenon that formed, *en masse*, a new wave in our modern literature' – the ten writers listed were all contributors to *Gallery 68*.[156] As for al-Rāwī's survey, there are several reasons why its

150 Yusrī Khamīs perceived oil money as a real temptation for young writers and in particular he mentioned the lure of the London-based Arab press, Y. Khamīs, taped interview, Cairo, 26 April 1996.

151 Aḥmad al-Shahāwī, taped interview, Cairo, 9 Nov. 1994.

152 Abū Bakr al-Saqqāf, *al-Ghad* (III), no. 2, Nov. 1985, pp. 8–9.

153 Interview with Amal Dunqul conducted by I'timād 'Abd al-'Azīz, *al-Ibdā'*, Oct. 1983.

154 M. I. Mabrūk, op. cit. (1982), pp. 10–11.

155 M. al-Rāwī, op. cit. (1982), p. 9.

156 Gh. Shukrī, *al-'Anqa' al-Jadīda: Ṣirā' al-Ajyāl fī al-Adab al-Mu'āṣir* (1977), p. 157.

conclusions might be flawed. First, those questioned as *udabā' al-jīl* were mostly contemporaries of *68*'s contributors rather than successors (despite the fact that *al-Ṭalī'a* had already dedicated a special issue of its literary supplement to the sixties generation's successors as early as 1973[157]). Those questioned by al-Rāwī therefore retained the older influences, and even *Gallery 68*'s more mature writers were not yet old enough or well known enough to approach the kind of influence wielded by long-established giants like Mahfouz and Idrīs. Kharrāṭ, for example, although he had been writing since the 1940s, only had his first short story collection published by an Egyptian publishing house in 1982.[158]

But why then were *Gallery 68*'s contributors not included as subjects of al-Rāwī's survey? Among those questioned, only 1 writer (out of 28) and 1 poet (out of 10) had contributed to *Gallery 68*. In fact, the Beirut journal *al-Miṣbāḥ*, in which many of the questionnaires were first published, admitted to the unfortunate omission of prominent writers like Jamāl al-Ghīṭānī, Yaḥyā al-Ṭāhir 'Abd Allāh and Muḥammad al-Bisāṭī (all *Gallery 68* contributors).[159] It is true that several of *Gallery 68*'s most talented contributors were no longer living in Egypt, but the survey's real stumbling block was that it focused on the more media-acceptable men of letters. Every survey aimed at establishing the hierarchy of writers inevitably predetermines that hierarchy through its selection of those whom it deems to have a legitimate say in the matter. Indeed, Salwā Bakr complained in *al-Miṣbāḥ* that al-Rāwī's survey dealt only with 'faces introduced into the arena of official culture'.[160] Bakr's comment raises an important point: that it is crucial to distinguish between the officially approved and independent faces of Egyptian literature or, in other words, between those whose status was measured according to the heteronomous principle operating at the dominant pole of the literary field and those whose status was gauged according to the autonomous principle at work in the avant-garde sub-field.

Critics too are participants in the struggle for legitimacy which, in this case, refers to the struggle for the monopoly of legitimate discourse about the literary work . Yet critics also play an essential role in the awarding of symbolic capital to the producers themselves through their power to consecrate. After all, literary works only exist as symbolic (as opposed to merely material) objects if they are known and recognized,[161] and it is the critics who must see fit to invest their own reputations in that of the producer (writer) or product (literary work).

157 *al-Ṭalī'a*, Feb. 1973.

158 *Ikhtināqāt al-'Ishq wa-l-Ṣabāḥ*, Cairo: Dār al-Mustaqbal al-'Arabī, 1982. Kharrāṭ had already published two other works in Cairo by this time: his short story collection *Ḥiṭān 'Āliya* was published in 1959 at his own expense, and his novel *Rāma wa-l-Tinnīn* was published by Dār al-Mustaqbal in 1979.

159 Cited in M. al-Rāwī, op. cit. (1982), p. 27.

160 Salwā Bakr commenting on the survey in the Beirut journal *al-Miṣbāḥ*, where the responses were initially published. Cited in M. al-Rāwī, op. cit. (1982), p. 24.

161 P. Bourdieu, *The Field of Cultural Production* (1993), p. 37.

This can then bring the producer himself into the cycle of consecration. For, once consecrated, the producer himself gains a legitimate right to consecrate another producer or product.[162] Nonetheless, even where the criticism is negative, the work has still been held up as an object worthy of legitimate discourse, and this helps to endow it with the recognition which the critic had attempted to prevent.

Although non-periodic journals enabled writers to express themselves more freely, winning the attention of critics was difficult – though not impossible – if one did not publish through the official apparatus. While government cultural policy marginalized much creative talent away from critics' attention, the domination of the commercial market also created difficulties for the broader development of a serious critical movement. Aḥmad Harīdī, writing in the independent journal *al-Ghad*, testified to the damaging onslaught of the commercial market on artistic life since 1975.[163] Salwā Bakr too complained that the official literary press had no interest in publishing criticism of works that had any real literary or intellectual value.[164] Many critics themselves appear to have agreed on the feeble quality of much literary criticism. In fact, complaints about the lack of a serious critical movement to keep apace of literary developments became a favourite slogan attached to talk of the literary crisis. Yet, as with talk of the general cultural crisis in the 1960s, the same watchwords could stem from radically different attitudes. Some, for example, berated the introduction of Western modes of criticism,[165] while others commended it as long overdue.[166] Others blamed the dearth of valid criticism on the literary brain-drain under Sadat, but attributed this to critics' pursuing wealth outside Egypt rather than to restrictions on freedom of expression.[167] Salwā Bakr strongly disagreed, listing a whole host of critics who remained in Cairo and maintaining that 'critical studies amass day after day in the desk drawers of critics who cannot find an outlet for their works'.[168]

Whatever the line of argument, many critics wasted space writing about the crisis in criticism and criticizing other critics, instead of filling pages with constructive literary criticism to help remedy the crisis. While *Gallery 68* might now appear guilty of this in places, one could argue that, at this early stage, the flaws in prevailing critical methods still needed pointing out. In general, *Gallery 68* did much to stir up debate about new terms like 'aesthetics' (*'ilm al-jamāl*), and it was

162 P. Bourdieu, *The Field of Cultural Production* (1993), pp. 37, 42, 77.

163 Aḥmad Harīdī, 'Akādimiyyat al-Funūn al-Miṣriyya ba'da Rub' Qarn', *al-Ghad* (III), no. 1, 1985 (no month).

164 Salwā Bakr writing in the Beirut journal *al-Miṣbāḥ* in the latter half of the seventies. Cited in M. al-Rāwī, op. cit. (1982), p. 25.

165 For example, Muṣṭafā 'Abd al-Laṭīf al-Saḥartī, *Dirāsa Naqdiyya fī al-Adab al-Mu'āṣir*, p. 14; and Rif'at Sallām, editorial to *Kitābāt*, no. 7, Jan. 1983.

166 For example, Interview with 'Abd al-'Azīz al-Sharaf conducted by Rashīd al-Dhawwādī, 1984, in R. al-Dhawwādī, op. cit. (1986), pp. 99–100.

167 See M. al-Rāwī, op. cit. (1982), p. 25.

168 Salwā Bakr writing in the Beirut journal *al-Miṣbāḥ* in the latter half of the 1970s. Cited in ibid.

in the following two decades that critical debate really came to fruition, initially in independent journals like *Iḍā'a 77*, and eventually with the launch of more mainstream publications like *Fuṣūl* (Seasons, 1980–), *Ibdā'* (Creativity, 1983–2002) and *Alif* ('A', 1981–).

In the meantime, however, the weak nature of literary criticism in general could lead to a somewhat distorted perception as to which young writers were at the heart of the creative literary scene, and al-Rāwī's bias towards more media-acceptable writers and poets for his survey of *udabā' al-jīl* bears witness to this. It would seem that publication among young writers proved easiest for those who furnished the best examples of prevailing taste, although innovators of exceptional talent were not excluded. The sometimes narrow distinction between imitator and innovator was expressed well by Ḥasan Sulaymān in *Gallery 68*: the former was 'a lowly wretched tinsmith who nevertheless excels at his art' and the latter 'a creative god, arrogant, cruel and obstinate, a perfectionist'. Sulaymān remarked perceptively, 'How easy it is for the craftsman to produce, and how difficult for the god to create.... There is a fine line between good and bad art'.[169]

Typical of the young writer favoured for publication was Rustum al-Kīlānī, who was included as representative of the younger generation in Rashīd al-Dhawwādī's *Aḥādīth fī al-Adab* (Conversations about Literature, 1986). Aged 26 at the inception of *Gallery 68*, he had published 20 collections by the time he was 40 years old. His role as Sulaymān's 'tinsmith' rather than 'creative god' is revealed in his conservative view of art, as expressed in the early 1980s: 'As for the new writers who invade the field of literature with an obscurity which we read without understanding much, and by which we suffer intensely, I support the opinion of my teacher and spiritual father...Maḥmūd Ṭaymūr'.[170] It was this kind of narrow adherence to the status quo which *Gallery 68* contributor Muḥammad Ibrāhīm Mabrūk was referring to when he complained of palaces of culture full of 'musty air' which had become like 'cramped cages for rearing the cubs of the popular established writers'.[171] This officially sanctioned literature was rooted in the past and failed to reflect Egypt's changed reality. Mabrūk asked despairingly, 'Do you not see the enormous and alarming gulf between what happens in reality and the superficiality and backwardness of these writings and works we see?'.[172]

Among *Gallery 68*'s contributors, it was those whose work did not pander to prevailing taste but who were less mature in their experimentation, though they might show great potential, who tended to lose out in the publication stakes. The critic al-Saḥartī noted that both publishers and critics dismissed new work

169 Ḥasan Sulaymān, 'Ilāh wa-Ṭifl wa-Samkarī', *Gallery 68*, no. 5, Feb. 1969, p. 4.
170 Rustum al-Kīlānī, in Rashīd al-Dhawwādī, op. cit. (1986), p. 118.
171 M. I. Mabrūk, op. cit. (1982), pp. 9–10.
172 Ibid., p. 6.

too quickly.[173] And, of course, all writers lost out, whether of exceptional or moderate talent, mature or maturing, when their work was deemed too inflammatory or critical for any publishing establishment to risk taking on. Several of *Gallery 68*'s contributors were, however, able to publish such work further afield, usually in Beirut, but also in Damascus or Baghdad, the latter especially after 1975 when war broke out in Lebanon.[174]

Among those frustrated by publication institutions was Muḥammad Ibrāhīm Mabrūk, the youngest member of *Gallery 68*'s editorial board. His bitterness was reflected in a harsh opening article in *al-Nadīm*, his own anti-establishment non-periodic journal of the early 1980s. His distinction between *kataba* (popular published writers who pandered to public taste) and *kuttāb* (talented innovators and hence true writers) was both poignant and severe, and it is consistent with Bourdieu's model of heteronomous and autonomous hierarchies respectively. Mabrūk warned of the former's 'deceptive dead end-roads, dense with frightened corpses…polluting the air with their cheap fame'. Yet he recognized the avant-garde dynamic as geared towards the future and stressed the temporary nature of the *kataba*'s dominating fame. While *kataba* grabbed all the attention on the surface of cultural life, *kuttāb* remained active at the heart of it, sacrificing the present in their attempt to shape the future. *Kuttāb* wore their own faces, whereas *kataba* donned an assortment of masks, depending on whom they were serving.[175] Mabrūk embodies Bourdieu's claim that 'a heretical break with the prevailing artistic traditions proves its claim to authenticity by its disinterestedness'.[176] Mabrūk's journal was located at the more autonomous pole of the avant-garde sub-field, where success entailing economic and political profit is symbolically excluded and discredited in favour of disinterested values. Here, practice is based on an inversion of the fundamental principles of all ordinary economies or systems: business (profit is not sought, nor do investments correspond to financial gain); power (honours and temporal greatness are shunned); even institutionalized cultural authority (the lack of formal academic training may be considered a virtue).[177]

That several of Mabrūk's fellow contributors to *Gallery 68* had penetrated the establishment by the early 1980s is alluded to in his extreme bitterness of tone when referring to the evolution from margin to mainstream. Temporal 'success' was portrayed as compromise and betrayal and blamed on 'the pressing demand

173 Muṣṭafā 'Abd al-Latif al-Saḥarṭī, *Dirāsa Naqdiyya fī al-Adab al-Mu'āṣir* (1979), p. 16.

174 Among *Gallery 68*'s Egyptian contributors to publish at least two books in Arab capitals other than Cairo were: the writers Yaḥyā al-Ṭāhir 'Abd Allāh, Sulaymān Fayyāḍ, Jamāl al-Ghīṭānī, Jamīl 'Aṭiyya Ibrāhīm, 'Abd al-Ḥakīm Qāsim, Majīd Ṭūbyā and 'Alī Zayn al-'Ābidīn al-Ḥusaynī; as well as the poets Amal Dunqul, Muḥammad 'Afīfī Maṭar and Muḥammad Mihrān al-Sayyid. *Gallery 68* contributing critic Ghālī Shukrī also published prolifically in Beirut and Baghdad.

175 M. I. Mabrūk, 'Zaman al-Kataba ya'ful wa-Azminat al-Kuttāb tajī' ', *al-Nadīm*, no. 2, Feb. 1982.

176 P. Bourdieu, *The Field of Cultural Production* (1993), p. 40.

177 Ibid., p. 39.

for stars, not writers', turning innovative writers into 'wax faces crouching in glass, air-conditioned rooms'. Mabrūk wrote of the hypocrisy of those writers who had been at the fringes of literary activity in the 1960s but who had by the early 1980s become the 'peacocks' of the literary scene. 'By responding as stars, they have turned into *kataba*, mummified corpses concealed in the remains of those who used to be *kuttāb*, without the lazy consumers being aware of it.' Official recognition was deemed to corrupt, for Mabrūk rejected the notion that a writer could reap the material benefits of his work and still remain truly creative; in fact, he compared the writer's attainment of material and official success to a man who has had his leg amputated.[178] The continuing integration of *68*'s contributors into the cultural establishment is clear from Mabrūk's renewed attack, three years later in the mid-1980s, on those writers who had abandoned counter culture, adopting instead – albeit subconsciously – the bourgeois way of life they had once fought against. He diagnosed them as schizophrenic – continuing to spout revolutionary language whilst living a bourgeois life.[179]

Mabrūk's attitude is startlingly harsh and uncompromising, but it is more comprehensible if one considers that, in the struggle for legitimacy, those operating in the avant-garde sub-field who are 'most concerned for their autonomy are considerably weakened by the fact that some of their competitors identify their interests with the dominant principles of hierarchization'.[180] In other words, those writers accepting state recognition were perceived to be endorsing the dominant power structure by acknowledging and responding to the cultural apparatus' interpellation of them as subjects. Yet, this fails to take account of the fact that these 'dominant principles of hierarchization' are not supra-historical and can accommodate change and progress – after all, some *Gallery 68* contributors such as Bahā' Ṭāhir and Jamīl 'Aṭiyya Ibrāhīm had eventually succeeded in striking a chord with a broader readership; or, likewise, one might argue that readership tastes had evolved over the three decades following *Gallery 68*. Even a staunch Marxist critic like Maḥmūd Amīn al-'Ālim eventually modified his dogmatic view of the subordination of literature to life, recognizing that a work should be judged by its aesthetical value and not just by its social and political intent;[181] a work was no longer obliged to address the masses of workers and peasants, it simply had to express the basic facts of life.[182] Thus the economic and symbolic capital won by sixties writers was not simply the result of yielding to prevailing literary norms and tastes. Rather, it was a case of plugging away at them over time

178 M. I. Mabrūk, 'Zaman al-Kataba ya'ful wa-Azminat al-Kuttāb tajī'', *al-Nadīm*, no. 2, Feb. 1982.

179 M. I. Mabrūk, 'Qiyām al-Nadīm', Editorial to *al-Nadīm*, no. 4, May 1985.

180 P. Bourdieu, *The Field of Cultural Production* (1993), p. 41.

181 Maḥmūd Amīn al-'Ālim, in the 1989 edition of his 1955 book, co-written with 'Abd al-'Aẓīm Anīs, *Fī al-Thaqāfa al-Miṣriyya*, p. 23. Cited in Maḥmūd Ghanayim, 'Maḥmūd Amīn al-'Ālim: Between Politics and Literary Criticism', *Poetics Today*, Vol. 15, no. 2, Summer 1994, p. 330.

182 Ibid., p. 222. Cited in Maḥmūd Ghanayim, op. cit., p. 335.

in a ceaseless struggle which nevertheless necessitated a more mature approach in terms of tolerance to the dominant pole of the field. In other words, these writers needed to demonstrate 'a particularly successful combination of the contradictory capacities specifically demanded by the law of the field'.[183] This gradual process of the canonization of some writers is a natural, though not always inevitable or predictable, part of the continuing avant-garde dynamic, propelling the literary scene forward.

As early as 1969, at the same time as praising the short story for flourishing as never before, Ibrāhīm Fatḥī had the foresight to warn of the transitory nature of avant-garde activity in *Gallery 68*:

> It appears that some of our writers consider this the end of the road. ... We have begun to run into definitive prepared patterns. ... The dividing line between renewal and stunts, between depth of the new view and pretentious craftsmanship, has been lost.[184]

While it is clear that *Gallery 68*'s contributors did not simply blend into the establishment, nevertheless, constant renewal at the fringe, together with the growing output and increasingly familiar names of several of *68*'s contributors, meant that they were beginning to be perceived as established writers. It is interesting to note, for example, that the independent non-periodic journal *al-Fikr al-Mu'āṣir* which probably published the greatest number of *Gallery 68* contributors[185] was criticized by *Kitābāt* for presenting only well-known writers.[186] Yet even this issue was deemed subversive enough to incur penalties in Cairo, and the journal was compelled to publish its next issue in Beirut.[187] It would seem that some kind of conflict is an inevitable symptom of progress and the ever-present struggle for symbolic capital, whether between establishment and fringe, or within the fringe itself. In the 1990s, for example, we encounter the same complaints of cultural strife: Aḥmad 'Abd al-Mu'ṭī Ḥijāzī wrote of 'a civil war in cultural life', complaining that Sabry Hafez had criticized Idwār al-Kharrāṭ in *Fuṣūl* for mentioning himself (in a recent edited volume on modern literature in the Middle East) more than Ḥaqqī, Idrīs or Mahfouz, and for commenting negatively on

183 P. Bourdieu, *The Field of Cultural Production* (1993), p. 83.

184 I. Fatḥī, 'Malāmiḥ Mushtaraka fī al-Intāj al-Qiṣaṣī al-Jadīd', *Gallery 68*, no. 6, April 1969, p. 114.

185 In the opening issue (May 1979) of *al-Fikr al-Mu'āṣir* – not to be confused with the 1960s journal of the same name, three of the four short story writers and two of the five poets published were *Gallery 68* contributors. In addition, the issue included a study translated by Ibrāhīm Manṣūr, a chapter of a novel by Idwār al-Kharrāṭ, and a study of Yaḥyā al-Ṭāhir 'Abd Allāh.

186 *Kitābāt*, Aug. 1979, p. 13.

187 Y. 'Abd Allāh in an interview with S. Gharīb, *al-Mustaqbal al-'Arabī*, n.d. Reprinted in *Khaṭwa*, no. 3, n.d. (1981?). This was a special issue commemorating Yaḥyā al-Ṭāhir 'Abd Allāh.

Mahfouz.[188] Yet this is inevitable as the continuing literary dynamic ensures that the victims of progress within the establishment relinquish their cultural monopoly.

The true and changed face of Egyptian literature after *Gallery 68* was acknowledged in the mid-1980s in a small book by Yusrī al-'Azab, who wanted to set the record straight. Al-'Azab sought to dispel the outmoded perception of many critics that there had been no novelist since Naguib Mahfouz, no short story writer since Yūsuf Idrīs and no poet since Aḥmad Shawqī. He also criticized as limited the view of those critics who recognized the advent of 'Abd al-Ḥakīm Qāsim and Jamāl al-Ghīṭānī after Mahfouz, Yaḥyā al-Ṭāhir 'Abd Allāh after Idrīs, and Ṣalāḥ 'Abd al-Ṣabūr, 'Abd al-Mu'ṭī Ḥijāzī and Amal Dunqul after Shawqī. That this second line of attack should involve contributors to *Gallery 68* demonstrates that they had by this stage thoroughly penetrated the establishment. The names cited by al-'Azab confirm the fact that *Gallery 68* made a greater impact on prose literature than on poetry, since both Ṣalāḥ 'Abd al-Ṣabūr and 'Abd al-Mu'ṭī Ḥijāzī had already been considered outmoded by Amal Dunqul and other *Gallery 68* poets. Yusrī al-'Azab's point of contention with the critics was that they ignored a whole host of talented new writers and poets; nearly all those named were contributors either to *Gallery 68* or to the non-periodic journals to follow it.[189]

It is a delusion, however, to consider this a clear-cut process with each new generation attempting to oust their predecessors in a neat cyclical manner. Several of *Gallery 68*'s contributors managed to participate in literary activity at both the fringe and the centre – and whatever else might come in between. While some had fully penetrated the literary establishment (e.g. Jamāl al-Ghīṭānī and Aḥmad Hāshim al-Sharīf), others remained active on the fringe (e.g. Muḥammad Ibrāhīm Mabrūk, Yaḥyā al-Ṭāhir 'Abd Allāh until his untimely death in 1983 and 'Izzat 'Āmir), and others still straddled the gap between the two (e.g. Idwār al-Kharrāṭ, Muḥammad al-Bisāṭī and Muḥammad 'Afīfī Maṭar), perhaps indeed forfeiting some of their autonomy as they matured and mastered the diplomacy needed to span both fringe and establishment.[190]

Whether the success of these sixties writers has necessarily entailed a loss of autonomy and a strategy of conservation, even if subconscious, to protect their now dominant position is still open to question. Either way, their current positions indicate that the cultural and political fields remain inexorably intertwined. As evidence against a loss of autonomy, one might cite *Gallery 68* contributor Jamāl al-Ghīṭānī, generally considered to be firmly part of the establishment as editor

188 A. Ḥijāzī, 'Kayfa Usammī Hādhihi al-Ma'raka?' *al-Ahrām*, 1 July 1992, in Fārūq 'Abd al-Qādir, *Min Awrāq al-Tis'īnāt* (1996).

189 Yusrī al-'Azab, *al-Qiṣṣa wa-l-Riwāya al-Miṣriyya fī al-Sab'īniyyāt* (1984), pp. 6–8.

190 I have discovered work by 25 of *Gallery 68*'s contributors in non-periodic journals of the late 1970s and early 1980s. Very few 'sixties' writers, such as Kharrāṭ, have defied generational categorization and tempered their 'establishment' image by publishing in *al-Kitāba al-Ukhrā* (Alternative Writing, 1991–2001), the organ of the 'nineties' generation.

of the weekly *Akhbār al-Adab* (The Literary News, 1993–). Yet he rallied against the authorities, taking on the dominant political field of power to protest against the widespread condemnation of Arabism in the wake of the 2003 Gulf War;[191] moreover, he publicly announced his refusal to be proposed for the Supreme Council of Culture's 2005 Arab Novel Prize, declaring that 'Official cultural policy sorely lacks credibility'.[192] Bahā' Ṭāhir also defended the writer's autonomy, refusing his position in the Egyptian delegation of writers to be honoured at the 2004 Frankfurt Book Festival and speaking out against the government-led organization process. Muḥammad al-Bisāṭī too defended the autonomy of the field when, as the editor-in-chief of the establishment sponsored *Ibdā'āt* series of books, he opposed the Ministry of Culture's decision to withdraw three novels that had been the target of an Islamist campaign in the late 1990s. Both Ṭāhir and al-Bisāṭī refused candidacy for the 2005 Arab Novel Prize.[193]

As evidence against a conservation strategy, one could cite *Gallery 68* founding editor Ḥasan Sulaymān, whose independent publishing house, *Dār Sharqiyyāt*, has played an important role in publishing avant-garde works since its establishment in 1991. His fellow *Gallery 68* founding editor, Idwār al-Kharrāṭ, remains equally active at the cutting edge, with indefatigable experimentation between the genres of the novel and poetry in recent years. He has retained his active interest in and encouragement of the work of the young generation.[194] For example, during a Cairo conference of young avant-garde writers which he organized in 2003, critics such as Ḥāmid Abū Aḥmad and Muḥammad Abū al-Aṭā dismissed most of the new work as unworthy while Kharrāṭ and fellow *Gallery 68* contributor Ibrāhīm Fatḥī defended the young writers, stressing the need for an open mind, for they recognized that new generations perceive the world in different ways which are not easily evaluated within prevailing critical paradigms. On the other hand, the very fact of accepting the legitimate right to organize such a conference and pronounce on its participants, quite apart from using funding from the broader field of economic and political power to rally these 'avant-gardists', is inevitably an act of conservation of one's own dominant position. Kharrāṭ in particular tries to steer the difficult course between the cultural and political fields, for example in his decision to act on behalf of the Ministry of

191 See 'Abduh Wāzin, *al-Hayāh*, 27 May 2003.

192 Gamal Nkrumah, 'Gamal al-Ghīṭānī: A Scent of History', *al-Ahram Weekly*, no. 733, 10–16 March 2005. Online. Available HTTP: http://weekly.ahram.org.eg/2005/733/profile.htm

193 In the previous round of the Arab Novel Conference in 2003, the Prize had been awarded to sixties novelist Sun' Allāh Ibrāhīm, who staged a spectacular rejection of it during the ceremony itself to thunderous applause. To prevent future embarrassment, those proposed as candidates for the 2005 Prize were made to sign an acceptance form in advance. But in a diplomatic move to restore the prize's credibility, it was awarded to Sudanese novelist al-Tayyib Ṣāliḥ, who had headed the 2003 panel of judges and would have been above such competition.

194 Appropriately, a book celebrating Kharrāṭ's seventieth birthday was entitled 'Adventurer to the End' (*Mughāmir hattā al-Nihāya*, Cairo: Arab Civilization Centre, 2000).

Culture as head of the panel of judges for the discredited 2005 Arab Novel Prize. One can see why critics in the popular press organ *al-Ahram Weekly* summed up the sixties generation as 'this generation of writers, who having started out as avant-garde, experimentalist and even revolutionary are now unequivocally "establishment"'.[195]

Whatever the judgement, it remains the case that the shifting position of sixties writers in the literary field inevitably affected the configuration of the field itself as rear-guard writers gradually relinquished their monopoly on the dominant aesthetics and other new avant-gardists emerged. However, Mabrūk's plea for a disinterested approach to one's art – giving up temporal riches in favour of future recognition – is, in a sense, outmoded, for the time of future recognition is now. It is only really in recent years – more than three decades since the *Gallery 68* venture – that the 'sixties generation' has been truly celebrated. Over the last decade, the repute of several of *Gallery 68*'s most talented contributors has spread more generally. In the *Cambridge History of Modern Arabic Literature*, Sabry Hafez lists 10 short story writers as particularly prominent in Egypt in recent years – 8 of these were contributors to *Gallery 68*; and indeed, of the 2 Jordanian writers similarly listed, Ghālib Halasā had been on the editorial committee of *Gallery 68*.[196] Mean-while, several of *Gallery 68*'s contributors have received broader recognition since developing into novelists, for example Idwār al-Kharrāṭ, Jamāl al-Ghīṭānī, 'Abd al-Ḥakīm Qāsim, Majīd Ṭūbyā, Muḥammad al-Bisāṭī, Ghālib Halasā, Ibrāhīm Aṣlān, Jamīl 'Aṭiyya Ibrāhīm and Bahā' Ṭāhir. Jacques Berque, in a footnote to the 1978 edition of his 1973 book, felt compelled to reassess his dim view of the recent Arab novel in the light of new developments in Egypt at the hands of young writers like Jamāl al-Ghīṭānī.[197] In fact, the impact of *Gallery 68* contributors on this genre has been great enough for Kilpatrick to identify a '*Gallery 68* generation' in the novel – such that it even encompasses contemporaries who did not contribute to the journal.[198]

Another indication of the start of the process of canonization of several of *Gallery 68*'s contributors is that the works they published in Baghdad, Beirut or Damascus during the difficult years of the 1970s and early 1980s have in recent years been republished in Cairo. Moreover, their collected works have started to appear: Yaḥyā al-Ṭāhir 'Abd Allāh and Amal Dunqul were the first to have their collected works published, in Cairo in 1983, owing to their premature deaths. Since 1990, the General Egyptian Book Organization has published the collected works of Sulaymān Fayyāḍ, Jamāl al-Ghīṭānī and Yūsuf al-Shārūnī, who was

195 Amina Elbendary and Youssef Rakha, 'Alive and Kicking', *al-Ahram Weekly*, no. 587, 23–29 May 2002. Online. Available HTTP: http://weekly.ahram.org.eg/2002/587/cu1.htm

196 S. Hafez, 'The Short Story', in M. M. Badawi (ed.) *Modern Arabic Literature* (1992), p. 326.

197 Jacques Berque, *Cultural Expression in Arab Society Today* (1978), p. 236.

198 For example, Yūsuf al-Qa'īd. Hilary Kilpatrick, 'The Egyptian Novel from *Zaynab* to 1980', in M. M. Badawi (ed.) *Modern Arabic Literature* (1992), p. 259.

awarded the State Prize for Merit in 2000; *Dār al-Hilāl* has published the collected works of Bahā' Ṭāhir, who in 1997 became the second of the sixties generation to receive the State Prize for Merit (after Ghālī Shukrī in 1996). Works by some sixties writers, such as Yaḥyā al-Ṭāhir 'Abd Allāh, Majīd Ṭūbyā and Ibrāhīm Aṣlān (who won the State Prize for Merit in 2003), have even been adapted for the big screen. Moreover, *Gallery 68* contributing poets 'Abd al-Raḥmān al-Abnūdī (who won the State Prize for merit in 2000) and Sayyid Ḥijāb have also achieved widespread fame since converting their talents for vernacular poetry into more popular songwriting.[199] *Gallery 68* was itself finally republished in two volumes in 1997. But the crowning recognition for the sixties generation and the avant-garde sub-field in general came in 1996 when Idwār al-Kharrāṭ, one of the founding editors of *Gallery 68* whose support of the young avant-gardists had and continues to have a sympathetic paternal quality, won one of the most prestigious literary awards in the Arab world.[200] It had taken him a quarter of a century of experimentation just to gain the recognition of a State Prize for Encouragement, let alone Merit, in 1973. Subsequently, he was awarded the Cafavy Award (1998), the Naguib Mahfouz Prize (1999), the State Prize for Merit (1999) and appointed Chair to the Fiction Committee of the Supreme Council for Culture. This latter is the current bastion of the Egyptian literary field and, significantly, it is largely managed by literary figures from the 'sixties generation'.

Perhaps the most obvious evidence, however, of *Gallery 68*'s crucial role in maturing and crystallizing writers is the fossilization of the notion of 'the sixties-generation' (*jīl al-sittīnāt*) itself. While some of the dangers of employing such a generalizing term were raised in Chapter 3 and Kharrāṭ himself recently reiterated that

> there is a logical problem in the classification of writers by decade of their appearance, and talk of a Sixties generation and a Nineties generation is rather pointless. But it is my feeling and that of others that this doesn't mean that there are no literary movements. The writers of the Sixties form a movement, or a trend.[201]

This wisdom notwithstanding, the fact is that 'sixties generation' has become completely embedded in Egyptian literary history and terminology, demonstrating again that the writers gathered in *Gallery 68*, far from being a fleeting aberration as many assumed or indeed hoped, have themselves infiltrated the literary canon to become part of the literary heritage.

199 Richard Jacquemond, op. cit. (2003), p. 111.

200 The Sultan 'Uways prize for literature.

201 Interview with I. al-Kharrāṭ. Cited in Amina Elbendary and Youssef Rakha, 'Alive and Kicking', *al-Ahram Weekly*, no. 587, 23–29 May 2002. Online. Available HTTP: http://weekly.ahram.org.eg/2002/587/cu1.htm

APPENDIX A

The blossoming of literary journalism in the early twentieth century

The following list does not claim to be exhaustive and is simply intended to give an indication of the explosion in literary journalism during the early years of the twentieth century. Journals are included in the list for their regular incorporation of material related to Egypt's literary and cultural life. Journals mentioned in the main body of this book are not included in this list. Unless otherwise noted, the information is taken mainly from the section 'Literary Reports' in *al-Ḍiyā'* (Light, 1898–1906) which introduced readers to new journals.

Mir'āt al-Ḥasnā' (The Beautiful Woman's Mirror, 1896) was a fortnightly journal founded by Salīm Sarkīs using the pen-name Mariyām Maẓhar, primarily to avoid censorship but also to encourage women to contribute to the press. Although mainly concerned with stereotypical women's interests, the journal also published fiction and poetry, including work by Najīb al-Ḥaddād, Ṣalāḥ Ḥāfiẓ, Aḥmad Shawqī, Tanyūs 'Abduh and Ilyās Fayyād, including at least one poem by Ḥāfiẓ Ibrāhīm that was never included in his *dīwān*. The journal also offered advīce and guidance to dramatists, favouring the comic over the tragic. It was in this and others of Sarkīs' journals (e.g. *al-Mushīr, al-Rāwī* and later in *Sarkīs*) that literary competitions for translation and original composition were first introduced as a means of encouraging young writers and the idea soon spread to other journals.[1]

Al-Ghazāla (The Gazelle, 1896) was published by Jufānī Zanānīrī until 1898, then revived in1900 by Idwār al-Qara'lī. This satirical fortnightly journal was published in the Egyptian vernacular and re-surfaced for a third time in April 1902 under Ya'qūb al-Jamāl.

Al-Ajyāl (The Generations, 1897) was founded by the Syrian Yūsuf Shulḥut who had previously been greeted on the pages of *al-Muqtaṭaf* as a 'great writer' and was known for his involvement in debates over linguistic reform.[2]

1 Aḥmad Ḥusayn al-Ṭamāwī, *Fuṣūl min al-Ṣiḥāfa al-Adabiyya* (1989), pp. 179–92, 199.
2 Dagmar Glaß, *Der Muqtaṭaf und seine Öffentlichkeit* (2004), p. 323.

Anīs al-Jalīs (The Intimate Friend, 1898) was founded in Alexandria by Alexandra Avierino and published monthly (for only 10 months of the year from 1902) until financial difficulties forced it to close in 1908. It is described as a scientific, literary and satirical journal for women.[3] It published poetry, encouraging that which broke with the traditional mould, and literary articles, as well as dealing with issues of women, education and society. Khalīl Muṭrān managed to combine literature and science in some of his work published in *Anīs al-Jalīs*; for example, in a story about a courting couple who sit in the moonlight and discuss x-rays in romantic terms.[4] There was also a section summarizing (rather than reviewing) recent publications. Among the journal's contributors were Labība Hāshim, Najīb al-Ḥaddād, Khalīl Muṭrān, Aḥmad Muḥarram, Felix Fāris, Aḥmad al-Kāshif and Nīqūlā Rizq Allāh.

Al-Mawsū'āt (The Encyclopedia, 1898), a fortnightly historical, scientific and literary journal, was the brainchild of the nationalist Muḥammad Farīd, but was supervised and edited by Aḥmad Ḥāfiẓ 'Awaḍ until October 1899 when Maḥmūd Abū al-Naṣr took over. It aimed to extend readers' interest to subjects beyond mere politics. Rudimentary critical comments introduced recent publications to readers, and the last section of each issue was set aside for stories and featured Aḥmad Shawqī among its contributers. Travel writing was particularly popular. At a time when much narrative literature in journals was translated or Arabized, *al-Mawsū'āt* encouraged original works drawing on Egyptian life. It even published some progressive debate on the issue of diglossia in Egypt with Luṭfī al-Sayyid advocating some development and simplification of the classical language.[5] Its contributors included Muḥammad 'Abduh, Luṭfī al-Sayyid, 'Alī Bahjat, Aḥmad Najīb, Muḥammad Tawfīq Rif'at, 'Abd al-Qādir Ḥamza, Ḥāfiẓ 'Awaḍ, Aḥmad Nasīm and Muṣṭafā 'Abd al-Rāziq. It ceased publication in July 1901.

Al-Kawthar (al-Kawthar: the name of a river in Paradise, 1899) was founded by Jūrj Ṭanūs and Tawfīq Faraḥ and published fortnightly.

Al-Ikhā' (The Brotherhood, 1900) was founded by Maḥmūd Kāmil and edited by Aḥmad al-Kāshif and the poet Aḥmad Muḥarram. It contained an entire section devoted to the publication of contemporary poetry. Originally published every ten days, it became monthly in February 1903.

3 Several more journals sprang up for women in the first decade of the twentieth century. Kallās counts 10 in Cairo and 2 in Alexandria. Jūrj Kallās, *Tārīkh al-Ṣiḥāfa al-Nisāwiyya: Nash'atu-hā wa-Taṭawwuru-hā, 1892–1932* (1996), pp. 46–8. Beth Baron concludes that the women's press in Egypt 'enlivened the intellectual environment and influenced the direction of social change'. B. Baron, 'Readers and the Women's Press in Egypt', *Poetics Today*, Vol. 15, no. 2, Summer 1994, p. 217. For those interested in the blossoming of the women's press in Egypt, see Beth Baron's comprehensive study. *The Women's Awakening in Egypt: Culture, Society and the Press* (1994).

4 B. Baron, *The Women's Awakening in Egypt* (1994), pp. 121, 142–5.

5 Ibid., pp. 54–7, 77–8.

Al-Khizāna (The Treasure Trove, 1900) was a monthly founded by Yūsuf al-Khāzin and was distinctive for its bulk (ca. 100 pages).

Al-Miftāḥ (The Key, 1900) was founded by Tawfīq 'Azzūz. Each issue of this monthly was supplemented with a 'literary narrative'.

Al-Nibrās (The Lantern, 1900), a weekly founded by Najīb al-Jāwīsh, reportedly published important literary and political studies.

Al-Tamaddun (Civilization, 1901) was a weekly founded by Ibrāhīm Ramzī.

Al-Majalla al-Madrasiyya, (The Scholarly Journal, 1903), founded by Sayyid Muḥammad, claimed to broaden the literary and scientific horizons of students.

Al-Imām (The Imam, 1903) was a weekly founded by Muḥammad Abū Shādī and Maḥmūd Wāṣif.

Al-Muṣawwir (The Illustrator, 1903) was a satirical weekly founded by Khalīl Zayniyya.

Al-Ṭarā'if (Curiosities, 1903) was a weekly founded by the poet and author Rashīd al-Maṣūb(?) who published much of his own poetry in it.

Al-Aqlām (Pens, 1906) was founded in response to a call by the writers Jūrj Ṭanūs and Maḥmūd Abū Ḥusayn. The editorial committee comprised a number of poets and writers who published poems, literary articles and stories in this monthly.

Fatāt al-Sharq (Young Woman of the East, 1906) was edited by the Lebanese woman writer Labība Hāshim, who contributed much of her own original and translated work, and ran until 1939. Her short narrative pieces told sentimental love stories and were closer to summaries of longer stories than short stories in the true sense. As in *al-Ḍiyā'*, these were published in the humour section. Hafez describes Labība Hāshim as 'the pioneer of a trend of simplistic narrative', popularizing narrative among women readers and familiarizing them with its conventions.[6] Although two longer stories serialized in the journal were later collected and published as books, her short stories were never gathered into a collection.[7]

Al-Shitā' (Winter, 1906) was founded by Salīm al-'Anḥūrī (an editor of *Mir'āt al-Sharq* before the British occupation) and was published monthly for only one Winter before al-'Anḥūrī again returned to Syria.[8]

Al-Iqdām (Enterprise, 1912) was a short-lived daily paper founded by Alexandra Avierino. As well as dealing with political issues, calling for social reform and discussing daring subjects such as socialism and poverty, it found space for literary content. It was edited by Walī al-Dīn Yakan, an aristocratic poet with a

6 S. Hafez, *The Genesis of Arabic Narrative Discourse* (1993), p. 137.

7 Abbās Khiḍr, 'Min Awā'il Kuttāb al-Uqṣūṣa fī Miṣr', *al-Qiṣṣa*, March 1965, p. 32.

8 Albert Kudseh-Zadeh, 'Salim Anhuri, Journalist, Poet and Social Critic'. In Donald Little (ed.) *Essays on Islamic Civilization* (1976), p. 183.

strong social conscience, and the poet Aḥmad Muḥarram and story writer Labība Hāshim featured among its contributors.[9]

'Abd al-Laṭīf Ḥamza also provides a list of Egyptian journals concerned specifically with prose narrative in the early twentieth century.[10] Unfortunately, the frequency of publication was not recorded; the editors appear after the parantheses:

Silsilat al-Riwāyāt[11] (Series of Stories, 1899). Muḥammad Khiḍr and Bashīr al-Ḥalabī.
al-Riwāya al-Shahriyya (The Monthly Story, 1902). Ya'qūb al-Jamāl
Musāmarat al-Nadīm (al-Nadim's Nightly Tales, 1903). Ibrāhīm Ramzī and 'Izzat Ḥilmī.
Musāmarat al-Sha'b (The Nation's Nightly Tales, 1904). Khalīl Ṣādiq.
al-Fukāhāt al-Miṣriyya (Egyptian Jokes, 1908). 'Abd Allāh 'Azālat al-Ḥalabī.
Al-Musāmarāt al-Usbū'iyya (Tales Weekly, 1909).[12]
al-Riwāya al-Jadīda (The New Fiction, 1910). Niqūlā Rizq Allāh.
al-Samīr (The Entertainer, 1911 in Alexandria). Qayṣar al-Shumayyil.
Musāmarāt al-Mulūk (The Nightly Tales of Kings, 1912).[13]
al-Riwāyāt al-Kubrā (The Greatest Stories, 1914). Murād al-Ḥusaynī.

9 A. H. al-Ṭamāwī, *Fuṣūl min al-Ṣiḥāfa al-Adabiyya* (1989), pp. 104–5.
10 'Abd al-Laṭīf Ḥamza, *al-Ṣiḥāfa wa-l-Adab fī Miṣr* (1955), p. 37.
11 Whereas the term *riwāya* is now held to mean 'novel', at this early stage in the development of this genre in Arabic, the term was much more fluid, referring to prose narrative and story telling more generally.
12 'Abd al-Muḥsin Ṭaha Badr, *Taṭawwur al-Riwāya al-'Arabiyya al-Ḥadītha fī Miṣr* (1983), p. 126.
13 Ibid., p. 127.

APPENDIX B

Gallery 68 particulars

Frequency and length of publication

Date	*No. of pages*
April–May 1968	78
June 1968	78
July 1968	78
Nov. 1968	78
Feb. 1969	78
April 1969	128[1]
Oct. 1969	116
Feb. 1971	100

List of editors

Nos. in which involved	*Name*
1–8	Aḥmad Mursī
1–8	Jamīl ‘Aṭiyya Ibrāhīm
1–8	Idwār al-Kharrāṭ
1–8	Ibrāhīm Manṣūr
1–4	Sayyid Ḥijāb
1–4	Ghālib Halasā
1–4	Dr Yusrī Khamīs
1–4	Ibrāhīm ‘Abd al-‘Āṭī
5–7	Muḥammad Ibrāhīm Mabrūk
1, 2	Ḥasan Sulaymān
1	Sa‘d ‘Abd al-Wahhāb
2	Mīlād ‘Abd al-Sayyid

1 Special issue: a selection of contemporary Egyptian short stories.

APPENDIX B

List of contributors and contributions

Contributors of short stories

(Where stories are known to have appeared in print prior to *Gallery 68*, this is noted.)

'Abd Allāh, Yaḥyā
- *Ḥadīth al-Ulfa* 5: 18–21

'Abd Allāh, Yaḥyā al-Ṭāhir
- *Jabal al-Shāy al-Akhḍar* 6: 105–9
  (Previously published in *al-Kātib*, Dec. 1968)
- *al-Raqṣa al-Mubāḥa* 7: 12–18
- *Ughniya al-'Āshiq Īliyā* 8: 15–22

'Abd al-'Āṭī, Ibrāhīm
- *Kull Shakhṣiyyāt fī-mā Yalī Takhayyuliyya, wa-Ayy Tashābuh Bayna-hā wa-Bayna Ayy Shakhṣ Ḥayy aw Mayyit Maḥḍ Taṣāduf* 1: 26–8
- *Da'd* 1: 58–64
- *Lūqā* 4: 55–67
- *Taqārīr Shāmila* 6: 9–15
- *Fuṣūl Munsiya min al-Qawānīn al-'Āmma li-l-Ra'b* 8: 38–42

'Abd al-Rāziq, 'Abd Allāh
- *Ughniya Khalf al-Jidār* 7: 53–5

al-Amīr, Ayman
- *Dhālika al-Laḥn* 5: 15–16, 75–8

Aṣlān, Ibrāhīm
- *Li-anna-hum Yarithūna al-Arḍ* 1: 17–24
- *Rā'iḥa al-Maṭar* 4: 48–53
- *Fī Jiwār Rajul Ḍarīr* 6: 5–8
- *al-Jurḥ* 8: 58–61
- *al-Raghba fī al-Bukā'* 8: 62–6
  (Previously published in *al-Jumhūriyya*, 27 April 1967)
- *al-Taḥarrur min al-'Aṭash* 8: 67–70
  (Previously published in *Ṣabāḥ al-Khayr*, Nov. 1966)
- *al-Baḥth 'An 'Unwān* 8: 70–4
  (Previously published in *Ḥiwār*, March 1966)
- *al-Malhā al-Qadīm* 8: 74–7
  (Previously published in *al-Majalla*, March 1968)

Three studies of Aṣlān by Kharrāt, Halasā and Kalfat 8: 78–99

'Aṭiyya, Na'īm
The following were presented as poems in *Gallery 68*, but Aṭiyya prefers to see them as short stories (taped interview, Cairo, 28 April 1996).

- *Fī al-Nihāya* 1: 34
- *al-Ḥāris* 1: 34

al-Bisāṭī, Muḥammad

- *Ibtisāmat al-Madīna al-Ramādiyya* 2: 52–6
- *Ḥadīth min al-Ṭābiq al-Thālith* 6: 94–9
  (Previously published in *al-Masā'*, 14 Aug. 1966)
- *Mughāmarāt Ḥamza* 7: 38–44

Study of Bisāṭī's collection *al-Kibār wa-l-Sighār* (1968) 2: 43–51

al-Buḥayrī, Aḥmad

- *al-Muharrij* 1: 35–7
- *Makān bi-lā Malāmiḥ Mumayyiza* 1: 37–9

Fahmī, al-Dasūqī

- *al-Jalabāb al-Abyaḍ* 5: 29–33

Translation of Kafka's *The Great Wall of China* 4: 11–25

Farīd, Māhir Shafīq

- *Mubārāt Shaṭranj* 3: 32–6

Fayyāḍ, Sulaymān

- *Raghīf al-Batānūhī* 6: 63–70
  (Previously published in *Wa-Ba'da-nā al-Ṭawfān*, 1968)

al-Ghiṭānī, Jamāl

- *Hidāyat Ahl al-Warā* 6: 46–51
  (Published same year in *Awrāq Shābb 'Āsha mundhu Alf 'Ām*, 1969)

Halasā, Ghālib

- *al-Khawf* 8: 8–14

Study of Bisāṭī's collection *al-Kibār wa-l-Ṣighār* 2: 43–51
Observations on obscurity in poetry 4: 75–8
Study of trends in 'the new literature' 6: 115–25
Study of philosophy and aesthetics 7: 70–3
Study of Ibrāhīm Aṣlān's short stories 8: 84–9

Ḥasab Allāh, Yaḥyā
A story was billed (without title) in the list of contents of no. 8, but it was not present in the journal.

Ḥusayn, ʻAlī Ḥusayn
- *Bi-Inkār* 7: 62–3

al-Ḥusaynī, ʻAlī Zayn al-ʻĀbidīn
- *Huwa* 1: 40–5

Ibrāhīm, Jamīl ʻAṭiyya
- *Alḥān Ghayr Mutaqābila* 2: 11
- *al-Murabbaʻ al-Dāʼirī* 6: 52–8
  (Previously published in *al-Majalla*, July 1965)
- *Kalimāt Rajul Ḥazīn* 8: 23–5

Juwaylī, Muḥammad Khālid
- *Baʻda Layla min al-Araq* 3: 49–50
- *Lam Yakun Thammata Dāʻ-in li-Dhālika* 5: 34–6

Kalfat, Khalīl Sulaymān
- *Māta Hamad Yawm ʻAwdati-hi min al-Qāhira* 3: 37–48
- *Wafāʼ al-Nīl* 6: 59–62
  (Previously published in *al-Masāʼ*, Dec. 1968)

Observations on *Gallery 68*'s writers 7: 73–82
Study of Ibrāhīm Aṣlān's short stories 8: 90–9

Kalfat, ʻAlī Sulaymān
- *al-Jidār* 2: 58–62
- *Picasso wa-ʻUṣfūra wa-Ḥidhāʼ* 5: 25–6

Kāẓim, Ṣāfī Nāz
- *Kullu-hā Wujahāt Naẓar* 3: 26

al-Kharrāṭ, Idwār
- *Ākhir al-Sikka* 6: 25–35
  (Previously published in *al-Majalla*, Feb. 1968)

Translation of five French poems by Paul Eluard and others 7: 112–116
Study of Aḥmad Mursī's art exhibition 7: 20–3
Translation of two avant-garde Indian poems 8: 43–4
Study of Ibrāhīm Aṣlan's short stories 8: 78–83

Mabrūk, Muḥammad Ibrāhīm
- *al-Rakḍ fī Sirdāb Muwaḥḥal* 4: 39–44
- *Nazafa Ṣawt Ṣamt Nisf Ṭāʼir* 6: 85–93
  (Previously published in *al-Majalla*, Oct. 1966)

Manṣūr, Ibrāhīm
- *Paul wa-Virginie* 3: 17–18
- *al-Ḥuzn min al-Jānib wa-min al-Amām* 3: 19
- *al-Yawm 24 Sā'a* 6: 16–19

Maqqār, Shafīq
- *Ru'yā Mahannā al-Ṭāghūṭī* 7: 24–31

Mus'ad, Ra'ūf
- *al-Ḥadīqa* 5: 11–13
- *wa-Daqīqa* 8: 45–6

Qāsim, 'Abd al-Ḥakīm
- *al-Ṣaffāra* 4: 32–4
- *Ḥikāyāt Ḥawla Ḥādith Saghīr* 6: 71–84
  (Previously published in *al-Majalla*, Aug. 1967)

al-Qiṭṭ, Yūsuf
- *'Ābid al-Thalātha* 3: 67–9
- *'Ayn al-Kāmīrā* 7: 48–52

Rajab, Muḥammad Ḥāfiẓ
- *al-Ab Ḥānūt* 6: 101–4
  (Previously published in *al-Kurra wa-Ra's al-Rajul*, 1968)

al-Sharīf, Aḥmad Ḥāshim
- *al-Luṣūṣ* 6: 20–4
  (Previously published in *al-Ahrām*, Jan. 1965 and included in *Wajh al-Madīna*, 1966)

al-Shārikh, Muḥammad
- *Qays wa-Layla* 2: 32–40

al-Shārūnī, Yūsuf
- *Lamaḥāt min Ḥayāt Mawjūd 'Abd al-Mawjūd, wa-Mulāḥaẓatāni* 8: 48–57
  (This is a more refined version of the same story previously published in *al-Ziḥām*, 1969)

Ṭāhir, Bahā'
- *al-Khuṭūba* 6: 36–45
  (Previously published in *Ṣabāḥ al-Khayr*, 9 May 1968

al-Takarlī, Fu'ād
- *al-Ṣamt wa-l-Luṣūṣ* 3: 64–72

Ṭūbyā, Majīd
- *Kull al-Anhār* 2: 74–8

Contributors of poems

ʻAbd Allāh, Naṣār
- *Qaṣā'id ilā Pavlov* 3: 51–2
- *al-Muḥākama* 3: 53–4
- *Fikra min Mudhakkirāt Muqātil ʻAjūz* 5: 7

al-Abnūdī, ʻAbd al-Raḥmān
- *al-Ashyā'* 4: 45–7

ʻĀmir, ʻIzzat
- *Madkhal al-Ḥadā'iq al-Ṭāghūriyya: al-Nashīd al-Sādis ʻAshar* 2: 9–10
- *Madkhal al-Ḥadā'iq al-Ṭāghūriyya: al-Nashīd al-Sādis wa-l-ʻIshrūn* 2: 10
- *Mā Yatabaqqā min al-Mawt* 5: 22–3
- *Qalb al-Aswāq* 5: 24
- *al-Barīq wa-l-Ṣamt* 7: 32–7

al-Baḥr, Tharwat
- *ʻUrūsat al-Mawlid* 4: 76
- *al-Taḥawwul* 4: 77–8

al-Bayyātī, ʻAbd al-Wahhāb
- Extract from *al-Kitāba ʻAlā al-Ṭīn* 1: 3–5
- Extract from *al-Kitāba ʻAlā al-Ṭīn* 5: 3
- *ʻAyn al-Shams* 8: 6–7

A self-study of his poetic experience/experiment 2: 62–73

Dunqul, Amal
- *al-Mawt fī Lawḥāt* 1: 65–6

Farghalī, Fatḥī
- *Min Malḥama al-Sanawāt al-ʻIjāf* 4: 69–71

al-Ghuzūlī, Usāma
- *al-Ḥajj* 7: 45

Ḥijāb, Sayyid
- *Ash'ār bi-l-ʻĀmmiyya al-Miṣriyya* 1: 25
- Extract from *al-ʻAtma* 7: 7–11

Study of specific poetic/folkloric rhythms and structures 3: 3–8

Study of poetic/folkloric rhythm and structure 4: 3–10

Kalfat, Khalīl Sulaymān (also listed under short story contributors)
- *'Ayn Sīn* 1: 46–8

Khamīs, Shawqī
- *al-Baḥr* 2: 57

Khamīs, Yusrī
- *Muta'akhkhir Dā'im-an* 2: 41

al-Kubaysī, Ṭarrād
- *'Aynāyya Tanẓurāni al-Ashyā' 'An-ī* 4: 54

Maṭar, Muḥammad 'Afīfī
- *Ughniya al-Mughannī al-Khā'if* 2: 42

al-Maṭba'ī, Ḥamīd
- *Abrāju-nā Mu'tima ka-l-Wujūh* 7: 19

Mursī, Aḥmad
- *al-Ṣawt* 2: 2
- *Sudan* 2: 21
- *Arabesque* 2: 22
- *'Ushshāq al-Madīna al-Mayyita* 2: 23
- *al-Manfā* 2: 24–5
- *al-Rūḥ al-Raqṣ* 4: 35–8

Article on sculptor Kamāl Khalīfa 4: 72–4
Translation of an interview with Henry Moore 3: 20–5

Nāfi', Sa'īd
- *Min Majmū'at Qaṣā'id bi-lā 'Unwān* 8: 47

Ṣādiq, Waṣfī
- *Fiqra min Shakwā Majhūla* 5: 14

Ṣalīb, Ṣalīb Kāmil
- *al-Qiṭār* 8: 36–7

Ṣāliḥ, Muḥammad
- *Min Asfār al-'Aṣr* 8: 26–7

Sayf, Muḥammad
- *al-Khandaq* 5: 27–8

al-Sayyid, Muḥammad Mihrān
- *'An al-Ṭuyūr al-Kharsā'* 3: 15–16
- *Wuqūf-an bi-hā Ṣaḥb-ī/ Ṣuḥbā* 7: 46–7

Contributors of plays

'Abd Allāh, Yaḥyā (also listed under short story contributors)
- *al-Kilāb Taḥta al-Mā'ida* 1: 68–78

Abū al-Naṣr, Muṣṭafā
- *Ughniya Mukarrira* 7: 56–61

Other contributors

Baṭūṭī, Māhir
Translation of play by Marguerite Duras 5: 37–61

Fahīm, Shawqī
Translation of article on Kafka, Gogol and Nathaniel West by Idris Bey 4: 26–31

Fahmī, Amānī
Translation of three plays by Harold Pinter 3: 9–14

Farīd, Fārūq
Translation of poem by Kostas Palamas 1: 67

Fatḥī, Ibrāhīm
Translation of a study of realism by F. D. Klingender 2: 26–31
Study of poetry 5: 71–4
Study of recent short stories in special issue no. 6 6: 110–4
Study of critical methods 7: 64–9

Hafez, Sabry
Study of the Egyptian short story and modernism 7: 83–90
Translation of three Russian poems 3: 30–1

Kāmil, Nadia
Translation of poetry by Apollinaire 5: 8–10

Majallī, Shafīq
Study of obscurity in poetry 2: 3–8

Naẓmī, Ra'ūf
Study of modern poetry 5: 62–6

al-Shafaqī, ʻAbd Allah
Translation of an interview with Norman Mailer 3: 55–63

Shafīq, Ṣubḥī
Translation of interview with Carlos Fuentos 1: 49–57

Shukrī, Ghālī
Study of the socialist approach to literature 5: 67–70

Sulaymān, Ḥasan
Subjective study of artistic inspiration 5: 4–6

APPENDIX C

List of Egyptian journals mentioned in the text

Secondary sources (listed in the bibliography) have had to be used for gleaning some of the following dates, especially for the earlier journals. These sources do not always concur on dates – discrepancies arise from the fact that journals frequently fell into neglect or were suppressed, only to be revived at a later date. Since these difficulties pertain particularly to the earlier journals, which emerged when collection and cataloguing procedures were less rigorous, generally only the date of appearance is provided for journals prior to 1920. In the few cases where discrepancies occur after 1920, I have generally opted for the widest span of dates on the assumption that more numbers of the journal came to light. Those journals listed in Appendix A are not listed again here. Not all titles are suited to translation. Nevertheless, translations have been provided here in the interests of those who do not read Arabic.

Jurnāl al-Khidīw (The Khedive's Journal, 1813)[1]
Abū Naḍḍāra (The Man with Spectacles, 1877; moved to Paris)[2]
Abū Zayd (Abu Zayd, 1901)
al-Ādāb (Refined Culture, 1887)
al-Adab (Literature, 1956–66)
Adabī (My Literature, 1936–7)
al-Adab wa-l-Tamthīl (Literature and Drama, 1916)
al-Adīb al-Miṣrī (The Egyptian Man of Letters, 1950)
al-Ahrām (The Pyramids, 1876)
Akhbār al-Adab (The Literary News, 1993–)
Akhbār al-Yawm (The News of the Day, 1944–)
Ākhir Sā'a (The Final Hour, 1934–83)

1 1813 according to 'Abd al-Laṭīf Ḥamza (1967); ca. 1822 according to Ibrāhīm 'Abduh (1982); 1827 according to P. J. Vatikiotis (1980). Although 1813 predates the establishment of the Bulaq press, the journal was originally handwritten.

2 Ṣanū' changed the name of this journal at least four times but it essentially remained *Abū Naẓẓāra*.

Apollo (Apollo, 1932–4)
al-Arghūl (The Musical Pipes, 1894)
al-'Aṣr al-Jadīd (The New Era, 1880)
al-Balāgh al-Usbū'ī (The Weekly Report, 1926–30)
al-Bashīr (The Herald, 1948–50)[3]
al-Bayān (Information, 1897–8)
al-Bayān (Information, 1911–21)
al-Ḍiyā' (Light, 1898–1906)
al-Fajr (The Dawn, 1925–7)
al-Fajr al-Jadīd (The New Dawn, 1945–6)
al-Fikr al-Mu'āṣir (Contemporary Thought, 1965–71)
al-Funūn al-Sha'biyya (The Folk Arts, 1965, 1967–71)
al-Fuṣūl (The Seasons, 1931)
al-Fuṣūl (The Seasons, 1944?–54?)
al-Ghad (Tomorrow, 1953, 1959, 1985–6)
Hā . . . Hā . . . Hā (Ha Ha Ha, 1907)
al-Hadaf (The Objective, 1956–8)
al-Hilāl (The Crescent Moon, 1892–)
Ḥimārat Munyatī (The Donkey of My Desire, 1897)
Ibdā' (Creativity, 1983–2002)
al-Jamāhīr (The Public, 1947–8)
al-Jāmi'a (The University, 1930–48)[4]
al-Jarīda (The Newspaper, 1907–14)
al-Jawā'ib al-Misriyya (Egyptian Responses, 1903–7)[5]
al-Jīl (The Generation, 1951–60)
al-Jumhūriyya (The Republic, 1953–)
al-Kātib (The Writer, 1937–8)
al-Kātib (The Writer, 1950–1)
al-Kātib (The Writer, 1961–80)
al-Kātib al-Miṣrī (The Egyptian Writer, 1945–8)
Kawkab al-Sharq (Star of the East, 1924–39)
al-Kawkab al-Sharqī (The Eastern Star, 1873)
Khayāl al-Ẓill (The Shadow Play, 1907–8)
al-Kitāb (The Book, 1945–53)
al-Laṭā'if (Jokes, 1886–96)

3 The issue dated 2 Oct. 1948 is actually no. 351. This is because an experimental group of writers rented the license of the already established *al-Bashīr*.

4 1930–48 according to Shalash (1988); 1932–9 according to Hafez (1979); 1934–48 according to al-Nassāj (1978). I have selected the widest possible dates on the assumption that additional runs were found.

5 Scholars disagree over the closure date: 1907 Badawi (1975); 1904 Mounah A. Khouri (1971); and 1905 Somekh (1976). Since the journal suffered from financial difficulties, it may be that it was suspended at times, but resurrected again.

al-Liwā' (The Standard, 1900)
al-Mahrajān (The Festival, 1947–8)
al-Maḥrūsa (The Protected One, 1880)
al-Majalla (The Journal, 1957–71)
al-Majalla al-Jadīda (The New Journal, 1929–31, 1933–44)[6]
al-Majalla al-Miṣriyya (The Egyptian Journal, 1900–2, 1909)
Majallat al-'Ashar Qiṣaṣ (The Ten Story Journal, 1936–7)
Majallat al-'Ishrīn Qiṣṣa (The Twenty Story Journal, 1937–45)
Majallatī (My Journal, 1934–45)[7]
al-Manār (The Minaret, 1898–1935)
al-Masā' (Tonight, 1956–)
al-Masraḥ (The Theatre, 1925–7)
al-Masraḥ (The Theatre, 1964–70)
al-Maymūn (The Monkey, 1879–1883)
Mir'āt al-Sharq (Mirror of the East, 1879)
al-Misalla (The Obelisk, 1919)
Miṣbāḥ al-Sharq (Light of the East, 1898)
Miṣr (Egypt, 1877)
Miṣr al-Fatāh (Young Egypt, 1879)
al-Miṣrī (The Egyptian, 1936–54)
al-Mu'ayyad (The Endorsed, 1889–1915)
al-Muqaṭṭam (The Muqaṭṭam Hills, 1889)
al-Muqtabas (Acquired Knowledge 1906; moved to Damascus 1909)
al-Muqtaṭaf (The Selection 1876 Beirut; moved to Cairo 1885–1952)
al-Mustaqbal (The Future, 1914)
Nādī al-Qiṣṣa (The Writing Club, 1970)
al-Nadīm al-Qiṣaṣī (al-Nadīm the Storyteller, 1946–7)
al-Nāqid (The Critic, 1927–8)
al-Nās (The People, 1951)
Nuzhat al-Afkār (The Recreation of Ideas, 1870)
al-Qāhira (Cairo, 1885)
al-Qiṣaṣ (Stories, 1922–3)
al-Qiṣaṣ (Stories, 1930–1)
Qiṣaṣ al-Shahr (Stories of the Month, 1945–6)

6 Scholars appear at odds over the date this journal ended. This doubtless results from confusion between the weekly (launched 1934) and the monthly, which carried the same name. The monthly ceased in 1941, but the weekly was taken over by the Society of Art and Freedom. The weekly ceased in late 1942 but was restarted by the same society in 1943 and eventually became monthly until its final closure in 1944. See Samīr Gharīb, *al-Siryāliyya fī Miṣr* (1986), pp. 26–7.

7 Most library collections mark *Majallatī*'s dates as 1934–7 and these are the only numbers to which I have gained access. However, both al-Nassāj and Shalash date the journal 1934–45 so one must assume that further runs appeared.

al-Qiṣṣa (The Story, 1945–6)
al-Qiṣṣa (The Story, 1949–55)
al-Qiṣṣa (The Story, 1964–5)
Rābiṭat al-Shabāb (The Youth League, 1947–50)[8]
Rawḍat al-Akhbār (News Pasture, 1874–8)
Rawḍat al-Madāris (The Schools' Training Ground, 1870–7)
al-Risāla (The Dispatch, 1933–53, 1963–5)
al-Risāla al-Jadīda (The New Dispatch, 1952–8)[9]
al-Riwāya (The Novel, 1937–9; 1952–3)
al-Riwāyāt al-Jadīda (New Novels, 1936–45)
Riwāyāt al-Usbū' (Stories of the Week, 1949–54)
Rūz al-Yūsuf (Rose al-Yūsuf, 1925–)
Ṣabāḥ al-Khayr (Good Morning, 1951–)
Sarkīs (Sarkīs, 1905–26)
al-Sha'b (The People, 1956–9)
al-Shahr (The Month, 1957–62)
al-Shā'ir (The Poet, 1950–1)
al-Shi'r (Poetry, 1930)
al-Shi'r (Poetry, 1964–5)
al-Siyāsa al-Usbū'iyya (Weekly Politics, 1926–31, 1937–49)
al-Sufūr (The Unveiling, 1915–24)
al-Ṭā'if (The Wanderer 1881–2)
al-Ṭalī'a (The Avant-Garde, 1965–77)
al-Tankīt wa-l-Tabkīt (Banter and Blame 1881)
al-Thaqāfa (Culture, 1939–53, 1963–5)
al-Taṭawwur (Development, 1940)
al-Tijāra (Trade 1878–9)
al-Usbū' (The Week, 1933, 1939–?)
al-Ustādh (The Master, 1892–3)
Wādī al-Nīl (The Nile Valley, 1866–74)[10]
al-Waqā'i' al-Miṣriyya (Egyptian Events, 1828)
al-Waqt (Time, 1879)
al-Waṭan (The Nation, 1877–84)
al-Zahrā' (The Most Brilliant, 1924–30)
al-Zuhūr (Blossomings, 1910–13)

8 These dates refer to the period during which this journal was taken over by the Wafdist Vanguard.
9 1952–7 according to Hafez (1979); 1954–8 according to Shalash (1988) and Sayyid Ḥāmid al-Nassāj, p. 363.
10 Scholars vary between 1867 (e.g. Ṭarrāzī) and 1966 (e.g. Ḥamza and 'Abduh).

Non-periodic journals

This list contains those non-periodic Egyptian journals mentioned in this book; it is not intended as a comprehensive list. The spontaneous nature and poor publication quality of many of these journals means that some numbers have not survived. Even dating those journals which I have been able to access is fraught with difficulty: not only did such journals tend to disappear as suddenly and as unannounced as they appeared (leaving uncertainty as to whether or not an issue is the final one), but some issues are neither numbered nor dated.

Abjadiyyāt (Elementary Truths, 1980)
Adab al-Ghad 1983–4 (2 issues)
Adab al-Jamāhīr (The Literature of the Masses, early 1970s)
al-Fikr al-Mu'āṣir (Contemporary Thought, 1979–81?)
Gālīrī 68 (Gallery 68, 1969–71)
Iḍā'a 77 (Illumination 77, 1977–88)
al-Jarād (The Locust, 1994–2000?)
Kāf Nūn (K. N., 1977–80)
al-Kalima (The Word, 1978?)
Kāmīrā 79 (Camera 79, 1979–?)
Khaṭwa (A Step, 1980–5)
al-Kitāba al-Sawdā' (Black Writing, 1988)
al-Kitāba al-Ukhrā (Alternative Writing, 1991–2001?)
Kitābāt (Writings, 1979–84)
al-Kurrāsa al-Thaqāfiyya (The Cultural Notebook, 1979–80)
Mawqif (Stance, 1981–?)
Miṣriyya (Egyptian, 1979?–86)
al-Naddāha (The Caller, 1978–9?)
al-Nadīm (al-Nadīm, 1980–5)
Nahār (Day, 1983–4?)
Qiṣṣa (Story, 1986–?)
Ruwwād (Pioneers, early 1980s)
Sanābil (Ears of Corn, 1969–72)
al-Shams al-Jadīda (The New Sun, 1984–)
al-Talī'a (The Avant-Garde, 1984–6)
al-Thaqāfa al-Jadīda (The New Culture, 1976)
al-Thaqāfa al-Waṭaniyya (The National Culture, 1980–1)

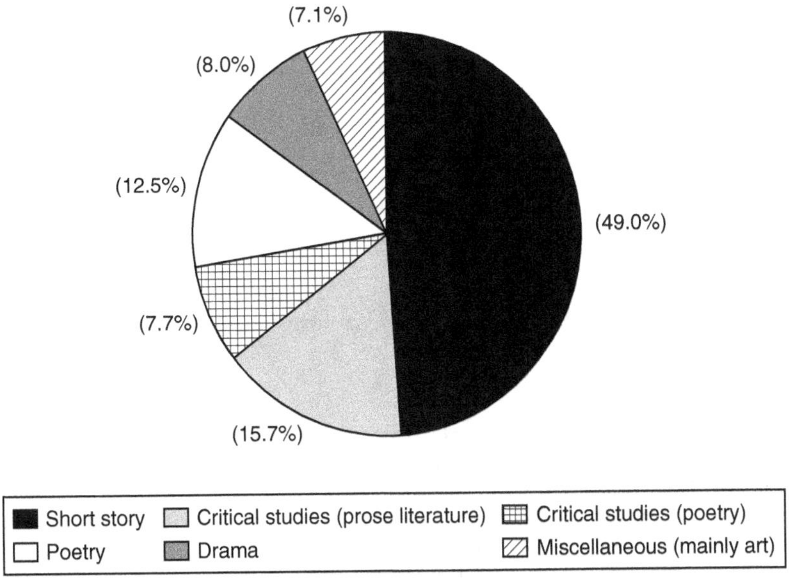

Figure 1 The literary emphasis in *Gallery 68*.

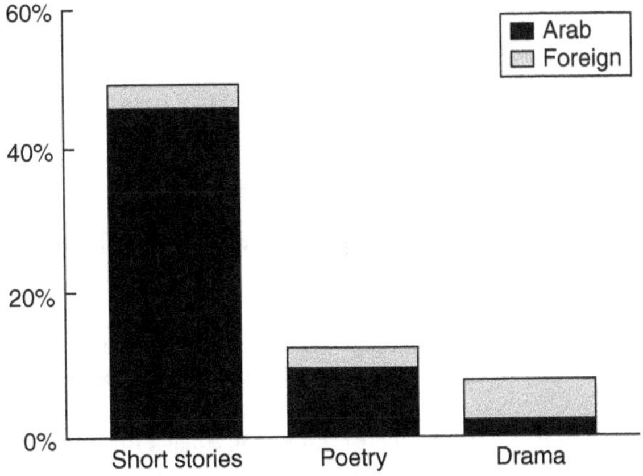

Figure 2 Proportion of Arab to foreign literature in *Gallery 68*.

BIBLIOGRAPHY

Works in European languages

Books

Abdel-Malek, Kamal and Hassan, Wael (eds) *Tradition, Modernity and Post-Modernity in Arabic Literature: Essays in Honour of Prof. Issa J. Boullata*, Leiden, Boston and Cologne: Brill, 2000.

Adūnīs/Adonis ('Alī Aḥmad Sa'īd), *An Introduction to Arab Poetics*, trans. Catherine Cobham, London: Saqi Books, 1990.

——, *The Pages of Day and Night*, trans. Samuel Hazo, Marlboro VT: Malboro Press, 1994.

Ahmed-Bioud, Abdelghani, Feki, Habib and Hanafi, Hassan, *3,200 Revues et Journaux Arabes, 1800–1965: titres arabes et titres translittérés*, Paris: National Library, 1969.

Allen Roger, 'Poetry and Poetic Criticism at the Turn of the Century', in Robin Ostle (ed.) *Studies in Modern Arabic Literature*, Warminster: Aris & Phillips, 1975.

—— (ed.) *Modern Arabic Literature*, New York: Ungar, 1987.

——, *A Period of Time*, Reading PA: Ithaca Press, 1992.

Aman, Muḥammad M., *Arab Periodicals and Serials – a Select Bibliography*, New York and London: Garland, 1979.

Asfour, John Mikhail, *When the Words Burn: An Anthology of Modern Arabic Poetry, 1945–1987*, Cairo: American University in Cairo Press, 1993.

Auchterlonie, Paul and Safadi, Yasin H., *Union Catalogue of Arabic Serials and Newspapers*, Lancaster PA: Mansell, 1977.

'Awaḍ, Louis (Lūwīs), *The Literature of Ideas in Egypt*, Part 1, Atlanta GA: The Scholars' Press, 1986.

Ayalon, Ami, *The Press in the Arab Middle East: A History*, Oxford and New York: Oxford University Press, 1995.

Badawi, Muhammad Mustafa, *A Critical Introduction to Modern Arabic Poetry*, Cambridge: Cambridge University Press, 1975.

——, *Modern Arabic Literature and the West*, London: Ithaca Press, 1985.

——, *Early Arabic Drama*, Cambridge: Cambridge University Press, 1988.

——, (ed.) *Modern Arabic Literature*, Cambridge History of Arabic Literature, Vol. IV, Cambridge: Cambridge University Press, 1992.

Barakat, Halim, *The Arab World: Society, Culture and State*, Berkeley and Oxford: University of California Press, 1993.

Baron, Beth, *The Women's Awakening in Egypt: Culture, Society and the Press*, New Haven and London: Yale University Press, 1994.

Berque, Jacques, *Cultural Expression in Arab Society Today*, Austin and London: University of Texas Press, 1978.

Bhabha, Homi, *The Location of Culture*, London and New York: Routledge, 1994.

Booth, Marilyn, *Bayram al-Tunisi's Egypt: Social Criticism and Narrative Strategies*, Exeter: Ithaca Press, 1990.

——, 'Poetry in the Vernacular', in M. M. Badawi (ed.) *Modern Arabic Literature*, Cambridge: Cambridge University Press, 1992, pp. 463–82.

Booth, Wayne C., 'Renewing the Medium of Renewal: Some Notes on the Anxieties of Innovation', in Ihab and Sally Hassan (eds) *Innovation / Renovation: New Perspectives on the Humanities*, Madison WI: The University of Wisconsin Press, 1983, pp. 131–59.

Boullata, Issa J. (ed.) *Critical Perspectives on Modern Arabic Literature*, Washington DC: Three Continents Press, 1980.

——, *Trends and Issues in Contemporary Arab Thought*, Albany NY: State University of New York Press, 1990.

Bourdieu, Pierre, *The Field of Cultural Production*, edited and introduced by Randal Johnson, Cambridge, UK: Polity Press, 1993.

——, *The Rules of Art*, trans. Susan Emanuel, Cambridge, UK: Polity Press, 1996.

Bradbury, Malcolm, 'Modernisms/Postmodernisms', in Ihab and Sally Hassan (eds) *Innovation/Renovation: New Perspectives on the Humanities*, Madison WI: The University of Wisconsin Press, 1983, pp. 311–27.

Brake, Laurel, Jones, Aled and Madden, Lionel (eds) *Investigating Victorian Journalism*, London: The Macmillan Press Ltd., 1990.

Brugman, J., *An Early History of Modern Arabic Literature in Egypt*, Leiden: Brill, 1984.

Buheiry, Marwan R. (ed.) *Intellectual Life in the Arab East, 1890–1939*, Beirut: American University of Beirut, 1981.

Bürger, Peter, *Theory of the Avant-Garde*, trans. Michael Shaw, foreword Jochen Schulte-Sasse, Minneapolis MN: University of Minnesota Press, 1984.

Butt, John and Tillotson, Kathleen, *Dickens at Work*, London: Methuen, 1957.

Cachia, Pierre, *An Overview of Modern Arabic Literature*, Edinburgh: Edinburgh University Press, 1990.

Chielens, Edward E., *The Literary Journal in America, 1900–1950*, Detroit MI: Gale Research Company, 1977.

Culler, Jonathan D., *The Pursuit of Signs: Semiotics, Literature, Deconstruction*, Ithaca, NY: Cornell University Press, 1981.

Dabous, Sonia, 'Nasser and the Egyptian Press', in Charles Tripp (ed.) *Contemporary Egypt through Egyptian Eyes*, London: Routledge, 1993, pp. 100–21.

Daiches, David, *Critical Approaches to Literature*, London: Longmans, 1961.

Dorigo, Rosella (ed.) *Literary Innovation in Modern Arabic Literature: Schools and Journals*, proceedings of the IV Emtar Congress, Venice, 21–4 April 1999, Rome: Herder, 2000 (=*Quaderni di Studi Arabi*, no.18).

Duman, Hasan and Ihsanoğlu, Ekmeleddin, *Istanbul Kütüphaneleri Arap Harflı Süreli Yayinlar Toplu Kataloğu, 1828–1928*, Istanbul: İslam Tarih, Sanat, ve Kültür Araştırma Merkezi, İslam Konferansı Teskilatı, 1986.

Elias, Elias Hanna, *La Presse Arabe*, Paris: Éditions Maisonneuve et Larose, 1993.

Eysteinsson, Astradur, *The Concept of Modernism*, New York and London: Cornell University Press, 1990.

Fanon, Frantz, *The Wretched of the Earth*, trans. Constance Farrington, Bungay, UK: Penguin, 1967.

Faraj, Nadia, *al-Muqṭataf 1876–1900: A Study of the Influence of Victorian Thought on Modern Arabic Thought*, unpublished D.Phil. thesis, University of Oxford, 1969.

Foucault, Michel, 'What is an Author?', trans. Josué V. Harari, in Josué V. Harari (ed.) *Textual Strategies: Perspectives in Post-Structural Criticism*, London: Methuen, 1980, pp. 141–60.

Galal, Kamal Eldin, *Entstehung und Entwicklung der Tagespresse in Ägypten*, Frankfurt am Main: Moritz Diesterweg, 1939.

Glaß, Dagmar, *Der Muqtaṭaf und seine Öffentlichkeit*, 2 Vols, Würzburg: Ergon Verlag, 2004.

Gonzalez-Quijano, Yves, *Les Gens du Livre: Édition et Champ Intellectuel dans L'Égypte Républicaine*, Paris: CNRS Édition, 1998.

Gruendler, Beatrice and Klemm,Verena (eds) *Understanding Near Eastern Literatures: A Spectrum of Interdisciplinary Approaches*, Wiesbaden: Reichert Verlag, 2000.

Hafez, Sabry, *The Rise and Development of the Egyptian Short Story, 1881–1970*, unpublished PhD thesis, London University, 1979.

——, *The Genesis of Arabic Narrative Discourse*, London: Saqi Books, 1993.

Harari, Josué V. (ed.) *Textual Strategies: Perspectives in Post-Structural Criticism*, London: Methuen, 1980.

Harlow, Barbara and Ghazoul, Ferial J. (eds) *The View from Within*, Cairo: The American University in Cairo Press, 1994.

Hartmann, Alfred Wilhelm Martin, *The Arabic Press of Egypt*, London: Luzac & Co., 1899.

Hassan, Ihab and Sally (eds) *Innovation/Renovation: New Perspectives on the Humanities*, Madison WI: The University of Wisconsin Press, 1983.

Hawthorn, Jeremy, *A Glossary of Contemporary Literary Theory*, London, New York, Melbourne, Auckland: Edward Arnold, 1992.

Hazo, Samuel, *The Blood of Adonis: Transpositions of Selected Poems of Adonis*, Pittsburgh PA: University of Pittsburgh Press, 1971.

Hegab, Sayed (Ḥijāb, Sayyid), *A New Egyptian: The Autobiography of a Young Arab*, New York, Washington and London: Praeger Publishers, 1971.

Hegazy, Samir, *Littérature et Société en Égypte de la Guerre de 1967 à celle de 1973*, Algiers: Entreprise National du Livre, 1986.

Herzog, Christoph, Motika, Raoul and Pistor-Hatam, Anja, *Presse und Öffentlichkeit im Nahen Osten*, Heidelberg: Heidelberger Orientverlag, 1995.

Hoffmann, Frederick J., Allen, Charles and Ulrich, Carolyn F. *The Little Magazine: A History and a Bibliography*, Princeton NJ: Princeton University Press, 1946.

Hopwood, Derek, *Egypt: Politics and Society 1945–1990*, London: Harper Collins Academic, 1991.

Hourani, Albert, *Arabic Thought in the Liberal Age, 1798–1939*, Cambridge: Cambridge University Press, 1983.

Huyssen, Andreas, 'The Search for Tradition: Avant-Garde and Post-Modernism in the 1970s', in Thomas Docherty (ed.) *Postmodernism: A Reader*, New York: Columbia University Press, 1993, pp. 220–36.

Isstaif, Abdul-Nabi, 'Going Beyond Socialist Realism, Getting Nowhere: Lūwīs 'Awaḍ's Cross-Cultural Encounter with the Other', in Kamal Abdel-Malek and Wael Hassan (eds) *Tradition, Modernity and Post-Modernity in Arabic Literature: Essays in Honour of Prof. Issa J. Boullata*, Leiden, Boston and Cologne: Brill, 2000, pp. 113–41.

Jabrā, Jabrā Ibrāhīm, 'Modern Arabic Literature and the West', in I. J. Boullata (ed.) *Critical Perspectives on Modern Arabic Literature*, Washington DC: Three Continents Press, 1980, pp. 7–22.

——, 'The Rebels, the Committed and the Others', in I. J. Boullata (ed.) *Critical Perspectives on Modern Arabic Literature*, Washington DC: Three Continents Press, 1980, pp. 190–205.

Jacquemond, Richard, *Entre Scribes et Écrivains*, Paris: Sindbad, Actes Sud, 2003.

Jayyusi, Salma Khadra, 'Contemporary Arabic Poetry – Vision and Attitudes', in Robin C. Ostle (ed.) *Studies in Modern Arabic Literature*, Warminster: Aris & Phillips Ltd., 1975, pp. 46–68.

Kedourie, Elie and Haim, Sylvia G. (eds) *Modern Egypt: Studies in Politics and Society*, London: Frank Cass, 1980.

Kelidar, Abbas, 'Shaykh 'Alī Yūsuf: Egyptian Journalist and Islamic Nationalist', in Marwan R. Buheiry (ed.) *Intellectual Life in the Arab East, 1890–1939*, Beirut: American University of Beirut, 1981, pp. 10–20.

Khouri, Mounah A., *Poetry and the Making of Modern Egypt*, Leiden: Brill, 1971.

Kilpatrick, Hilary, *The Modern Egyptian Novel: A Study in Social Criticism*, London: Ithaca Press, 1974.

Klemm, Verena, 'Literary Commitment Approached through Reception Theory', in B. Gruendler and V. Klemm (eds) *Understanding Near Eastern Literatures*, Wiesbaden: Reichert Verlag, 2000, pp. 145–53.

Kostelanetz, Richard (ed.) *The Avant-Garde Tradition in Literature*, New York: Prometheus Books, 1982.

Kudseh-Zadeh, Albert, 'Salim Anhuri, Journalist, Poet and Social Critic', in Donald Little (ed.) *Essays on Islamic Civilization*, Leiden: Brill, 1976.

Little, Donald (ed.) *Essays on Islamic Civilization*, Leiden: Brill, 1976.

Lyotard, Jean-François, 'Answering the Question: What is Postmodernism?', in Ihab and Sally Hassan (eds) *Innovation/Renovation: New Perspectives on the Humanities*, Madison WI: The University of Wisconsin Press, 1983, pp. 329–41.

Makarius, Raoul, *La Jeunesse Intellectuelle d'Égypte au Lendemain de la Deuxième Guerre Mondiale*, Paris: Mouton & Co., 1960.

Manzalaoui, Mahmoud (ed.) *Arabic Writing Today: The Short Story*, Cairo: Dār al-Ma'ārif, 1968.

Mead, Donald C., *Growth and Structural Change in the Egyptian Economy*, Homewood, IL: Richard D. Irwin, 1967.

Mehrez, Samia, Introduction to 'Abd al-Ḥakīm Qāsim, *Rites of Assent*, trans. Peter Theroux, Philadelphia PA: Temple University Press, 1995.

Meyer, Stefan G., *The Experimental Arabic Novel: Postcolonial Literary Modernism in the Levant*, New York: State University of New York, 2001.

Moosa, Matti, *The Origins of Modern Arabic Fiction*, Washington DC: Three Continents Press, 1983.

Moreh, Shmuel, *Modern Arabic Poetry, 1800–1970: The Development of its Forms and Themes Under the Influence of Western Literature*, Leiden: Brill, 1976.

Muhawi, Ibrāhīm and Suleiman, Yasir (eds) *Literature and Nation in the Middle East*, Edinburgh: Edinburgh University Press, 2006.

Munier, Jules, *La Presse en Égypte, 1799–1900*, Cairo: Imprimerie de l'Institut Français d'Archéologie Orientale, 1930.

Mūsā, Salāma, *The Education of Salāma Mūsā*, trans. L. O. Schuman, Leiden: Brill, 1961.

al-Musawi, Muhsin Jassim, *The Postcolonial Arabic Novel: Debating Ambivalence*, Leiden and Boston: Brill, 2003.

Nasser, Munir K., *Press, Politics and Power: Egypt's Heikal and al-Ahram*, Ames, Iowa: The Iowa State University Press, 1979.

Ostle, Robin (ed.) *Studies in Modern Arabic Literature*, Warminster: Aris & Phillips, 1975.

—— (ed.) *Modern Literature in the Near and Middle East, 1850–1970*, London and New York: Routledge, 1991.

Philipp, Thomas, *Jūrjī Zaydān: his Life and Thought*, Beirut: Orient-Institut der Deutschen Morgenländischen Gesellschaft, 1979.

——, *The Syrians in Egypt, 1725–1975*, Stuttgart: Franz Steiner Verlag, 1985.

Pistor-Hatam, Anja (ed.) *Amtsblatt, Vilayet Gazetesi und Unabhängiges Journal: die Anfänge der Presse im Nahen Osten*, Frankfurt am Main and New York: Peter Lang, 2001.

Poggioli, Renato, *The Theory of the Avant-Garde*, Cambridge MA and London: The Belknap Press of Harvard University Press, 1968.

Sadgrove, Philip, *The Development of the Arabic Periodical Press and its Role in the Literary Life of Egypt, 1978–1882*, Unpublished PhD Thesis, University of Edinburgh, 1984.

——, *The Egyptian Theatre in the Nineteenth Century, 1799–1882*, London: Ithaca Press, 1996.

——, 'Journalism in Muḥammad 'Alī's Egypt, 1805–49', in Jakob Skovgaard-Petersen (ed.) *The Introduction of the Printing Press in the Middle East*, Oslo: Scandinavian University Press, 1997 (=*Culture and History* no. 16), pp. 89–99.

Said, Edward, *The World, the Text, and the Critic*, Cambridge MA: Harvard University Press, 1983.

Sakkut, Hamdi, *The Egyptian Novel and its Main Trends from 1913 to 1952*, Cairo: American University in Cairo Press, 1971.

Scheunemann, Dietrich (ed.) *European Avant-Garde: New Perspectives*, Amsterdam and Atlanta: Rodopi, 2000.

Seikaly, Samir, 'Damascene Intellectual Life in the Opening Years of the 20th Century: Muḥammad Kurd 'Alī and *al-Muqtabas*', in Marwan R. Buheiry (ed.) *Intellectual Life in the Arab East, 1890–1939*, Beirut: American University of Beirut, 1981.

Selim, George Dimitri, *Arab-World Newspapers in the Library of Congress*, Washington DC: Library of Congress, 1980.

Selim, Samah, *The Novel and the Rural Imaginary in Egypt, 1880–1985*, London and New York: RoutledgeCurzon, 2004.

Shaheen, Mohammad, *The Modern Arabic Short Story: Shahrazad Returns*, London: Macmillan Press, 1989.

Shattock, Joanne and Wolff, Michael (eds) *The Victorian Periodical Press: Sightings and Soundings*, Leicester University Press and University of Toronto Press, 1982.

Skovgaard-Petersen, Jakob (ed.) *The Introduction of the Printing Press in the Middle East*, Oslo: Scandinavian University Press, 1997 (=Culture and History no. 16).

Smith, Charles D., *Islam and the Search for Social Order in Modern Egypt: A Biography of Muhammad Husayn Haykal*, Albany NY: State University of New York Press, 1983.

Spivak, Gayatri Chakravorty, 'Subaltern Studies: Deconstructing Historiography', in Ranajit Guha and Gayatri Chakravorty Spivak (eds) *Selected Subaltern Studies*, Oxford: Oxford University Press, 1988, pp. 1–32.

Stagh, Marina, *The Limits of the Freedom of Speech: Prose Literature and Prose Writers in Egypt under Nasser and Sadat*, Stockholm: Almquist & Wiksell International, 1993.

Stehli-Wehrbeck, Ulrike, 'Referenz und Selbstreferenz: Strategien des Erzählens in Ṣun'allāh Ibrāhīm's *Tilka r-Rā'iḥa*', in B. Gruendler and V. Klemm (eds) *Understanding Near Eastern Literatures*, Wiesbaden: Reichert Verlag, 2000, pp. 203–14.

Swallow, Alan, *An Editor's Essays of Two Decades*, Seattle WA: Experiment Press, 1962.

Terterov, Marat, 'Egypt under Mubarak: Lessons from Political Liberalisation', Unpublished M Phil. Thesis, St. Antony's College, Oxford, 1996.

Tomiche, Nada, *Histoire de la Littérature Romanesque de L'Égypte Moderne*, Paris: Maisonneuve et Larose, 1981.

Unbehaun, Horst (ed.) *The Middle Eastern Press as a Forum for Literature*, Frankfurt am Main and Oxford: Peter Lang, 2004.

Vatikiotis, P. J., *The History of Egypt from Muḥammad 'Alī to Sadat*, Baltimore MD: John Hopkins University Press, 1980.

Wahba, Majdi, *Cultural Policy in Egypt*, Paris: Unesco, 1972.

Warren, Austin and Wellek, René, *Theory of Literature*, Reading: Penguin, 1986; First edition, 1949.

Wechssler, Eduard, *Die Generation als Jugendreihe und ihr Kampf um die Denkform*, Leipzig: Quelle und Meyer, 1930.

Weisstein, Ulrich, *Comparative Literature and Literary Theory: Survey and Introduction*, trans. William Riggan, Bloomington and London: Indiana University Press, 1973.

Williams, Raymond, 'Language and the Avant-Garde', in Nigel Fabb, Derek Atteridge, Alan Durant and Colin MacCabe (eds) *The Linguistics of Writing: Arguments Between Language and Literature*, Manchester: Manchester University Press, 1984, pp. 33–47.

Yapp, Malcolm, 'Modernization and Literature in the Near and Middle East, 1850–1914', in Robin Ostle (ed.) *Modern Literature in the Near and Middle East, 1850–1914*, London and New York: Routledge, 1991, pp. 3–16.

Ziegler, Antje, 'Arab Literary Salons at the Turn of the 20th Century', in Beatrice Gruendler and Verena Klemm (eds) *Understanding Near Eastern Literatures: A Spectrum of Interdisciplinary Approaches*, Wiesbaden: Reichert Verlag, 2000, pp. 241–53.

Articles

Allen, Charles, 'The Advance Guard', *Sewanee Review*, Vol. 51, no. 3, Summer 1943, pp. 410–29.

Allen, Roger, 'Egyptian Drama and Fiction in the 1970s', *Edebiyat*, Vol. 1, no. 2, 1976, pp. 219–35.

——, 'Muḥammad al-Muwayliḥī's Coterie: The Context of *Ḥadīth 'Īsā Ibn Hishām'*, *Quaderni di Studi Arabi*, no. 18, 2000, pp. 51–60.

Allen, Roy F., 'The Tradition of the Avant-Garde', *Visible Language*, Vol. 21, nos. 3–4, Summer/Autumn 1987, pp. 456–94.

Amireh, Amal, 'Edwar al-Kharrāṭ and the Modernist Revolution in the Egyptian Novel', *al-Jadīd*, Vol. 2, no. 9, July 1996, p. 13.

Andary, Nizar, 'Arab Journals Provide Rich but Neglected Sources for Study of the Arab World', *al-Jadīd*, Vol. 2, no. 12, Oct. 1996, pp. 8–9, 21.

Baker, Harry T., 'Periodicals and Permanent Literature', *North American Review*, Vol. 212, no. 6, Dec. 1920, pp. 777–87.

Baron, Beth, 'Readers and the Women's Press in Egypt', *Poetics Today*, Vol. 15, no. 2, Summer 1994, pp. 217–40.

Bennett, David, 'Periodical Fragments and Organic Culture: Modernism, the Avant-Garde, and the Little Magazine', *Contemporary Literature*, Vol. 30, no. 4, Winter 1989, pp. 480–502.

Bixler, Paul, 'Little Magazine, What Now ?' *The Antioch Review*, Vol. 8, no. 1, Spring 1948. Reprinted in *The Antioch Review*, Vol. 50, nos. 1–2, Winter 1992, pp. 75–88.

Bohde, Cheryl D., 'Magazines as a Powerful Element of Civilization', *American Periodicals*, Vol. 1, no. 1, Fall 1991, pp. 34–45.

Booth, Marilyn, 'Colloquial Arabic Poetry, Politics and the Press in Modern Egypt', *International Journal of Middle Eastern Studies*, Vol. 24, 1992, pp. 419–40.

Bourdieu, Pierre, 'The Peculiar History of Scientific Reason', *Sociological Forum*, Vol. 6, no. 1, March 1991, pp. 3–26.

Chalala, Elie, 'Egyptian Ideological Press Continues Decline', *al-Jadīd*, Vol. 2, no. 3, Jan. 1996, p. 3.

De Moor, Ed, 'The Rise and Fall of the Review *Shi'r*', *Quaderni di Studi Arabi*, no. 18, 2000, pp. 85–96.

Dillon, George, 'The 'Little Magazine' Gimmick', *Poetry*, Vol. 71, no. 1, Oct. 1947.

Elberendary, Amina and Rakha, Youssef, 'Ālive and Kicking', *al-Ahram Weekly*, no. 587, 23–29 May 2002. Online. Available HTTP: http://weekly.ahram.org.eg/2002/587/cu1.htm (accessed 17 July 2003).

Francesca M. Corrao, '*Shi'r*: Poetics in Progress', *Quaderni Di Studi Arabi*, no. 18, 2000, pp. 97–104.

Gershoni, Israel, 'The Evolution of National Culture in Modern Egypt: Intellectual Formation and Social Diffusion, 1892–1945', *Poetics Today*, Vol. 13, no. 2, Summer 1992, pp. 325–50.

Ghanayim, Mahmud, 'Maḥmūd Amīn al-'Ālim: Between Politics and Literary Criticism', *Poetics Today*, Vol. 15, no. 2, Summer 1994, pp. 321–38.

Gibb, H. A. R., 'Studies in Contemporary Arabic Literature: I. The Nineteenth Century', *Bulletin of the School of Oriental Studies*, Vol. 4, no. 4, 1928, pp. 745–60.

——, 'Studies in Contemporary Arabic Literature: IV. The Egyptian Novel', *Bulletin of the School of Oriental and African Studies*, Vol. 7, no. 1, 1933, pp. 1–22.

Gonzalez-Quijano, Yves, 'Pour une Sociologie du Fait Littéraire dans le Monde Arabe: à propos de *The Limits of Freedom of Speech* par Marina Stagh', *Arabic and Middle Eastern Literatures*, Vol. 3, no. 1, 2000, pp. 87–93.

Günter, Paul and Joost, Nicholas, 'Little Magazines and the Cosmopolitan Tradition', *Papers on Language and Literature*, Vol. 6, no. 1, 1970, pp. 100–10.

Hafez, Sabry, 'Literary Innovation: Schools and Journals', *Quaderni di Studi Arabi*, no. 18, 2000, pp. 17–39.

Halim, Hala, 'Ibrahim Fathi: Curbstone Critic', *al-Ahram Weekly*, no. 602, 5–11 Sept. 2002. Online. Available HTTP: http://weekly.ahram.org.eg/2002/602/profile.htm (accessed 18 Sept. 2005).

Hallaq, Boutros, 'Articulation du Particulier et de l'Universel chez Yaḥyā Ḥaqqī et *al-Madrasa al-Ḥadītha*', *Quaderni di Studi Arabi*, no. 18, 2000, pp. 61–72.

Hassan, Fayza, 'Gamil Attiya Ibrahim: Keeping the Books', *al-Ahram Weekly*, 20–26 June 1996, p. 26.

Hoffman, Frederick J., 'Little Magazines and the Avant-Garde', *Arts in Society*, vol. 1, no. 5, Fall 1960.

Ibrahim, Sonallah, 'The Experience of a Generation', trans. and introduction by M. Booth, *Index on Censorship*, Vol. 16, no. 9, 1987, pp. 19–22.

Isstaif, Abdul-Nabi, 'Forging a New Self, Embracing the Other: Modern Arabic Critical Theory and the West – Luwis 'Awad', *Arabic and Middle Eastern Literatures*, Vol. 5, no. 2, 2002, pp. 161–80.

Jacquemond, Richard, 'La Liberté Surveillée des Intellectuels Égyptiens', *Liber*, no. 26, March 1996. Supplement to *Actes de la Recherche en Sciences Sociales*, nos. 111–12.

Jameson, Frederic, 'Third World Literature in the Era of Multinational Capital', *Social Text*, no. 15, 1986, pp. 65–88.

Jayyusi, Salma Khadra, 'Freedom and Compulsion: The Poetry of the Seventies', *Journal of Arabic Literature*, Vol. 26, nos. 1–2, March–June 1995, pp. 105–19.

Khallaf, Rania, 'Of Jeans and Self-Belief', *al-Ahram Weekly*, no. 730, 17–23 Feb. 2005. Online. Available HTTP: http://weekly.ahram.org.eg/2005/730/cu2.htm (accessed 2 Dec. 2004).

——, 'A Questionable Reincarnation', *al-Ahram Weekly*, no. 737, 7–13 April 2005. Online. Available HTTP: http://weekly.ahram.org.eg/2005/737/cu1.htm (accessed 12 April 2005).

Khouri, Mounah, 'Lūwīs 'Awaḍ: A Forgotten Pioneer of the Free Verse Movement', *Journal of Arabic Literature*, Vol. 1, 1970, pp. 137–44.

Klemm, Verena, 'Different Notions of Commitment (*Iltizām*) and Committed Literature (*al-adab al-multazim*) in the Literary Circles of the Mashriq', *Arabic and Middle Eastern Literatures*, Vol. 3, no. 1, 2000, pp. 51–62.

Kostelanetz, Richard, 'Avant-Garde (1984)', *New England Review and Bread Loaf Quarterly*, Vol. 7, no. 1, Autumn 1984, pp. 24–39.

Mehrez, Samia, 'Experimentation and the Institution: The Case of *Iḍā'a* and *Aṣwāt*', *Alif*, no. 11, 1991, pp. 115–40.

Milman, Estera, 'The Text and the Myth of the Avant-Garde', *Visible Language*, Vol. 21, nos. 3–4, Summer/Autumn 1987, pp. 335–63.

Nkrumah, Gamal, 'Gamal al-Ghitani: A Scent of History', *al-Ahram Weekly*, no. 733, 10–16 March 2005. Online. Available HTTP: http://weekly.ahram.org.eg/2005/733/profile.htm (accessed 15 March 2005).

Ostle, Robin C., 'The *Apollo* Phenomenon', *Quaderni di Studi Arabi*, no. 18, 2000, pp. 73–84.

Pollak, Felix, 'The World of the Little Magazines', *Arts in Society*, Vol, 2, no. 1 Spring/Summer 1962, pp. 50–66.

——, 'Landing in Little Magazines – Capturing (?) a Trend', *Arizona Quarterly*, Vol. 19, no. 2, Summer 1963, pp. 101–15.

Rakha, Youssef, 'Our Revolution' (Interview with 'Abd al-Raḥmān al-Abnūdī), *al-Ahram Weekly*, no. 595, 18–24 July 2002. Online. Available HTTP: http://weekly.ahram.org.eg/2002/595/sc15.htm (accessed 4 Aug. 2003).

Rayyan, Amgad, 'Les Revues Non-Periodiques dans les Années 70', *Bulletin du CEDEJ*, no. 25, 1er semestre 1989, pp. 117–21.

Salt, Jeremy, 'Strategies of Islamic Revivalism in Egypt', *Journal of Arabic, Islamic and Middle Eastern Studies*, Vol. 1, no. 2, 1994, pp. 90–100.

Spivak, Gayatri Chakravorty, 'Can the Subaltern Speak?', *Wedge*, nos. 7–8, Winter/Spring 1985, pp. 120–30.

Taufiq, Suleman, 'Kaffee trinken – und Gott verschlingen: Zu Besuch bei der jungen literarischen Szene Kairos', *Neue Zürcher Zeitung*, no. 61, 14–15 March 1998, p. 67.

Van Leeuwen, Richard, 'Literary Journalism and the Field of Literature: The Case of *Akhbār al-Adab*', *Quaderni di Studi Arabi*, no. 18, 2000, pp. 151–67.

Walker, Dennis, 'Turks and Iraq's Impact on Early Egyptian Pan-Arabs: Ahmad Hasan al-Zayyat', *Journal of Arabic, Islamic and Middle Eastern Studies*, Vol. 2, no. 1, 1995.

Weightman, John, Williams, Raymond, Nadeau, Maurice, Howe, Irwing, Weightman, John, d'Amico, Masolino, Bromwich, David, Steiner, George, Pinsky, Robert, Rutschky, Michael, Josipovici, Gabriel and Nkosi, Lewis, 'The Role of the Literary Magazine', *Times Literary Supplement*, no. 4028, 6 June 1980, pp. 637–40.

Zabel, Morton Dauwen, 'The Way of Periodicals', *Poetry*, Vol. 34, no. 6, Sept. 1929, pp. 330–4.

Works in Arabic

Books

'Abd Allāh, Yaḥyā al-Ṭāhir, *al-Kitābāt al-Kāmila*, Cairo: Dār al-Mustaqbal al-'Arabī, 1983.

'Abd al-Qādir, Fārūq, *Min Awrāq al-Tis'īnāt: Nafaq Mu'tim wa-Maṣābiḥ Qalīla*, Cairo: al-Markaz al-Miṣrī al-'Arabī li-l-Ṣiḥāfa wa-l-Nashr, 1996.

'Abd al-Raḥmān, 'Abd al-Jabbār, *Kashshāf al-Dawriyyāt al-'Arabiyya, 1876–1984*, 4 vols, Beirut: al-Dār al-'Arabiyya li-l-Mawsū'āt, 1989.

'Abduh, Ibrāhīm, *Taṭawwur al-Ṣiḥāfa al-Miṣriyya, 1798–1981*, Cairo: Maktabat al-Ādāb, 1982.

al-Amīn, 'Izz al-Dīn, *Nash'at al-Naqd al-Adabī al-Ḥadīth fī Miṣr*, Cairo: Dār al-Ma'ārif, 1970.

'Awaḍ, Lūwīs, *Blūtūlānd wa-Qaṣā'id Ukhrā*, Cairo: Maṭba'at al-Karnak, 1947.

——, *al-Thawra wa-l-Adab*, Cairo: Dār al-Kātib al-'Arabī, 1967.

'Ayyād, Shukrī, *al-Qiṣṣa al-Qaṣīra fī Miṣr*, Cairo: Ma'had al-Buḥūth wa-l-Dirāsāt al-'Arabiyya, 1968.

al-'Azb, Yusrī, *al-Qiṣṣa wa-l-Riwāya al-Miṣriyya fī al-Sab'īniyyāt*, Cairo: General Egyptian Book Organization, 1984.

'Azīz, Sāmī, *al-Ṣiḥāfa al-Miṣriyya wa-Mawqifu-hā min al-Iḥtilāl al-Injilīzī*, Cairo: Dār al-Kātib al-'Arabī li-l-Ṭibā'a wa-l-Nashr, 1968.

——, Ṣābāt, Khalīl and Rizq, Yunān Labīb, *Ḥurriyyat al-Ṣiḥāfa fī Miṣr, 1798–1924*, Cairo: Maktabat al-Wa'y al-'Arabī, 1972.

Badr, 'Abd al-Muḥsin Ṭaha, *Taṭawwur al-Riwāya al-'Arabiyya al-Ḥadītha fī Miṣr*, Cairo: Dār al-Ma'ārif, 1983.

al-Dasūqī, 'Umar, *Nash'at al-Naqd al-Ḥadīth wa-Taṭawwuru-hu*, Cairo: Dār al-Fikr al-'Arabī, 1976.

Dhawwādī, Rashīd, *Aḥādīth fī al-Adab*, Cairo: General Egyptian Book Organization, 1986.

Dunqul, Anīs, *Aḥādīth Amal Dunqul*, Cairo: New Look, 1992.

Ghānim, Fatḥī, *Ma'raka bayna al-Dawla wa-l-Muthaqqafīn*, Cairo: General Egyptian Book Organization, 1995.

Gharīb, Sāmīr, *al-Siryāliyya fī Miṣr*, Cairo: General Egyptian Book Organization, 1986.

Ḥamrūsh, Aḥmad, *Qiṣṣat al-Ṣiḥāfa fī Miṣr*, Cairo: Dār al-Mustaqbal al-'Arabī, 1989.

Ḥamza, 'Abd al-Laṭīf, *al-Ṣiḥāfa wa-l-Adab fī Miṣr*, Cairo: Maṭba'at al-Barlamān, 1955.

——, *Adab al-Maqāla al-Ṣuḥufiyya fī Miṣr*, vols I-VIII, Cairo: Dār al-Fikr al-'Arabī, 1957–63.

——, *al-Ṣiḥāfa al-Miṣriyya fī Mi'at 'Ām*, Cairo: al-Maktaba al-Thaqāfiyya, 1960.

——, *Qiṣṣat al-Ṣiḥāfa al-'Arabiyya fī Miṣr*, Baghdad: Maṭba'at al-Ma'ārif, 1967.

——, *al-Ṣiḥāfa al-'Arabiyya fī Miṣr mundhu Nash'ati-hā ilā Muntaṣaf al-Qarn al-'Ishrīn*, Baghdad: Maṭba'at al-Ma'ārif, 1967.

Ḥamza, Ṣalāḥ al-Dīn, *Majallat al-Risāla wa-Dawru-hā fī al-Nahḍa al-Adabiyya al-Ḥadītha 1933–53*, Cairo: Dār al-Nahḍa al-'Arabiyya, 1982.

Ḥaqqī, Yaḥyā, *Fajr al-Qiṣṣa al-Miṣriyya*, Cairo: General Egyptian Book Organization, 1975.

al-Hawwārī, Aḥmad Ibrāhīm, *Naqd al-Riwāya al-'Arabiyya fī Miṣr*, Cairo: General Egyptian Book Organization,1978.

Jundī, Anwar, *Taṭawwur al-Ṣiḥāfa al-'Arabiyya fī Miṣr*, Cairo: Maṭba'at al-Risāla, 1967.

Kallās, Jūrj, *Tārīkh al-Ṣiḥāfa al-Nisāwiyya: Nash'atu-hā wa-Taṭawwuru-hā, 1892–1932*, Beirut: Dār al-Jīl, 1996.

Kharrāṭ, Idwār, *al-Ḥassāsiyya al-Jadīda: Maqālāt fī al-Ẓāhira al-Qiṣaṣiyya*, Beirut: Dār al-Ādāb, 1993.

Khūrshīd, Fārūq, *Bayna al-Adab wa-l-Ṣiḥāfa*, Beirut: Dār Iqra', 1980, First edition, Cairo: al-Dār al-Miṣriyya, 1962.

Mabrūk, Murād 'Abd al-Raḥmān, *al-Ẓawāhir al-Fanniyya fī al-Qiṣṣa al-Qaṣīra al-Mu'āṣira fī Miṣr, 1967–1984*, Cairo: General Egyptian Book Organization, 1989.

al-Maghāzī, Aḥmad, *al-Ṣiḥāfa al-Fanniyya fī Miṣr, Nash'atu-hā wa-Taṭawwuru-hā, 1798–1924*, Cairo: General Egyptian Book Organization, 1978.

Maḥfūẓ, 'Iṣām, *al-Riwāya al-'Arabiyya al-Ṭalī'iyya*, Beirut: Dār Ibn Khaldūn, 1982.

Mahrān, Ḥusayn, *Ghālī Shukrī: Dhākirat al-Jīl al-Ḍa'i'*, Cairo: al-Hay'a al-'Āmma li-Quṣūr al-Thaqāfa, 1996.

Manṣūr, Ibrāhīm, *al-Izdiwāj al-Thaqāfī wa-Azmat al-Mu'āraḍa al-Miṣriyya*, Beirut: Dār al-Ṭalī'a, 1981.

Mikhā'īl, Ramzī, *al-Ṣiḥāfa al-Miṣriyya wa-l-Ḥaraka al-Waṭaniyya min al-Iḥtilāl ilā al-Istiqlāl, 1882–1922*, Cairo: General Egyptian Book Organization, 1996.

Muḥammad, Fāṭima Yūsuf, *al-Masraḥ wa-l-Ṣulṭa fī Miṣr, 1952–1970*, Cairo: General Egyptian Book Organization, 1994.

Muḥammad, Muḥammad Sayyid, *al-Ṣiḥāfat bayna al-Tarīkh wa-l-Adab*, Cairo: Dār al-Fikr al-'Arabī, 1985.

al-Nassāj, Sayyid Ḥāmid, *Ittijāhāt al-Qiṣṣa al-Miṣriyya al-Qaṣīra*, Cairo: Dār al-Ma'ārif, 1978.

Nawfal, Yūsuf, *al-Fann al-Qiṣaṣī bayna Jīlay Ṭaha Ḥusayn wa-Naguib Mahfouz*, Cairo: General Egyptian Book Organization, 1988.

al-Qabbānī, 'Abd al-'Alīm, *Nash'at al-Ṣiḥāfa al-'Arabiyya bi-l-Iskandariyya, 1873–1882*, Cairo: General Egyptian Book Organization, 1973.

al-Qiṭṭ, 'Abd al-Qādir, introduction to Muḥammad Mihrān al-Sayyid, *Badal-an min al-Kidhb*, Cairo: Dār al-Kātib al-'Arabī, 1967.

al-Ramādī, Jamāl al-Dīn, *Khalīl Muṭrān: Shā'ir al-Aqṭār al-'Arabiyya*, Cairo: Dār al-Ma'ārif, n.d. 1959?

al-Rāwī, Muḥammad, *Udabā' al-Jīl Yataḥaddathūna*, Alexandria: Dār al-Maṭbū'āt al-Jadīda, 1982.

Rayyān, Amjad, *Ghālī Shukrī: Bayna al-Ḥadātha wa-Mā Ba'da al-Ḥadatha*, Cairo: General Egyptian Book Organization, 1986.

al-Rayyis, Riyāḍ Najīb, *al-Fatra al-Ḥarija: Naqd fī Adab al-Sittīnāt*, London: Riad El-Rayyes Books, 1992.

al-Saḥartī, Muṣṭafā 'Abd al-Laṭīf, *Dirāsa Naqdiyya fī al-Adab al-Mu'āṣir*, Cairo: General Egyptian Book Organization, 1979.

al-Sa'īd, Rif'at, *al-Ṣiḥāfa al-Yasāriyya fī Miṣr, 1925–1948*, Beirut: Dār al-Ṭalī'a li-l-Ṭibā'a wa-l-Nashr, 1974.
——, *al-Ṣiḥāfa al-Yasāriyya fī Miṣr, 1950–1952*, Cairo: Dār al-Thaqāfa al-Jadīda, n.d.
al-Ṣāwī, Aḥmad Ḥusayn, *Fajr al-Ṣiḥāfa fī Miṣr*, Cairo: General Egyptian Book Organization, 1975.
Shalabī, Muḥammad, *Ma' Ruwwād al-Fikr wa-l-Fann*, Cairo: General Egyptian Book Organization, 1982.
Shalash, 'Alī, *Dalīl al-Majallāt al-Adabiyya fī Miṣr: Bibliyūghrāfiyya 'Āmma, 1939–1952*, Cairo: General Egyptian Book Organization, 1985.
——, *al-Majallāt al-Adabiyya fī Miṣr: Taṭawwuru-hā wa-Dawru-hā, 1939–1952*, Cairo: General Egyptian Book Organization, 1988.
al-Sharīf, Aḥmad Hāshim, *Naguib Mahfouz: Muḥāwarāt Qabl Nobel*, Cairo: Rūz al-Yūsuf, 1989.
al-Shārūnī, Yūsuf, *Dirāsāt fī al-Qiṣṣa al-Qaṣīra*, Damascus: Dār Ṭalāl, 1989.
Shukrī, Ghālī, *Shi'ru-nā al-Ḥadīth ilā Ayn?*, Cairo: Dār al-Ma'ārif, 1968.
——, *Ṣirā' al-Ajyāl*, Cairo: Dār al-Ma'ārif, 1971.
——, *Min al-Arshīf al-Sirrī li-l-Thaqāfa al-Miṣriyya*, Beirut: Dār al-Ṭalī'a, 1975.
——, *al-'Anqā' al-Jadīda: Ṣirā' al-Ajyāl fī al-Adab al-Mu'āṣir*, Beirut: Dār al-Ṭalī'a, 1977.
——, *Muḥāwarāt al-Yawm*, Beirut: Dār al-Ṭalī'a, 1980.
Sulaymān, Ḥasan, *Ḥurriyyat al-Fannān*, Cairo: General Egyptian Book Organization, 1980.
al-Ṭamāwī, Aḥmad Ḥusayn, *Fuṣūl min al-Ṣiḥāfa al-Adabiyya*, Cairo: Dār al-Farjānī, 1989.
——, *al-Hilāl: Mi'at 'Ām min al-Taḥdīth wa-l-Tanwīr, 1892–1992*, Cairo: Dār al-Hilāl, 1992.
Ṭarrāzī, Philippe de, *Ta'rīkh al-Ṣiḥāfa al-'Arabiyya*, 4 vols, Beirut: Dār Ṣādir, 1967; originally published 1913–33.
'Umar, Muṣṭafā 'Alī, *al-Qiṣṣa al-Qaṣīra fī al-Adab al-Miṣrī al-Ḥadīth*, Cairo: Dār al-Ma'ārif, 1986.

Articles

'Abd Allāh, Maḥmūd 'Abd al-Ḥalīm, 'Mushkilāt fī Ḥayāti-nā al-Adabiyya', *al-Qiṣṣa*, no. 1, Jan. 1964, pp. 63–6.
——, 'Qaṣṣāṣ min Jīl bi-lā Asātidha', *al-Qiṣṣa*, no. 7, July 1964, pp. 100–3.
'Abd al-Qādir, Fārūq (Chair) 'Nadwat *al-Ṭalī'a* ḥawla Azmat al-Thaqāfa al-Miṣriyya', *al-Ṭalī'a*, Dec. 1974, pp. 147–56.
——, 'Ittiḥād al-Kuttāb: Mulāḥaẓāt ḥawla al-Qānūn', *al-Ṭalī'a*, Nov. 1975, pp. 132–8.
——, 'Ittiḥād al-Kuttāb: al-Munāqasha Mustamirra', *al-Ṭalī'a*, Dec. 1975, pp. 168–77.
'Abd al-Rāziq, Muḥammad Maḥmūd, 'Damā' Jadīda fī Nādi al-Qiṣṣa', *Nādi al-Qiṣṣa*, no. 2, June 1970, pp. 68–72.
'Abd al-Ṣabūr, Ṣalāḥ, 'al-Majallāt al-Adabiyya wa-l-Ibdā' al-Fannī', *al-Ādāb*, Dec. 1974, p. 23.
Abū 'Awf, 'Abd al-Raḥmān, al-Baḥth 'an Ṭarīq Jadīd li-l-Qiṣṣa al-Miṣriyya al-Qaṣīra', *al-Hilāl*, Vol. 77, no. 8, Aug. 1969, pp. 80–91.
——, 'Trājīdiyyāt al-Thawra wa-l-Qahr fī Riwāyat Jīl al-Sittīniyyāt', *Fuṣūl*, Vol. 12, Fall 1993, pp. 169–84.
Abū Rayya, Yūsuf, 'Mādha Baqiya min Yaḥyā?', *Khaṭwa*, no. 3, n.d. 1981? (special issue commemorating Yaḥyā al-Ṭāhir 'Abd Allāh), pp. 48–56.
Ādam, Aḥmad, 'Jawlat al-Funūn al-Sha'biyya bayna al-Majallāt', *al-Funūn al-Sha'biyya*, Jan. 1965, pp. 133–5.

al-Ahwānī, 'Abd al-'Azīz, 'al-Siyāsa wa-Fann al-Qiṣṣa', *al-Kātib*, no. 81, Dec. 1967, pp. 7–9.

Amīn, 'Alī Muṣṭafā, 'al-Mu'tamar al-Awwal li-l-Udabā' al-Shabbān', *al-Kātib*, no. 106, Jan. 1970, pp. 118–23.

al-'Asharī, Jalāl, 'al-Qiṣṣa al-Qaṣīra min al-Azma ilā al-Qaḍiyya', *al-Fikr al-Mu'āṣir*, no. 52, June 1969, pp. 62–76.

——, 'Jīl mā Ba'da Naguib Mahfouz', *al-Fikr al-Mu'āṣir*, no. 66, Aug. 1970, pp. 78–90.

'Āshūr, Nu'mān, 'al-Jumhūr fī al-Adab wa-l-Fann', *al-Kātib*, no. 141, Dec. 1972, pp. 112–6.

'Āṣī, Mīshāl, 'Dawr al-Majallāt al-Adabiyya al-Lubnāniyya fī-l-Khalq al-Fannī wa-l-Ibdā'', *al-Ādāb*, Dec. 1974, pp. 24–6.

Aṣlān, Ibrāhīm and others, 'al-Qiṣṣa al-Qaṣīra min Khilāl Tajāribi-him' (responses to questionnaire), *Fuṣūl*, Vol. 2, no. 4, July–Sept. 1982, pp. 257–309.

'Aṭiyya, Na'īm, '68 Majalla Tajrībiyya', *al-Majalla*, July 1967, pages unnumbered.

'Awaḍ, Lūwīs', al-Khūlī, Luṭfī', Khashaba, Sāmī' and others, 'Hākadhā Yatakallamu al-Udabā' al-Shabāb' (discussion of young writers responses to questionnaire), *al-Ṭalī'a*, Sept. 1969, pp. 61–92.

'Ayyād, Shukrī, 'al-Qiṣṣa al-Miṣriyya al-Mu'āṣira', *al-Majalla*, June 1969, pp. 94–7.

——, 'Hādhā al-'Adad wa-Qiṣaṣ Ukhrā' (introduction to special issue on the short story), *al-Majalla*, Aug. 1969, pp. 2–5.

'Ayyād, Shukrī', Bāsīsū, Mu'īn', al-Khūlī, Luṭfī' and others, 'Hākadhā Yatakallamu al-Udabā' al-Shabāb fī-l-Waṭan al-'Arabī' (discussion of young writers responses to questionnaire), *al-Ṭalī'a*, Dec. 1969, pp. 73–94.

Badawī, Muḥammad, 'Mughāmarāt al-Shakl fī Riwā'ī al-Sittīnāt', *Fuṣūl*, Vol. 2, no. 2, Jan.–March 1982, pp. 125–42.

Barakāt, Ḥalīm, Hafez, Sabry, Ḥaqqī, Yaḥyā, Kanafānī, Ghassān, Tāmir, Zakariyya, 'Nadwat *al-Majalla*: al-Mawqif al-Ḥādir fī-l-Qiṣṣa al-'Arabiyya', *al-Majalla*, June 1968, pp. 5–11.

Fāris, Muḥammad, 'Hākadhā Yatakallamu al-Udabā' al-Shabāb', *al-Ṭalī'a*, Nov. 1969, pp. 107–13.

Fayyāḍ, Sulaymān, 'Arba'ūn 'Ām-an ma' al-Qiṣṣa', *al-Hilāl*, Vol. 77, no. 8, Aug. 1969, pp. 170–83.

al-Ghaffārī, Amīn, 'Taḥiyya ilā Dhikrā Mīlād al-Ustādh Aḥmad Bahā' al-Dīn', *al-'Arabī*, Year 11, no. 895, 8 Feb. 2004. Online. Available HTTP: http://www.al-araby.com/articles/895/040208-11-895-opn01.htm (accessed 17 Sept. 2005).

Ghīṭānī, Jamāl, 'Tajribatī fī Kitābat al-Qiṣṣa', *al-Hilāl*, March 1977, pp. 58–63.

Hafez, Sabry, 'Azmat al-Ḥurriyya fī al-Riwāya al-'Arabiyya al-Mu'āṣira', *Ḥiwār*, May–June 1964, pp. 52–63.

——, 'Naẓra fī Ba'ḍ Majmū'āt 1968 al-Qiṣaṣiyya', *al-Majalla*, no. 147, March 1969, pp. 62–71, 85.

——, 'Ḥawla Mu'tamar al-Udabā' al-Shubbān: Ab'ād al-Ru'ya al-Shābba li-l-Wāqi' al-Adabī', *al-Majalla*, no. 157, Jan. 1970, pp. 51–5.

——, 'al-Mawja al-Jadīda fī-l-Riwāya al-Miṣriyya wa-l-Muqāwama al-Waṭaniyya', *al-Ṭalī'a*, Aug. 1971, pp. 29–40.

——, 'Khiṭṭat 70/71 bayna al-Fikr wa-l-Taṭbīq', *al-Ṭalī'a*, Jan. 1972, pp. 156–9.

al-Hawwārī, 'Abd al-Ḥalīm, Zubaydī, Taysīr, 'Hākadhā Yatakallamu al-Udabā' al-Shabāb fī-l-Waṭan al-'Arabī', *al-Ṭalī'a*, Feb. 1970, pp. 155–9.

al-Ḥusaynī, Maḥmūd, 'Malāmiḥ al-Wāqi'iyya fi al-Adab al-Lā-Ma'qūl', *al-Nadīm*, no. 3, March 1982, pp. 35–9.

Idrīs, Suhayl, 'al-Ṣiḥāfa wa-Ifsād al-Adab', *al-Ādāb*, Jan. 1975, editorial.

'Īsā, Ṣalāḥ, 'Ta'līq 'alā al-Taḥqīq: al-Kahana wa-l-Jallādhūn', *al-Thaqāfa al-Waṭaniyya*, no. 2, Jan. 1981.

Ismā'īl, 'Izz al-Dīn, 'al-Mushkilāt allatī tuwājihu al-Majallāt al-Adabiyya fī Miṣr', *al-Ādāb*, Dec. 1974, pp. 33–7.

——, 'Qirā'a fī Waḍ'iyyat al-Qiṣṣa al-Qaṣīra min Khilāl Taṣawwurāt Kuttābi-hā', *Fuṣūl*, Vol. 2, no. 4, July–Sept. 1982, pp. 311–18.

Kāmil, 'Alī, 'al-Fikr fī Khidmat al-Mujtama'', *al-Taṭawwur*, no. 1, Jan. 1940, pp. 20–2.

Kashīk, Muḥammad, ''Alāmāt al-Taḥdīth fī al-Qiṣṣa al-Miṣriyya al-Qaṣīra, 1925–80', *Miṣriyya*, no. 6, Jan. 1984, pp. 17–33.

al-Kharrāṭ, Idwār, Introduction to *al-Karmal*, no. 14, 1984, pp. 4–14.

Khashaba, Sāmī, 'al-Nash'a al-Thaqāfiyya fī-l-Waṭan al-'Arabī', *al-Ādāb*, July 1968, pp. 74–6 and Dec. 1969, pp. 58–61.

——, 'Jīl al-Sittīnāt fī al-Riwāya al-Miṣriyya', *Fuṣūl*, Vol. 2, no. 2, Jan.–March 1982, pp. 117–23.

Khiḍr, 'Abbās, 'Min Awā'il Kuttāb al-Uqṣūṣa fī Miṣr', *al-Qiṣṣa*, no. 15, March 1965, pp. 27–34.

al-Khūlī, Luṭfī, 'Dawr al-Majallāt al-Thaqāfiyya al-Taqaddumiyya fī-l-'Ālam al-Thālith', *al-Ādāb*, Dec. 1974, pp. 3–10.

Mabrūk, Muḥammad Ibrāhīm, 'Zaman al-Kataba ya'ful wa-Azminat al-Kuttāb tajī', *al-Nādīm*, no. 2, Feb. 1982, pp. 2–16.

al-Mīrghanī, Rijā'ī, '*Iḍā'a 77* wa-Tajribatu-hā al-Jamāliyya', *Kitābāt*, no. 8, 1984 (no month), pp. 52–107.

al-Miṣrī, Ibrāhīm, 'Ayna huwa al-Adab al-Miṣrī?', *al-Majalla al-Jadīda*, Dec. 1929, pp. 228–34.

Mūsā, Shams al-Dīn, 'Malāmiḥ al-Thaqāfa al-Miṣriyya bayna al-Qiṭā'ayn al-'Āmm wa-l-Khāṣṣ: al-Nashr, Tarāju' al-Dawla wa-Hijrat al-Kuttāb wa-l-Mu'allifīn', *al-Ṭalī'a*, Oct. 1975, pp. 160–5.

al-Muṭī'ī, Lam'ī, 'al-Ṭalī'a al-Wafdiyya Wajh Taqaddumī li-l-Wafd', on the Wafd Party website. Online. Available HTTP: http://hezb.alwafd.org/index.php?option=com_content&task=view&id=124&Itemid=67 (accessed 20 Sept. 2005).

Najīb, 'Izz al-Dīn, 'al-Fann al-Tashkīlī: min Shāri'a al-Haram ilā *Gallery 68*. Li-man tudaqqu al-Ajrās?' *al-Ṭalī'a*, Aug. 1975.

Nash'at, Kamāl, 'Dawr Madrasat *Apollo* wa-Mabādi'u-hā', *al-Majalla*, June 1967, pp. 34–9.

al-Nassāj, Sayyid Ḥāmid, 'Ḥawla Qaḍiyyat al-Riyāda fī-l-Qiṣṣa al-Miṣriyya', *Nādi al-Qiṣṣa*, no. 2, June 1970, pp. 34–43.

al-Qaṣīr, Aḥmad, 'Kamāl 'Abd al-Ḥalīm: Basāṭat al-'Umq', *Akhbār al-Adab*, no. 560, 4 March 2004. Online. Available HTTP: http://www.akhbarelyom.org.eg/adab/issues/560/1000.html (accessed 18 July 2004).

Rayyān, Aḥmad, ''Abd Allāh al-Nādīm wa-*l-Tankīt wa-l-Tabkīt*', *al-Naddāha*, no. 2, n.d. 1979?, pp. 9–11.

Ṣafūrī, Rizq, 'Min A'lām al-Fikr al-'Arabī: Faraḥ Anṭūn wa-l-Fikr al-'Arabī fī al-'Aṣr al-Ḥadīth', *al-Bayādir*, no. 845, n.d. Online. Available HTTP: http://albayader.com/index.asp?cat=27&issue=845 (accessed 3 Oct. 2005).

Sālim, Ḥilmī, 'Dunquliyyūn wa-Adūnīsiyyūn', *al-Kurrāsa al-Thaqāfiyya*, no. 2, March 1980, pp. 3–11.

——, 'Amal Dunqul Kawwana "Jamāhiriyya" bi-Shi'ri-hi al-Ṣādiq', *al-Ḥayāh*, 25 April 2003. Online. Available HTTP: http://www.jehat.com/ar/amal/page-8-2.htm (accessed 15 Sept. 2005).

Sallām, Rif'at, 'Bībliyūghrāfiyyat Shu'arā' al-Sab'īniyyāt fī Miṣr', *Alif*, no. 11, 1991, pp. 158–86.

Shablūl, Aḥmad Faḍl, 'al-Mashhad al-Shi'rī al-Skandarī', Middle East Online, 19 Sept. 2002. Online. Available HTTP: http://www.middle-east-online.com/?id=8267 (accessed 4 Aug. 2003).

al-Shahāwī, 'Abd al-Khāliq, ''Ashar Sana min Ḥayāt *al-Kātib*', *al-Kātib*, no. 106, Jan. 1970, pp. 124–35.

al-Shārūnī, Yūsuf, 'al-Lā-Ma'qūl fī Adabi-nā al-Yawma wa-Mawqif al-Naqd min-hu', *al-Majalla*, Dec. 1964, pp. 62–8 and Jan. 1965, pp. 62–8.

——, 'al-Nādira al-'Arabiyya fī al-Adab al-Miṣrī', *al-Hilāl*, March 1977, pp. 102–10.

Shukrī, Ghālī, 'Malāmiḥ al-Wajh al-Fāji'', *al-Ṭalī'a*, May 1972, pp. 180–7.

Ṣidqī, Muḥammad, 'Sa-ya'tī Dā'im-an' (Obituary of Ḥasan Fu'ād), *al-Ghad* (III), no. 2, Nov. 1985, pp. 114–18.

Yass, al-Sayyid, 'al-Shahādāt al-Wāqi'iyya li-l-Udabā' al-Shabāb', *al-Kātib*, no. 104, Nov. 1969, pp. 161–74.

al-Zayyāt, Laṭīfa, 'Malāmiḥ al-Qiṣṣa al-Miṣriyya al-Jadīda fī-l-Sab'īniyyāt', *al-Ṭalī'a*, Feb. 1973, pp. 147–50.

Unattributed articles

'Aḥmad Ḥamrūsh: Rūḥ al-Taḥaddī warā' Izdihār Masraḥ al-Sittīniyyāt', interview, *al-Bayān*, 22 July 2002. Online. Available HTTP: http://www.albayan.co.ae/albayan/2002/07/22/sya/34.htm (accessed 15 Aug. 2004).

'al-Bayān al-Khitāmī li-Nadwat al-Majallāt al-Adabiyya wa-l-Thaqāfiyya', *al-Ādāb*, Dec. 1974, pp. 53–5.

'Ittiḥād al-Kuttāb', *al-Ṭalī'a*, Dec. 1975, Jan. and Feb. 1976.

'al-Jumhūr fī-l-Adab wa-l-Fann', *al-Kātib*, no. 141, Dec. 1972, pp. 112–16.

'Jumhūr 1975: Mādhā Qara'a? Hal Hiya Bidāyat Ḥiqba Jadīda?' *al-Ṭalī'a*, Feb. 1976, pp. 164–70.

'Malāmiḥ al-Qiṣṣa al-Ḥadītha fī al-Sab'īnāt', *al-Ṭalī'a*, Feb. 1973, pp. 147–50.

'Milaff al-Majallāt Ghayr al-Dawriyya: Ḥadīth ma' Idwār al-Kharrāṭ', *Kitābāt*, no. 9, Nov. 1984, pp. 37–43.

'al-Tajriba al-Shi'riyya al-Miṣriyya: al-Tawāṣul lā al-Inqiṭā'', *al-Ṭalī'a*, April 1973, pp. 152–70.

'Ẓilāl Azmat 5 Yūniyū wa-l-Qiṣṣa al-Qaṣīra al-Miṣriyya', *al-Ṭalī'a*, March 1971, pp. 71–8.

Personal taped interviews

'Abd al-Ḥalīm, Kamāl	Cairo, 3 May 1996
al-'Ālim, Maḥmūd Amīn	Cairo, 3 May 1996
'Aṭiyya, Na'īm	Cairo, 28 April 1996
'Ayyād, Shukrī	Cairo, 29 April 1996
al-Farghālī, Nāṣir	London, 28 Nov. 1994
Farīd, Māhir Shafīq	Cairo, 30 April 1996

al-Ghīṭānī, Jamāl	Cairo, 30 April 1996
Ibrāhīm, Jamīl 'Aṭiyya	Cairo, 30 April 1996
Khamīs, Yusrī	Cairo, 26 April 1996
Manṣūr, Ibrāhīm	Cairo, 1 May 1996 and 3 May 1996
Mutawallī, Muḥammad	Cairo, 1 May 1996
al-Qaṣṣāṣ, Jamāl	Cairo, 4 Nov. 1994
Ṣāliḥ, Muḥammad	Cairo, 27 April 1996
al-Shahāwī, Aḥmad	Cairo, 9 Nov. 1994
Shukrī, Ghālī	Cairo, 3 May 1996
Ṭāhir, Bahā'	Cairo, 1 May 1996

Film

Ibrāhīm, Jamīl 'Aṭiyya. *Ughniya fī al-Manfā* (Geneva, 1995).

NAME INDEX

Abāẓa, Fikrī 41
Abāẓa, Tharwat 79, 123, 149, 154
'Abbās I (1848–54) 9, 11
'Abbās II (1892–1914) 27
'Abbās, Aḥmad 61
'Abd Allāh, 'Abd al-Ḥalīm 124
'Abd Allāh, Maḥmūd 'Abd al-Ḥalīm 79–80
'Abd Allāh, Yaḥyā al-Ṭāhir 62, 119, 129, 142, 148, 154 n.54, 157, 164 n.104, 170, 175–6, 191–2, 202, 216, 222 n.174, 224–5, 227–8
'Abd al-'Āṭī, Ibrāhīm 104, 131, 148, 169, 172, 192
al-'Abd, Muḥammad Imām 18
'Abd al-'Āl, Sa'd 197 n.39
'Abd al-Hādī, Ibrāhīm 63
'Abd al-Ḥalīm, Ibrāhīm 62, 64
'Abd al-Ḥalīm, Kamāl 62, 64
'Abd al-Qaddūs, Iḥsān 19, 65, 67, 124 n.80
'Abd al-Qādir, Fārūq 81, 203–4, 225 n.188
'Abd al-Rāziq, 'Abd Allāh 190 n.5
'Abd al-Rāziq, 'Alī 38 n.145, 41 n.161
'Abd al-Rāziq, Maḥmūd 194 n.27
'Abd al-Rāziq, Muṣṭafā 35
'Abd al-Ṣabūr, Ṣalāḥ 50, 54, 56, 65, 67, 124, 184, 195, 225
'Abd al-Sayyid, Mikhā'īl 13, 119
'Abd al-Wahhāb, Sa'd 119
'Abduh, Ibrāhīm 10 n.6
'Abduh, Mary 41
'Abduh, Muḥammad 11, 13, 14, 25, 28
al-Abnūdī, 'Abd al-Raḥmān 73, 119, 129, 179, 181–2, 216, 228
Abū Aḥmad, Ḥāmid 226
Abū al-Aṭā, Muḥammad 226
Abū 'Awf, 'Abd al-Raḥmān 117
Abū Ghāzī, Badr al-Dīn 75 n.127
Abū Ḥadīd, Muḥammad Farīd 24, 41 n.161, 44, 78
Abū al-Najā, al-Sayyid 196
Abū Rayya, Yūsuf 157 n.69, 164, 185 n.196, 202
Abū Shādī, Aḥmad Zakī 29, 31, 38 n.145, 48–50, 58 n.34
Abū al-Su'ūd, 'Abd Allāh 10–12
Abyaḍ, Jūrj 33
Ādam, Aḥmad 80 n.161
Adham, 'Alī 38 n.145, 82 n.168
Adonis *see* Adūnīs
Adūnīs 58, 87, 105 n.80, 140, 184, 185
al-Afghānī, Jamāl al-Dīn 13
'Afīfī, 'Alī 197
Aḥmad, Muḥammad Yusrī 57 n.27, 62, 68
al-Ahwānī, 'Abd al-'Azīz 169
'Alī, 'Abd al-Wahhāb 197 n.39
'Alī, Muḥammad 8–9, 11
'Alī, Muḥammad Kurd 28, 30 n.112, 32
al-'Ālim, Maḥmūd Amīn 58 n.33, 61–3, 66–9, 165, 166 n.111, 175, 223
Allāh, Anwar Fatḥ 58 n.34
Allen, Roger 25, 149 n.29, 154 n.56, 160 n.84, 213 n.119
Amīn, Aḥmad 39, 42, 65, 66
Amīn, 'Alī 66
Amīn, 'Alī Muṣṭafā 195 n.29
al-Amīn, 'Izz al-Dīn 11 n.10, 12 n.13, 28 n.100

Amīn, Muṣṭafā 66
Amīn, Qāsim 28, 31, 42 n.168, 127
'Āmir, 'Izzat 127 n.102, 183, 202, 225
al-'Anḥūrī, Salīm 14 n.26
Anīs, 'Abd al-'Azīz 66, 67
al-'Antablī, 'Uthmān 61
al-'Antīl, Fawzī 80 n.161
Anṭūn, Faraḥ 24, 27
al-'Aqqād, 'Abbās Maḥmūd 19, 31, 34, 39, 41, 49, 51 n.221, 58 n.29, 59, 66
al-'Aqqād, Salīm 26
al-'Aryān, Muḥammad Sa'īd 58 n.34
al-'Asharī, Jalāl 82 n.168, 92 n.37, 132 n.132, 149 n.28, 192, 193 n.16
'Āshūr, Nu'mān 58 n.34, 60 n.45, 63, 68, 76
Aṣlān, Ibrāhīm 80, 98, 154 n.54, 170, 172–3, 175, 227, 228
Aṭiyya, Na'īm 82 n.168, 113 n.11, 119, 125, 130, 154 n.54, 189
Aṭiyya, Riḍā 197 n.39
'Awaḍ, Ḥāfiẓ 18 n.48, 28, 40 n.150
'Awaḍ, Lūwīs 12 n.18, 40 n.150, 49, 55–6, 58–9, 71, 76, 78, 91, 114, 136 n.149, 145 n.14, 154, 155 n.59, 161, 174 n.147, 180, 196
'Awaḍ, Ramsīs 76
Ayyād, Shukrī 46, 58 n.29, 67, 69, 70, 75, 81, 83, 94 n.45, 113, 147, 148 n.21, 149, 151, 153, 158–9, 174, 191, 192 n.15, 213, 215
al-'Azab, Yusrī 225 n.189
'Azīz, Sāmī 13 n.22, 20
'Azmī, Maḥmūd 43 n.175, 66
al-'Azzāwī, Fāḍil 190

Badawī, 'Abduh 78
al-Badawī, Maḥmūd 79 n.152
Bahā' al-Dīn, Aḥmad 61, 65
Bahjat, Aḥmad 194
al-Baḥr, Tharwat 133 n.135
Bakr, Salwā 217, 219, 220
Baqshīsh, Maḥmūd 199, 202, 205
Barakāt, Ibrāhīm 26
al-Barqūqī, 'Abd al-Raḥmān 34
al-Bayyātī, 'Abd al-Wahhāb 58, 124, 182, 190 n.5
Bellow, Saul 149
Benét, Stephen Vincent 89 n.20
Berque, Jacques 122, 227
Bey, Idrīs 149 n.26, 162 n.95
Bint al-Shāṭi', 'Ā'isha 70
al-Bisāṭī, Muḥammad 80, 148, 154 n.54, 168, 170, 172, 173, 175, 196 n.32, 219, 225–7
Bixler, Paul 106 n.86
Booth, Wayne 93, 102 n.68
Bourdieu, Pierre 110–11, 115 n.23, 117–18, 120 n.54, 131, 138, 139, 191 n.11, 196, 198–9, 209–10, 217, 219 n.161, 220 n.162, 222–3
Bradbury, Malcolm 106 n.82
al-Buḥayrī, Aḥmad 103
Bürger, Peter 87 n.5, 88, 95–6, 106
Butor, Michel 76 n.132

Camus, Albert 56, 149
Chekhov, Anton 66, 149
Christie, Agatha 45
Conrad, Joseph 79
Corneille, Pierre 24
Cromer (Lord) 18, 20, 27

Darwīsh, 'Abd al-Karīm 83
al-Dasūqī, 'Abd al-'Azīz 203
al-Dasūqī, 'Umar 11 n.12
Dawwāra, Fu'ād 75 n.127
Ḍayf, Aḥmad 35
de Moor, Ed 1, 177 n.157
des Combe, Paul Jacot 60
al-Dhawwādī, Rashīd 43 n.176, 158 n.70, 160 n.85, 161 n.94, 220 n.166, 221
al-Dīb, Badr 61–2, 137, 160, 191
al-Dīdī, 'Abd al-Fattāḥ 75 n.127, 82 n.168
al-Dīn, Amīn Taqī 32
al-Dīn, Khālid Muḥyī 67
Diyāb, Maḥmūd Tawfīq 41 n. 161, 215 n.133
Douek, Raymond 60
Dufferin (Lord) 20–1
Dunqul, Amal 91, 112, 113 n.6, 129, 180, 183 n.190, 184–7, 196, 218, 222 n.174, 225, 227

Eliot, T. S. 55–6, 62, 142
Eluard, Paul 59

Fahmī, 'Abd al-'Azīz 43 n.175
Fahmī, 'Abd al-Raḥmān 54, 67, 70

Fahmī, Manṣūr 34, 38 n.145
Fanon, Frantz 142,
Faraj, Alfred 67, 71
Farghalī, Fatḥī 183 n.190
Farḥāt, Muḥammad Muḥyī al-Dīn 55 n.8
Farīd, Māhir Shafīq 130, 132, 176, 215
Farīd, Muḥammad Sāmī 75 n.127
al-Fatḥ, Aḥmad Abū 61, 66
Fatḥī, Ibrāhīm 78, 92, 113 n.12, 115, 119, 124, 131, 157–8, 164–5, 167, 170, 172–3, 183, 191, 195, 204, 224, 226
Faulkner, William 79
Fawzī, Ḥusayn 28 n.105, 34, 36, 47–8, 70
Fāyid, Fakhrī 73 n.117, 84
Fayyāḍ, Sulaymān 93, 148, 154 n.54, 159 n.79, 168, 191–2, 194 n.26, 206, 222 n.174, 227
Foucault, Michel 143
Francis, Raymond 55
Freud, Sigmund 59
Fu'ād, Ḥasan 64–6, 91, 214 n.131

al-Ghaḍbān, Ilyās 26
al-Ghaḍbān, 'Ādil 57
al-Ghaffārī, Amīn 61 n.50
Ghānim, Fatḥī 61, 62, 65
Gharīb, Sāmīr 41 n.164, 52 n.224, 60 n.41, 176 n.155, 216 n.138, 244 n.6
al-Ghīṭānī, Jamāl 73–4, 80, 87, 88 n.9, 109, 113 nn.10, 12, 114, 119, 129 n.113, 142, 146, 154 nn.54–55, 165, 170, 191–2, 194, 196, 206, 219, 222 n.174, 225, 227
Ghurāb, Yūsuf 67
al-Ghuzūlī, Usāma 96 n.57, 181, 183 n.190, 202
Glaß, Dagmar 10 n.5, 22 nn.68, 72, 23, 39 n.147, 229 n.2
Goethe, Johann Wolfgang 153
Gogol, Nicolai 149, 161–2
Gorky, Maxim 45, 66, 152

al-Ḥaddād, Najīb 26, 229–30
Hafez, Sabry 16 n.37, 17 n.39, 21, 22 n.69, 27, 28, 35, 43, 45–6, 48, 62, 65, 68, 73, 74, 91, 119–20, 131–2, 145, 148–51, 155, 157, 160, 167, 179, 182 n.182, 184, 191, 195, 196 nn.28, 32, 224, 227
Ḥāfiẓ, Maḥmūd 41 n.160
Ḥāfiẓ, Ṣalāḥ 57 n.27
al-Ḥafnī, Aḥmad 80 n.161
al-Ḥakīm, Tawfīq 44, 46, 58 n.29, 59, 66, 114, 158
Halasā, Ghālib 114, 119, 126, 127 n.107, 147–8, 151, 154 n.54, 155–6, 159 n.79, 165–9, 171–2, 177–8, 180, 191–2, 227
al-Ḥamasī, Qastakī 26
Ḥamdi, 'Abd al-Ḥamīd 34
Ḥamdī, Kamāl Mamdūḥ 75 n.127
al-Ḥamrāshī, Muḥammad 49
Ḥamrūsh, Aḥmad 18 n.49, 61, 65, 75
al-Ḥamwī, 'Abduh 13
al-Ḥamwī, Salīm 13
Ḥamza, 'Abd al-Laṭīf 10–13, 15, 25, 29, 41, 63
Ḥamza, 'Abd al-Qādir 40, 230
Ḥanafī, Ḥasan 199
Ḥaqqī, Yaḥyā 35 n.135, 47 n.200, 48, 70 n.102, 71, 73–7, 82–4, 93, 113–14, 123–5, 128, 137, 169, 170, 218, 224
al-Harāwī, Muḥammad 49 n.214
Harīdī, Aḥmad 220
Ḥasan, 'Abd al-Rāziq 170
Ḥasan, Fayza 91 n.26
Ḥasan, Muḥammad 'Abd al-Ghanī 53
Ḥasan, Zakī Muḥammad 41 n.161
Hāshim, Labība 26, 230
al-Ḥātim, Ḥasan 49 n.213
Ḥātim, Muḥammad 'Abd al-Qādir 81 n.162, 145
al-Hawwārī, 'Abd al-Mun'im 'Abd al-Ḥalīm 23 n.73, 171
al-Hawwārī, Aḥmad Ibrāhīm 13 n.23
Haykal, Muḥammad Ḥasanayn 91
Haykal, Muḥammad Ḥusayn 29, 34, 39–40, 43, 81
Hegab, Sayed 181 nn.175, 177; *see also* Ḥijāb, Sayyid
Hegazy, Samir 83 nn.172, 175, 179, 94
Hemingway, Ernest 145, 148–9, 152
al-Ḥifnī, 'Abd al-Mun'im 76
Ḥijāb, Sayyid 68, 73, 119, 156, 177, 180–2, 184, 216, 228; *see also* Hegab, Sayed
al-Ḥijāwī, Zakariyyā 57 n.27
Ḥijāzī, 'Abd al-Mu'ṭī 124, 174, 174 n.144, 184, 190–1, 196 n.10, 224, 225
Ḥijāzī, Aḥmad 50, 136 n.149, 161, 225 n.188
Ḥijāzī, Fu'ād 197 n.38
Ḥijāzī, Maḥmūd Fahmī 80 n.161
Hishām, Muḥammad 202
Hollander, Bernard 59

Homer 33
Houghton, Walter E. 44 n.184
Ḥunayn, Jūrj 59–60, 89, 210
Ḥusayn, Ṭāhā 29, 34, 38 n.145, 39, 41 n.161, 42 n.168, 44, 46, 55, 56 n.16, 58 n.29, 64–6, 114, 122 n.70, 176 124 n.80, 210
al-Ḥusaynī, 'Alī Zayn al-'Ābidīn 222 n.174
al-Ḥusaynī, Maḥmūd 174, 175 n.148
Ḥusnī, As'ad 54 n.4
Ḥusnī, Ḥasan 20 n.59
Hussein, Saddam 190

Ibn Danyāl 66
Ibrāhīm, Fahmī 50 n.217
Ibrāhīm, Ḥāfiẓ 22, 25, 31, 32, 41 n.161, 50
Ibrāhīm, Jamīl 'Aṭiyya 69 n.93, 73, 91, 95, 118–19, 137–8, 152, 189, 196 n.32, 204, 213, n.118, 215–16, 222 n.174, 223, 227
Ibrāhīm, Nabīla 80 n.161
Ibrāhīm, Sun' Allāh 2, 84 nn.184–185, 85 n.186, 146, 226 n.193
Ibsen, Henrik 70
Idrīs, Suhayl 65 n.73
Idrīs, Yūsuf 57, 65, 67–8, 71, 76, 113–14, 159, 163–4, 195–6, 218, 225
al-Imām, Amfīd 76
Isḥaq, Adīb 13 n.26, 14–15
Ismā'īl, 'Izz al-Dīn 54, 70 n.101, 75, 77
Ismā'īl, Maḥmūd Ḥasan 78
'Izzat, 'Alī Jamāl al-Dīn 82 n.168

Jabrā, Jabrā Ibrāhīm 56, 142, 175–6
Jacquemond, Richard 50 n.217, 110 n.1, 120, 122 nn.67, 70
Jāhīn, Ṣalāḥ 64, 181
Jalāl, Muḥammad 'Uthmān 10, 12, 33
al-Jamal, 'Abd al-Fattāḥ 67, 73, 74, 93, 124, 129
James, Henry 148
Jameson, Frederic 144
Jawdat, Ṣāliḥ 49–50
al-Jāwīsh, Khalīl 26
al-Jazā'irī, Ṭāhir 32
Jibrān, Faraj 55 n.8
Jibrān, Jibrān Khalīl 24, 38, 49 n.206
Joyce, James 56, 69, 150
Jum'a, Muḥammad Luṭfī 19, 43 n.180
al-Jumayyil, Anṭūn 32
Juwaylī, Muḥammad 100

Kafka, Franz 56, 62, 69, 79, 145, 148, 149, 150, 161, 162
Kalfat, Khalīl Sulaymān 101, 104, 131, 162, 166, 171–3, 182, 191–2
Kāmil, Anwar 59
Kāmil, Fu'ād 59
Kāmil, Maḥmūd 24, 45–6, 55, 57, 79
Kāmil, Muṣṭafā 28
Kanafānī, Ghassān 179
al-Kāshif, Aḥmad 29, 31
Kashīk, Muḥammad 168 n.122, 175, 202
Kātū, 'Azīza 50 n.217
Kāẓim, Ṣāfī Nāz 196
Khaffāja, Ṣaqr 76
Khalaf Allāh, Muḥammad Aḥmad 73
Khalaf, Muḥammad 202
Khalīl, Muḥammad Rafīq 50 n.217
Khamīs, Shawqī 182 n.182
Khamīs, Yusrī 112, 116 n.28, 120, 177, 181, 182 n.181, 186, 194, 218 n.150
al-Kharrāṭ, Idwār 63, 87, 90 n.22, 96–7, 100, 105 n.78, 107 n.90, 108 n.92, 113, 118 n.36, 127, 132, 134, 136, 144, 146, 151, 154 nn.54–55, 159 n.79, 178, 182, 184, 194 n.26, 197–8, 202, 206, 217, 224, 225–8
Khashaba, Sāmī 121, 131, 149, 151, 155, 157, 194, 215–16
al-Khaṭīb, Aḥmad Shawqī 61
al-Khaṭīb, Muḥibb al-Dīn 38 n.145
al-Khayyāṭ, Rif'at 75
al-Khayyāṭ, Yūsuf 20
Khiḍr, 'Abbās 24, 26 n.91, 80 n.156, 231 n.7
al-Khūlī, Amīn 69, 70
al-Khūlī, Luṭfī 115, 134 n.140, 162–3, 170, 196
Khūrshīd, Fārūq 54, 160, 195
Khūrshīd, Ibrāhīm Zakī 70 n.102
al-Kīlānī, Rustum 43 n.176, 221
Kitchener (Lord) 18
Klemm, Verena 65 n.73, 122 n.70, 142 n.4, 176 n.153
Klingender, Francis Donald 173
Kostelanetz, Richard 106–7, 108 n.95
al-Kubaysī, Ṭarrād 133 n.135, 181–2, 190 n.5

al-Laqqānī, Ibrāhīm 14 n.26, 28
Lāshīn, Maḥmud Ṭahir 44, 47, 80, 156
Lawrence, D. H. 58, 70
Lenin, Vladimir Ilyich 59, 175

Libedinsky, Yuri Nikolaevich 148
Lorca, Federico Garcia 152

Mabrūk, Muḥammad Ibrāhīm 18, 92 n.32, 113 n.12, 133, 175, 183, 195, 200, 202, 205, 218, 221–2
al-Ma'dāwī, Anwar 73, 75 n.127
Māḍī, al-Sayyid Sa'd 204 n.78
Maghāzī, Aḥmad 9 n.3, 13 n.25, 20–1, 30, 36
Mahfouz, Naguib 44 n.180, 46, 51, 67 n.80, 70, 83, 93, 95, 113–14, 123, 124 n.80, 128–9, 137, 150, 155, 160, 195, 198 n.44, 217, 218–19, 225
Māhir, Muṣṭafā 82 n.168
Maḥmūd, Ḥasan 41 n.161, 56 n.18
Maḥmūd, Zakī Najīb 3, 82
Majallī, Shafīq 177–9
Majdī, Ṣalāḥ 10, 12 n.17
Makāriyūs, Shāhīn 22
al-Makhzanjī, Muḥammad 202
Makkāwī, 'Abd al-Ghaffār 67, 75 n.127
Makkāwī, Sa'd 60 n.45
al-Malā'ika, Nāzik 58
Mandūr, Muḥammad 61 n.48, 69–70, 75–6
al-Manfalūṭī, Muṣṭafā Luṭfī 22, 28, 35
Mann, Thomas 70
Manṣūr, Ibrāhīm 61 n.52, 93, 99, 109, 113, 116–20, 131, 133, 137–8, 148, 152 n.46, 162, 169, 172, 184, 189, 192, 194, 196, 198
al-Manzalaoui, Mahmoud 159 n.79
Maqqār, Muḥammad 196 n.32
Maqqār, Shafīq 94, 114–15, 138, 147 n.17, 153–4, 173, 191–2
al-Marṣafī, Muḥammad 40 n.150
al-Mash'alānī, Nasīb 26
Maṭar, Muḥammad 'Afīfī 70, 124, 182–4, 186, 195, 197 n.39, 222 n.174, 225
al-Maṭba'ī, Ḥāmid 181, 190 n.5
Maupassant, Guy de 46, 66, 149
Mayakovsky, Vladimir 142
Maẓhar, Ismā'īl 40 n.150, 54
al-Māzinī, 'Abd al-Qādir 31, 39
al-Māzinī, Ibrāhīm 19, 34, 58 n.29, 66
Mehrez, Samia 152, 177 n.158, 182 n.183, 202 n.66
Milman, Estera 86 n.3
al-Mīrghanī, Rijā'ī 214
al-Miṣrī, Ibrāhīm 29, 42
Mubārak, 'Alī 8, 12
Mubārak, Zakī 41 n.161
Muḥammad, Aḥmad al-Ṣāwī 41 n.161, 42
Muḥammad, Muḥammad 'Awaḍ 70
Munīr, Murād 201
Munīr, Walīd 202
Mu'nis, Ḥusayn 70
Mursī, Aḥmad 119, 134, 177, 196 n.32, 198
Mursī, Rajab 70
Mūsā, Muṣṭafā 61 n.46
Mūsa, Nabawiyya 41 n.161
Mūsā, Salāma 21, 27, 29, 34, 36, 37 n.141, 39, 40 n.158, 41–2, 43 n.175, 51, 55, 58–9, 63
Mūsā, Shams al-Dīn 196 n.36, 215 n.133
Mus'ad, Ra'ūf 84, 97
al-Muṭī'ī, Lam'ī 61 n.46
Muṭrān, Khalīl 24, 30–2, 38 n.145, 58 n.29
al-Muwayliḥī, Ibrāhīm 10, 18, 25
al-Muwayliḥī, Muḥammad 17, 22, 24, 25, 31, 114

al-Nadīm, 'Abd Allāh 1, 14–18, 21, 25, 28, 35, 70
Nāfi', Sa'īd 50 n.217
Nājī, Ibrāhīm 40 n.155, 50, 56, 57, 58 n.34
Najīb, 'Izz al-Dīn 198–9, 202, 204–5
al-Najjār, Muḥammad 18
al-Naqqāsh, Salīm 13, 15
Nash'at, Kamāl 49 n.207, 51 n.221
al-Nashshār, Aḥmad 202
Nasīm, Maḥmūd 202
al-Nassāj, Sayyid Ḥāmid 35 n.136, 42 n.171, 45 n.189, 46 n.193, 47 n.198, 67 n.184, 71 n.109, 72, 158, 245 n.9
Nasser, Gamal Abdel 54, 64 n.63, 71–3, 83, 91–2, 94, 95, 119, 123, 127, 133
Naẓīr, Khalīl 18
Naẓmī, Ra'ūf 153, 165, 177–8
Nimr, Fāris 22, 23, 27
Nu'ayma, Mīkhā'īl 49 n.206, 58 n.29

Poggioli, Renato 86–90, 95 n.52, 97, 101–2, 105–6, 108 n.93
Pollak, Felix 89, 90 n.21, 137 n.151

al-Qabbānī, Aḥmad Abū Khalīl 20, 33
al-Qabbānī, Ḥusayn 55 n.8
al-Qādir, Zakī 'Abd 61, 66

al-Qaffāsh, Muntaṣar 197 n.37
al-Qa'īd, Yūsuf 227 n.198
Qalash, Kamāl 84
al-Qardāḥī, Sulaymān 20
al-Qashāshī, Muṣṭafā 45
Qāsim, 'Abd al-Ḥakīm 84, 114, 119, 129, 138, 152 n.44, 154 n.54, 161 n.92, 162–3, 168, 192, 194 n.26, 196 n.32, 216, 222 n.174, 225, 227
al-Qaṣīr, Aḥmad 64
al-Qaṣṣāṣ, Jamāl 93, 96, 186, 197 n.39, 201 n.61, 202
Qa'ūd, Fu'ād 181
Qindīl, 'Alī 197 n.39
Qishṭa, Hishām 59 n.40, 60
al-Qiṭṭ, Muḥammad 'Abd al-Qādir 75–7
al-Qiṭṭ, Yūsuf 133 n.135
Quṣayrī, Albert 59

Raḍwān, Fatḥī 68, 70 n.102, 91 n.28
al-Rāfi'ī, Muṣṭafā Ṣādiq 22, 24, 29, 38 n.145, 41
al-Rā'ī, 'Alī 58 n.34, 66, 71
Rajab, Muḥammad Ḥāfiẓ 80, 114, 144, 154 n.54, 157, 159 n.79, 175, 194–5
Ramaḍān, 'Abd al-Jawād 49 n.213
Ramaḍān, 'Abd al-Mun'im 180, 185, 186 n.200
al-Ramādī, Jamāl al-Dīn 30 n.116
Rambeau, Arthur 59
Ramlī, Fatḥī 62
al-Rāwī, Muḥammad 150 n.38, 158 n.72, 159 n.77, 162, 163 n.102, 217 n.148, 218, 219, 221
Rayyān, Aḥmad 17, 202
al-Rayyis, Riyāḍ Najīb 91 n.27, 128
Riḍā, Rashīd 28
Riḍwān, Abū al-Futūḥ Muḥammad 8 n.1
Rifā'a, 'Alī Fahmī 12
al-Rīḥanī, Amīn 24
Robbe-Grillet, Alain 76 n.132, 127, 145, 150
al-Ruṣāfī, Ma'rūf 22
Rushdī, Rashād 55, 71, 154

Ṣābāt, Khalīl 20 n.55
Ṣabrī, Mūsā 67
Sa'd, Ṣādiq 60
Sadat, Anwar 82, 87, 91, 95, 127, 152, 154, 188, 195, 197, 199, 207, 220
al-Saḥartī, Muṣṭafā 'Abd al-Laṭīf 220 n.165, 221, 222 n.173
Sa'īd, Aḥmad Khayrī 46, 47
al-Sa'īd, Amīna 65
al-Sa'īd, Rif'at 59 n.35, 62 n.59
Saintesbury, George 44
Saint-Simon, Henri de 4, 86
Ṣāliḥ, Aḥmad 'Abbās 58 n.34, 61, 76
Ṣāliḥ, Muḥammad 116, 118, 183 n.190, 194
Ṣāliḥ, Rushdī 51, 60–1, 66, 70 n.102, 80 n.161
Salīm, 'Abd al-Ḥamīd 47
Sālim, Ḥilmī 182, 185–7, 201, 202, 205
Sallām, Rif'at 182–3, 185–6, 202, 205, 207, 214, 220 n.165
Samāḥa, Aḥmad 197 n.39
Ṣanū', Ya'qūb 1, 14–18, 25, 36
al-Saqqāf, Abū Bakr 218
Ṣaqr, 'Izzat 18
Ṣarrūf, Ya'qūb 22–3, 27
Sartre, Jean-Paul 56, 58, 122 n.70
al-Sayyid, Luṭfī 29, 35
al-Sayyid, Muḥammad Mihrān 77 n.142, 186, 222 n.174
Scheunemann, Dietrich 96
Schulte-Sasse, Jochen 87–8, 106
Selim, Samah 13, 17
Shablūl, Aḥmad Faḍl 50 n.217
al-Shādhilī, Maḥmūd 181
Shafīq, Aḥmad 38 n.145
al-Shahāwī, Aḥmad 180, 218
Shaheen, Mohammad 79, 80, 89, 92, 123, 196
al-Shaḥḥāt, Muḥammad 208 n.99
Shaḥḥāṭa, Tawfīq 55
Shahīn, Aḥmad 'Umar 207 n.95
Shākir, Maḥmūd 78
Shalabī, Muḥammad 28 n.105, 158 n.71, 196 n.35
Shalash, 'Alī 39–40, 42–5, 49–51, 69, 85
al-Sharaf, 'Abd al-'Azīz 220 n.166
al-Sharīf, Aḥmad Hāshim 80, 95 n.50, 113, 128 n.109, 149 n.30, 150, 158–9, 162–3, 194, 217 n.144, 225
al-Sharqāwī, 'Abd al-Raḥmān 60 n.45, 65–7, 70 n.102, 71
al-Shārūnī, Yūsuf 52 n.223, 58 n.34, 59, 61–2, 75, 92–3, 113, 120 n.56, 144, 154 n.54, 171, 190 n.70, 192, 217
Shawqī, Aḥmad 19, 22, 24, 29, 38 n.145, 40 n.155, 50, 61, 225

al-Shaykh, Aḥmad 'Abd al-'Aẓīm 50 n.217
al-Shidyāq, Salīm Fāris 11, 14 n.26
al-Shimālī, Tawfīq 55 n.8
al-Shūbāshī, Mufīd 58, 70 n.102
Shukrī, 'Abd al-Raḥmān 29, 31
Shukrī, Ghālī 62 n.56, 66, 67, 73, 76–7, 80–1, 91–2, 94, 109, 113, 118–19, 127 n.107, 130, 132, 138, 150–1, 153, 156, 158, 161, 165, 170, 174, 177–9, 182 n.182, 184, 196, 217, 222, 228
al-Ṣibā'ī, Muḥammad 34, 41 n.161
al-Ṣibā'ī, Yūsuf 65, 67, 80 n.156, 120, 124 n.80, 133, 217
Ṣidqī, Muḥammad 64 n.64, 65 n.69, 66 n.77
al-Sīwī, 'Ādil 205, 209
Spivak, Gayatri Chakravorty 143 nn.6, 7
Stagh, Marina 64 n.63, 68, 72, 90, 92, 119, 196
Steinbeck, John 79, 148
Strindberg, August 62
Sulaymān, Ḥasan 83, 106, 114, 117–18, 125–6, 129–30, 162, 167, 175, 180, 184, 214, 221, 226
Sulaymān, Khālid A. 83–4
Sulaymān, Muḥammad 180

al-Ṭābi'ī, Muḥammad 66
Ṭaha, 'Alī Maḥmūd 40, 50
Ṭaha, Maḥmūd Ṭaha 79
Ṭāhir, Bahā' 56, 64, 92, 95, 109, 113 n.7, 116, 120, 123–4, 127, 131, 138, 145–6, 153–4, 172, 183, 192, 194, 196, 206, 213, 223, 226–7
Ṭāhir, 'Umar 182
al-Ṭaḥṭāwī, Rifā'a Rāfi' 8, 11–12
al-Takarlī, Fu'ād 154 n.54, 190 n.5
Ṭalīma, 'Abd al-Mun'im 204
al-Ṭamāwī, Aḥmad Ḥusayn 24 nn.78, 82, 31 n.121, 32, 33 n.125, 40 n.152, 41 n.160, 65
Taqlā, Salīm 14 n.26
Ṭarābīshī, Jūrj 70
Tawfīq, Muḥammmad 18
Taymūr, Aḥmad 22, 32, 38 n.145
Taymūr, Maḥmūd 41 n.161, 47, 58 n.29, 65, 70 n.102, 79, 158, 221
Taymūr, Muḥammad 35
Thābit, 'Ādil 75 n.127
Ṭilib, Ḥasan 202 n.69
al-Tilmisānī, Kāmil 59
al-Ṭināḥī, Ṭāhir 65
Ṭūbyā, Majīd 152, 154, 159 n.79, 162, 170, 222 n.174, 227–8
Ṭulaymāt, Zakī 19, 66
al-Tūnisī, Bayram 19
Turgenev, Ivan 34

'Unsī, Muḥammad 11–12

Virgil 33

Wahba, Sa'd al-Dīn 68–9, 120, 137, 189, 203
al-Wakīl, Mukhtār 49
West, Nathaniel 149, 162
al-Wirdānī, Maḥmūd 202
Woolf, Virginia 69
Wright, Richard 56

Yass, al-Sayyid 159–60
al-Yāzijī, Ibrāhīm 25–6
al-Yāzijī, Tawfīq 38 n.145
Yūnan, Ramsīs 41 n.164, 52, 59–60, 210
Yūnus, 'Abd al-Ḥamīd 58 n.34, 66, 70, 81
Yūsuf, Abū Sayf 60
al-Yūsuf, Fāṭima 19
Yūsuf, Muḥammad Kamāl al-Dīn 70
Yūsuf, Shaykh 'Alī 14 n.26, 28

Zaghlūl, Sa'd 28, 127
al-Zahāwī, Jamīl Ṣidqī 28, 38 n.145, 40 n.155
Zakariyyā, Fu'ād 75 n.127, 82 n.168
Zakī, Aḥmad 32
Zalzāl, Bashāra 25
Zaydān, Jūrjī 23–4, 31
al-Zayyāt, Aḥmad Ḥasan 43–4, 46, 52, 54, 78
al-Zayyāt, Laṭīfa 81, 163, 170
Zhdanov, Andrei Aleksandrovich 165
al-Zīn, Aḥmad 49 n.213
Zubaydī, Taysīr 171

SUBJECT INDEX

1904 Entente/*entente cordiale* 18, 28
1919 revolution 37
1923 constitution 19, 37
1948 Palestinian tragedy/war 53, 56, 63
1952 revolution in Egypt 53, 63–4
1960s literary rebellion 175
1967 defeat by Israel 3, 82 n.166, 84, 111, 128, 132, 134, 178, 203, 214; and 1960s literary experiments 76, 83, 109, 116, 164; adjustment to habitus 111; campaign to shape the future 108; effect on intellectuals 83, 93; *Gallery 68* 93, 117–18, 214, *see also Gallery 68/Gālīrī 68/jīl 68*; literary explosion 190; nationalist feelings 163, *see also* nationalism/nationalist; overt political commitment 169; repercussions of 118; writers' isolation from society 94
1970s and beyond 177, 188–228
2003 Gulf War 226
2004 Frankfurt Book Festival 2, 154, 226
2005 Arab Novel Prize 2, 226–7
68 generation/68's contributors *see Gallery 68/Gālīrī 68/jīl 68*

absurdism/absurdist 100–1; new literature of the sixties generation 76 n.133, 175; response to new patterns of life 123; stories 192; in Western literature 157
adab 30, 30 n.113, 47
aesthetic paradigms/aesthetics (*'ilm al-jamāl*) 166, 167, 177; *see also* art/artists/artistic
Alexandria 9, 16, 24, 27
Alexandria University 63
alienation 151, 165, 167
America/Americans 27 n.94, 45, 128, 207; *see also* United States
American Civil War (1860–5) 9
American imperialism/imperialist 82 n.166, 207; *see also* imperialism/imperialist
Apollo society/poets: group of 1930s 31, 48, 88; romantic movement 58
Arab National Theatre 11
Arabic literature: first steps to revolutionize 12, 47; modern, development of 56; penetration of 74; political–literary overlap 1; short story, disappearance of 76, *see also* short stories/short story; surrealist tendencies in 59; and Western literature, critical studies of 76
art/artists/artistic 49 n.6, 128, 129, 135, 136, 167, 173, 198, 210; Artists' Union 199 n.46, 205; fine arts (*al-funūn al-jamīla*) 30; political role 119, 175; renaissance 49; society, cycle of isolation 214
avant-garde assertion 94; after nationalization in 1960 90; by sixties generation 6, 87, 110, *see also* sixties writers; isolation of the writer 94
avant-garde dynamic/dynamism 97, 181, 222; experimentation 97; movements 95; objective stance 115; poets in the 1970s 60, 185–6
avant-garde journals 2, 17, 60, 107–8, 116–17, 129, 133, 135, 138, 166; *Gallery 68*; see *Gallery 68/Gālīrī 68/jīl 68*; goals of 89; Marxist programme 52, 64, *see also* Marxism/Marxist; non-periodic 6, 93, 120, 183, 198–9, 201–3, 215;

avant-garde journals (*Continued*)
polarized standpoints 117; stream of 6, 85; Western literature, reluctance to engage with 208
avant-garde writers (*al-ṭala'i'*) 80, 125, 174; Cairo conference 226; canonization of 60, 211, 224; *see also* *Gallery 68/Gālīrī 68/jīl 68*; sixties writers
avant-gardism/avant-gardist 5; function of 108; literary avant-garde 51, 62, 63, 86 n.1; obscurity 107, *see also* obscurity; other points of view, openness to 208; post-modernism 87, 105; sectarian spirit of 107, sixties generation of 5, *see also* sixties writers; tolerance and criticism 128; will to change 96
'Ayn al-Shams University, Cairo 63

Baghdad 222, 227
Beirut 10, 12, 22, 84, 141, 177, 222, 224
Bolshevism 34
Bourdieu, P. 131, 139 n.62, 209–10; conservation, succession and subversion 111, 115, 196–7, 225–6; 'field' of cultural production 191 n.11, 196, 212 n.115, 217 n.149, 219 n.161, 222 n.176, 223 nn.180, 183; model 138–9; model of heteronomous and autonomous hierarchies 222, *see also* heteronomous principle/hierarchy; model of the cultural field 217; terminology 199; theory of fields 2, 6; three different types of strategy 111, 196
bourgeoisie 86–7
British/British colonialism/British occupation 15 n.33, 17, 25, 27; in 1904 28; liberation from, British Protectorate 19; literary journalism under 20; profile of publications 20
Bulaq press *see under* press/publishing

Cafavy Award *see* Prize(s)
Café Riche see literary cafés/clubs/salons
Café Sphinx see literary cafés/clubs/salons
Cairo University 156, 177, 182 n.181, 215
Capitulations System, immunities under 20
Casino Opera 129; *see* literary cafés/clubs/salons
censors/censorship 5, 59, 63, 72, 106, 197; effects of 161; exercised by editors themselves 123; hampered development of journalism 36; institutionalized/officially lifted 95; mechanisms of 92
China 43, 54, 69
colonial/colonialism 15 n.33
commitment (*al-iltizām*)/committed literature (*al-adab al-multazim*) 122 n.70; powerful surge in 66; social and political 64; and 'socialist realism' 163–4; watchword 69; wave of 121
Committee/Council for Composition, Translation and Publication 46, 54
communism/communists 115 n.23, 120, *see also* Marxism/Marxists/communists; campaign against 157; Communist Party/Egyptian Communist Workers Party 65, 204; hard-line literature 65
Conferences: Arab Novel Conference in 2003 226; Conference for Young Writers in December 1969 162, 203
culture/cultural activities 68, 94; anti-Union strategy 205; apparatus/Sadat's grip/oppression 146, 197, 223; capital 111–12, 115 n.53, 136, 139, 197; crisis 82, 199–202, 206, 220; establishment 6, 61, 88, 90, 143, 188, 201, 223; fragmentation 75; globalization 141; hegemony, European/foreign/Western 6, 45, 140, 145, 178; journals/journalism/periodicals 25, 29–30, 38, 44, 57, 204–5; lean years of the 1970s 77, 160; literary journals/publications, state control of 84, 94, 166, 207; policy, government/official 119, 199, 220; production, concept/strategies 110, 196; radio station/Programme Two 68, 204; renaissance (*nahḍa*) 10, 36, 38, 122; renewal sponsored by *Gallery 68* 198; revolution, awakening the masses 72, 145, 165; stagnation of 72, 207, 216–17; surge in 68

Damascus 30, 222, 227
Damascus conference of Arab writers in 1957 65
Danshaway 18, 18 n.49
Dār al-Fikr publishing house 64
Dār al-'Ulūm teachers' college 9

Democratic Movement for National Liberation (HDTW) *see* HDTW
didacticism/didactic 16–17, 18, 48, 22–3, 29 n.111, 35, 41, 71
Dīwān al-Madāris (the Schools' Bureau) 9
drama/dramatics *see* theatre/theatrical/drama/dramatists

education/educational 9, 10, 12, 13, 28
Egyptian: of the 1960s 111; development/experimentation 4, 16, 89, 109, 153, 218; heritage 140, 143, 145; independent journal as a tool 197; influential Marxist work 63; literary field 6, 112, 141, 188, 212, 228; scene 67, 129, 140, 145, 146, 147, 188; strategies of succession and subversion 111
Egyptian Communist Workers' Party 204
Egyptian identity 93, 140, 143, 146; demand for stronger 13; nurturing 42; specific, giving expression to 142
Egyptian national consciousness/ nationalism/nationalist 14, 29, 42; *see also* national/nationalism/nationalist
Egyptianize/Egyptianization 1
escapism/escapist 116, 150–1, 169, 205; through art and literature 36, 208; from critical Arab issues 148; fiction 20; from war realities 53, 67
Europe/European 4–5, 8–9, 13, 79; avant-garde activity 5, 88, 95–6; books 9; cultural hegemony 178, *see also* culture/cultural activities; domination 13; fiction 79; imperialism 141; journals in Egypt 14; literature 29, 171; mission schools 9; modernity 47
existentialism/existentialist philosophy 56, 71, 151
experimentation/experimental writers 115; in the 1960s 128; Egyptian 6, *see also* Egyptian; encourage, train and criticize 56; Lebanese and Syrian journals 65; narrative and poetry 92; poetry journal 183; writers/writings 65, 84

fallāḥ/fallāḥīn 16, 17 n.40, 180–1
filiation 144, 145
financial difficulties of publications 36, 160; *al-Adīb al-Miṣrī* (The Egyptian Man of Letters, 1950) 58; *Anīs al-Jalīs* (The Intimate Friend, 1898) 230; *Apollo* 50; *Gallery 68 see Gallery 68/Gālīrī 68/jīl 68*; *al-Jawā'ib al-Miṣriyya* (Egyptian Responses, 1903–7) 31; *al-Mustaqbal* (The Future, 1914) 36
First Conference for Young Writers in 1969 195, 216
First World War 13, 19, 37
folk arts/folklorists 155–6
folk literature/folk poets/folk songs 180
France/French 30, 55, 56 n.16, 59, 71, 74, 152, 212 n.115; countering *Al-Ahrām's* support 28; departure from Egypt 10; educational missions in 8; influence 12, 27; introductions to the Egyptian novel 76; poetry 31; student uprisings in 127; translated stories 79, 145

Gallery 68/Gālīrī 68/jīl 68 2–3, 6, 73, 76–7, 81, 111, 113, 116, 120–2, 125, 132, 176–7, 198, 196, 207; antagonism between generations 80, 94, 113, 161; avant-garde activity, mother-figure to 133; avant-garde/ avant-garde tendencies 122–3, 135–6, 138, 155 n.61, 174, 189, 224; canonization of writers 227; ceased in 1971 138; contemporary generation (*al-jīl al-mu'āṣir*) 125, 132; contributors 196–7, 206; criticism of 131–2; disappearance 137; diversity within 155; editorial style 131; experimentation/contemporary literary experimentation 113, 125, 130, *see also* experimentation/experimental writers; financial difficulties 120, 128, 135, 137, 198, *see also* financial difficulties of publications; five new literary trends 155; generation of 68/generation of writers, the 107, 114–15, 126, 132, 136, 147, 193, 227; *jīl al-sittīnāt* (the generation of the 1960s) *see* sixties writers; launch of 112; limitations of role 134; no serialized novels 86 n.2; origins of 129; paradigms 177, 188, 196, 201, 226; poems/poetry 177–8, 181–2, 186, 190, 190 n.5, 196, *see also* poems/ poetry; Poetry Committee 77–8, 124; political and literary neutrality/stance 120–1, 207; profile of content 130–1;

Gallery 68/Gālīrī 68/jīl 68 (*Continued*)
respect for freedom of choice and variation 176; revival 198 n.43; Sartrian utopia 122; and socialist realism 126, 164–5, 167–71; Western imperialism 156
generation/*jīl* 121, 123, 226; appeal of *al-adab* 69; important role of weeklies 66; independent union of writers 121; inter-generational antagonism 158, 194; *jīl al-sittīnāt* 2, 93, 96, 228; linked by common human experience 130; literary generation 109, 112, 157, 190, journals 3, 55; literary salons, strong influence of 61; new 132, 134; nineties 2, 109, 225, 228; poetry 140, 141, 185, 186; rigid chronological periodization 3; rising young writers 75, 80; seventies 2, 109; sixties 2, 3, 109, 121, 136, 140, 146, 147, 151–2, 155, 156, 193, 228
genres 24, 36, 63, 178; antagonism between 3, 157; Arabic narrative 48; blurring of distinctions between 4; development/formation 17; drama/dramatics *see* theatre/theatrical/drama/dramatists; of literary journalism 8; novels *see* literary forms; of poetry 49, 179; short story *see* short stories; theatre *see* theatre/theatrical/drama/dramatists
Germany/German 46, 127

habitus 110–11, 121
al-ḥassāsiyya al-jadīda (the new sensibility) 96, 105–6, 118, 217; avant-garde of the 1960s and 1970s 87; patterned formulations 105–7; voice of writers 90
HDTW, *al-Ḥaraka al-Dīmūqrāṭiyya li-l-Taḥrīr al-Waṭanī* (The Democratic Movement for National Liberation) 62, 64
heritage: Arab 6, 81, 102, 140, 154, 184; culture 75; folklore 102, 115, 145, 146, 152, 153, 154, 155, 156, 208, 209, 228
heteronomous principle/hierarchy 212, 216, 219

imperialism/imperialist 183–5
independent journals 1, 2, 197, 199; avant-garde journals 208; culture of negation 199; non-periodic journals 120
India 43, 54, 71, 79, 128
Industrial Revolution 88
Iraq/Iraqi 199; attention to *Gallery 68* 189; dispute with Nasser 72, 181; poets 28, 38, 133 n.135, 181, 190; short story writers 129
Islam/Islamic/Islamist: Arab direction for Egyptian culture 38; campaign in the late 1990s 226; literature and history 43; reformist journal *al-Manār* 28
Israel/Israeli 14; anti-Israeli feelings 163; cultural death after American treaty 82 n.16; defeat by 96, 111; dissociation of intellectuals from establishment 85; effects on political life 84; *Gallery 68*'s approach 214; nationalistic sentiments 185, 207; tensions, effects of 83; writers' role in the war 169

Jamā'at al-Fann wa-l-Ḥurriyya (The Society of Art and Freedom) 41 n.64, 59, 60–1, 89, 210, 244 n.6
Jamā'at al-Khubz wa-l-Ḥurriyya (The Society of Bread and Freedom) 59
Jamā'at al-Madrasa al-Ḥadītha (The Modern School) in 1920s 28, 34, 46
Jam'iyyat Anṣār al-Tamthīl (The Society for the Friends of Drama) 33
Jam'iyyat Kuttāb al-Ghad (The Society of Tomorrow's Writers) 204
Jam'iyyat al-Ma'ārif (The Society of Knowledge) 9
Japan 54
journals/journalism/journalistic 2, 4, 9–11, 13, 26, 36, 39, 61, 120, 181; article as a separate genre 26; autonomous sub-field 6, 188–9, 197–9, 205; dedicated to poetry 58, 181; development of the theatre 9, *see also* theatre/theatrical/drama/dramatists; impact of *Gallery 68* 193, 227; literary experimentation, hotbed of 2, 107, 116, 125, 133, 135, 218; mainstream journals/press 58, 188, 193, *see also* press/publishing; non-periodic 6, 93, 120, 183, 198–9, 201–3, 215; organ of political/cultural dissemination 2; populist 45–6; satirical cartoons, inclusion of 10; short fictional forms 17; specializing in literature or theatre/poetry 20, 49;

traditional forum for avant-garde literature 2
June war/June defeat *see* 1967 defeat by Israel

Kafkaesqe trend 131, 148
Khedive 11, 16, 18, 28; hostility towards 15; *Jurnāl al-Khidīw* (The Khedive's Journal, 1813) 10

Lebanon/Lebanese 14, 23, 27, 30–1, 65 n.73, 189, 222, 231
Levant 24, 58
literacy level/rate 10, 15; in the 1880s 14; of Egyptians 38; increases in 88
literary cafés/clubs/salons 32, 61, 124; *Café Riche* 113, 120, 124, 129, 131, 189, 217 n.148; *Café Sphinx* 129; *Casino Opera* 113, 129; of Damanhūr 204 n.78; of Dimyāṭ 133 n.135, 197 n.39; on Fridays 113 n.12
literary criticism 23, 29, 166
literary dynamic 146, 209; by non-periodic avant-garde journals 188, 225
literary experimentation 2; in the 1970s and 1980s 135; contemporary significance 125; Egyptian forward momentum 218; inspired by *Gallery 68* 107; launch of a new era in 116; pushed underground 1; writers in their twenties 133
literary field 72, 76; areas of culture 74; controversies, three main areas 6; dominant positions in 217; literary concerns 23; literary heritage, Egyptian/Arab/international 209; nationalist struggle 63; nationalization, double-edged sword 72; polarization of 42, 63; political power 63; strategy, three different types of 111; structure, fundamental/internal 117, 139, 211
literary field/scene 34, 46, 80, 116, 135, 149, 181, 182, 191, 194, 196, 224; Egyptian 2, 6, 67, 129, 145–7, 188, 197, 201, 218; *Gallery 68* 189, 193; 'peacocks' of the 129, 223; penetration onto international scene 74; for young writers 95, 221, cultural scene 6, 63, 84, 94, 161, 210, field of power 1, 6, 78, 146, 212, 217, 226, political scene 121, 140
literary forms 12, 18; evolution/development of 1, 35; modern/new 145, 160; *muwashshaḥ* 12, 26 n.92; novels 22–4, 29, 44, 79, 226; role played by journalism 25; and techniques 145, 164, 175, 208; travelogues and short stories 34; *zajal* 12, 18, 19
literary generations/genres *see* genres
literary identity: embryonic phases 146; developments in narrative technique 150
literary journals/journalism 1, 4, 28, 35, 54, 63, 71, 73, 230; committed literature *see* commitment (*al-iltizām*)/committed literature (*al-adab al-multazim*); definition of 5; didactic/direct didacticism/didactic principles 28, 41, 71, *see also* didacticism/didactic; during the 1940s/during the First World War/during the Second World War 36, 53, 63; Egypt's intellectual renaissance 40; embryonic 8, 11; focus on society's alienation 151; French literature bias/new generation/growing politicization of 55; fresh/political impetus/rise of 15, 47, 73, 40 n.150; golden age of 5, 37–52; home-grown 36, 70; imitation of Western modernist trends 148; intertwinement of cultural and political fields 61; Leftism/leftist/leftist influence 59 n.35, 61, 67, 73, 77, 81, 167, *see also* Marxism/Marxists/communists; mainstream 6, 108, 110, 117, 139, 184, 188, 222; manifestos *see* manifestos; of the Ministry of Culture *see under* Minister/Ministry of Culture; most influential 19, 55, 61, 69; occidentalist perspective of 27; popularity of 22–3, 41, 45; post-war decline 54; role of 31, 35, 48; satire *see* satire/satirical journalism/satirical journals; specialist *see* specialist literary journals; splintering of 38; successful brand of/models of 36, 51; twentieth century, first major journals of 32; under British occupation 20–7
literary movements 64–5
literary renewal 134–5, 207; development of new styles and techniques 121; in established forums 112; launch of journals 34; renaissance 47

Majlis al-Sha'b (The National Assembly) 203
manifestos/opening manifestos 32, 49, 58, 89, 112, 132, 136, 166; approach of *Gallery 68* 176; breaking with tradition 197 n.37; call for national Egyptian literature 40; collective statement of opinion 134; frustration of young writers 84; -like opening editorials/opening 42, 55, 62, 69, 75, 169
Marxism/Marxists/communists 60, 65, 115 n.23, 120, 157, 175, 211, 223; closure by military decree in 1944 52; crackdown on communists 65; ideology 59; influence, *al-Fajr al-Jadīd* (The New Dawn, 1945–6) 60, 60 nn.43–4, 133–4, 202 n.65; journal, *al-Jamāhīr* (The Public, 1947–8) 60; leftist journals 61, *see also* literary journals/journalism; Partisans of Peace 60; principles/programme 59; private publishing house run by communists 120; tendencies 92; theory/thought 59, 165; writers 64
Minister/Ministry of Culture 72, 75, 79, 145, 216 n.141, 217; achievements/policies 81; attitude to communism/leftists 72–3, 76, 78; books 190, 226; cultural journals 73, 91, 120, 189; dismantling Nasser's edifice 95; distribution apparatus 213; dominant positions, control of/support of 112, 135; *Gallery 68*, editorial intrusions 120; grants scheme (*tafarrugh*)/subsidy 70, 84, 128; high-profile folk arts, recognition of 80, 156; literary establishment, domination of 110; recommendations of Conference for Young Writers 195; sixties writers 117, *see also* sixties writers; sponsored monthly, launch of 70, 76, 78, 84, 120; translations from foreign sources 79; writers unions 195, 203, 206
Ministry of National Guidance 68

Nasser/Nasserism/Nasserist 87; Free Officers' movement 61, 64–5; nationalization 94, *see also* nationalization; persecution of writers/intellectuals 119, 123; state, social and political agenda 71–2
national/nationalism/nationalist 14, 34, 42; consciousness 39; Egyptian literature 29, 44; movement 15, 28; national literature (*adab qawmī*) 47; political identity, quest for 37; sentiments 29, 18, 33; struggle 63
National Library 94 n.47
National Theatre during the 1960s 18 n.49, 61
National Union of Writers 112
nationalization 94; massive government investment in culture 90; of press and publishing houses 69
new literature (*al-adab al-jadīd*) 155, 160–1, 201 n.65; censorship 161, *see also* censors/censorship; contributions to *Gallery 68* 168–75, 190, 193–4; foreign literature 14, 155, 207–8; institutionalization of 72–85; journals/journalistic 2, 10, 72, 188–9, 209, 217; a new literary dynamic 188; novels 128; in the post-Revolutionary era 67; principal trend of social realism 167; social and political content of 66; three main areas of debate 6; Western influence 140–53
newspapers 9, 11–14, 20, 29, 65; Egyptian 27; nationalistic sentiments 18, 28–9; promoting new literature 67
nihilism/nihilists/alienation 97, 134; *see also* alienation
non-periodic journals *see* journals/journalism
novels *see* literary forms

obscurity 82, 100, 108, 148, 158, 185, 221; attack on 171; avant-garde 107; definition, attempt at 178, 185; in *Gallery 68* 184; in modern poetry 177–8, 184; of new forms 171
'the Offset Revolution' (*thawrat al-masṭar*) 129
oil money 218, 218 n.150
opening editorials 32–3, 38 n.145, 40, 49, 82, 123, 131, 133–4, 197, 200; manifesto-like 55; shared objectives 42; on socialism 82, 210; view of the short story 79; Western cultural hegemony 45, 58, 208; *see also* culture/cultural activities

Palestine/Palestinian 142; plight 207; tragedy 5, 53, 207; war 56, 63; writers/poets 129, 152 n.45, 171, 179
pan-Arab/pan-Arabism 48 n.174, 54 n.5, 81, 83; nationalism/nationalist struggle 28, 63, *see also* national/nationalism/nationalist; support for socialism 76; under Nasser 54
Pan-Islamism 25
Partisans of Peace *see* Marxism/Marxists/communists
Persia 43, 54
poems/poetry 2, 21, 49–50, 180, 184, 214; aesthetic renewal, society and its politics 179, 186; Apollo group/Apollo society/*Apollo* 31, 46, 48–50, 49 nn.208–210, 212–213, 50, 58, 88; Arab Heritage 102, 181; in Arabic 1, 22, 145; chain of evolution 178; *Dīwān* poets 31; experimentation in 182–3, 186; *fallāḥ* 180–1; framework of/genealogy of 178; *Gallery 68* and poetry 177–87; monopoly of the monorhyme 177; *muwashshaḥ* 12, 26 n.92; obscurity, validity of 177–8, 184, *see also* obscurity; opportunism 185; political protest 179; pre-Islamic 33, 178; revolution in form 193; sixties ideal 185–6; strophic forms/verse 12, 18, 31; theory, variety of schools of 77; *zajal* 12, 18, 19
Poetry Committee 78
politics/political *see also* Minister/Ministry of Culture; Nasser/Nasserism/Nasserist; nationalization; confrontation 5; subordinating creativity to 123; unrest 19
post-modern/post-modernism; *mā ba'da al-ḥadātha* (that which comes after Modernism) 4, 87, 105
press/publishing 88, 95, 122, 189, 205, 218 n.150, 220, 227; bridge between politics and literature 67; Bulaq press 8, 8 n.1, 10, 243 n.1; cultural 154; development of 9; freedoms/restrictions 20; mainstream 188, 191, 193; national 156; photocopiers and stencils, *thawrat al-masṭar* (the Offset Revolution), phenomena of 197; women's 230 n.3
Press Law, 1881 20, 42 n.65
Prize(s): 2005 Arab Novel Prize 2, 226–7; Arab Novel Prize in 2003 2; Cafavy Award 228; Naguib Mahfouz Prize (1999) 228; State Prize for Encouragement 288; State Prize for Merit in 2000 227–8; The Sultan 'Uways Prize for literature 228 n.200; Supreme Council for Culture's 2005 Arab Novel Prize 226

realism/realist school 163–87, 174; basic tenet of 173; in a contemporary framework 123; discussions of 211
rebellion 85, 105, 115, 138, 176; against linguistic conventionality 86; literary 175; need of the literary scene 80; as opposed to 'disagreement' 157; 'of outstanding individuals' 129; radical 133
Romantic Movement 58
Russian influence/literature 48, 57, 79, 208; Arabic translation 145; short stories 43; writers 34, 47

satire/satirical journalism/satirical journals 1, 15, 63; against traditional forms of discourse 19; cartoons 10, 18 n.48; figures and contemporary policies 18; political 14, 25; Ṣanū' and al-Nadīm, two pioneers of 14; sketches 15
School of Languages 8–10
Second World War 8, 53
serialize/serialization: of books 12, 40; of Danshaway incident 18; novels/short stories 4, 23–9, 31, 44, 57, 66, 67 n.80, 79, 86 n.2, 231; plays 33
short stories 3, 44, 47–8, 54, 59, 84, 94, 115, 138, 177, 193; aimed to reflect social reality 35; birth of the 115; campaign against the communists 157; collection 219; creative literature 48; in Egypt 96, 134; English translations 154; *Gallery 68* 86, 94, 115–17, 134–5, 138, 157, 174, 190, 190 n.5, 192–3; genre 86, *see also* genre; popularity 123; revolution in form 193; serialized novels 4, 23, 31, 44, 86 n.2; of the sixties generation 140; turning point in history 62; *Weltanschauung* (*ru'ya*)/new developments in 116; writers 35, 79, 131, 190

sixties writers 2–3, 6, 8, 18, 112, 138, 140–1, 143, 146, 152, 156–7, 154, 157, 162–4, 177, 223, 227–8; alienation of/sense of alienation 147, 172, *see also* alienation; Arab literary heritage 146, 152, 154–6; canonization of writers 6, 189, 212, *see also* avant-garde writers; *Gallery 68/ Gālīrī 68/jīl 68*; clash of generations/ new versus old/struggle between generations 56, 140, 161–2; contemporary reality, negative portrayal of 164; Egyptian literary scene, present domination of 145–6; experimentation and innovation 152; literary controversies, three main issues 140; literary identity of 143, 147; modernist developments 140, 161, 164; new literature, absurdist or surrealist 175; overt political engagement 121; primary influence 155; represented in *Gallery 68* (1968–71) 143; socialist realism, abandonment of 164; 'strategic essentialism' 141, 143; three models of resistance, amalgamation of 146; Western absurdism/techniques/ influence 140, 152, 157
socialist realism (*al-wāqi'iyya al-ishtirākiyya*)/socialism 78, 81, 163, 167–8, 172; Arab society's adoption of 81; of the avant-garde 106; devotion to the people 168; expression, changing modes of 163; lexicon 169; literature, advocators of 174; and Marxism 164; outlived its usefulness 171; principles, identification with 173; struggle for 170
societies *see Jamā'āt*
Soviet Union 64, *see also* Russian influence/literature
specialist literary journals 5, 20, 36, 57, 88, 156; aim of bridging East and West 46; avant-garde/ approaching avant-garde 33, 34, 38, 50–1; cultural establishment, guerrilla warfare against 88; demise of 51; experimental literary techniques 45; extreme modernism 37; financial support 51, *see also* financial difficulties of publications; general educational impact 41
Spring Exhibition 198
Stalinist approach *see* literature
state control *see* cultural activities; Minister/Ministry of Culture; Nasser/Nasserism/Nasserist; nationalization
struggle for legitimacy 6, 189, 223
Suez Canal 9
Supreme Council for Arts and Letters 67 n.80
Supreme Council for Culture 63, 228; Chair to the Fiction Committee of the Supreme Council for Culture 228
Supreme Council for the Arts, Letters and Sciences 68
surrealism/surreal 121, 171, 175; in literature and art 52; response to new patterns of life 123; tendencies in Arabic literature 59
symbolic capital 219, 224
syncretism/syncretic 146
Syria/Syrians 9–10, 13, 36

tafarrugh grants *see* Minister/ Ministry of Culture
theatre/theatrical/drama/dramatists 36, 66; one-act plays/verse dramas 70; prominent men in 15, 69; rights of dramatists 31; sketches/pieces 2, 15, 17
translations/translated literature 4, 9, 14, 16, 155, 207–8; Arabization of European poetry 33; from French poetry 12; journals published in Egypt 10, 26; narrative fiction 20, 22, 29; novels 128; of plays 24; stories 79; Western influence 20, 26, 32
Turkey/Turkish 10–11, 13, 54

UNESCO study: Progress of Literacy in Various Countries 14
Union of Journalists 65
Union of Writers 129, 203–6
United States 2, 5, 86, 90, 198; *see also* America/Americans
'Urābī revolt 14–16, 20, 125

Victorian England 39, 88
Victorian periodicals 44

Wafd government of 1951–2 64
Wafdist Vanguard 61, 61 n.46, 245 n.8; *Rābiṭat al-Shabāb* (The Youth League, 1947–50) 60–1; *al-Nās* (The People, 1951) 61
West/Western: critique 4; cultural hegemony 45, 145, *see also* culture/cultural activities; dialectical relationship with 145; imperialism, effects of 147; -influenced national Egyptian(ist) literature 38; influences, ambivalent attitude towards 149; literature 47, 142, 149, 154, 207; writers union 195, 203, 206

Yawmiyyāt Na'ib fī-l-Aryāf (The Diary of a Country Prosecutor, 1937) 45
Yemen 84
Youth Secretariat of the United Arab Republic 195

zajal poets 18–19
Zionism/Zionist: accusations of 56, 127, 207; aggression 207; American aggression/imperialist agenda 127, 170; encroachment 142; fiction 207; opposition to 118; Palestinian plight 207; plot 141

For Product Safety Concerns and Information please contact our EU representative GPSR@taylorandfrancis.com
Taylor & Francis Verlag GmbH, Kaufingerstraße 24, 80331 München, Germany

www.ingramcontent.com/pod-product-compliance
Lightning Source LLC
Chambersburg PA
CBHW052217300426
44115CB00011B/1717
* 9 7 8 0 4 1 5 5 9 7 4 0 1 *